Brands, Geographical Origin, and the Global Economy

Indications of geographical origin for foodstuffs and manufactures have become an important source of brand value since the beginnings of globalisation during the late nineteenth century. In this work, David M. Higgins explores the early nineteenth-century business campaigns to secure national and international protection of geographical brands. He shows how these efforts culminated in the introduction of legal protocols which protect such brands, including Champagne, Sheffield, Swiss-made watches, and 'Made in the USA'. Higgins explores the major themes surrounding these indications, tying in the history of global marketing and the relevant laws on intellectual property. He also questions the effectiveness of EU policy to promote 'regional' and 'local' foods and why such initiatives brought the European Union into conflict with North America, especially the United States. He extends the study with a reflection on contemporary issues affecting globalisation, intellectual property, less developed countries, and supply chains.

David M. Higgins is Professor of Accounting and Finance at Newcastle University Business School.

Cambridge Studies in the Emergence of Global Enterprise

The world economy has experienced a series of globalisations in the past two centuries, and each has been accompanied by and shaped by business enterprises, by their national political contexts, and by new sets of international institutions. Cambridge Studies in the Emergence of Global Enterprise focuses on those business firms that have given the global economy many of its most salient characteristics, particularly regarding how they have fostered new technology, new corporate cultures, new networks of communication, and new strategies and structures designed to meet global competition. All the while, they have accommodated to changes in national and international regulations, environmental standards, and cultural norms. This is a history that needs to be understood because we all have a stake in the performance and problems of global enterprise.

Editors

Louis Galambos, *The Johns Hopkins University*
Geoffrey Jones, *Harvard Business School*

Other Books in the Series:

Teresa da Silva Lopes, *Global Brands: The Evolution of Multinationals in Alcoholic Beverages*

Christof Dejung and Niels P. Petersson, *The Foundations of Worldwide Economic Integration: Power, Institutions, and Global Markets, 1850–1930*

William J. Hausman, *Global Electrification: Multinational Enterprise and International Finance in the History of Light and Power, 1878–2007*

Christopher Kobrak, *Banking on Global Markets: Deutsche Bank and the United States, 1870 to the Present*

Christopher Kobrak, *National Cultures and International Competition: The Experience of Schering AC, 1851–1950*

Christopher D. McKenna, *The World's Newest Profession: Management Consulting in the Twentieth Century*

Johann Peter Murmann, *Knowledge and Competitive Advantage: The Coevolution of Firms, Technology, and National Institutions*

Neil Rollings, *British Business in the Formative Years of European Integration, 1945–1973*

Andrew L. Russell, *Open Standards and the Digital Age: History, Ideology, and Networks*

Jonathan Silberstein-Loeb, *The International Distribution of News: The Associated Press, Press Association, and Reuters, 1848–1947*

Brands, Geographical Origin, and the Global Economy

A History from the Nineteenth Century to the Present

DAVID M. HIGGINS

Newcastle University

CAMBRIDGE
UNIVERSITY PRESS

CAMBRIDGE
UNIVERSITY PRESS

University Printing House, Cambridge CB2 8BS, United Kingdom

One Liberty Plaza, 20th Floor, New York, NY 10006, USA

477 Williamstown Road, Port Melbourne, VIC 3207, Australia

314-321, 3rd Floor, Plot 3, Splendor Forum, Jasola District Centre, New Delhi - 110025, India

79 Anson Road, #06-04/06, Singapore 079906

Cambridge University Press is part of the University of Cambridge.

It furthers the University's mission by disseminating knowledge in the pursuit of education, learning and research at the highest international levels of excellence.

www.cambridge.org
Information on this title: www.cambridge.org/9781107032675
DOI: 10.1017/9781139507059

First published 2018

A catalogue record for this publication is available from the British Library

Library of Congress Cataloging in Publication data
NAMES: Higgins, David M., author.
TITLE: Brands, geographic origin, and the global economy : a history from the nineteenth century to the present / David M. Higgins, University of York.
DESCRIPTION: Cambridge [UK] ; New York : Cambridge University Press, 2018. |
SERIES: Cambridge studies in the emergence of global enterprise
IDENTIFIERS: LCCN 2017045877 | ISBN 9781107032675 (hardback)
SUBJECTS: LCSH: Marks of origin – Law and legislation – History. | Trademarks – Law and legislation – History. | Names, Geographical – Law and legislation – History. | BISAC: BUSINESS & ECONOMICS / Economic History.
CLASSIFICATION: LCC K1562 .H54 2018 | DDC 346.04/88–dc23
LC record available at https://lccn.loc.gov/2017045877

ISBN 978-1-107-03267-5 Hardback

To My Parents, Samuel and Isabel Higgins

Contents

Figures

Tables

Acknowledgements

Many of the books I read as a student were prefaced by the comment: 'If I had known what this book entailed at the outset, I would never have taken it on.' Having completed this project, I now know exactly what this statement means! It is appropriate that full recognition is given to the many who have helped me while writing this book. Sincere thanks are due to Eric Crahan, who was the commissioning editor for Cambridge University Press, and the series editors, Geoff Jones and Lou Galambos. I am also indebted to Kristina Deusch, who was my production editor. For different reasons, I am particularly indebted to Dev Gangjee and Geoff Tweedale. Dev provided continuous advice on the innumerable legal issues that had to be addressed in my research and he responded with alacrity to my many queries. Geoff gave me the confidence to begin scoping out this project and he has been consistently supportive. I relish the prospect of buying them a small, suitably dry sherry. Other scholars who have had an influence on my thinking about indications of geographical origin include Felicity Barnes, Lionel Bently, Paul Duguid, Teresa da Silva Lopes, Mads Mordhorst, and Richard Perren. I have benefitted from collaboration with Aashish Velkar and David Clayton, and I received advice on accounting issues, marketing, and strategic management from Andy Holden and Steve Toms, Matt Gorton, and Tom McGovern, respectively. Angela Tregear supplied copies of DOLPHIN reports, and Phillip Leat sent various RIPPLE reports. Thanks are also due to the participants at the Association of Business Historians conferences in 2003 and 2014, the Business History conferences in 2008 and 2012, the Economic History Society conference in 2017, and the European Business History Association conferences in 2005 and 2009.

Many institutions have supported this project over the years and I am deeply indebted to them. Financial assistance was provided by the Nuffield Foundation (SGS/33846). The Business History Unit at Copenhagen Business School was a generous host during my tenure as a visiting fellow in 2009. Tony Morrow granted me unrestricted access to various publications held by The Worshipful Company of Butchers in London. At various times, I have benefitted from communications with the UK Department for the Environment, Food and Rural Affairs, the European Parliament, the Federal Trades Commission, and the US Department of Agriculture.

It is quite possible that my requests for obscure primary and secondary material drove many archivists and librarians to the verge of insanity. My apologies. It is with pleasure that I record the help of those based at the British Library, especially Beverley and Sarah at the Document Supply Centre, the librarians at the now defunct Newspaper Library (Colindale), the bulk order team and their colleagues at the National Archives, and the Modern Records Centre, University of Warwick. At the University of York, Margaret Dillon and Lisa Hopwood facilitated the submission of innumerable interlibrary loans. Since moving to Newcastle University, Catherine Dale and her colleagues in the Law Library have been particularly industrious in tracking down legal cases, statutes, and other official documents – they never failed. Mark Callan, a librarian in the Robinson Library (University of Newcastle), provided helpful translation. Ronald Richenburg (Bodleian) located obscure statutes, Richard Ward (House of Lords) supplied various Standing Committee debates, and Robin Hampton, librarian at the Ministry of Primary Industries, New Zealand, provided electronic access to the Appendices to the Journals of the House of Representatives. Phillippe Vierra (Federation of the Swiss Watch Industry) has helped me locate relevant online documents pertaining to the Swiss watch industry. I should also thank David Cutler (Rolex), Francis Fay (European Commission), Bernard Magrez (Château Pape Clément), Hugh Alexander (The National Archives), and Petr Samec (Budweiser Budvar) for permission to reproduce their brands.

On a personal level, a large debt is owed to Peter and Marta, and Victor, for unlimited opportunities to 'crash-over' when visiting London to conduct research, and to Kenny Mac, for the same reason when visiting Sheffield. Indubitably, the biggest personal debt I owe is to my family, Louise, Matilda and Caleb – aka the 'Cheeky Monkeys' – who have experienced mercurial swings in my disposition while I was completing this work.

Geographical Origin in the Global Economy

Do you consider yourself a savvy consumer? In purchasing a pair of leather shoes, would you select an Italian brand or one carrying a 'Made in USA' label? ... Do you prefer the Italian brand because of a belief that Italian leather is superior in quality or craftsmanship? Or do you prefer the shoes made in the United States out of a sense of national pride and responsibility in keeping Americans employed?

B. L. Bade, 'Beyond Marking: Country of Origin Rules and the Decision in CPC International'. *The John Marshall Law Review* 179 (1997): 179

A powerful force drives the world toward a converging commonality ... The result is a new commercial reality – the emergence of global markets for standardised consumer products on a previously unimagined scale of magnitude ... Gone are accustomed differences in national or regional preference ... The world's needs and desires have been irrevocably homogenized.

T. Levitt, 'The Globalization of Markets'. *Harvard Business Review* 61 (1983): 92–93

Champagne is probably the most illustrious alcoholic beverage in the world. Its allure is based on its association with the rich and famous – both fictional and real-life. James Bond's preferred brands included Bollinger and Dom Pérignon. Winston Churchill claimed, 'A single glass of champagne imparts a feeling of exhilaration. The nerves are braced; the imagination is stirred; the wits become more nimble.' Celebrations in Formula 1 car racing involve obligatory Champagne-spraying from the podium. Champagne is used to celebrate christenings and weddings: 'In short, popping a bottle of bubbly is about making a statement.'[1] Although producers of Champagne own famous brands, the beverage itself is a geographical indication (GI). Despite its global fame, one feature of Champagne is rarely recognised, let alone appreciated: its renown required recognition by the various Champagne houses that they had a common interest and that protection of this GI called for collective action. In a landmark decision in the Chancery Division of the High Court, Justice Dankwerts ruled in 1961 that '[t]he test is the existence of a common interest between the plaintiffs and the persons on whose behalf they sue. The twelve plaintiffs were appointed at a meeting in 1958 by the 46 houses which produce virtually all the Champagne imported into England and Wales.'[2]

Within fifty years of this ruling, brands became ubiquitous. It is impossible to visit a supermarket, retail outlet, or airport lounge without being bombarded by major brands. According to the social activist Naomi Klein, recent decades have been characterised by 'a considerable increase in spending on advertising … a renewed interest in puffing-up brand identities [which has sent] manufacturers on a cultural feeding frenzy … In the process virtually nothing has been left unbranded'.[3] Similarly, Douglas Holt, founder of the Cultural Strategy Group and L'Oréal Professor of Marketing at the University of Oxford, argued that branding is a core activity of capitalism: 'it is a distinctive mode of capital accumulation'.[4] Many famous brands are also global brands. A ranking of the top 100 global brands by the brand agency Interbrand in 2016 listed Apple, BMW, Siemens, Sony, and Toyota.[5] Such brands, and most of the others appearing on the list, are owned by multinational companies.

The Interbrand ranking includes Jack Daniels and Möet & Chandon, which are directly relevant to this book: both are associated with alcoholic beverages produced in specific geographical locations the boundaries of

---

[1] http://firstwefeast.com/drink/2014/10/champagne-quotes-from-the-famous-drinkers-who-loved-it-best

[2] *J. Bollinger and Others* v. *The Costa Brava Wine Company Limited, Reports of Patent, Design and Trade Marks Cases* (hereafter, RPC), 1961, No. 5: 117.

[3] N. Klein, *No Logo, No Space, No Choice, No Jobs* (London: Flamingo, 2001), 7–8. Klein's views helped launch a global anti-branding movement that links firms' branding efforts to the central concerns of those opposed to rampant globalisation. D. B. Holt, 'Why Do Brands Cause Trouble? A Dialectical Theory of Consumer Culture and Branding', *Journal of Consumer Research*, 29 (2002): 70.

[4] D. B. Holt, 'Toward a Sociology of Branding', *Journal of Consumer Culture*, 6 (2006): 300.

[5] The rankings are based on brand value. http://interbrand.com/best-brands/best-global-brands/2016/ranking/

which are legally defined and fiercely protected. Jack Daniels can only be produced in Lynchburg, Tennessee. State legislation stipulates that Tennessee Whiskey and Tennessee Sour Mash Whiskey labelling can only be used on whiskey produced in Tennessee according to criteria governing the composition of grain and the distilling, barrelling, and bottling processes.[6] Similarly, Möet & Chandon is renowned for its champagne. It is one of the biggest-selling marques and it holds a Royal Warrant. Authorised use of the GI Champagne requires, inter alia, that it is produced within the eponymous region and that it satisfies the regulations of Le Comité Interprofessionnel du vin de Champagne.[7]

My intention in writing this monograph is to provide an interdisciplinary history of indications of geographical origin (IGOs) in the global economy from the nineteenth century to the present. Adopting an integrative approach is necessary because the evolution of these indications reflects many overlapping themes. From an economic perspective, protection of IGOs is necessary because manufacturers and agriculturalists recognised that misrepresentation had adverse consequences, including loss of reputation and market share. Passing-off exploited the relationship between a product's geographical origin and price, and substantial returns were earned by unscrupulous traders, which simultaneously affected producers and consumers. Passing-off also blurred the correct operation of markets and price signals: did demand for New Zealand lamb increase because consumers appreciated its quality, or because there were greater opportunities to misrepresent it as Welsh? A related theme is how quickly and effectively did national and international law respond to the fraudulent use of IGOs, and to what extent did the law protect the relationship between geographical indication and location? This question is closely aligned to debates about whose interests – consumers' or producers' – matter most. Finally, without adequate legal protection, advertising campaigns promoting IGOs would have been ineffectual. It is no coincidence that during the interwar period the New Zealand government was aggressive in its prosecution of fraudsters when it engaged in a saturation-marketing campaign promoting New Zealand lamb in Britain.

---

[6] *State of Tennessee: An Act to amend Tennessee Code Annotated, Title 57, Chapter 2, relative to the manufacturing of intoxicating liquors.* Public Chapter No. 341, House Bill No. 1084, 2013.

[7] K. M. Guy, *When Champagne Became French* (Baltimore, MD: Johns Hopkins University Press, 2003), 8.

This book had its genesis in the mid-1990s when I began researching the trademarks used by Sheffield cutlers and the emergence of 'Sheffield'. Subsequently, collaboration with Geoff Tweedale, Mads Mordhorst, and Dev Gangjee, and participation in conferences and workshops, extended my interest in IGOs. Over time, I realised that this subject had been comparatively neglected by business historians. There were, of course, exceptions. Paul Duguid, for example, is prominent in debates on how and why regulatory and institutional change affected the development of IGOs in the port industry during the nineteenth and early twentieth centuries.[8] Nonetheless, it is fair to say that research on these indications has been dominated by scholars in legal history, marketing, and agricultural–rural development.[9]

Debates on IGOs extend far beyond the academic sphere. Producers and consumers, local and national governments, and international organisations, such as the World Trade Organization (WTO), became involved. The value attached to IGOs necessitated intervention by jurists to define the legal properties of these indications and their demarcation from other branches of intellectual property. Sometimes, the results of litigation appear bizarre: Feta and Basmati are recognised as GIs despite the fact that the geographical locations to which they refer do not exist. Other litigation has pitted the small company against the colossal multinational.[10] Finally, every conceivable grocery we buy signals its

---

[8] P. Duguid, 'Networks and Knowledge: The Beginnings and End of the Port Commodity Chain, 1703–1860', *Business History Review*, 79 (2005): 493–526. See also T. Mollanger, 'The Effects of Producers' Trademark Strategies on the Structure of the Cognac Brandy Supply Chain during the Second Half of the 19th Century: The Reconfiguration of Commercial Trust by the Use of Brands', forthcoming, *Business History*; J. Simpson, 'Cooperation and Cooperatives in Southern European Wine Production', *Advances in Agricultural History*, 1 (2000): 95–126; J. Simpson, 'Selling to Reluctant Drinkers: The British Wine Market, 1860–1914', *Economic History Review*, LVII (2004): 80–108; A. Stanziani, 'Wine Reputation and Quality Controls: The Origin of the AOCs in 19th Century France', *European Journal of Law and Economics*, 18 (2004):149–167; A. Stanziani, 'Information, Quality and Legal Rules: Wine Adulteration in Nineteenth Century France', *Business History*, 51 (2009): 268–291.

[9] See, especially, E. Barham and B. Sylvander (eds.), *Labels of Origin for Food: Local Development, Global Recognition* (Wallingford: CAB International, 2011); N. Papadopoulos and L. Heslop, 'Country Equity and Country Branding: Problems and Perspectives', *Journal of Brand Management*, 2 (2002): 294–314; D. Rangnekar, 'The Socio-Economics of Geographical Indications', *International Centre for Trade and Sustainable Development*, 4 (2004).

[10] C. Heath, 'The Budweiser Cases: A Brewing Conflict', in C. Heath and A. Kamperman (eds.), *Landmark Intellectual Property Cases and Their Legacy* (Biggleswade, The Netherlands: Kluwer Law International, 2011), 181–244.

provenance: wines from Burgundy and Rioja, Czech and German beers, French cheeses, Spanish and Italian hams, as well as Scotch beef and Welsh lamb.

It is useful at the outset to demarcate the terms used throughout this book. This is not an easy task. Dev Gangjee noted that the nomenclature resembles 'alphabet soup'.[11] The main difficulty is that international definitions of appellation, appellation of origin, geographical indications, and indications of source (IoS) were not clearly defined until the mid-twentieth century. Subsequently, the definition of appellation blurred into geographical indication. Regulations for correct nomenclature are currently governed by the Agreement on Trade-Related Aspects of Intellectual Property Rights (TRIPS), which defines GIs as

indications which identify a good as originating in the territory of a Member, or a region or locality in that territory, where a given quality, reputation or other characteristic of the good is essentially attributable to its geographical origin.[12]

In broad terms, and at the risk of exasperating specialist legal historians, the TRIPS definition of a GI is equivalent to appellation.[13] Throughout this book I use the terms GI and appellation interchangeably. However, for the sake of historical accuracy, I endeavour to use appellation until the TRIPS Agreement (1994), and GI thereafter. The key point to be cognisant of is that both terms require that a product possesses certain attributes that are *unique* and that can only be derived from a *specific* geographical region. The role of terroir provides classic examples of such products. Thus, the Chardonnay grape when cultivated in a particular subsoil in the region of Chablis produces the renowned Chablis wine, but when grown in other regions the wine does not possess the same characteristics and cannot be described as Chablis.[14] The most famous French examples of GIs are Burgundy, Champagne, and Cognac, for which, literally, 'the product is the place'. Many GIs have considerable lineage: Roquefort cheese was consumed by the ancient Romans and

---

[11] D. Gangjee, *Relocating the Law of Geographical Indications* (Cambridge: Cambridge University Press, 2012), 3.

[12] Article 22. TRIPS Agreement. This definition is similar to appellation. The TRIPS Agreement is binding on all Member States belonging to the World Trade Organization.

[13] The issue of whether geography per se imparts these specific qualities is hotly contested. Cultural factors and the role of human skill are considered equally important.

[14] M. A. Devlétian, 'The Protection of Appellations and Indications of Origin', *Industrial Property Quarterly*, 1 (1957): 12.

legislation passed by the Toulouse Parliament in 1666 reserved the sole rights to this name for cheese cured in the natural caves at Roquefort.[15]

The World Intellectual Property Organization (WIPO) defines an IoS (or indication of origin) as

an indication referring to a country (or to a place in that country) as being the country or place of origin of a product. In contrast to a geographical indication, an indication of source does not imply the presence of any special quality, reputation or characteristic of the product essentially attributable to its place of origin. Indications of source only require that the product on which the indication of source is used originate in a certain geographical area. Examples of indications of source are the mention on a product of the name of a country, or indications such as 'made in ... ', 'product of ... '.[16]

Indications of origin, which include country of origin and 'Made in', *only* indicate geographical location: they do not denote that the products emanating from that location have special characteristics due to geography (soil, climate, humidity). For example, Denmark and New Zealand, as applied to butter, are indications of source, and farmers based in Aarhus and Esbjerg, or the North and South Island, can use Denmark and New Zealand, respectively.[17] Throughout this book, I use the terms 'indication of origin' and 'country of origin', interchangeably, and use the term 'indications of geographical origin' (IGO) in a general sense when the distinction between GIs and indication of origin is unimportant.

IGOs are becoming increasingly visible in the twenty-first century and operate on three distinct geographical levels. At the national level, Swiss-made as applied to watches is a GI. Similarly, at the regional level, many European cheeses and meats are sold in wrappers imprinted with small yellow and red or yellow and blue labels indicating 'Protected Designation of Origin' (PDO) or 'Protected Geographical Origin' (PGI), respectively. These are also GIs and their boundaries are strictly demarcated and fiercely protected. Turning to indications of origin, New Zealand and Danish are renowned when applied to lamb and bacon, respectively. Likewise, 'Made in Germany' is valuable when applied to automobiles and engineering, and 'Made in Italy' has a cache when embossed on footwear.

Trademarks, brands, and IGOs are closely related. At the most basic level, a trademark indicates the manufacturer or trade source of a product.

[15] Gangjee, *Relocating the Law of Geographical Indications*, 32.
[16] www.wipo.int/geo_indications/en/faq_geographicalindications.html
[17] Subject to compliance with any state legislation.

A trademark may have other functions, but it must indicate trade origin. This essential function was central to trademark legislation introduced by many countries during the nineteenth century, and it remains valid today.[18] Prior to this legislation litigation for 'passing-off' – a broader class of action involving misrepresentation in its widest sense – was well established and, at least in a British context, can be dated to the early nineteenth century. But such actions were expensive and the outcome uncertain.[19] By creating legal property, registration facilitated action for infringement. Unsurprisingly, there was a rapid and substantial response to the Trademark Registration Acts.[20]

Trademarks are related to brands in the sense that both indicate trade origin. Additionally, a symbiotic relationship exists between them: 'Changes in trademark laws affect what sorts of signs will be registrable as trademarks and likely to attract investment and become brands, and changes in branding practices have repeatedly led to significant restructurings of trademark laws.'[21] Thus, Cadbury succeeded in registering a specific shade of purple which was indicative of its chocolate and Nike is the registered owner of the catchphrase 'Just do it.' However, in other respects, brands communicate more complex and nuanced information than trade origin. In broad terms, a brand represents a set of values or characteristics that are advertised to, and appreciated by, consumers.[22] Essentially, brands transform a commodity or product by adding associations. Culture, in its broadest sense, is central to this process. For Martin Kornberger,

[t]he movement from product-commodity to brand is a semiotic transformation . . . [with] important implications: first, brands become mental constructs that evoke

---

[18] D. Kitchin, D. Llewelyn, J. Mellor, R. Meade, T. Moody-Stuart, and D. Keeling, *Kerly's Law of Trade Marks and Trade Names* (London: Sweet & Maxwell, 2005), 8.

[19] T. A. Blanco-White, *Kerly's Law of Trade Marks and Trade Names* (London: Sweet & Maxwell, 1966), 1–10.

[20] P. Duguid, T. da Silva Lopes, and J. Mercer, 'Reading Registrations: An Overview of 100 Years of Trademark Registrations in France, the United Kingdom, and the United States', in T. da Silva Lopes and P. Duguid (eds.), *Trademarks, Brands and Competitiveness* (Abingdon: Routledge, 2010), 9–30.

[21] A. George, 'Editorial Brands: Interdisciplinary Perspectives on Trade Marks and Branding', *Brand Management*, 13 (2006): 175.

[22] S. Anholt, *Competitive Identity: The New Brand Management for Nations, Cities and Regions* (London: Palgrave Macmillan, 2006); J. Davis and S. Maniatis, 'Trademarks, Brands and Competition', in Silva Lopes and Duguid, *Trademarks, Brands, and Competitiveness*, 119–137; G. McCracken, *Culture and Consumption* (Bloomington: Indiana University Press, 1988); M. Schultz, Y. Antorini, and F. Csaba, *Corporate Branding* (Copenhagen: Copenhagen Business School, 2005).

different meanings; second, brands are powerful because they influence the social and cultural fabric of our world . . . In short, brands are cultural expressions and not just corporate enterprises . . . cultural codes constrain and enable the production of meaning.[23]

IGOs are different from 'proper' or 'technical' trademarks because they denote geographical, not trade origin.[24] In many common law countries, for example, these indications were traditionally registered as certification trademarks which required that a trade body or association certify that a product possessed certain attributes.[25] Nonetheless, many IGOs are powerful brands, especially when heritage is an important determinant of consumer choices. It is claimed that interest in heritage became prominent towards the end of the twentieth century, which was characterised by a 'nostalgia boom'.[26] David Lewis and Darren Bridger argue that during this period a new group of consumers emerged whose 'attitudes, aspirations and purchasing patterns are unlike any before them'. Because their basic needs were quickly and easily satisfied, these new consumers 'tend-[ed] to reject mass-produced and mass-marketed commodities in favour of products and services that can claim to be in some way authentic'.[27] For IGOs, authenticity involves a connection to time and place which affirms tradition; authenticity is also a core component of successful brands because it forms part of a unique brand identity.[28]

'Heritage' brands denote longevity; they are proof that key attributes of a product do not change through time. Recent scholarship in heritage branding has claimed:

Historical culture provides a rich foundation for branding processes and practices; and deploying history and heritage in brand development hardly requires a leap of faith given how deeply and extensively the past infiltrates everyday life . . .

[23] M. Kornberger, *Brand Society: How Brands Transform Management and Lifestyle* (New York: Cambridge University Press, 2010), 42–43.

[24] Though trademarks and IGOs may complement each other. Thus, a product may be marked with an IGO and a trademark. The former denotes geographical origin; the latter identifies the products of a particular manufacturer. V. Mantrov, *EU Law on Indications of Geographical Origin* (London: Springer, 2014), 64.

[25] N. Dawson, *Certification Trademarks: Law and Practice* (London: Intellectual Property Publishing Limited, 1988); J. Belson, *Certification Marks* (London: Sweet & Maxwell, 2002).

[26] S. Brown, R. V. Kozinets, and J. F. Sherry Jr., 'Teaching Old Brands New Tricks: Retro Branding and the Revival of Brand Meaning', *Journal of Marketing*, 67 (2003): 19.

[27] D. Lewis and D. Bridger, *The Soul of the New Consumer* (London: Nicholas Brealey, 2001), 3–4.

[28] M. B. Beverland, 'Crafting Brand Authenticity: The Case of Luxury Wines', *Journal of Management Studies*, 42 (2005): 1003, 1007.

Although the impact of history and the past assumes many different forms, looking at cultural and historical codes of strong brands can provide particularly useful insights into branding practices ... our approach to branding and brand development is deeply indebted to this particular understanding of the past and the present as being mutually inclusive of each other.[29]

The importance of heritage is complemented by human geographers. Andrew Pike has argued that '[o]rigination means the attempts by actors – producers, circulators, consumers and regulators inter-related in spatial circuits – to construct geographical associations for goods and services'.[30] However, the temporal and spatial signals communicated by brands are not always constant or robust: they are 'inherently unstable' and may be falsely reinvented.[31] Consider, for example, Newcastle Brown Ale. This beer is currently produced in Tadcaster (North Yorkshire), but it retains Newcastle in the brand because this is where the beer was originally produced and where it has a strong local allegiance. By the early twenty-first century, the United States had become the biggest market for this beer. Because American consumers had no interest where in England the beer was produced, the company decided to add the legend 'Imported from England'.[32]

Concerns have also been raised that interpreting 'place' as a static concept is misguided: 'If places can be conceptualised in terms of the social interactions which they tie together, then it is also the case that these interactions themselves are not motionless things, frozen in time.'[33] Other

---

[29] J. Schroeder, J. Borgerson, and Z. Wu, 'A Brand Culture Perspective on Global Brands', in F. D. Riley, J. Singh, and C. Blankson (eds.), *The Routledge Companion to Contemporary Brand Management* (Abingdon: Routledge, 2016), 155. Brand heritage is recognised as important in a diverse range of industries. See, for example, B. T. Hudson, 'Brand Heritage and the Renaissance of Cunard', *European Journal of Marketing*, 45 (2011): 1538–1556; T. da Silva Lopes, *Global Brands: The Evolution of Multinationals in Alcoholic Beverages* (New York: Cambridge University Press, 2007); K.-P. Wiedmann, N. Hennigs, S. Schmidt, and T. Wuestefeld, 'Drivers and Outcomes of Brand Heritage: Consumers' Perception of Heritage Brands in the Automative Industry', *Journal of Marketing, Theory and Practice*, 19 (2011): 205–220.

[30] A. Pike, *Origination: The Geographies of Brands and Branding* (Chichester: Wiley-Blackwell, 2015), 17.

[31] Pike, *Origination*, 21; E. Hobsbawm, 'Introduction: Inventing Traditions', in E. Hobsbawm and T. Ragnger (eds.), *The Invention of Tradition* (Cambridge: Cambridge University Press, 1983), 1–14.

[32] A. Pike, 'Placing Brands and Branding: A Socio-Spatial Biography of Newcastle Brown Ale', *Transactions of the Institute of British Geographers*, 36 (2011): 213–216. The decision to relocate production out of Newcastle meant the beer ceased to be classed as a PGI.

[33] D. Massey, 'A Global Sense of Place', *Marxism Today* (June 1991): 29.

geographers have enhanced this perspective to incorporate GIs. Using the example of Champagne, Bronwyn Parry questions whether it is meaningful to claim that the qualities of this wine were determined by terroir. In Parry's view, the current emphasis on GIs is 'completely outmoded' and may hinder the development of 'more outward-looking and progressive approaches to the protection of unique communal products'.[34]

It is incontrovertible that cultural, social, and political forces have had a direct bearing on GIs. Consider the term 'appellation d'origine contrôlée' (AOC), which is central to French wine regulations and underpinned by the concept of 'usages locaux, loyaux, et constants' ('local, loyal, and constant usages'). Erica Farmer has shown how the combination of these three elements provides a judicial benchmark that incorporates qualitative values which help differentiate an AOC wine in one location from that of its neighbours: 'Boundaries of local communities are defined socially ... the social perceptions of the product in connection to it are just as important.' The role played by sociocultural forces in demarcating the boundaries of wine appellations is crucial. The interaction of these forces creates 'an enforceable legal framework that allows for the interpretation of culturally based evidence'.[35]

The economics literature indicates that trademarks can generate numerous advantages to producers and consumers. Benefits to the former include the creation of monopoly rents, incentives to maintain quality, facilitating entry into new markets, and generating inertia in consumer preferences.[36] It is claimed that trademarks are useful because they reduce search costs, which helps consumers match their individual preferences to specific products, and because they overcome the problem of asymmetric information, which can lead to quality dissipation and

---

[34] B. Parry, 'Geographical Indications: Not All "Champagne and Roses"', in L. Bently, J. Davis, and J. C. Ginsburg (eds.), *Trade Marks and Brands: An Interdisciplinary Critique* (Cambridge: Cambridge University Press, 2008), 379–380.

[35] E. A. Farmer, 'Local, Loyal, and Constant: The Legal Construction of Wine in Bordeaux', in R. E. Black and R. C. Ulin (eds.), *Wine and Culture: Vineyard to Glass* (London: Bloomsbury, 2013), 145–146, 148–149.

[36] A. Griffiths, 'A Law-and-Economics Perspective on Trade Marks', in L. Bently, J. Davis, and J. C. Ginsbur (eds.), *Trade Marks and Brands: An Interdisciplinary Critique* (Cambridge: Cambridge University Press, 2010), 241–266; B. Klein and K. B. Leffler, 'The Role of Market Forces in Assuring Contractual Performance', *Journal of Political Economy*, 89 (1981): 615–641; W. M. Landes and R. A. Posner, 'Trademark Law: An Economic Perspective', *Journal of Law and Economics*, 30 (1987): 265–309; G. B. Ramello, 'What's in a Sign? Trademark Law and Economic Theory', *Journal of Economic Surveys*, 20 (2006): 547–565.

'false trading'.[37] In theory, there is no reason why the benefits trademarks afford consumers and producers cannot be obtained from IGOs. Thus, demarcation of specific areas ensures that the produce of one region is not identical with produce from another. Terroir means that wine bearing the appellation Pauillac is different from that labelled St Estèphe. Only wine producers in the former are entitled to mark their wine Pauillac and thereby enjoy the premia that this singular appellation commands. Similarly, only indigenous farmers are lawfully permitted to mark New Zealand on their lamb. In both cases, governance by a cooperative, trade association, or national body seeks to prevent individual members debasing quality and 'freeriding' on the reputation of the IGO.

Trademarks and IGOs are a form of monopoly and only the proprietors are lawfully entitled to use them. Consider, for example, Champagne. The owners of this appellation cannot prevent competitors producing sparkling wine from Chardonnay, Pinot Meunier, or Pinot Noir grapes, which are also used to make Champagne. Nor can they prevent the labelling of such wine as 'French sparkling wine' (if it satisfies relevant regulations). Indeed, a famous type of French sparkling wine made according to the 'Champagne method' of fermentation in the bottle, sometimes using different grape varieties, is Crémant de Loire, which has its own appellation. Other non-French sparkling wines, for example, Cava and Prosecco, also have considerable repute. Similarly, there is nothing to prevent companies producing high-quality, luxury automobiles, using materials identical to those of Rolls Royce. But rival producers of sparkling wine or high-end motor cars are prohibited from marking their products Champagne and Rolls Royce, respectively. For this reason, appellations are protected from any misuse 'which misleads the public as to the geographical origin of the good'. Additional protection is afforded appellations for wines and spirits, which must not be accompanied by the words, 'kind', 'like', or 'style'. Similarly, trademarks are protected from dilution, blurring, and tarnishing because of the 'likelihood of consumer confusion'.[38]

---

[37] G. A. Akerlof, 'The Market for "Lemons": Quality Uncertainty and the Market Mechanism', *Quarterly Journal of Economics*, 84 (1970): 488–500. Recent scholarship provides a critique of the benefits that consumers are alleged to derive from trademarks. P. Duguid, 'Information in the Mark and Marketplace: A Multivocal Account', *Enterprise and Society*, 15 (2014): 1–30.

[38] See, for example, W. M. Landes and R. A Posner, *The Economic Structure of Intellectual Property Law* (Cambridge, MA: Belknap Press, 2003): 201–209; I. S. Fhima, 'The Actual

Because of their monopoly characteristics, IGOs can be viewed through the lens of strategic management. According to the resource-based view of the firm, producers in a given industry have different resources. Firms are heterogeneous, not homogeneous. Consequently, competition does not lead to convergence in rents. Imperfect imitation is one component of these resources which is particularly relevant to GIs. Restrictions on imitation include property rights to scarce resources which can depend on time and space: 'Once this particular unique time in history passes, firms that do not have space- and time-dependent resources cannot obtain them, and thus these resources are imperfectly imitable.'[39] GIs in particular are exemplars of non-imitable resources which are gaining recognition in the strategic management literature. Using a telling example, Michael Beverland showed that the 2000 release of Chateau Latour sold for around $500 a bottle, whereas a neighbouring estate – Chateau Haut Paulliac – which is less than a metre from the boundary of Latour, sold its wine for $20. Beverland explained why authenticity is integral to the branding strategies employed by luxury French winemakers: 'The idea of terroir was responsible for providing products with uniqueness and allure that would be difficult for competitors to replicate (uniqueness is an important form of authenticity).'[40] Similarly, Maxim Voronov and collaborators have shown how the establishment of the Vitners Quality Alliance (VQA) was important to the growth of fine wine production in Ontario. This Alliance is responsible for the award of VQA which is a controlled designation of origin and a valuable legitimising mechanism.[41]

Dilution Requirement of the United States, United Kingdom and European Union: A Comparative Analysis', *Boston University Journal of Science & Technology Law*, 12 (2006): 271–309.

[39] J. Barney, 'Firm Resources and Sustained Competitive Advantage', *Journal of Management*, 17 (1991): 107–108; M. A. Peteraf, 'The Cornerstones of Competitive Advantage: A Resource Based View', *Strategic Management Journal*, 14 (1993): 181–182. These classic articles on the RBV launched a substantial debate among strategic management scholars which remains current.

[40] Beverland, 'Crafting Brand Authenticity', 1008. The release of wine on a given date does not indicate vintage because the best wines are stored for many years. If Latour looks expensive, readers should not enquire too closely into the price of Romanée-Conti.

[41] M. Voronev, D. De Clercq, and C. R. Hinings, 'Conformity and Distinctiveness in a Global Institutional Framework: The Legitimation of Ontario Fine Wine', *Journal of Management Studies*, 50 (2013): 607–645. Owning valuable and rare resources may be insufficient to generate sustained advantage in wine production. J. Barthélemy, 'The Impact of Technical Consultants on the Quality of Their Clients' Products: Evidence from the Bordeaux Wine Industry', *Strategic Management Journal*, 38 (2017): 1174–1190.

A further similarity between trademarks and IGOs is the need to protect consumers from deception. Infringement of a competitor's trademark is comparable to misrepresenting an IGO. It is immaterial if the substitute product is identical in all other respects, for example, price and quality, to the genuine article. Even if consumers do not care about provenance and are equally content with French or New Zealand wine, they must not be deceived into buying the former if they request the latter. Moreover, from a legal perspective, it is irrelevant if consumer preferences stand on base motives. In 1963, the Singer Manufacturing Company successfully appealed the decision permitting Birginal-Bigsby to register the brand American Beauty for its Japanese sewing machines. The court acknowledged that 'it may well be true that some segment of the American public prefers sewing machines of American manufacture to Japanese machines. We think that nothing more is required. That segment is entitled to buy according to its prejudices and preferences without the danger of being deceived or confused by geographically misdescriptive marks.'[42]

The adverse effects of trademark fraud on individual firms were reported in evidence given before a British Select Committee in 1862. Bass, Spear & Jackson, and other leading British manufacturers, complained that fraud had severely damaged their reputation and weakened their prospects in export markets.[43] It was claimed misrepresentation of Balbriggan (Ireland) almost eradicated the hosiery trade in that town.[44] Allegations involving the substitution of US beef for Scottish were made by British farmers, and Harald Faber, the Danish Agricultural Commissioner to Britain, investigated the passing-off of Russian and Siberian butter as Danish.[45] The consequences of misrepresentation were early recognised in the courts. In 1898 a judge presiding over a leading US case stated:

---

[42] *The Singer Manufacturing Company and Singer Sewing Machine Company* v. *Birginal-Bigsby Corporation*, 319 F.2d, US Court of Customs and Patent Appeals, 1963, 277.

[43] Select Committee on Trade Marks Bill, and Merchandize Marks Bill. Parliamentary Papers (hereafter, P.P.) XII.431 (1862): QQ. 8–33; QQ. 2489–2506.

[44] Special Report from the Select Committee on Merchandize Marks Act (1862) Amendment Bill. P.P. X.357 (1887): QQ. 2997–3172.

[45] D. M. Higgins and M. Mordhorst, 'Reputation and Export Performance: Danish Butter Exports and the British Market, c. 1880–c. 1914', *Business History*, 50 (2008): 185–204; D. M. Higgins and D. Gangjee, '"Trick or Treat?" The Misrepresentation of American Beef Exports in Britain during the Nineteenth Century', *Enterprise & Society*, 11 (2010): 203–241.

Such practices often inflict the most deplorable damage upon the genuine and reputable products of those places, not only in that they rob them of a good part of the revenue directly, but the greatest damage consists in the depreciation which the indifferent wares, entirely foreign to the nature of the place from which they are said to come, inflict upon the entire locality.[46]

It is no coincidence that misrepresentation of brands and IGOs first became internationally prominent from the late nineteenth century. From an economics perspective, globalisation during this period was characterised by four defining features: trade liberalisation and the integration of national currencies via the gold standard; transport and communication revolutions which lowered the cost of transport and the barrier of distance; industrial revolutions which powered economic growth, and trade-stimulating peace in the era of Pax Britannica.[47] The integration of 'markets across space', or 'hard globalisation', resulted in the international convergence of commodity and factor prices.[48] This economic interpretation of globalisation has been criticised on its own terms: the available data used to test convergence may suffer from statistical bias, differences in prices do not accurately reflect inherent quality variation in the traded products, and it is not clear whether the benefits claimed for integration affected long-term economic growth.[49]

Additionally, this focus on four key themes overlooks the importance of institutional developments which helped markets function. Management scholars have suggested that cultural and institutional forces have also been fundamental to the process of globalisation. It was argued that transnational organisations such as the WTO exerted 'trickle-down' effects which altered the ways in which national governments interpreted the 'legal rules of the game', and that globalisation required global, not national, organisational structures.[50] Business historians have emphasised the importance of

---

[46] *Pillsbury-Washburn Flour-Mills Co., Limited, et al.* v. *Eagle.* 86 *Federal Reporter*, 627.

[47] K. H. O'Rourke and J. G. Williamson, 'Introduction: The Spread of and Resistance to Global Capitalism', in L. Neal and J. G. Williamson (eds.), *The Cambridge History of Capitalism.* Vol. II: *The Spread of Capitalism from 1848 to the Present* (Cambridge: Cambridge University Press, 2014), 4–5.

[48] J. de Vries, 'The Limits to Globalization in the Early Modern World', *Economic History Review*, 63 (2010): 713–714; K. H. O'Rourke and J. G. Williamson, 'Once More: When Did Globalization Begin?', *European Review of Economic History*, 8 (2004): 109–117.

[49] G. Federico, 'How Much Do We Know about Market Integration in Europe?', *Economic History Review*, 65 (2012): 488–490. Quality differences also enfeeble reliance on the 'law of one price'. At various times the best-quality Danish and Australian butter were reserved solely for export.

[50] M. L. Djelic and S. Quack, 'Institutions and Transnationalization', in R. Greenwood, C. Oliver, R. Suddaby, and K. Sahlin (eds.), *The Sage Handbook of Organisational*

the proliferation of international business networks as global trade expanded.[51] The growth of national legislation to prohibit fraudulent transactions and the establishment of an international architecture to protect market exchange when there was quality uncertainty were equally critical but 'softer' features of globalisation.[52]

The transport revolution removed the barrier of distance and eliminated proximity between buyer and seller. Mira Wilkins argued that trademarks were the solution to the problem of quality uncertainty caused by this separation; that trademarks were indispensable to the growth of the 'modern multifunctional, multiplant, multiproduct, multiregional, multinational enterprise', and, 'The trademark becomes a fundamental and absolutely essential property ... when the firm must find means to increase its own sales to lower average unit costs to realise the advantages of economies of scale'.[53] But trademarks were not vital only to large-scale multinational enterprises: they are essential whenever there is quality uncertainty. IGOs share a key characteristic of trademarks and brands because they create trust in anonymous, market-based exchanges.[54]

Creating trust in brands and IGOs requires that proprietors have effective legal remedies for misrepresentation. Nationally, many common and civil law countries created domestic regimes for their protection during the nineteenth century. Registration, which created legal property in trademarks, was an integral feature of such schemes. But the first wave

---

Institutionalism (Los Angeles, CA: Sage, 2008), 299–323; G. S. Drori, 'Institutionalism and Globalisation Studies', in Greenwood, Oliver, Suddaby, and Sahlin, *The Sage Handbook of Organisational Institutionalism*, 455.

[51] J. E. Robins, 'A Common Brotherhood for Their Mutual Benefit: Sir Charles Macara and Internationalism in the Cotton Industry, 1904–1914', *Enterprise & Society*, 16 (2015): 847–888; E. Buchnea, 'Transatlantic Transformations: Visualising Change over Time in the Liverpool–New York Trade Network, 1763–1833', *Enterprise & Society*, 15 (2015): 687–721.

[52] See, especially, A. Stanziani, *Rules of Exchange: French Capitalism in Comparative Perspective, Eighteenth to Early Twentieth Centuries* (New York: Cambridge University Press, 2012).

[53] M. Wilkins, 'The Neglected Intangible Asset: The Influence of the Trade Mark on the Rise of the Modern Corporation', *Business History*, 34 (1992): 66, 71. In business history, similar themes have been discussed by A. D. Chandler, *Scale and Scope: The Dynamics of Industrial Capitalism* (Cambridge, MA: Harvard University Press, 1994); R. Church and A. Godley, *The Emergence of Modern Marketing* (Abingdon: Routledge, 2003); da Silva Lopes, *Global Brands*. The relevance of Wilkins' arguments to IGOs is critiqued in Chapter 2.

[54] Kornberger, *Brand Society*, 52. However, this need not mean there is equal bargaining power between consumers and producers. C. Lury, *Brands: The Logos of the Global Economy* (London: Routledge, 2004), 127.

of globalisation meant the international protection of all forms of intellectual property became imperative. In principle, there was no reason why domestic legislation could not be extended abroad via bilateral treaties. However, there was considerable variation between countries in what constituted a trademark and unease that protection afforded foreign citizens exceeded that available to domestic citizens.

Despite their similarities it is necessary to recognise key differences between brands and IGOs. Perhaps the single most important difference is that there is a collective interest in IGOs. For this reason, they are intrinsically related to collective and certification marks. The latter denote a common relationship among the enterprises and/or a common characteristic of the products sold by the members. A collective mark is owned by an association for the use of its members: it is an indication which distinguishes the output of members from non-members. Certification marks are different: they can be used by any producer demonstrating that their products comply with the standard specified by the proprietor of the IGO.[55] It is well established that IGOs cannot be exclusively appropriated by an individual because this would create a monopoly and debar others located in the same area from using it.[56] Collective ownership is the source of another difference between trademarks and IGOs: the latter serve a public interest which may deserve additional protection.

In Europe, creation of PDO and PGI in 1992 was part of a comprehensive strategy designed to enhance the competitiveness of European agriculture, reduce dependence on subsidies, and prevent rural depopulation. By appealing to heritage and reputation the PDO and PGI schemes were designed to establish a robust link between place – or terroir – and product. Foodstuffs registered under either scheme are rigorously defended within the EU. Globally, protection is afforded under the TRIPS Agreement. Within the EU, the PDO and PGI schemes are justified because they generate a number of public benefits, for example, greater investment in the locality. To achieve these benefits a clear relationship must be established between the characteristics of the product and its locality. This quality assurance function, which is enshrined in law, does not apply to trademarks, the proprietors of which have only a private incentive to establish and maintain a certain

[55] Belson, *Certification Marks*, 20–21.
[56] J. L. Hopkins, *The Law of Trademarks, Trade Names and Unfair Competition* (Cincinnati, OH: W. H. Anderson, 1924), 93–94, 164.

level of quality.[57] A related issue is that it would be unjust for an individual trademark owner who has not contributed to the reputation of a GI to deprive a community of its use. Accurate demarcation of the boundaries from which a GI takes its name is vital to prevent consumer deception. But again, and unlike trademarks, a broader range of interests are involved. For example, determination of the boundaries of a GI incorporates the interests of the local population.[58]

A further substantial difference between brands and IGOs is that the latter cannot be delocalised. As noted earlier in this chapter, the boundaries demarcating an appellation are rigorously determined. Proprietors of GIs, for example, must establish that the quality or characteristics or reputation of a product are attributable to a particular region. Indications of origin cannot be delocalised either, though they do not benefit from the same level of protection afforded GIs. In contrast, most brands are frequently delocalised: Apple, Nike, and Sony do not indicate geographical origin; they are owned by multinational companies and their products are produced across the globe.

Subsequent debates within the WTO emphasised further differences between trademarks and GIs. It was claimed that the former can be acquired almost instantaneously, simply by an 'intent to use' or the lodging of an application with a registration system. In contrast, the creation of a GI requires the establishment of a link between a region and a product's characteristics, which may require many years. Indeed, as is often the case in the EU, such a link is the result of centuries of tradition. Consequently, it is argued the 'first-in-time, first in right' principle provides an unfair advantage to trademark owners.[59] It is also claimed that because the choice of a trademark is arbitrary, there is a virtually unlimited range of names that can be chosen, and by deliberately selecting a geographical name as a trademark, a firm accepts the risk that the same name may be used concurrently as a GI. In contrast, GIs are 'necessary' because the range of names is limited a priori by well-established usage. Rights holders to GIs may not easily change the name given by the public to the geographical area in which they are located. Consequently, it

---

[57] Economic analyses of trademarks suggest quality assurance is endogenised within the firm. Klein and Leffler, 'The Role of Market Forces'.

[58] R. W. Benson, 'Toward a New Theory for the Protection of Geographical Indications', *Industrial Property*, 4 (1978): 130.

[59] Essentially, this principle ensures that between competing users in the same geographic market, the exclusive right to use a mark belongs to the first to establish trademark rights in that market. Problems emerge when the trademark includes a geographic name.

is more difficult to find an alternative GI than it is to find an alternative trademark.[60]

The rapid growth of international trade meant national legislation was no longer sufficient to protect intellectual property. Common law countries such as Britain and the United States viewed GIs as a subset of trademarks, whereas France, a civil law country, afforded sui generis[61] protection. Another problem was how to determine which category of intellectual property took precedence. Thus, if the name of a place was registered as a trademark, did this prevent subsequent registration of the name as a GI? Similarly, whose interests – consumers' or producers' – were paramount? Lori Simon has argued that the United States has been more concerned with protecting consumers from deception. Conversely, in France, protection of GIs is primarily designed to protect producers.[62] Viewed from one perspective, such differences appear inconsequential: lawful use of GIs ensures that consumers and genuine producers benefit. Such conflicts were aired regularly following the Paris Convention for the Protection of Industrial Property in 1883. This Convention was the first attempt to build an international architecture for the protection of all forms of intellectual property. Disagreement between civil and common law countries on how to categorise and protect GIs remains a source of conflict today and has the potential to undermine the Transatlantic Trade and Investment Partnership.

It may appear self-evident that the prevention of consumer deception automatically benefits producers. In the absence of deception, producers are unaffected by the direct loss of sales generated by fraudulent activity. Similarly, the elimination of misrepresentation involving substitution of inferior (low-quality) products for the genuine article ensures that there is no dilution of goodwill. However, with GIs, it does not always hold that consumer protection necessarily benefits producers. It is argued that even if consumers are not deceived by 'California Champagne' or 'British Sherry', the goodwill attached to wines from these regions is undermined.[63] Unchecked, dilution can result in genericide, meaning

[60] WTO, Dispute Settlement Board, 'First Written Submission by the European Communities', 25 May 2004 (document WT/DS174/R/Add.2).

[61] In this context, sui generis means that GIs benefit from protection as a distinct class of intellectual property.

[62] L. E. Simon, 'Appellations of Origin: The Continuing Controversy', *Northwestern Journal of International Law & Business*, 5 (1983): 151–152.

[63] Other problems arise from this type of dilution. For example, how to reclaim the goodwill lost through usurpation without infringing the rights of the usurpers? Benson, 'Toward a New Theory', 129–130.

a GI refers to the mode of manufacture or a type of product. Classic examples include Brussels pâté, Brie, and Frankfurters, which are now globally produced. Of course, genericide is also a problem confronting brands. Nonetheless, there are grounds for believing that the threat of genericide is more pronounced for GIs. For example, from the late nineteenth century, Italian emigrants to the United States started producing their own versions of Parmesan and Mozzarella. Currently, the United States considers these names generic and it has resisted attempts by the EU to reclassify them as GIs. Resolution of this particular dispute is hindered by the problem of how to determine net economic costs: 'Attempts to limit the use of such terms to specific producer groups would be viewed as a restriction on commercial speech and would impede the signalling of competitive substitutability in the marketplace [but] generic use serves as "free advertising" for the original regional speciality and should be permitted.'[64]

Country of origin, or 'Made in', has featured prominently in campaigns to restore national economic prosperity. Usually, these initiatives were prompted by concerns that consumer deception in the domestic market undermined the competitiveness of indigenous manufacturers. In Britain, for example, the Merchandise Marks Act of 1887 prohibited the application of false trade descriptions which included 'any description, statement, or other indication, direct or indirect ... as to the place or country in which any goods were made or produced'.[65] This legislation was followed by other countries. France, Germany, and Spain introduced similar legislation in 1892, 1894, and 1902, respectively.[66] In the United States, the McKinley Report noted, 'The admitted superiority of certain lines of American goods has induced the importation of foreign imitations of inferior quality, with American brands, to be put on our market as the superior goods of American manufacture.'[67] Subsequently, the McKinley tariff of 1890 mandated compulsory origin marking on *all* products imported to the United States.[68]

---

[64] D. S. Gangjee, 'Genericide: The Death of a Geographical Indication', in D. S. Gangjee, (ed.), *Research Handbook on Intellectual Property and Geographical Indications* (Cheltenham: Edward Elgar, 2017), 510–511.

[65] 50 & 51 Vict., Ch. 28, *Merchandise Marks Act*, 1887. s.3 (b).

[66] League of Nations. CEI 20. International Economic Conference. *Marks of Origin.* Geneva, May (1927): 37–39, 52.

[67] US International Trade Commission, *Country of Origin Marking: Review of Laws, Regulations, and Practices.* Investigation 332–366, Washington, DC (1996) 3–5.

[68] Tariff Act, 1890, Ch. 1244 26 Stat, s.6.

The requirement to mark imports with an indication of origin is complementary to tariffs and other quantitative restrictions.[69] Both categories of obstacle are intended to prevent unfair competition, though each is premised on different criteria. The former is based on the legal construct of consumer deception and ensures that consumers do not buy the products of one country in the belief that they originate from another. The latter are deployed to prevent 'dumping', which belongs to economic theories of unfair competition and does not rely on consumer deception. However, customs determination of source is based on rules of origin for the purpose of levying duties which may not correspond with consumer perception of origin. Despite this complementarity, it is fair to state that scholars in business and economic history have focused more on tariffs and have all but neglected non-tariff barriers, especially indications of origin.[70]

Such oversight is absent from the marketing literature. The study of country of origin by marketing scholars began in the early 1960s. Ernest Dichter stated, 'The little phrase "Made in ... " can have a tremendous influence on the acceptance and success of products over and above the specific advertising techniques used by themselves.'[71] But it was not until Schooler's seminal study in 1965 that empirical testing of the country of origin effect emerged.[72] Among marketing scholars there is general agreement that, 'One of the oldest and most persistent concerns in international marketing is whether the origin of a product makes it more or less favourable to consumers.'[73]

---

[69] Marking imports with an indication of origin can be viewed as a 'soft' defensive mechanism to protect domestic producers. It does not extol the virtues of domestic products but relies on prejudice towards imports.

[70] Tariffs are discussed in D. A. Irwin, 'Higher Tariffs, Lower Revenues? Analyzing the Fiscal Aspects of "The Great Tariff Debate of 1888"', *Journal of Economic History*, 58 (1998): 59–72; D. A. Irwin, 'Did Late-Nineteenth Century U.S. Tariffs Promote Infant Industries? Evidence from the Tinplate Industry', *Journal of Economic History*, 60 (2000): 335–360; A. Marrison, *British Business and Protection, 1903–1932* (Oxford: Clarendon Press, 1996); M.-W. Palen, 'Protection, Federation and Union: The Global Impact of the McKinley Tariff upon the British Empire, 1890–94', *Journal of Imperial and Commonwealth History*, 38 (2010): 395–418; M-W. Palen, *The Conspiracy of Free Trade: The Anglo-American Struggle Over Empire and Economic Globalization, 1846–1896* (Cambridge: Cambridge University Press, 2016).

[71] E. Dichter, 'The World Customer', *Harvard Business Review*, 40 (1962): 116.

[72] R. Schooler, 'Product Bias in Central American Common Market', *Journal of Marketing Research* 2 (1965): 394–397.

[73] N. Koschate-Fischer, A. Diamantopoulos, and K. Oldenkotte, 'Are Consumers Really Willing to Pay More for a Favourable Country Image? A Study of Country-of-Origin Effects on Willingness to Pay', *Journal of International Marketing*, 20 (2012): 19.

Until the early 1980s, much of the literature simply replicated Schooler: 'single-cue' studies – in which only the country of origin is used to assess consumer preferences – appeared to generate convincing results.[74] However, accelerating globalisation encouraged marketing scholars to question the validity of this methodology. The pioneering study by Nicolas Papadopoulos and Louise Heslop was critical of traditional country-of-origin literature because it was narrow and misleading: it assumed a *single* place of origin. It was also recognised that a country's image need not be positive for all products.[75] Subsequently, more emphasis was placed on multiple-cue studies in which country of origin was one of many variables. A study by Bruno Godey and colleagues on the determinants of luxury product consumption in seven countries revealed that design and brand were ranked first and second, respectively, while country of origin had the lowest rank.[76] It was argued that country of origin needed to be unpacked into: country of design, country of assembly, country of parts, and country of manufacture.[77] Other scholars claimed country of origin was increasingly considered to be that which consumers typically associated with the product. In other words, what mattered was consumer *perception* of origin.[78]

One theme which emerges from the marketing literature is that the interaction between company brands and country of origin is sufficiently complex to cast doubt on whether it is meaningful to distinguish the effects of either. It is in this context that studies on the growth of

---

[74] J. M. Pharr, 'Synthesising Country-of-Origin Research From the Last Decade: Is the Concept Still Salient in an Era of Global Brands?', *Journal of Marketing, Theory and Practice*, 34 (2005): 34.

[75] N. Papadopoulos and L. A. Heslop, *Product Country Images: Impact and Role in International Marketing* (New York: International Business Press, 1993), 4–8; E. Jaffe and I. Nebenzahl, *National Image and Competitive Advantage* (Copenhagen: Copenhagen Business School, 2001), 53–55.

[76] B. Godey, B. Pederzoli, G. Aiello, R. Donvito, P. Chan, H. Oh, R. Singh, I. I. Skorobogatykh, J. Tsuchiya, and B. Weitz, 'Brand and Country of Origin Effect on Consumers' Decision to Purchase Luxury Products', *Journal of Business Research*, 65 (2012): 1461–1470.

[77] T. Aichner, 'Country-of-Origin Marketing: A List of Typical Strategies with Examples', *Journal of Brand Management*, 21 (2014): 81–93.

[78] J-C. Usunier, 'Relevance in Business Research: The Case of Country-of-Origin Research in Marketing', *European Management Review*, 3 (2006): 62; P. Magnusson, S. A. Westjohn, and S. Zdravkovic, '"What? I Thought Samsung Was Japanese": Accurate or Not, Perceived Country of Origin Matters', *International Marketing Review*, 28 (2011): 468; L. Hamzaoui-Essoussi, D. Merunka, and B. Bartikowski, 'Brand Origin and Country of Manufacture Influences on Brand Equity and the Moderating Role of Brand Typicality', *Journal of Business Research*, 64 (2011): 973.

multinational companies (MNCs) are complementary. Geoffrey Jones argued that during the late nineteenth century and in the post-1945 period, MNCs were pivotal to the trade which characterised globalisation. Jones' research revealed that the total number of British-based single and multi-plant manufacturing subsidiaries owned by US companies grew from 48 in 1907 to 264 in 1935 and reached 728 by 1962. Moreover, between 1913 and 2010, world foreign direct investment as a percentage of world trade increased from 9 per cent to 30.3 per cent. By 2009, intra-firm trade accounted for 48 per cent of US manufactured imports and approximately 30 per cent of US exports of manufactures.[79]

The global cosmetics industry provides a potent example of the ambiguity that exists in the relationship between company brands and country of origin. For Jones, '[o]ne of the peculiarities of the global economy was that country, or city, of origin assumed an even greater importance as an indication of quality and prestige', even though many leading cosmetics brands, for example, Ponds, Max Factor, L'Oréal, and Nivea, are produced in multiple countries, and employ generic terms such as 'eau de cologne', 'eau de parfum', and 'eau de toilette'.[80] Recent work on the Italian textile industry suggests that other problems can arise when country of origin becomes product-centric. The Prato region in Italy is home to 3,000 Chinese-owned textile companies specialising in low-end fashions which threaten to 'undermine the prestige of "Made in Italy" in traditional high-end markets'.[81]

If origin clues are firmly embedded within well-known brand names the effect of the former cannot be eliminated by changing country of manufacture. Informing consumers that Toyota cars are manufactured in the United States may not prevent them believing that Toyota is a Japanese brand. Conversely, the decisions of MNCs to alter the location of their manufacturing/assembly operations can undermine the importance of country of origin, especially if consumers use brand name as a proxy for country of origin. It is recognised that many important brands are associated with countries possessing strong country-of-origin images. This observation may explain why multinationals do not support origin labelling since global sourcing is partly based on low-cost countries with

---

[79] G. Jones, *Entrepreneurship and Multinationals: Global Business and the Making of the Modern World* (Cheltenham: Edward Elgar, 2013), 93.

[80] Jones, *Entrepreneurship and Multinationals*, 63, 66, 143.

[81] G. Bertoli and R. Resciniti, *International Marketing and the Country of Origin Effect: The Global Impact of 'Made in Italy'* (Cheltenham: Edward Elgar, 2012), xi.

weaker country-of-origin image. For example, it has been claimed that Mazda and Honda became less attractive when these automobiles were produced in Mexico and the Philippines.[82]

Re-assessing the role of indications of origin enhances our understanding of how 'fair' and 'free' trade were perceived. From the late nineteenth century until 1914, Britain was a 'free-trade' nation. Analysis of British tariff levels during this period led Douglas Irwin to conclude that '[t]he British tariff was an extension of the domestic excise system, levied only on a select number of commodities to raise fiscal revenue without discriminating against foreign goods in favour of domestic goods'.[83] More recently, Frank Trentmann asserted, 'Britain gave free trade to the world.'[84] But this 'free' trade regime did not mean 'fair' trade. Misrepresenting the provenance of agricultural produce, for example, featured prominently in official investigations. In Britain, a Select Committee in 1893 reported: 'That misrepresentation exists the Committee have no doubt, chiefly in the substitution of American chilled beef for English and Scotch', and '[o]ther cases abound of "passing-off" River Plate mutton as "New Zealand"'.[85] Similar complaints were made about American Cheddar cheese and Wiltshire bacon, and Canadian and New Zealand Cheddar.[86] In other words, free trade was not always fair trade: consumers were deceived and genuine producers adversely affected.

Standard models of comparative advantage show that trade can be mutually advantageous: greater quantities of all products are available for trade when countries specialise in those products where their opportunity cost is lowest. But this result does not necessarily take account of genuine quality differences which exist between imported and domestically made products. Prejudice towards imports can undermine the gains

---

[82] S. A. Ahmed and A. d'Astous, 'Antecedents, Moderators, and Dimensions of Country-of-Origin Evaluations', *International Marketing Review*, 25 (2008): 79; M. V. Thakor and C. S. Kohli, 'Brand Origin: Conceptualisation and Review', *Journal of Consumer Marketing*, 13 (1996): 31–32; Hamzaoui-Essoussi, Merunka, and Bartikowski, 'Brand Origin', 974; Godey, Pederzoli, and Aiello, 'Brand and Country of Origin Effect'; S. Samiee, 'Resolving the Impasse Regarding Research on the Origins of Products and Brands', *International Marketing Review*, 28 (2011): 473–474.

[83] D. A. Irwin, 'Free Trade and Protection in Nineteenth Century Britain and France Revisited: A Comment on Nye', *Journal of Economic History*, 53 (1993): 152.

[84] F. Trentmann, *Free Trade Nation* (Oxford: Oxford University Press, 2008), 2.

[85] Select Committee of House of Lords on Marking of Foreign Meat. P.P. XII.341 (1893): ix.

[86] Report and Special Report from the Select Committee on the Agricultural Produce (Marks) Bill. P.P. VIII.227 (1897): QQ. 1872–1886; QQ. 2434–2436; QQ. 2734–2738.

from trade even when tariffs and other quantitative restrictions are absent. For example, the perception that Australasian lamb and US beef were not perfect substitutes for the same products originating from Wales or Scotland artificially limited the growth in demand for these imports. Conversely, if imports were of lower quality, price differentials provided an incentive for unscrupulous vendors to pass-off Australasian lamb as Welsh, or American beef as Scotch, thereby artificially increasing demand and prices for imported products.

A related theme is that comparative advantage is overlooked when appeals are made to national sentiment. Indeed, sometimes it is precisely because free trade is adversely affecting an economy that national senti- ment is mobilised. Clearly, if price differentials were the only factor affecting consumer purchases, the balance of trade could easily be rectified by imposing tariffs. But national efforts to promote the purchase of domestic products were governed by a much broader range of factors. Dana Frank has shown that the 'Buy American' Act of 1933 originated during the Great Depression and was based on economic nationalism designed to protect the US economy and domestic employment. The broader context of this initiative, and later campaigns during the 1970s and 1980s, involved an 'import panic attack', concerns about the economic infiltration of immigrants, and the exercise by the populace of democratic control over their economic lives.[87] Similarly, the 'Buy British' and 'Buy Empire' campaigns of the 1930s were an attempt to promote imperial unity.[88]

To be effective, such initiatives require that products are marked to indicate domestic origin. Currently, there are significant differences between countries on the reliability of 'Made in'. In the United States, for example, all imported products are required to be marked with an indication of their country of origin. A major exception to this is when the imported product is 'substantially transformed' within the United States. Even then, marking the transformed product 'Made in the USA' is usually prohibited unless it is 'all or virtually all' made in the United States. In Britain, by contrast, once imported products have satisfied customs regulations they do not need to be marked with country of origin.

---

[87] D. Frank, *Buy American* (Boston, MA: Beacon Press, 1999), ix.
[88] S. Constantine, 'Bringing the Empire Alive: The Empire Marketing Board and Imperial Propaganda, 1926–33', in J. MacKenzie (ed.), *Imperialism and Popular Culture* (Manchester: Manchester University Press, 1986), 192–231; S. Constantine, 'The Buy British Campaign of 1931', *Journal of Advertising History*, 10 (1987): 44–59.

Marking 'Made in Britain' on domestic products is entirely voluntary, so British consumers may be unable to differentiate between unmarked domestic and imported products. Refining the concept of 'Made in' to include 'Made entirely in Britain', 'Made in Britain', 'Mostly made in [Germany], finished in Britain', and 'Assembled in Britain' provides more information about the precise composition of the final product, but is potentially confusing for consumers.

This book is organised as follows. The next chapter discusses the role of the guilds in establishing a link between place and quality. In many ways the guilds pioneered some of the institutional regulations which underpin modern collective and certification marks. For example, they exercised control over apprentices and raw materials; only products which attained the required quality were permitted to bear the guild's mark; searchers were employed to detect low-quality products, and miscreants could be excised from their profession. Following the demise of the guilds two developments occurred in the nineteenth century which determined how IGOs could be used. First, France pioneered the demarcation and protection of GIs applied to wine and foodstuffs. Second, individual firms sought to use geographical names as trademarks. Conflict between manufacturers had a direct bearing on the viability of other types of indication of origin. I show that attempts to create a 'British' trademark failed, whereas the French mark *UNIS* did secure registration in Britain. The penultimate section of this chapter discusses the international trade in watches and the ambiguous message conveyed by 'Made in'.

Chapters 3 and 4 discuss the misrepresentation of indications of origin on agricultural products between the late nineteenth century and the 1930s. The analysis focuses on Britain, which was the world's biggest importer of foodstuffs during this period. Misuse of country of origin was prolific. Price differentials between domestic and imported produce encouraged misrepresentation. Differences in relative prices indicated real and perceived differences in the quality and characteristics of a typical basket of groceries. Danish bacon was especially valued because of its leanness and regular supply, whereas there was an ingrained prejudice towards frozen meat from Australasia and Latin America. I argue that cooperatives were a key feature of many food-exporting nations such as Denmark and New Zealand which also used country of origin to differentiate and promote their products. This was especially pronounced during the interwar period. Recognising the goodwill attached to country of origin, and the damage caused by misrepresentation, major food-exporting nations became highly litigious.

Chapter 5 presents a case study of the British Merchandise Marks Act of 1926 and the mandatory requirement that some imported manufactures indicate their country of origin. The demand for this legislation was long-standing and can be traced to campaigns originating from the Merchandise Marks Act, 1887, and the 'Made in Germany' debacle of the 1890s. The First World War reignited Anglo–German rivalry and concern about 'unfair competition'. However, the British response was neither comprehensive or compulsory. Each request for marking was treated on its merits and many of the industries involved were not economically significant. I argue that this initiative was motivated by nationalism. A related argument is that the growth of trade in semi-manufactured products, the activities of MNCs, and customs' determination of 'substantial transformation' were beginning to undermine the accuracy of 'Made in'.

Prior to the Paris Convention for the Protection of Industrial Property, 1883, intellectual property was protected at the domestic level and via bilateral treaties. The rapid growth of multilateral trade during the nineteenth century required the creation of an international architecture for the protection of IGOs. Chapter 6 discusses the creation and evolution of the Paris Convention to 1938. It becomes apparent that dissonance between national legislation was the principal reason why a truly global accord proved unobtainable. Having pioneered GI protection, it was practically inevitable that France sought to ensure that international regulations governing GIs closely imitated its domestic legislation. Another argument of this book is that France and other wine-producing countries benefitted from 'regulatory capture'.[89] French insistence on the absolute protection of 'products of the vine' threatened to fracture the Paris Convention. The favourable treatment of wine – which continues today – meant other beverages, such as Czech beers, did not obtain equivalent protection until much later. Moreover, French tactics generated some bizarre consequences. For example, Britain was not a renowned wine producer before 1945, but it acceded to the Madrid Agreement for the Repression of False or Deceptive Indications of Source of Goods (1891), to safeguard 'Sheffield' edge tools and other manufactures produced in geographically renowned locations.

---

[89] Regulatory capture in the food industry is discussed in M. French and J. Phillips, *Cheated not Poisoned? Food Regulation in the United Kingdom, 1875–1938* (Manchester: Manchester University Press, 2000), 2–10.

Chapter 7 discusses the renewed efforts made after 1945 to reinforce international protection of GIs. For the first time, the Lisbon Conference of 1958 defined the term 'appellation' and provided for their registration. However, like earlier periods, the fundamental problem of how to appease the interests of wine producers remained. Between the 1960s and early 1990s, the EU introduced a battery of regulations governing wine and food appellations which brought into sharp relief the conflict between EU and common law countries, especially the United States. A further argument in this book is that different types of protection afforded GIs raise fundamental questions about the nature of market exchange and 'honest trade'. From an economics perspective, at least, 'honest' trade requires the absence of asymmetric information: lawful and accurate use of GIs ensures that consumers and producers are protected against misrepresentation. But although use of a qualifying statement such as 'Californian Burgundy' is unlikely to mislead consumers about the true origin of the wine, it can injure genuine producers of Burgundy by creating the impression that this appellation is generic.

The EU's initiatives on foodstuffs generated international discord on how best to protect GIs. It is appropriate, therefore, to assess the EU regulations governing the PDO and PGI schemes. Chapter 8 indicates that there was a rapid increase in the number of registrations following this initiative. However, as might be anticipated, the response to these schemes was dominated by a few countries – France, Italy, Portugal, and Spain. A review of the empirical evidence provides grounds for believing that the EU scheme was only partially successful. I argue that the fundamental weakness in the EU scheme is that 'quality' was never defined. Consequently, the basic premise of the initiative – that quality depended on geographic location – remains questionable.

In the penultimate chapter, 'Swiss made', 'Made in the US', and 'Made in the EU' are examined. Each of these schemes became prominent in the past twenty years or so because of industry and government concern about consumer confusion. Offshoring to take advantage of lower production costs raised fundamental questions about the meaning of 'Made in. I argue that 'Swiss made' was a particularly effective geographical indication because watch manufacturers and the Swiss federal government agreed the technical regulations permitting a watch to be marked 'Swiss made'. In contrast, I show that the Federal Trade Commission's qualifying standard for 'Made in the US' is sufficiently prohibitive that most US manufacturers rely only on their brands. Attempts to launch a 'Made in the EU' scheme were totally unsuccessful because this was viewed by leading manufacturers in Britain and Germany as a badge of inferiority: it threatened the reputation of 'Made in Britain', 'Made in Germany', and the brands belonging to their leading companies. In Chapter 10 general conclusions are presented.

2

Firms and Indications of Geographical Origin in the First Global Economy

I claim that the right of the community to the reputation which its artisan population has acquired is complete, and should not be allowed to be trenched on by others.

Herbert Hughes, Special Report from the Select Committee on Merchandize Marks Act (1862) Amendment Bill (1887).P.P. X.357: Q.2537.

The appellant was no more entitled to the exclusive use of the word 'Columbia' as a trade-mark than he would have been to the use of the word 'America', or 'United States', or 'Minnesota', or 'Minneapolis'. These merely geographical names cannot be appropriated and made the subject of an exclusive property. They do not, in and of themselves, indicate anything in the nature of origin, manufacture or ownership.

Columbia Mill Co v. Alcorn, 150 U.S. 460

This chapter discusses the evolution of IGOs in manufacturing prior to 1914. These indications have been dated to at least the medieval period and, it has been claimed, 'Marks indicating the geographical origins of goods were the earliest type of trade mark.'[1] Many IGOs, for example, 'Worsted from Ipswich' and 'Malines-style cloth', were collectively used and policed by occupational guilds which proliferated throughout Europe from the twelfth century; they simultaneously indicated geographical

---

[1] M. Blakeney, 'Geographical Indications and Trade', *International Trade Law and Regulation*, 6 (2000):48. Recent scholarship has indicated that marks bearing animal and geometric motifs were imprinted on pottery made in the Indian city of Harappa and exported to Mesopotamia around 2600 BC, but it is not clear whether these marks indicated geographical origin or simply the name of the manufacturer. K. Moore and S. Reid, 'The Birth of Brand: 4000 Years of Branding', *Business History*, 50 (2008): 422.

origin and quality.[2] This final characteristic was a function of the skills of the craftsmen and their control over the quality of raw materials and apprenticeships. By the later eighteenth century many guilds had either vanished or their privileges had been rescinded and the collective ownership of marks indicating the geographical origin of manufactures had largely disappeared.

This void would have been of little consequence if the scale and scope of international trade remained at medieval levels, but this was not the case. During the nineteenth century global trade in manufactures grew rapidly. Between 1899 and 1913, world trade in manufactures grew by 61 and 105 per cent by value and volume, respectively.[3] Similarly, there were pronounced changes in the distribution of international production and supply. Thus, between 1870 and 1914, the proportion of global industrial production accounted for by the United States increased from 23 to 36 per cent, while Britain's declined from 32 to 14 per cent.[4] These broad shifts were reflected in export performance. During the period 1876 to 1913, Britain's share of global manufacturing exports declined from 37.8 to 25.3 per cent, while that of the United States and Canada, and the rest of the world, increased from 4.4 to 10.6 per cent, and 1.5 to 7.9 per cent, respectively.[5] Between 1899 and 1913, trade in manufactures between industrial countries and the rest of the world increased by 91 per cent at constant prices.[6]

One repercussion of growing international trade was greater scope to misuse IGOs. In India, Madras customs detained cases of 'Fine Old Highland Whisky', because they were made in Germany.[7] The Board of Trade informed the Manchester Chamber of Commerce that cloth manufactured in Italy was being sold as 'AMERICANI' in Uganda.[8] London-made cigarettes were passed-off as 'Egyptian', tweed was misrepresented as 'Donegal', and watches made in Geneva and the United States were passed-

[2] G. Richardson, 'Brand Names before the Industrial Revolution', *National Bureau of Economic Research*, Working Paper No. 13930 (2008): 22.
[3] Calculated from H. Tyszynski, 'World Trade in Manufactured Commodities', *Manchester School*, 19 (1951): 282.
[4] Chandler, *Scale and Scope*, 4.
[5] A. G. Kenwood and A. L. Lougheed, *The Growth of the International Economy, 1820–1990* (London: Routledge, 1992), 86.
[6] Calculated from A. Maizels, *Industrial Growth and World Trade* (Cambridge: Cambridge University Press, 1963), table 4.4, 89.
[7] *Times of India*, 7 December 1892, 4.
[8] Greater Manchester Country Record Office. M8/2/13. Proceedings of the Manchester Chamber of Commerce. 12 October 1904.

off as 'English' and 'Swiss', respectively.[9] Similarly, German lamp holders and French cycle chains were sold as Austrian and English, while Austrian fountain pens were purchased as 'Irish'.[10] Cuban cigars were particularly susceptible to misrepresentation. British and German cigar manufacturers were accused of filling genuine Havana cigar boxes with spurious cigars. It was also alleged that cigar manufacturers in Europe were entitled to label their cigars Havana if they used genuine Havana tobacco because the cigars were equal in every respect to cigars fully manufactured in Cuba. An 'extravagant profit' based on a 300 per cent markup could be obtained from this dubious practice.[11]

Exacerbating matters, some IGOs had become generic, denoting the mode, not place, of manufacture. Consequently, irrespective of their geographic location, firms were at liberty to apply generic marks because no fraud was perpetrated.[12] In Britain, Brussels Carpets was considered a generic term, and it was claimed that Havana cigars '[do] not indicate the place of origin ... it had no meaning whatever to the public, or to anybody else, as indicating the place of origin'.[13] In late nineteenth-century France Marseilles soap, Eau de Cologne, and Malines lace were judged generic,[14] as were Copenhagen (snuff), Gibralter (chimneys), Lackawanna (coal), Moline (ploughs), and Worcestershire (sauce) in the United States.[15] Subsequently, the Federal Trade Commission 'would not recognize that such names as Irish potatoes, Bermuda onions, Brussels sprouts, or Holland gin purport to indicate geographical origin of the products in question'.[16]

The expansion of national and international markets during the nineteenth century meant growing geographical separation between producers

---

[9] *Times*, 16 May 1900, 4; 6 March 1907, 3; *Report from the Select Committee on Hall Marking* (Gold and Silver). P.P. X.365 (1878–1897): QQ. 174–75.

[10] L. B. Sebastian, *The Law of Trade Marks* (London: Stevens & Sons, 1911), 676.

[11] *Special Report from the Select Committee on Merchandize Marks Act* (1862) *Amendment Bill* (1887). P.P. X.357: QQ. 2763–2798; QQ. 2809–2817.

[12] The major exception was when the use of generic terms was intended to deceive consumers. H. L. Pinner, *World Unfair Competition Law: An Encyclopedia*. Volume 1 (Leyden: A. W. Sijthoff, 1965), 636.

[13] *Special Report from the Select Committee on Merchandize Marks Act* (1862) *Amendment Bill* (1887). P.P. X.357: Q. 2927; Q. 2537.

[14] Pinner, *World Unfair Competition Law*, 636.

[15] Hopkins, *The Law of Trademarks*, 101–113; N. F. Hesseltine, *A Digest of the Law of Trade-Marks and Unfair Trade* (Boston, MA: Little Brown, 1906), 64; C. E. Coddington, *A Digest of the Law of Trade Marks* (New York: Ward and Peloubet, 1878), 245–246, 248.

[16] S. P. Ladas, *Patents, Trademarks and Related Rights: National and International Protection* (Cambridge, MA: Harvard University Press, 1975), 1609.

and consumers. To realise the benefits of large-scale production offered by growing markets, manufacturers needed to overcome the problems of asymmetric information and quality uncertainty. According to Mira Wilkins, trademarks – subsequently brands – were the means by which manufacturers instilled confidence amongst their distant consumers.[17] Although Wilkins deserves credit for alerting business historians to this 'neglected intangible asset', her arguments are not universally accepted. Paul Duguid has shown that for many years before obtaining property rights to them, manufacturers protected their trademarks in the courts.[18] Doubts have also been raised about the extent to which trademarks were only associated with modern corporations: their use was prevalent in the Sheffield cutlery trades in which small-scale firms predominated.[19]

This chapter develops a further critique of Wilkins' argument by discussing IGOs, which do not indicate the output of a *particular* producer. The focus on brands and their association with the modern corporation overlooks the fact that during the nineteenth century IGOs were an integral part of trademarks, for example, Huntley & Palmers 'Reading' biscuits, the 'Elgin National Watch Company', and the 'Waltham Watch Company'. Some companies attempted – successfully – to obtain exclusive use of IGOs. However, unlike trademarks, IGOs had a rather paradoxical development:

> [They] were the only means for many centuries of designating *quality products* far from their region of origin, [and] only received legal protection recently, while trademarks have been protected much longer ... despite the facts that trade had considerably increased the need for quality signs and that trademarks were often used to indicate geographical source.[20]

The decline of the guilds undermined the collective ownership of IGOs and prompts the question: to what extent was it possible for individual firms to re-establish this connection? Providing an answer is not straightforward because it involves a conflict between economic incentives and the prevailing legal environment. From a purely economic perspective it is recognised that guilds provided social benefits in return for some degree of monopoly power, but there was no guarantee that individual firms would

---

[17] Wilkins, 'The Neglected Intangible Asset'.
[18] P. Duguid, 'Developing the Brand: The Case of Alcohol', *Enterprise and Society*, 4 (2003): 405–441.
[19] D. M. Higgins and G. Tweedale, 'Asset or Liability? Trade Marks in the Sheffield Cutlery and Tool Trades', *Business History*, 37 (1995): 1–27.
[20] Emphasis added. E. Thévenod-Mottet and D. Marie-Vivien, 'Legal Debates Surrounding Geographical Indications', in Barham and Sylvander, *Labels of Origin for Food*, 14.

generate similar externalities. Although the economics literature indicates that such firms have a strong incentive to maintain the quality of their own products, nineteenth-century law severely restricted individual ownership of IGOs. Moreover, in common law countries, certification and collective marks were not recognised until the twentieth century. The apparently bizarre consequence of these legal restrictions was that individual firms could own geographical terms provided they 'clearly could not be regarded as indicative of the place of manufacture or sale'.[21]

Two further themes are discussed towards the end of this chapter. First, IGOs are examined using case studies of 'Made in Britain' and UNIS. Both proved controversial because they highlighted the conflict between maintaining quality in trademarks and the incentive to 'freeride' and debase quality in collective marks. The second theme explores the ambiguities inherent to the international supply chain for watches. The nineteenth-century watch industry highlights the recurring problem of defining 'substantive transformation' and raises doubts about the reliability of country of origin when watches were assembled from multiple components, each having a different geographical origin.

THE GUILDS

A guild has been defined as 'an association of people who share some common characteristic and pursue some common purpose'.[22] The geographical and chronological coverage of guilds was pronounced: they existed in ninth-century Cairo, Damascus, and Samarkand, and grew rapidly in medieval Europe. Occupational or craft guilds produced bread, cutlery, edge tools, leather goods, pewter wares, and woollen clothes; they existed in the gold- and silversmiths' trades as well as in cordwain, haberdashery, masonry, and stationery.[23] Some of the European guilds declined from the mid-fifteenth century, but in Germany and Sweden, local monopolies and privileges were not abrogated until 1879 and 1846, respectively.[24]

---

[21] Patent Office Inquiry. *Report of the Committee Appointed by the Board of Trade to Inquire into the Duties, Organization, and Arrangements of the Patent Office under the Patents, Designs, and Trade Marks Act, so Far as Relates to Trade Marks, and Designs* (1888). P.P.LXXXI.37: xi.

[22] S. Ogilvie, *Institutions and European Trade: Merchant Guilds, 1000–1800* (Cambridge: Cambridge University Press, 2011), 19.

[23] W. Cunningham, *The Growth of English Industry and Commerce during the Early and Middle Ages* (Cambridge: Cambridge University Press, 1905), 340.

[24] G. I. H. Lloyd, *The Cutlery Trades* (London: Longman, 1913), 6–7, 354.

Medieval craft guilds ensured a robust connection between IGOs and quality. A key feature of the guilds is that they authorised the use of *collective* marks on products which met the required standard:

The guild's mark would provide assurance that goods were the result of true guild workmanship. The guild mark was the mark of the association as a whole. As such it bore resemblance to a modern collective mark that is owned by and symbolises an association of producers, the members of which use the mark under the control of the association, to distinguish the goods of members from those of other undertakings.[25]

Occupational guilds were founded on a series of rules governing apprenticeships, membership, technical knowledge, the regulation of sales, wages, and prices, and penalties for fraudulent activity.[26] Control of quality was fundamental to all of the craft guilds[27] and is partly explained by interurban rivalry and the civic pride of the municipalities: 'The quality of the wares produced within their limits ... called for regulation [and] led to the establishment of a standard quality for local products and the use of the municipal mark.'[28] Another explanation was the need to secure stable incomes and higher welfare.[29] Differences in the skill and dexterity of individual craftsmen required that the guilds guarantee minimum levels of quality. Regulations governing the composition of inputs were particularly rigorous. The London Cutlery Guild stipulated that only sterling silver be used in the embellishment of knife hafts. The Hanse towns in Germany ensured that inferior qualities of wool were not used in the textile crafts, that hair was not mixed with wool, and that dyers used appropriate quantities of dye.[30]

Although recent scholarship questions the extent to which the guilds exercised monopoly power,[31] it has reaffirmed their efforts to control

---

[25] J. Belson, *Special Report: Certification Marks* (London: Sweet & Maxwell, 2002), 7.

[26] Cunningham, *Growth of English Industry*, 336–353; Lloyd, *The Cutlery Trades*, 78–79, 130–139.

[27] S. A Epstein, *Wage Labour and Guilds in Medieval Europe* (Chapel Hill: University of North Carolina Press, 1991), 125–129; F. Consitt, *The London Weavers' Company* (Oxford: Clarendon Press, 1933), 89.

[28] L. E. Daniels, 'The History of the Trademark', *Bulletin of the US Trademark Association*, 7 (1911): 247.

[29] B. Gustafsson, 'The Rise and Economic Behaviour of Medieval Craft Guilds: An Economic-Theoretical interpretation', *Scandinavian Economic History Review*, XXXV (1987): 9.

[30] Lloyd, *The Cutlery Trades*, 79; Gustafsson, 'The Rise and Economic Behaviour of Medieval Craft Guilds', 13.

[31] G. Richardson, 'Guilds, Laws and Markets for Manufactured Merchandise in Late Medieval England', *Explorations in Economic History*, 41 (2004): 1–25.

quality.[32] In the medieval era, adverse selection and asymmetric information were chronic and extensive. In this environment the guilds implemented strict rules governing the manufacture of a range of textile and metal goods. The growth of long distance trade in manufactures exacerbated the problem of quality uncertainty because producers were selling to anonymous buyers. The consequences of faulty products could be lethal: in 1347, the Heaumers stipulated that only those craftsmen who had their work proved by the guild warden could make helmets: 'some persons who are strangers [to the guild] have meddled in the making of helmetry – and as they do not know the trade, many great men have been slain'.[33] It is unsurprising that this industry was the first to overcome the problems of conveying accurate messages about the unobservable attributes of its products.[34]

Moreover, searchers employed by the guilds were tasked with detecting low-quality products bearing the guilds' marks. Anders Gadd and Patrick Wallis have demonstrated that between 1636 and 1702, searchers belonging to the London Pewterer's guild made at least one tour of England each year. Their investigations encompassed Cornwall, Cumberland, and even Wales, and petitions were made to extend their powers of search to Scotland. Gadd and Wallis provide a positive verdict on the efforts this guild made to maintain the quality of its products and to reduce asymmetric information. Their appraisal is most relevant to searches made within London, as they admit that some caution needs to be exercised in believing that higher local detection rates were replicated nationally.[35]

Quality was enforced by strict sanctions because fraudulent sale directly undermined guild reputation and municipal revenues. In medieval Belgium, affixing the mark of the City of Brussels to tapestries woven outside the city resulted in confiscation of the cloth and the offender was barred from practising his profession for one year.[36] Thomas Jupp, a London cloth worker, was fined £1,000 and condemned to stand in the pillory at Cheapside (London) and Colchester for affixing

[32] S. R. Epstein and M. Prak, *Guilds, Innovation, and the European Economy, 1400–1800* (Cambridge: Cambridge University Press, 2008), 4, 13. For a different view, see A. Caracausi, 'Information Asymmetries and Craft Guilds in Pre-Modern Markets: Evidence from Italian Proto-Industry', *Economic History Review*, 70 (2017): 397–422.

[33] C. Ffoulkes, *The Armourer and His Craft* (New York: Benjamin Bloom, 1967), 171.

[34] Richardson, 'Brands Names before the Industrial Revolution'.

[35] I. A. Gadd and P. Wallis, 'Reaching behind the City Wall: London Guilds and National Regulation, 1500–1700', in Epstein and Prak, *Guilds, Innovation*, 294–298.

[36] Daniels, 'The History of the Trademark', 264.

counterfeit Colchester seals to cloth made in Bocking.[37] The judgements of the London guild courts could result in the whipping of apprentices or the imprisonment of journeymen. The blacksmiths of Bologna appointed inquisitors who subjected guild members to public praise or humiliation depending on whether their products were judged commendable or inferior. *Rattening* empowered guilds with the authority to sell the tools of debtors to enforce payment of fines. To maintain confidence in their IGOs, guild ordinances sometimes permitted dissatisfied consumers the right to seek redress without taking court action.[38]

The quality of guild production was communicated by IGOs: 'by the medieval period the collective goodwill enjoyed by a given locality or organisation and the protection of a mark or seal as the symbol of that goodwill was very common', and 'the trademark ... identified beside quality and producer, often also place of origin ... both producer, guild, and place of origin were tied to the commodity, which increased the marketability of the product'.[39] In textiles, Parisian weavers sought to prevent misuse of 'façon de Paris'; the mark of the town of Osnabrück – the centre of the Westphalian linen industry – was held in such esteem that linen bearing this IGO achieved a 20 per cent price premium compared to other linens. Weavers in Barcelona and Torroela enjoyed similar collective goodwill.[40] The British cloth trade has been cited as a classic example of the development of IGOs. By the end of the fifteenth century, cloths made in Bristol, Norwich, and Kendal had 'acquired individual reputations, which naturally enhanced the value of cloths made not only in [these] particular towns ... but in cloth making settlements in proximity to these towns'.[41] From the second half of the sixteenth century, the national and international repute of the Colchester baize industry was rigorously protected by the Privy Council. In the reign of Queen Anne (1702–1714),

---

[37] F. I. Schechter, *The Historical Foundations of the Law Relating to Trade-Marks* (New York: Colombia University Press, 1925), 91.

[38] R. H. Britnell, *The Commercialisation of English Society* (Manchester: Manchester University Press, 1996), 176; Consitt, *The London Weavers' Company*, 88; Epstein, *Wage Labour*, 128; J. T. Smith, *English Guilds* (Oxford: Oxford University Press, 1870), cxxvii; G. Unwin, *The Gilds and Companies of London* (London: George Allen & Unwin, 1938), 28.

[39] Schechter, *Historical Foundations*, 79; Gustafsson, 'The Rise and Economic Behaviour of Medieval Craft Guilds', 22. For a contrary view, see Caracausi, 'Information Asymmetries'.

[40] Schechter, *Historical Foundations*, 79–80.

[41] Schechter, *Historical Foundations*, 82. The importance of town of origin as an indicator of value is emphasised by Epstein, *Wage Labour*, 126.

a charter was granted to the manufacturers of Witney blankets (Oxfordshire), for which products it was said, 'The name Witney itself was a guarantee of the excellence of the manufacture.'[42]

In the armour and cutlery industries, Milan and Cologne were famous for their hauberks and halberds, respectively. Swords from the Haute-Savoy region of Bordeaux, Passau, Solingen, and Toledo were especially prized, as were the schools of armour located in Augsburg, Brescia, Innsbruck, and Nuremberg.[43] The swords and daggers produced in Damascus and Toledo 'represented the acme of workmanship and of temper'.[44] In the cutlery trades, the Act of Incorporation in Hallamshire (Sheffield), 1624, noted the 'reputation of great skill and dexterity' of Sheffield cutlers who had 'made knives of the best edge, wherewith they served the most [parts] of this kingdom and other foreign countries'.[45] The relationship between IGO and quality affected the geographic sourcing of inputs. In cutlery, a general statute of 1549 forbade the use of 'Bilbow' (Bilbao) iron because its use in the manufacture of edge tools and armour undermined quality. Conversely, 'Cullen' (Westphalian) steel was highly prized by 1640.[46] During the early sixteenth century, 'Innsbruck' iron was sought by German armourers. To preserve the reputation of this iron they specified that substandard qualities be branded 'Milanese'.[47]

However, by the nineteenth century, the guilds did not enjoy the same privileges or operate on the same scale. The rise of proto-industrial activity and merchant capitalism in the seventeenth and eighteenth centuries undermined craft guilds and their concentration in towns and cities. The decline of the guilds undermined the symbiotic relationship between geographical origin and quality. Michael Fitzsimmons argued that the introduction of alternative institutional structures in France to ensure guild-level quality were futile: 'more than anything else, the introduction of ... occupational licenses became inextricably linked with ... an abrupt deterioration in quality ... fraud, charlatanry, and deceit [were] long lasting, and ... became a major element of efforts to re-establish guilds'.[48]

---

[42] *Times*, 20 March 1909, 3.   [43] Ffoulkes, *The Armourer*, 12–13.

[44] Lloyd, *The Cutlery Trades*, 352.

[45] Lloyd, *The Cutlery Trades*, 114. During this period cutlery produced in Paris and Salisbury was also renowned for its quality.

[46] Lloyd, *The Cutlery Trades*, 69–70, 92, 114, 358.   [47] Ffoulkes, *The Armourer*, 38.

[48] M. Fitzsimmons, *From Artisan to Worker* (Cambridge: Cambridge University Press, 2010), 60.

FRANCE: THE PIONEER IN PROTECTION

France was an innovator in the protection of IGOs. Michael Blakeney argued that the relevant French law can be traced to the medieval period and the conferment of advantages upon Bordeaux wine producers to give them an advantage when dealing with the lucrative English market.[49] It is also recognised that France introduced the doctrine of unfair competition (*Concurrence Déloyale*).[50] Articles 1382 and 1383 of the Code Civil, promulgated in 1804, stated, respectively:

Any person who causes injury to another by any act whatsoever is obligated to compensate such person for the injury sustained;
And
A person is responsible for damages not only for these acts which he has actually committed, but also for any damages caused by his negligence or imprudence.

French legislation enacted in 1824 stipulated that only the place name where a product was manufactured could be used to indicate origin.[51] However, despite this statute, French courts and jurists grappled with key questions: how were geographical boundaries to be demarcated? Were these boundaries constant? How did wine and other 'natural' products differ from other types of manufacture? Some judicial decisions held that the right to use the name of a locality to indicate origin belonged to those who lived within the formal boundaries of the town and its environs. The latter were entitled to use the name of the town because their products enhanced the town's reputation. For example, space restrictions had forced some manufacturers of 'Sedan' cloth to establish their factories outside the city.[52]

However, with 'natural' products, a much tighter demarcation of boundaries was required because the qualities of wine and food depended on a specific location. 'Appellation d'origine' was protected because natural conditions such as soil, water, fauna, and climate were unique to particular regions.[53] The precision required for accurate

---

[49] M. Blakeney, *The Protection of Geographical Indications* (Cheltenham: Edward Elgar, 2014), 4.

[50] W. J. Derenberg, 'The Influence of the French Code Civil on the Modern Law of Unfair Competition', *American Journal of Comparative Law*, 4 (1955): 1–34; Ladas, *Patents, Trademarks and Related Rights*, 1691–1692.

[51] A. Taillefer and C. Claro, *Traité des Marques de Fabrique et de la Concurrence Déloyale en Tous genres, d'Eugène Pouillet* (Paris: Marchal et Godde, 1912), 625.

[52] Taillefer and Claro, *Traité des Marques de Fabrique*, 622–623.

[53] L. Lenzen, 'Bachus in the Hinterlands: A Study of Denominations of Origin in French and American Wine-Labelling Laws', *Trademark Reporter*, 58 (1968): 178.

delimitation raised fundamental questions: where is the place of production (*lieux de fabrication*) for a particular wine? Was it the place where the grapes were harvested – or was it the location where the grapes were pressed and transformed into wine? By the mid-nineteenth century, a considerable volume of case law had established that 'wines belong to the class of manufactured products, and the places where they are harvested and where they are prepared are the places of production'.[54]

Nonetheless, considerable litigation ensued, partly because delimiting a region proved contentious. What did the term 'place of fabrication' mean? It could refer to a private domain, a city, or a region, such as Cognac or Saint Émilion. Alessandro Stanziani argued: 'uncertain legal definitions of the "origin" made litigations increase while encouraging free-riding'.[55] In any event, the spread of phylloxera[56] during the 1870s fundamentally altered the balance between the supply of and demand for wine and encouraged substantial fraud. Thus, wine was produced from raisins and adulterated with gypsum, and Algerian wine was sold as 'Burgundy'.[57] In Champagne,

With phylloxera spreading and grape production falling, vignerons were stunned to learn that sales of champagne continued to grow ... Questions were raised about the origin of these wines ... Considerable amounts of falsified 'champagnes' had allegedly been sent to Paris from the Marne in 1889 ... wines were 'egregiously' altered with wines from outside the region. National papers hinted at an attempted cover-up by the négociants.[58]

In these circumstances it was imperative that confidence was restored in wine GIs lest the ensuing quality debasement adversely affected all but the lowest-quality producers. The earliest initiatives sought to establish a clearer link between product and place. A law addressing Fraud and Falsification in the Matter of Products or Services was enacted in 1905,

---

[54] Taillefer and Claro, *Traité des Marques de Fabrique*, 625.

[55] Stanziani, 'Wine Reputation and Quality Controls', 158. Of interest, the same author argues that during the nineteenth century, the courts refused to take into consideration collective marks. Stanziani, 'Information, Quality, and Legal Rules', 285.

[56] Phylloxera is a microscopic louse that lives on vine roots. By 1900, almost 75 per cent of French vineyards were affected. J. Simpson, *Creating Wine: The Emergence of a World Industry, 1840–1914* (Princeton, NJ: Princeton University Press, 2011), 94.

[57] Gangjee, *Relocating the Law of Geographical Indications*, 94; Simpson, *Creating Wine*, 59–62.

[58] Guy, *When Champagne Became French*, 106.

Le Pape Clément V (1264 et 1314) fut le 1ᵉ Pape d'Avignon.

L' ICÔNE.

CHÂTEAU
PAPE CLÉMENT

Depuis 1252, l'année des premières vendanges du Château Pape Clément,
nous travaillons toujours sur ce même terroir.

www.bernard-magrez.com

L'abus d'alcool est dangereux pour la santé, à consommer avec modération.   PROPRIÉTAIRE

FIGURE 2.1 'Ever since 1252, the year of the first grape harvest at Château Pape
Clément, we've been working on the same terrain.'
© Bernard Magrez

and in 1908 a decree was issued which established the Appellation d'
Origine. However, these initiatives proved controversial and violent dis-
order erupted in Champagne.[59]

---

[59] Gangjee, *Relocating the Law of Geographical Indications*, 96–101; Guy, *When Champagne Became French*, 158–185.

A further problem was how to link quality with place. This issue was, and remains, fundamental. Again a number of questions were raised which are central to the subsequent discussion. For example, was location sufficient to guarantee quality? Although a 1919 law provided formal legal protection for GIs, other factors required consideration, for example, the concept of *'usages locaux, loyaux, et constants'* ('local, loyal, and constant use'). In the 1930s, the Court of Cassation in France rejected litigation brought by the Syndicate of Wine Producers of Châteauneuf-du-Pape against winemakers in a neighbouring locality who were using this GI. The Court held that the plaintiff had not proved local, loyal, and constant use of the term.[60] To demonstrate that a local method fulfilled these requirements, certificates from chambers of commerce, proof of ancient working technique, and communal records and registers could be adduced.[61]

Although later scholarship emphasised the sociocultural foundations inherent in the 1919 law, and raised doubts about the extent to which terroir guaranteed 'quality',[62] by the 1920s France had developed a legal and institutional framework that protected GIs. As a pioneer, France almost inevitably would determine international protection of GIs. However, as I indicate later, this influence was not always benign.

FIRMS, TRADEMARKS, AND GEOGRAPHICAL NAMES

Fundamentally, trademarks distinguish the merchandise of different producers. To fulfil this role it is imperative that trademarks are 'distinctive', that they are 'adapted to distinguish the goods of the proprietor of the trademarks from those of other persons'. All the major contemporary legal authorities were agreed on this, and distinctiveness was a key requirement of registration which enabled a proprietor to acquire legal property in a trademark.[63] However, during the nineteenth century, it was thought undesirable that trademarks should encompass geographical names. One explanation for this conflict was that 'distinctiveness' is inapposite when discussing IGOs because they do not distinguish the output of different producers. A second reason was that use of a geographical name was not always equivalent to an IGO. Finally,

---

[60] Ladas, *Patents, Trademarks and Related Rights*, 1577.
[61] Lenzen, 'Bachus in the Hinterlands', 177–178.
[62] See, especially, Parry, 'Geographical Indications'; Farmer, 'Local, Loyal, and Constant'.
[63] D. M. Kerly, *The Law of Trade Marks and Trade Name* (London: Sweet & Maxwell, 1913), 179; Sebastian, *The Law of Trade Marks* (1911), 20; J. L. Hopkins, *The Law of Unfair Trade* (Chicago: Callaghan and Company, 1900), 2.

appropriation of an IGO by an individual was permitted only under specific circumstances.

It is useful to distinguish 'primary' and 'secondary' geographical trademarks. The former refer to a particular locality and are recognised as a geographical word.[64] In this sense they could function as IGOs. However, such trademarks were barred from registration because it was considered unacceptable that monopoly rights to their use should be acquired by a specific firm:

> Their nature is such that they cannot point to the origin (personal origin) or ownership of the articles of trade to which they may be applied … It must be considered as sound doctrine that no one can apply the name of a district or country to a well-known article of commerce, and obtain thereby such an exclusive right to the application as to prevent others inhabiting the district, or dealing in similar articles coming from the district, from truthfully using the same designation.[65]

Other commentators claimed that granting individuals monopoly rights to geographical trademarks would 'greatly embarrass trade, and secure exclusive rights to individuals in that which is the common property of many'.[66] For these reasons, 'York' (stoves and ranges), 'Alabamatube' (iron and steel tubes), 'Clinton' (paint), and 'Amherst' (cotton and worsted dress goods) were debarred from registration in the United States. In Britain, similar restrictions applied to 'Eboline' (silk piece goods), 'Melrose' (hair restorer), 'Ben Ledi' (whiskey), 'Glengowrie Blend of Fine Old Highland Whiskey', and 'Manor' (tin plates).[67] The fundamental issue raised by the above, and similar cases was that use of these IGOs was legitimate only when employed by *all* firms in a particular region.

Nonetheless, individual firms continued to use geographical names as part of their trademarks and rivals employed various methods to divert sales from them. In effect, this type of fraud was similar to the more common situation where manufacturers attempted to imitate the 'get-up' of their rivals.[68] Even though ownership of primary geographical

---

[64] Sebastian, *The Law of Trade Marks* (1911), 60.
[65] Hopkins, *The Law of Unfair Trade*, 96.   [66] Coddington, *A Digest*, 247.
[67] Hesseltine, *A Digest*, 61–63; L. B. Sebastian, *The Law of Trade Marks* (London: Stevens and Sons, 1899), 72. For similar statements by the courts, see, for example: *'Pocahontas Coal' Coffman* v. *Castner, et al.*, 87 Federal Reporter, 457; *'Montserrat Lime-Fruit Juice'*, *Evans and another* v. *Von Laer*, 32 Federal Reporter, 153; *'Sonman Coal'*, *Appeal of Laughman et al.*, 128 Pa.1, 18 A.415; *'Rossendale Cement'*, 44 Federal Reporter, 277.
[68] Strictly, *passing-off* refers to attempts to divert trade using means which are unrelated to a trademark, for example, use of similar coloured wrappings, or legends, whereas *infringement* only applies to registered trademarks.

trademarks was severely restricted, litigation was possible – and successful – when intent to deceive consumers was proved. In *Wotherspoon* v. *Currie*, the plaintiff was originally based in the town of Glenfield (Scotland). Their starch, marked 'Glenfield Starch', was renowned. The plaintiff left this town and another manufacturer located there and began selling their product as 'Glenfield Starch'. The court ruled that the actions of the successor were intended to deceive consumers and an injunction was obtained.[69]

Sometimes, manufacturers misrepresented their location to divert trade from firms legitimately using a place name to designate their products. For example, Anheuser-Busch, based in St. Louis, Missouri, exported their bottled beer as 'St. Louis Lager Beer' to South America, where 'it had acquired a considerable market for its product'. The defendant, Piza, based in New York, labelled his beer '"St. Louis Lager Beer" ... so as to represent that his beer is made at St. Louis'. The plaintiff secured an injunction against Piza in 1885.[70] Equally successful actions against this type of misrepresentation were launched by A. F. Pike Manufacturing Co., for 'Lamoille' and 'Willoughby Lake' (as applied to scythe stones), Pillsbury-Washburn Flour Mills Co., over misuse of 'Minneapolis', 'Minneapolis, Minn.', and 'Minneapolis, Minnesota', and the California Fruit Association for 'California'.[71]

Another type of fraud involved rival manufacturers established in the same location. It was frequently the case that a firm would commence business in a locality and over time its name became synonymous with location. If this relationship became famous, competing firms moved to this area and used its name for their own products, thereby freeriding on the goodwill established by the original firm. In *Huntley & Palmer*[72] v. *The Reading Biscuit Company*, 1893, it was reported:

[The plaintiff's] biscuits had obtained a considerable reputation, and the only reputation of the town of Reading in the biscuit trade had been acquired by, and was in connexion with, the trade of the Plaintiff's, and of no one else ... their

---

[69] *Wotherspoon* v. *Currie*. R. Cox, *A Manual of Trade Mark Cases: Comprising Sebastian's Digest of Trade-Mark Cases* (Boston, MA: Houghton, Mifflin and Company, 1881), 188.

[70] *Anheuser-Busch Brewing Association* v. *Piza*, 24 *Federal Reporter*, 149.

[71] *A. F. Pike Manufacturing Co.,* v. *Cleveland Stone Co., et al.*, 35 *Federal Reporter*, 896; *Pillsbury-Washburn Flour-Mills Co., Limited., et al.,* v. *Eagle*, 86 *Federal Reporter*, 608; *California Fruit Canners' Association et al.,* v. *Myer et al.*, 104 *Federal Reporter*, 82.

[72] Thomas Huntley and George Palmer began their partnership in 1841. In 1921, the company merged with Peek Frean, another leading biscuit manufacturer, to form Amalgamated Biscuit Manufacturers Limited (ABM). T. A. B. Corley, *Quaker Enterprise in Biscuits* (London: Hutchinson and Company, 1972), 3, 268. In 1960, ABM acquired W. & R. Jacob. The group was subsequently bought by Nabisco in 1982.

biscuits, all of which were manufactured at Reading, were known throughout the world as 'Reading Biscuits' ... The Plaintiff's stated their belief that it was the intention of the Defendant Company to commence and carry on a biscuit trade, under the title of *The Reading Biscuit Company*, and thus to appropriate the reputation of the Plaintiff's, and that they would thus pass-off, and enable other persons to pass-off, the Defendant Company's goods fraudulently as being the goods of the Plaintiff's.[73]

In this case the court admitted that the defendant was entitled to set up in Reading and to mark their biscuits as 'Reading Biscuits', but 'you must not do that in such a manner as to take away unlawfully and illegitimately an established trade in the town', otherwise they would 'be depriving the Plaintiff's of part of their legitimate trade'.[74] The injunction prevented the defendant using 'Reading' unless their biscuits were clearly distinguished from those of Huntley & Palmer.

The ability of an individual firm to obtain exclusive rights to a primary geographical name was restricted to situations in which it possessed the sole privilege of producing particular merchandise and usually involved natural products. In coalmining, for example, use of the term 'Radstock Coal Company' was reserved for the Countess of Waldegrave, who practically owned all the collieries within the parish of Radstock (Somerset). Other collieries wishing to sell their coal with this designation were enjoined until they could demonstrate that they were owners or lessees of collieries within the parish. Similar cases included 'Leopoldshall' (Germany), applied to salt, and 'Cromac Springs' (Belfast), for mineral water.[75]

Conversely, 'secondary' geographical trademarks were not primarily understood as indicating geographical origin. They were used in a 'fictitious sense merely to indicate ownership, independent of location'; their geographical connotations are entirely arbitrary: 'When geographical names are used as trademarks they are in that application to be understood, not as ascribing the goods to which they are affixed to any special section of the earth's surface, but as expressing the works at which, or the manufacturer by whom, those goods have been produced.'[76] For this reason, secondary geographical trademarks do not act as IGOs. Consequently, 'Defiance' (writing paper), 'Dublin' (soap), 'Dover'

---

[73] *Reports of the Patent Commissioners* (hereafter, *RPC*) Vol. X (1893): 277–278.
[74] *RPC*, Vol X, 1893: 280.
[75] Cox, *A Manual of Trade Mark Cases*, 343–344; Hesseltine, *A Digest*, 68–69.
[76] Hopkins, *The Law of Trademarks* (1924), 161; Sebastian, *The Law of Trade Marks* (1911), 87.

(household products), 'Gibraltar' (belting), and 'Waverly' (bicycles) were permitted registration in the United States.[77] 'Defiance' was unusual: it had been used as a trademark long before the town of Defiance (Ohio), became economically important. The decision of the Examiner of Trade Marks to refuse registration was overturned because '[t]he geographical meaning of the word does not overshadow its original meaning and take from it its arbitrary significance as a trade-mark for paper'.[78] In all of these cases, the fundamental issue the Courts had to consider was: in the mind of the 'ordinary consumer', did such marks indicate trade or geographical origin?

Once again, the renown achieved by some secondary trademarks encouraged fraudulent behaviour. In Britain, two cases were notable: 'Ethiopian' (black stockings) and 'Persian' (cotton thread). Lewis Boyd Sebastian, an eminent British barrister in intellectual property law, asserted: 'no one could affirm that the use of [these] names . . . had induced [the consumer] to suppose that the articles in question were imported from these countries'.[79] In both cases it was acknowledged that the plaintiffs had established a considerable reputation for their products. Thus, 'said stockings . . . with said trade mark, had gained great repute for their excellence, and were in great demand in the market, where they were commonly called and known by the name of "The Ethiopian black cotton stockings" or "Ethiopians"'.[80] In the latter, the plaintiff claimed that infringement had cost them £5,000 in sales to the West Indian market and they secured an injunction on the grounds that '[i]n all these cases if parties were as desirous as they professed to be not to resemble other trademarks, they could always find a very ready mode of carrying their wishes into effect'.[81]

However, the distinction between primary and secondary geographical trademarks was rarely watertight. Frequently, trademarks which originally indicated geographical origin acquired secondary signification. This blurring of boundaries also encouraged fraud. Thus, in the 'Stone Ales' case, the plaintiffs were long-established brewers in the town of Stone (Staffordshire). In 1888, a rival established a brewery in this town and sought to sell their ales as 'Stone Ale' or 'Stone Ales', but the court recognised that these terms:

---

[77] These, and numerous other cases, are reported in Hesseltine, *A Digest*, 69–73.
[78] Byron Weston Company, *ex parte*, *Official Gazette*, US Patent Office, 861.
[79] Sebastian, *The Law of Trade Marks* (1911), 88.   [80] *Hine v. Lart*, 10 *Jurist* o.s. 106.
[81] *Taylor v. Taylor*, 23 L.J.Ch., 255–256.

all come from the Plaintiff's brewery, which is said to have been established in Stone for a hundred years, and to have flourished there all that time without a rival, and even without any attempt at rivalry worth mentioning. Whatever reputation, therefore, is attached to 'Stone Ales' or 'Stone Ale' above other ales known in the district is due to Plaintiffs and their predecessors [these terms do] not merely convey the idea that the beer was manufactured at Stone, but that it was the ale of the Respondents' manufacture.[82]

In the United States, this conflict is best exemplified by the 'watch cases' involving the Elgin National Watch Company and the Waltham Watch Company. For both, the courts recognised that although 'Elgin' and 'Waltham' were originally used in a geographical sense to indicate location, they subsequently acquired a secondary meaning: consumers understood that watches stamped with 'Elgin' or 'Waltham' were watches made by these companies. Both had expended considerable sums advertising their products. The former had spent $75,000 per annum for many years, and by 1899 the total advertising expenditure of the latter was $1 m. The scale of the frauds was equally significant. The Elgin company was in danger of losing between $30,000 and $50,000 of sales revenues, while the market for the Waltham concern was flooded with 25,000 imitation watches of inferior quality.[83]

INDICATIONS OF ORIGIN AT THE NATIONAL LEVEL

The previous section discussed the problems confronting individual firms seeking to acquire property in indications of origin and the extent to which secondary meaning could be used to secure protection from passing-off. Most of these cases involved the names of towns, cities, or regions. This section extends the analysis to the national level and contrasts British failure with French success. Attempts to launch a 'British' or 'British Empire' mark foundered largely because of objections based on economic grounds, especially the belief that it would damage private trademarks. In contrast, attempts to prevent the application by the Union Nationale Inter-Syndicate des Marques Collectives to register 'UNIS' and 'UNIS France' focused on legal objections and were unsuccessful.

---

[82] *Montgomery v. Thompson*, RPC, VIII., No. 40: 367, 369. See also *Worcester Royal Porcelain Company Ltd v. Locke & Co.*, RPC, XIX, (1902): 479.

[83] *American Waltham Watch Co. v. Sandman*, 96 *Federal Reporter*, 330; *Elgin Nat. Watch Co. v. Illinois Watch-Case Co., et al.*, 89 *Federal Reporter*, 487; *Illinois Watch-Case Co., v. Elgin Nat. Watch Co.*, 94 *Federal Reporter*, 667; *Elgin Nat. Watch Co. v. Loveland et al.*, 132 *Federal Reporter*, 41.

The concept of a 'British' or 'British Empire' trademark appears to have originated from a suggestion made by the Glasgow Chamber of Commerce to the British Empire Trade Mark Association (BETMA). Part of the justification for this initiative was the 'Made in Germany' debacle following the introduction of the British Merchandise Marks Act, 1887. It was recognised that 'Made in Germany' had been beneficial for German exports and it was believed that a British equivalent would generate similar benefits for British manufacturers: 'It is now proposed to substitute a positive for the negative sign and, instead of proclaiming that an article is made elsewhere . . . simply to attract our fellow countrymen by a recognised mark proving that it is British made.'[84] Other explanations that were advanced included that it would benefit small firms who did not have their own trademarks – or who did not have the resources to defend them against infringement abroad, and the identification of 'British' products would be facilitated enabling domestic consumers to exercise a 'voluntary preference' in favour of British manufactures.[85]

In Britain, legislation permitting the registration of an indication of origin was first enacted by the Trade Marks Act, 1905:

Where any association or person undertakes the examination of any goods in respect of origin, material . . . quality, or other characteristic, and certifies the result of such examination by mark used upon or in connection with such goods, the Board of Trade may, if they shall judge it to be to the public advantage, permit such association or person to register such mark as a trade mark in respect of such goods.[86]

The regulations governing indications of origin differed from those applied to ordinary trademarks. For example, the Board of Trade had to be satisfied that the former were 'to the public advantage'.[87] As a result of this Act and the Trade Marks Act, 1919, national and regional indications of origin were registered by the Irish Industrial Development Association, the Danish butter industry, La Union de Fabricantes de Tabacos de la Isla de Cuba, and the Scottish Woollen Trade Mark Association.[88]

---

[84] Merchandise Marks Committee, 1919–1920. Minutes of Evidence, 1919–1920: Q. 4540.

[85] Dominions Royal Commission. *Royal Commission on the Natural Resources, Trade, and Legislation of certain portions of His Majesty's Dominions. Minutes of Evidence Taken in London during October and November, 1912. Part II. Natural Resources, Trade, and Legislation* (1912). P.P. XVI.393: QQ. 2220, 2874.

[86] 5 Edw.7, Ch.15, s.62. Trade Marks Act, 1905.

[87] Trade Marks Act, 1905; 9 & 10 Geo. 5, Ch.79, s.62. Trade Marks Act, 1919.

[88] The National Archives (hereafter, TNA). BT 11/13. *Registration of the Mark UNIS: Report*: 10–11.

The BETMA proposal attracted criticism from manufacturers who feared that it would undermine the value of their trademarks:

The opponents of the mark maintain that such a mark in use could not fail to become regarded as a mark of quality, and that if it were used indiscriminately on goods of all qualities, inferior goods would receive an unfair advantage at the expense of the better class goods. The use of the mark with private trade marks would, it is said, lessen their distinctiveness and thus impair their value, a value which they have acquired as the result of considerable effort and expenditure on the part of the firms whose goods they identify.[89]

Firms opposing BETMA included Lever Bros. Ltd., J. & P. Coats Ltd., Cadbury Bros. Ltd., and Arthur Guinness, Son & Co. Ltd., all of whom owned famous trademarks, as well as the Federation of British Industries and the Association of British Chemical Manufacturers. Some renowned firms, for example, Webley & Scott (firearms) and Pilkington's Tile & Pottery Co. Ltd., did support the BETMA proposal. Nonetheless it is clear from the evidence given before the Select Committee on Merchandise Marks Act, 1919–1920, that in terms of market capitalisation, opponents substantially outnumbered supporters.[90]

The relationship between origin and quality featured prominently in debates on a 'British' or 'British Empire' mark. BETMA argued that its proposed mark only indicated origin. But this side-stepping only exacerbated matters. To the extent consumers believed British products were superior, the proposed mark might indicate quality; this signal would be amplified if products were also imprinted with private trademarks. However, the indication of origin might be undermined if it was adopted by firms producing low-quality goods, making it less likely that firms owning reputable trademarks would agree to BETMA's proposals. It was also possible that the indication of origin would foster the belief that the products to which it was affixed would be the best *wherever* they were produced, which would fatally undermine its ability to identify country of origin. Finally, there was the problem of 'certifying' the products: which body would be responsible, and how practicable and desirable was this procedure given the scale and diversity of British manufacturing? This was a crucial consideration because it highlighted

---

[89] *Report to the Board of Trade of the Merchandise Marks Committee* (1920). P.P. XXI.615: x.

[90] This observation is based on L. Hannah, *The Rise of the Corporate Economy* (London: Methuen, 1983), table A5, 189. This table includes major tobacco companies which were not represented before the Select Committee of 1919–1920.

the tension between individual firms and trade associations. The former are responsible for protecting their own trademarks because they directly bear the costs of infringement, but misuse of certification and collective marks imposes costs on an entire industry, region, or nation. Given this conflict, firms owning renowned trademarks objected to the proposed indication of origin because they had little confidence their private interests were aligned with its objectives:

The registration of a British mark of origin was refused in its inception ... The strong objections which were raised ... by the opponent firms ... made it clear that to hand control of a general mark of origin of this kind to a private institution, which had not received the support of a large and important body of English traders, would be detrimental to public interests.[91]

Because of these competing arguments it was impossible for the Merchandise Marks Committee, 1919–1920, to recommend that a 'British' or 'British Empire' mark was to the public advantage, and the scheme collapsed.

The opposition of British manufacturers against a national indication of origin in the early twentieth century extended to those originating from abroad and is perhaps best exemplified by the struggle of the Union Nationale Inter-Syndicate des Marques Collectives (UNIS) to register 'UNIS' and 'UNIS France' as trademarks in Britain. This organisation was founded in 1915 under the patronage of the Paris chamber of commerce to establish a trademark guaranteeing French origin. The UNIS mark was to be reserved for manufacturers who were French citizens by birth or who had been naturalised for more than fifteen years. The fact that a firm was established in France was not sufficient to establish its right to use 'UNIS': situations might arise where a French product was not manufactured exclusively in France by French workmen, or where raw or semi-finished materials entered its manufacture which were not sourced in France or French colonies. In these circumstances, each case would be treated on its merits.[92]

The UNIS application commenced in 1917, and it was opposed by many of the companies who had objected to BETMA's proposals, for

---

[91] In the matter of an application by Union Nationale Inter-Syndicate des Marques Collectives to register trademarks, *RPC*, XXXIX. (1922): 107–108. For a broader analysis of this debate, see D. M. Higgins, '"Made in Britain?" National Trademarks and Merchandise Marks: The British Experience from the Late Nineteenth Century to the 1920s', *Journal of Industrial History*, 5 (2002): 50–70.

[92] TNA, BT 11/13, Registration of the Mark UNIS, Cahill to Director General of Overseas Trade, 20 May 1922.

example, Bass, Ratcliff & Gretton Ltd., J & P Coats Ltd., and Joseph
Crosfield & Sons Ltd. The opponents appealed against the decision of the
Comptroller General as Registrar of Trade Marks in 1921, and the
High Court of Justice in 1922. It was not until 1923 that the Court of
Appeal ruled in favour of UNIS. At first sight opposition by British
manufacturers seems strange: if national indications of origin were
a 'badge of inferiority' – the main criticism levelled at the proposed
'British' mark – then British manufacturers should have welcomed the
UNIS application, believing that the adverse consequences of using it
would rebound on French manufacturers. However, the UNIS case illus-
trates that many of the grounds for objection were based on an erroneous
understanding of national indications of origin.

Among the principal economic objections to registration of the 'UNIS'
marks were that they adversely affected the interests of British manufacturers and traders; they were not to the public advantage; such marks did not
provide any guarantee that the products to which they were affixed were of
French origin; the ability of British traders to source supplies from French
firms was restricted; the marks reflected quality, not origin, without providing any effective guarantee of a particular quality; they excluded British
firms with operations in France from using the 'UNIS' mark. Finally, '[t]he
marks are open to the greatest objection [that] they are going to drive out
a great quantity of British goods that go to France to be finished'.[93]

The court overruled these objections because they were based upon
'inference or supposition'. For example, there was no substantial evidence
that any particular injury would be inflicted on British trademarks if
'UNIS' was registered: 'the opponents have been unable to find a single
trader who has been injured by these marks'. Turning to the
quality–origin nexus, it was admitted that 'UNIS' marks could communicate quality, but, '[i]t is difficult to see how a person who purchases
goods with the mark "UNIS France" on them, can suppose that they have
been produced elsewhere than in France'. Many of the objections were
'objections which might be taken to the registration of any trade mark,
and, if accepted, would seriously interfere with the general registration of
marks'. In fact, even if successful, opposition to the 'UNIS' marks was
pointless: they would continue to be used in France and Britain.
Moreover, they had been affixed to products for between six and seven
years and were 'among the best known marks in Europe'. The Board of

[93] In the matter of an application by Union Nationale Inter-Syndicate des Marques
Collectives to register trademarks, *RPC*, XXXIX, 1922: 99–100, 115.

Trade could exercise the ultimate sanction independent of the courts: it had the power to cancel the marks on public interest grounds – including evidence that the marks directly injured British trade.[94]

'UNIS' and 'UNIS France' were not owned by the French government but they received official approval. In fact, the French authorities were keen to devolve these marks to a trade association to ensure their use was not compulsory or a symbol of quality.[95] The UNIS marks were not a general mark of origin open to all, but qualified indications of origin advanced by a specific trading association. Any firm was at liberty to indicate the origin of their products by marking them 'Made in France', 'Product of France', or 'French Make', but not all French manufacturers were entitled to use 'UNIS'.

The UNIS marks did more than indicate French origin: they also denoted that the products were made in France using French capital or labour under the supervision of one of the syndicates comprising the Union. The Union recognised that many companies incorporated according to French law with headquarters in France were subsidiaries of foreign companies and that 'it would be really excessive to give them the character of French business'. Regulations governing use of the 'UNIS' marks overcame obstacles inherent to the origin–quality nexus: the Union prohibited the use of its marks on 'notoriously defective products, whose sale would be likely to injure the reputation of the interested industry's current products'.[96]

In the end, the UNIS application was heard by the Court of Appeal. It was recognised that the UNIS marks '[do] not obviously indicate the characteristics of the goods being certified [and] that the public may come to think of it as a mark of quality when it may not be so'.[97] Nonetheless, the court left the matter to the Board of Trade, which allowed the UNIS marks to proceed to registration.

Comparing the two examples, it is apparent that in Britain many famous companies opposed national indications of origin, fearing they would adversely affect their renowned trademarks. In France, it was recognised that several syndicates representing the perfume, wine, and pharmaceutical industries were unwilling to use the UNIS marks because such use would create confusion with their own trademarks. However,

---

[94] In the matter of an application by Union Nationale Inter-Syndicate des Marques Collectives to register trademarks, *RPC*, XXXIX, 1922, 113, 116, 118, 129; The National Archives, 'Registration of the mark UNIS', BT 11/13:6.

[95] *Propriété Industrielle*, 11 (1934): 192–194.

[96] *Propriété Industrielle*, 11 (1934): 193–194 [author's translation].

[97] Dawson, *Certification Trade Marks*, 20.

these syndicates did not oppose others desirous of using 'UNIS' marks. An explanation for this divergence may be that France had greater experience of the coexistence of private and collective trademarks.

'WHERE IS THE LINE TO BE DRAWN?' INTERNATIONAL SUPPLY CHAINS AND THE WATCH INDUSTRY

The general trends in the growth of international trade in manufactures were discussed at the beginning of this chapter. Simultaneously, the need to control quality along the vertical supply chain became more important. Paul Duguid and James Simpson have demonstrated how producers of port and claret, as well as champagne and cognac, battled fraudulent misrepresentation which threatened to undermine the reputation of their trademarks.[98] British, Swiss, and US watch manufacturers were not immune to these practices.

A watch is comprised of two parts: the movement, which provides the time, and the casing within which the movement is placed.[99] The assaying of products made with gold and silver was compulsory from the reign of Edward I (1239–1307). In the watch industry it was a common practice for the watch case to be assayed in England even though the movement might be American or Swiss:

The chief complaint against the operation of the existing law comes from the manufacturers of watches and watch cases. They have established by evidence that within the last few years a practice has sprung up, and is rapidly increasing, under which foreign made watch-cases are sent to this country to be hall-marked with the British hall-mark, and are afterwards fitted with foreign movements, and are then not unfrequently sold and dealt in as British-made watches.[100]

Originally, the hallmark denoted the fineness or quality of products made from precious metal, but the practice of inserting foreign movements into British hallmarked watch cases meant the assay mark had become a mark of quality and an indication of origin for the watch. Legislation to prevent this misrepresentation was provided by various Customs Acts which required that in addition to British hallmarks, foreign

---

[98] Duguid, 'Developing the Brand'; Duguid, 'Networks and Knowledge'; Simpson, 'Selling to Reluctant Drinkers'.

[99] For the remainder of this chapter, 'watch' refers to the movement and the case.

[100] *Report from the Select Committee on Hall Marking* (Gold and Silver) (1878–1879). P.P. X.365: iv–v.

plate had to bear the letter 'F' in an oval escutcheon.[101] But this legislation was ineffective because assay offices were not required to ask depositors whether their cases were domestic or foreign. Financial gains provided a further incentive to misrepresentation. For example, it was reported that some British watches commanded a premium of 10–15 per cent, and sometimes as much as 200 per cent, compared to foreign and Swiss watches, respectively. It appears that the Waltham Watch Company were an exception to this practice: their British subsidiary imported all movements from the United States and although these might be enclosed in British hallmarked cases, the watch face or plate clearly indicated 'American Watch Company, Waltham, Mass'.[102]

The principal methods Swiss and US manufacturers used to pass-off their watches as 'British' appear straightforward. Foreign movements were either sent to Britain to be placed inside British hallmarked cases, or British hallmarked cases were exported abroad, finished with foreign movements, and re-exported to Britain.[103] Closer examination of these practices reveals more complex issues of misrepresentation. For example, one reason why US watch manufacturers wanted their watches inserted into British hallmarked cases was to prevent Swiss manufacturers using US cases and passing-off their watches as 'Made in the US'. It also appears that US manufacturers objected to their watches being passed-off as 'Swiss', but not 'English'. Conversely, some British producers were known to obtain watches from Geneva and mark these with legends such as 'Smith, Bond Street', to induce the belief that they were indigenous.[104] If consumers believed a hallmark indicated that the case *and* the movement were British, the scope for misrepresentation increased, with concomitant damage to the British watch industry.[105]

---

[101] An Act to Alter Certain Duties and to Amend the Laws Relating to the Customs, 1867, Vict., Ch.82, s.24; Customs (Tariff) Act, 1876, 39 & 40 Vict., Ch.35, s.2; Revenue Act, 1883, 46 & 47 Vict., Ch. 55, s.10.

[102] *Special Report from the Select Committee on Merchandize Marks Act* (1862). Minutes of Evidence (1887). P.P. X.357: QQ. 73–74; QQ. 184–202; QQ. 485–87; QQ. 712–75; QQ. 813–18; QQ. 1636–1703.

[103] *Special Report from the Select Committee on Merchandize Marks Act* (1862). Minutes of Evidence (1887). P.P. X.357: QQ. 1327–29; QQ. 1475–78. Evidence given before this Committee refers to 'English' hallmarks, but assay offices also existed in Dublin, Edinburgh, and Glasgow. For this reason, 'British' is used throughout this chapter, unless a citation refers specifically to 'English'.

[104] *Report from the Select Committee on Hall Marking* (Gold and Silver). P.P. X.365, (1878–1897): QQ. 243–49; Q. 302; Q. 849.

[105] *Special Report from the Select Committee on Merchandize Marks Act* (1862). Minutes of Evidence (1887): P.P. X.357: 712–20; 742–45

The misrepresentation of watches raised a series of problems about how to delineate the boundaries between truthful and misleading indications of origin. These problems became acute in the debates preceding the Merchandise Marks Act, 1887. This Act defined the expression 'false trade description' as 'a trade description which was false in a material respect'. But how was 'material respect' to be defined? Was it possible for a competent jury of watchmakers to distinguish the British and Swiss components of a watch? If not, uncertainty might deter litigation even when the abuse was flagrant. Should the boundary be set in terms of value added? It was claimed that the value added to movements imported and subsequently processed in Britain represented the greatest value, therefore the practice of applying British assay marks to foreign movements was justified. Additionally, there was recognition that consumer perception of origin could affect the revenues of the domestic watch industry. Thus, if a Swiss movement was inserted into a British case and the final watch was marked 'Swiss', a consumer, believing the entire product was Swiss, would only pay the Swiss price even though two-thirds of the labour cost was British. But the opposite also applied: if the final product was marked to indicate British origin, consumers were overpaying by one-third for this watch. Finally, were Swiss watch movements really 'Swiss'? Swiss-made watch springs were known to be made from wire produced in Sheffield.[106]

In the United States, concern about the importation of foreign watches and their sale as 'US' resulted in legislation which preceded the general marking requirements of the McKinley tariff by almost twenty years. In 1871 a bill was passed stipulating that US customs prohibit the import of watches or watch movements unless they were legibly marked with the place and country of manufacture.[107] British regulations to eradicate misleading indications of origin were contained in the Merchandise Marks Act, 1887. This Act also required that all watch cases – imported or domestic – sent to be stamped or marked at a British assay office had to be accompanied by a declaration of their place or country of manufacture. It also distinguished 'watch' from 'watch cases', and stipulated that if the watch did not indicate its country of origin, then the words or marks on

---

[106] *Special Report from the Select Committee on Merchandize Marks Act* (1862). Minutes of Evidence (1887). P.P. X.357: Q. 108; QQ. 932–933; Q. 1021; QQ. 1022–1029; QQ. 1349–53; QQ. 1521–1529.
[107] *Report of the Commissioners Appointed to Revise the Statutes Relating to Patents, Trade and other Marks, and Trade and Commercial Names* (Washington, DC: Government Printing Office, 1902), 99.

the watch case would be interpreted as indicating the country where the watch was made.[108] Subsequently, this provision was strengthened by a Customs General Order.[109] It appears that the Merchandise Marks Act, 1887, did result in successful prosecutions when foreign watches were falsely described as 'English'. However, in some cases, for example, *Williamson* v. *Tuerney*, 1901, the court accepted that it was not fraudulent to describe a watch as 'English' when it contained foreign parts. The fundamental issue here was whether the watch was *substantially* made in England.[110]

CONCLUSIONS

In medieval Europe the guilds were responsible for using collective marks to signal manufacturing and geographical origin, and quality. During the nineteenth century individual manufacturers were prevented from acquiring exclusive rights to primary geographical trademarks, though they did use geographical names as part of their brands. When the law did permit individual firms to acquire property in geographical trademarks this was usually on the condition that they primarily indicated trade, not geographical origin.

The key difference between the use of indications of origin on manufactures compared to agricultural produce is that the role of location-specific factors was less important to the former. In the medieval era many towns, cities, and regions were renowned for their manufactures. This stature was not a function of location but stringent regulations governing materials and labour, both of which were geographically mobile. Thus, Colchester's reputation for baize depended on the settlement of Flemish weavers between 1570 and 1571. Other Flemish weavers, based in Halstead, were responsible for the infringement of Colchester's mark.[111] Similarly, skilled armourers benefitted from royal patronage and travelled across Western Europe, and the revocation of the Edict of Nantes in 1685 resulted in the exodus of skilled craftsmen to Britain and Holland.[112]

---

[108] 50 & 51 Vict., Ch.28. *Merchandise Marks Act, 1887*: s.7, s.8.

[109] Customs General Order 9/188. 32nd Report of the Commissioner of Her Majesty's Customs on The Customs for the Year Ended 31 March 1888. P.P. XXXIV.159. London: HMSO (1888), 77–78.

[110] Sebastian, *The Law of Trade Marks* (1911), 681.

[111] Schechter, *Historical Foundations*, 88–90.

[112] Ffoulkes, *The Armourer*, 14; R. Reith, 'Circulation of Skilled Labour in Late Medieval and Early Modern Central Europe', in Epstein and Prak, *Guilds, Innovation*, 142.

A further conclusion to emerge from this chapter concerns the conflict between private trademarks and indications of origin. Reputable manufacturers perceived 'Made in Britain' as a badge of inferiority and were concerned that the goodwill established in their trademarks would be undermined by using such an indication. This tension raised other questions, for example, are private trademarks and indications of origin mutually exclusive? The marketing literature offers possible answers. The opposition of British firms to 'British' was justified if they believed it was of negligible value or that it would damage their trademarks. However, this opposition may have harboured a sting in its tail: 'Countries with stronger product than country images may be faced with weaker demand if suitable alternatives become available to buyers at some point in the future.'[113] Conflict between private brands and indications of origin continues today.[114]

The penultimate section of this chapter discussed the problems that arise when assay marks were perceived as indications of origin. A key feature of contemporary debates on the watch industry was how to ensure that such indications accurately represented provenance. This topic involved 'value added' and 'false in a material respect' – precursors to modern definitions of 'substantive transformation'. A related problem which also has contemporary relevance was determining the factors that affected consumer perceptions of provenance. Country of origin, or 'Made in', might convey the impression that a manufactured product was wholly made in one location. But the growth of complex value-added chains in global manufacturing meant such indications were potentially misleading. Because manufacturing operations need not be location-specific, any restriction on geographical diversity might undermine long-term competitiveness based on securing low-cost inputs and/or being located in lower-cost countries.

---

[113] Papadopoulos and Heslop, 'Country Equity and Country Branding', 300.
[114] In Chapter 9 I discuss 'Swiss made' as applied to watches and 'Made in the US'.

3

Country of Origin and Agricultural Trade during the Nineteenth Century

In my opinion, though our trade has suffered and may possibly still suffer from selling the pick of our meat as English and Scotch, because that deprives us of the good advertisement that this excellent meat would be to us, still any injury so caused is merely trifling compared to the harm that is done by fraudulent sales of River Plate or Australian ... The meat marking law, so far from injuring us, would, I think, be a positive advantage to us.

Henry Charles Cameron, Agent General for New Zealand, 1898.[1]

It is a matter of considerable satisfaction to find that the wholesale merchants in Great Britain are of the opinion that some of the butter produced in Ireland is superior in quality to butter from any other country which supplies British markets. If, therefore ... its average quality can be levelled up to the standard which is already reached by the most careful and skilled manufacturers, Irish butter should establish its superiority against all competitors.

Department of Agriculture and Technical Instruction for Ireland:
Report of the Departmental Committee on the Irish Butter Industry.
P.P. VIII.1 (Dublin: HMSO, 1910), 23

The first wave of globalisation had a direct impact on the production and trade of agricultural produce. Previously, it was too expensive to transport all but expensive, 'colonial' foodstuffs such as spices, sugar, and tobacco.[2] The changes which occurred during the late nineteenth century included rapid urbanisation and growing per capita incomes, both of which

---

[1] The Agent General for New Zealand to the Hon. Minister of Agriculture, 25 September 1897, *Appendix to the Journals of the House of Representatives*, 1898, Session I, H-17: 2.

[2] O'Rourke and Williamson, 'Introduction', 6.

presented a severe test for the global agricultural supply function. Fortunately, '[w]orld agriculture met the challenge brilliantly'.[3] Between 1850 and 1913, world trade in agricultural products grew at an average yearly rate of 3.4 per cent and by 1913, food accounted for 27 per cent of world exports.[4] Britain occupied a central position within this global trading network. John Hanson estimated that from the mid-nineteenth century until 1900, Britain was the biggest market for the aggregate exports, of Asia, Africa, and South America. In the years 1860, 1880, and 1914, Britain imported 49, 40, and 24 per cent, respectively, of the aggregate exports of these three continents and between 1860 and 1880, their aggregate exports to Britain were greater than their exports to Western Europe (excluding Britain) and North America combined.[5] By 1913, the UK and Ireland accounted for 19 per cent of global imports of primary products.[6]

This broad geographical picture conceals the fact that the British market was of paramount importance for specific produce and the countries exporting it. This market was more than simply a 'vent for surplus': it is no exaggeration to state that for certain produce Britain was effectively a monopsonist. Thus, between 1880 and 1907, on average, the British market absorbed 81.3 and 98.6 per cent, respectively, of US live cattle and beef exports, by volume. Similarly, between 1881 and 1914, Britain absorbed an average of 96.3 per cent, by value, of all meat exports from New Zealand, and by 1905, British imports of cheese, eggs, bacon, and ham, by value, accounted for 99.4, 92.6, 99.8, and 95.5 per cent, respectively, of the total value of Canadian exports of these products. Finally, similar trends are also observed for British imports of Danish butter, which were never below 80 per cent of total Danish butter exports between 1880 and 1913.[7]

---

[3] G. Federico, 'Growth, Specialization, and Organization of World Agriculture', in L. Neal and J. G. Williamson (eds.), *The Cambridge History of Capitalism*. Vol. II: *The Spread of Capitalism from 1848 to the Present* (Cambridge: Cambridge University Press, 2014), 47.

[4] A. Nützenadel, 'A Green International? Food Markets and Transnational Politics, c. 1850–1914', in A. Nützenadel and F. Trentmann (eds.), *Food and Globalization: Consumption, Markets and Politics in the Modern World* (Oxford: Berg, 2008), 157; F. Trentmann, 'Before Fair Trade Empire, Free Trade and the Moral Economies of Food in the Modern World', in Nützenadel and Trentmann, *Food and Globalization*, 254.

[5] J. R. Hanson, *Trade in Transition: Exports from the Third World, 1840–1900* (New York: Academic Press, 1980), 55.

[6] Kenwood and Lougheed, *The Growth of the International Economy*, 86.

[7] Canadian data were calculated from *Report of the Minister of Agriculture for the Dominion of Canada for the Year Ended October, 31, 1905*: 5–6 Edward VII, Sessional Paper 15 (Ottawa, 1906): xxv; Danish data were obtained from Higgins and Mordhorst,

Concomitant with the emergence of global food supply chains was growing concern about authentication, especially the relationship between product and place.[8] Thus, when consumers specified Danish butter or Irish ham, what assurance did they have that they were buying the genuine article? Because Britain was by far the biggest importer of produce during this period, it offered the greatest opportunities for misrepresenting the geographical origin of produce. In this context, passing-off raised a number of issues which directly affected the economic prosperity of those countries most reliant on exporting to Britain. One problem concerned the use of generic terms which undermined the link between product and place. For example, from medieval times, cheddar was originally understood to mean cheese produced by a particular method in the village of Cheddar, and surrounding districts in the southwest of England, but by the late nineteenth century, Canadian cheddar, principally from Ontario, accounted for 70 per cent of Britain's cheese imports.[9] Similar problems occurred when 'Wiltshire' and 'Canterbury' were applied to US and Canadian hams, and New Zealand lamb, respectively. In the United States, dairy research laboratories investigated the manufacture of Swiss, cheddar, and Roquefort types of cheeses. It was claimed that: 'The experiments with European varieties of soft cheese have been carried far enough to indicate the possibility of making cheese of the Camembert type in this country.'[10]

Major food-exporting regions such as Australasia, Canada, and Denmark used country of origin to differentiate their produce on foreign markets. But as competition intensified, misrepresentation had the potential to damage their agricultural sectors by reducing earnings. Moreover, a reduced market share was unable to support large-scale specialisation in the produce-exporting country. The signals communicated by country of

'Reputation and Export Performance', 188; New Zealand data were calculated from F. H. Capie, 'The Development of the Meat Trade between New Zealand and the United Kingdom, 1860–1914'. Unpublished MSc thesis, London University (1969): table 6; US data were obtained from Higgins and Gangjee, 'Trick or Treat?', 208.

[8] A. Nützenadel and F. Trentmann, 'Introduction: Mapping Food and Globalization', in Nützenadel and Trentmann, *Food and Globalization*, 13. Reinforcing this trend was growing prohibition of adulteration of which the 'Margarine Laws' are probably the best genre.

[9] L. M. Mason and C. Brown, *Traditional Foods of Britain: A Regional Inventory* (Totnes: Prospect Books, 2004), 118–119; H. Menzies, *By the Labour of Their Hands: The Story of Ontario Cheddar Cheese* (Ontario: Quarry Press, 1994), 11.

[10] *Yearbook of the United States Department of Agriculture* (hereafter, *USDA*) (1912), 50. Investigations into the feasibility of producing 'Cheddar', 'Swiss'-type cheeses, and Roquefort are reported in *Yearbook of the USDA* (1911), 47.

origin varied according to the type of foodstuff. Applied to meat, they denoted the absence of diseases, such as tuberculosis. Butter was more complex. Passing-off margarine as butter adversely affected all dairy producers, irrespective of their location, and threatened to erode price differentials between high- and low-quality butters. This practice also threatened the reputation of newly emerging butter exporters such as Russia and Siberia.[11] Turning to cheese, the Canadian government was particularly aggrieved that 'margarine cheese' was passed-off as genuine Canadian cheese.[12] Similarly, Demerara was recognised to be cane sugar originating from the British West Indies, but this term was frequently applied to artificially dyed white beet sugar produced in France and Germany.[13]

Discontinuity in food supply chains encouraged deliberate misrepresentation of indications of origin. The United States was concerned that its bacon was imported into Ireland and re-sold in England as 'Irish'.[14] The Irish acknowledged that it was customary for creamery proprietors to purchase foreign and colonial butters and to re-sell these without any indication that they were not Irish.[15] It was alleged that Danish merchants passed-off Russian butter as 'Danish', which infuriated Harald Faber. Similarly, complaints were made that Russian and Siberian butter were exported to Denmark and then re-shipped to Germany as 'Danish'. The United States complained that: 'Once in the hands of the trade, our butter was repeatedly sold as English, Canadian, or Australian.' New Zealand protested that '[a]n English dealer bought New Zealand cheese at 54/-; repacked it and returned it to the colony at 78/- as best Cheddar'.[16]

This chapter focuses on state intervention in agriculture to improve quality and to protect country of origin. Such indications could be ambiguous, referring to quality, composition, and/or geographical origin. The growth of the international economy in the late nineteenth and early twentieth centuries presented new opportunities for fraud. For most of the period covered in this chapter, fraudulent use of indications

---

[11] *The Grocer*, 17 February 1912, 498.   [12] *The Grocer*, 29 October 1904, 1099.

[13] *The Grocer*, 29 August 1903, 558; *The Grocer*, 30 July 1904, 283; *The Grocer*, 4 August 1906, 303; *The Grocer*, 28 November 1908, 1413; *The Grocer*, 6 April 1912, 1011; *Report from the Select Committee on Merchandise Marks Act*, 1887. P.P. 15. 334 (1890): QQ. 3203–3204.

[14] *Yearbook of the USDA* (1899), 46.

[15] Department of Agriculture and Technical Instruction for Ireland, *Report of the Departmental Committee on the Irish Butter Industry*. P.P. VIII.1, (1910): 10.

[16] *The Grocer*, 15 August 1903, 446; *The Grocer*, 24 December 1910, 1699; *Yearbook of the USDA* (1897), 15; *New Zealand Country Journal*, XVIII, No. 3, 1 May 1894: 357.

of origin in Britain was prohibited by the Merchandise Marks Act, 1887. Analysis of unreported[17] cases under this statute indicates that foreign governments were aggressive litigants. However, not all actions were successful. The courts grappled with the new case law: for example, was long-established trade employment of a term legitimate, and therefore innocent, or was it calculated to deceive? In the majority of cases, only small or nominal fines were imposed.

STATE INTERVENTION

A substantial literature exists on the economic advantages conferred on individual owners of trademarks. In theory, these advantages extend to groups of firms selling products with an indication of origin. But for this extension to be successful it is imperative that high and uniform levels of quality are achieved. Whereas an individual producer has a strong incentive to protect its own goodwill, it is not certain that each producer will take the same interest in upholding the integrity of an indication of origin: there may be private incentives to cheat by secretly lowering quality. The solution to this free-riding problem was provided by the emergence of cooperatives in agriculture. Recent scholarship on this organisational form has shown that cooperative production of wine was associated with 'improved quality and consistency of wines produced by better management and technical skills', and that in the Italian wine industry, 'cooperative associations had a strong ideological basis which prevented opportunistic behavior among members'.[18]

However, during the nineteenth century, it was in the dairy industry that cooperatives featured most prominently, and Denmark and New Zealand are considered exemplars.[19] In Denmark, 1,168 cooperative dairies existed by 1914, accounting for 85 per cent of all dairies at this date. Harald Faber

---

[17] Unreported cases are not considered legally significant and usually appear in the trade press, rather than law reports. The distinction between 'reported' and 'unreported' cases continues today. I am grateful to Catherine Dale, law librarian at Newcastle University, UK, for this observation.

[18] F. J. Medina-Albaladejo and T. Menzani, 'Co-operative Wineries in Italy and Spain in the Second Half of the Twentieth Century: Success or Failure of the Cooperative Business Model', *Enterprise and Society*, 18 (2017): 64; Simpson, 'Cooperation and Cooperatives in Southern European Wine Production', 113.

[19] I. Henriksen, M. Hviid, and P. Sharpe, 'Law and Peace: Contracts and the Success of the Danish Dairy Cooperatives', *Journal of Economic History*, 72 (2012): 197–224; I. Henriksen, E. McLaughlin, and P. Sharp, 'Contracts and Cooperation: The Relative Failure of the Irish Dairy Industry in the Late Nineteenth Century Reconsidered', *European Review of Economic History*, 19 (2015): 412–431. The economic perspective in these papers is complemented by research showing that cooperatives played an important

attributed the success of dairy cooperatives to each member's recognition of the common interest: 'These cooperative dairies had this advantage over those under private ownership, that the people who delivered milk to the former were interested in the result; therefore they took care to deliver the milk in good condition, and to see that their neighbours did the same.'[20] Similarly, from the late nineteenth century, the production of New Zealand butter was organised on a cooperative basis. According to Charles Fay, 'We have in New Zealand, the England-cum-Denmark of the South, a rare opportunity for observing the place of cooperation in the organization of agriculture.' If New Zealand was to develop a thriving export trade with Britain, it was imperative that its butter was comparable to that supplied by Denmark. According to Fay, the growth of cooperatives facilitated the production of such butter because 'there is a premium on intimacy between producer and processor and thus on the cooperative form'.[21] Indeed, the pioneer companies in the New Zealand dairy industry were cooperatives, for example: Flemington Cheese and Butter Factory and the Greytown Cooperative Dairy Company, formed in 1882 and 1883, respectively. In 1886, Henry Reynolds established the first butter factory in Waikato and used the Anchor brand; in 1896, Reynolds sold the business and the Anchor brand to the New Zealand Dairy Association. Although individual entrepreneurs initiated the factory system of production, they were quickly replaced by farmers who combined their resources in cooperative production. By 1890, of 150 butter factories operating in New Zealand, 40 per cent were cooperatives, directly owned by the farmers; by 1900, cooperatives outnumbered all other types of butter factory.[22]

Official intervention in Australasian, Canadian, Danish, and US agriculture from the later nineteenth century occurred for two reasons. First, agriculture's share of GDP meant that export success was

---

role in the formation of Danish identity. M. Mordhorst, 'Arla and Danish National Identity: Business History as Cultural History', *Business History*, 56 (2014): 116–133.

[20] H. Faber, *Cooperation in Danish Agriculture* (London: Longmans, Green & Company, 1918), 38–39, 41.

[21] C. R. Fay, *Co-operation at Home and Abroad. Volume II, 1908–1938* (London: P. S. King & Son, 1939), 349, 358.

[22] H. Philpott, *A History of the New Zealand Dairy Industry* (Wellington: New Zealand Government Printer, 1937), 41–61; F. Steel, '"New Zealand Is Butterland": Interpreting the Historical Significance of a Daily Spread', *New Zealand Journal of History*, 39 (2005): 4; H. Stringleman and F. Scrimgeour, 'Dairying and Dairy Products: The Beginnings of New Zealand's Dairy Industry', *Te Ara – the Encyclopedia of New Zealand*, 3. Downloaded from www.teara.govt.nz/en/dairying-and-dairy-products/page-1.

fundamental to national economic prosperity. Second, the state played an important role because it had the legislative power to enforce national minimum quality standards.[23] Reinforcing this commitment to quality was recognition that the British market had exacting standards. In 1878, John Dyke, Liverpool Agent for the Canadian Minister of Agriculture, warned: 'I cannot ... impress too forcibly upon the minds of our Canadian exporters of all classes, that, whereas, the primest quality of any class of goods will realize the best prices anywhere in the world, in this country, second or third-class qualities cannot be disposed of at a price to return profit. This rule applies to ... everything that we export.'[24] In fact, Britain imported the highest-quality produce whereas citizens in exporting countries consumed lower-quality foodstuffs. In the case of Danish butter it was claimed: 'By far the greatest part of the butter consumed in Copenhagen is of Russian origin, as this can be had so much cheaper than Danish butter, which is exported to the United Kingdom.'[25]

There can be no doubt that state involvement was crucial to the development and maintenance of high quality in dairy and meat products. Even a cursory examination of contemporary official publications testifies to improvements in herds and technical instruction; the establishment of experimental stations; provision of state bounties to accelerate agricultural improvements, as well as financial aid for chilled distribution and storage of produce.[26] Complementing these developments, 'best practice' was diligently monitored. The careful attention that the Danes devoted to the bacon requirements of British customers – and the higher prices thereby commanded – was reported in the United States.[27] In Canada, the Minister of Agriculture was informed of the superior methods of butter production in Wisconsin and Minnesota, and the Canadian Commissioner of Agriculture and Dairying was instructed to visit Britain, 'to see the existing conditions of the markets for perishable farm

---

[23] A further condition was that the state had the resources to instigate litigation to deter misrepresentation.

[24] *Report of the Minister of Agriculture for the Dominion of Canada for the Calendar Year 1878.* 42 Victoria, Sessional Papers: 103.

[25] *The Grocer*, 15 August 1903, 446. Similar claims were made for Australian butter. *Royal Commission on the Butter Industry.* Victoria (1905): Q. 733; QQ. 944–952.

[26] See, for example, Australia: 1 Geo.V. No. 10. The Meat and Dairy Produce Encouragement Acts Amendment Act of 1910; *Report of the Minister of Agriculture for the Dominion of Canada for the Calendar Year 1896.* 60 Victoria, Sessional Papers No. 8: xiii.

[27] *Yearbook of the USDA* (1895), 15–16; *Yearbook of the USDA* (1896), 32.

products there, to learn the newest preferences for ... qualities of goods ...
and to start two agents of the department in their work for the extension
and improvement of trade in Canadian farm products'.[28]

The efforts national governments made to improve the international
competitiveness of their agricultural exports would have been nullified
unless their produce was differentiated from rivals'. Numerous publications
documented the prices of a diverse range of agricultural products on the
British market, including the *Agricultural Returns* of the Board of
Agriculture, the *Meat Trades Journal and Cattle Salesman's Gazette*, and
Weddel's *Review of the Frozen Meat Trade*. Complementing these sources
were ad hoc reports issued by various Departments of Agriculture.[29]
Contemporaries were thus informed of the relative prices of produce –
which also provided an incentive to misrepresent. Two types of misrepresentation of country of origin were practised, each with substantially
different adverse consequences. The first type occurred when products
from country A were misrepresented as those of country B. In this case,
and assuming there were no perceived or actual quality differences between
the two products, country B lost sales to country A. The second category
relaxes the assumption that actual or perceived differences in quality did not
exist. For example, assume that the produce of country B was superior to
that of country A. Now, the consequences of misrepresentation for country
B were more severe: not only did it lose sales to country A, but its reputation
for quality was also damaged because low quality was substituted for high
quality. In this case, misrepresentation of geographical origin was simultaneously a misrepresentation of quality. New Zealand was concerned that
inferior Australian and Argentine meat were passed-off as 'New Zealand',
but it was untroubled by having its butter and cheese passed-off because 'the
Australian and Canadian article is usually as good as ours'.[30]

---

[28] *Report of the Minister of Agriculture for the Dominion of Canada for the Calendar Year
1879.* 43 Victoria, Sessional Papers No. 10: 136; *Report of the Minister of Agriculture for
the Dominion of Canada for the Calendar Year 1897.* 61 Victoria, Sessional Papers No. 8:
10. For New Zealand, see, for example, *Frozen Meat Committee*, Appendix to the
Journals of the House of Representatives, Session I, I-10, 1902: 3; *Report by J L Kelly
on the Possibilities of Trade between New Zealand and the West Coast Ports of the
United Kingdom*, Appendix to the *Journals of the House of Representatives*, Session I,
H-34a, 1908: 1–41.

[29] *Yearbook of the USDA* (1895), 14–18; *Yearbook of the USDA* (1897), 16; *Industries and
Commerce Report*, New Zealand, Appendix to the *Journals of the House of
Representatives*, Session II, H-17, 1906: 6.

[30] *The New Zealand Produce Trade in England* Appendix to the *Journals of the House of
Representatives*, Session I, H-17, 1898: 2.

Country of origin marking was a possible solution to origin and quality misrepresentation in the international meat industry. Rivalry between Canada and the United States to supply the British market featured prominently in reports to the Canadian Minister of Agriculture. The Canadian agent in Nottingham stated:

This important trade, which is still in its infancy, must be made to assume very great proportions, if judiciously carried on and encouraged; but in order that Canada may get her fair share of credit, I think it would be well if some means were taken to impress upon dealers the advisability and propriety of making their 'Canadian' meat known as such, instead of having it included in the general term 'American'.[31]

Similarly, in 1878, the Canadian agent in Liverpool complained: 'It often happens that American goods of inferior quality find a market over our better class goods, simply because of the ingenuity and taste shown in their outside decoration.'[32] These fears were especially relevant to the Canadian cheese industry, which had established a firm reputation: 'Now that the superiority of Canadian cheese has been so thoroughly demonstrated, I would again urge the advantage to be derived by having the word "Canada" placed upon packages of all kinds. The Americans have been very particular in this respect.' Similarly, it was 'an admitted fact ... that Canadian cheese has been of the finest quality of late, being considered superior to anything produced in the United States'.[33]

New Zealand's lamb and mutton exports experienced substantial misrepresentation in the British market from the late nineteenth century. The sources of this problem were twofold. First, it was recognised that Argentine competition created powerful financial incentives to misrepresent:

Complaints have again this year been frequently made by butchers selling New Zealand meat of the severe handicap they experience in their business from the fraudulent practice of competitors in the trade selling River Plate mutton and lamb as 'New Zealand' or 'prime Canterbury' ... The little advantage that may be gained in price (if any) by the sale of English butchers of New Zealand mutton

---

[31] *Report of the Minister of Agriculture for the Dominion of Canada for the Calendar Year 1876.* 40 Victoria, Sessional Papers No. 8: 146–147; *Report of the Minister of Agriculture for the Dominion of Canada for the Calendar Year 1877.* 41 Victoria, Sessional Papers No. 9: 155.

[32] *Report of the Minister of Agriculture for the Dominion of Canada for the Calendar Year 1878.* 42 Victoria, Sessional Papers No. 9: 109–110.

[33] *Report of the Minister of Agriculture for the Dominion of Canada for the Calendar Year 1885.* 49 Victoria, Sessional Papers No. 10: 322, 347.

as English is infinitesimal compared with the loss sustained by the substitution of River Plate meat for New Zealand.[34]

Second, it was claimed that 25 per cent of New Zealand's meat sales to Britain were accounted for by passing-off the former as domestic produce. However, it did not necessarily follow that an indication of origin was the correct, or even appropriate solution to misrepresentation: if New Zealand meat was branded as such, the same 25 per cent of sales might be lost as a result of prejudice: 'There is a lot of New Zealand meat consumed by English people as English meat, and if you branded that I think it would stop its consumption a good deal' and 'I know that a good deal of [this] meat is sent to the West-end of London and the person who puts it on his table does not want to see "New Zealand lamb" stamped on it when he wants his friends to believe that it is the best Welsh mutton.'[35]

In the New Zealand meat industry proponents of country-of-origin marking had to convince sceptics that the long-term gains exceeded short-term costs. Henry Cameron, New Zealand's Produce Commissioner based in London, was a forceful exponent of this view. He claimed that an extensive advertising campaign extolling the benefits of New Zealand mutton would undermine the fraudulent practices by which New Zealand meat was passed-off and '[b]utchers who now sell New Zealand meat as English would either have to sell it on its merits or fight opposition from those who would be then in a position to [offer] to their customers the genuine New Zealand article at a fair price'.[36] By 1907 – some twenty-five years after the SS *Dunedin* landed the first consignment of frozen New Zealand mutton in Britain – the case was still being made that an indication of origin was necessary to protect the reputation of New Zealand's meat: 'there is no means by which consumers can distinguish New Zealand meat when they desire to obtain it, and when they ask for it they often get inferior stuff supplied to them, which disgusts them, and destroys the reputation of the New Zealand article'.[37]

---

[34] *Second Annual Report, Department of Industries and Commerce.* Appendix to the *Journals of the House of Representatives*, Session I, H-17. New Zealand, 1903: 16.

[35] *Frozen Meat Committee*, Appendix to the *Journals of the House of Representatives*, Session I, I-10, New Zealand, 1902: 41, 64–65, 72.

[36] *Frozen Meat Committee*, Appendix to the *Journals of the House of Representatives*, Session I, I-10, New Zealand, 1902: 88.

[37] *Sixth Annual Report of the Department of Industries and Commerce by James McGowan.* Appendix to the *Journals of the House of Representatives*, Session I, H-17, New Zealand, 1907: 21, 26.

Evidence given before the New Zealand Frozen Meat Committee indicates that private firms were at the forefront of branding and quality grading and that the government was reluctant to interfere. Charles Cresswell, the secretary of the Wanganui Meat-Freezing Company, claimed, 'I am not in favour of Government grading, because the various companies have learnt by experience how to grade the particular sheep treated at their respective works. The bulk of the sheep treated in one part of New Zealand are of a very different class to those treated at works in another part [any] attempt to grade the whole of the sheep in different parts on the same lines would prove disastrous.'[38] Indeed, it was firms' private brands which featured prominently in attempts to differentiate produce. For example, the Christchurch Meat Company used the Eclipse brand for first quality and the C. M. Co. and Crown brands for second and third quality, respectively.[39] Opposition to government grading was sufficiently strong that the Committee could not recommend any change to existing marking arrangements.[40]

Private brands also featured prominently in US beef exports, an inevitable extension of the marketing activities of leading firms such as Armour, Cudahy, Morris, and Swift. Alfred Chandler demonstrated how these companies pioneered the mass slaughter and distribution of perishable meat products, involving rail networks and chilled storage and distribution, all coordinated by a national network of branch offices.[41] Economies of scale and scope extended from national to international markets. By the late 1890s, Eastman's Ltd., controlled an American cattle and shipping business and nearly 350 retail shops in Britain. In 1897, it was reported that all the beef exported from the United States was controlled by firms who slaughtered and chilled it and that its sale in Britain was 'controlled exclusively by the English representatives of Eastman's, ... Morris, Swifts, etc'.[42] This extensive vertical integration

---

[38] *Frozen Meat Committee*, Appendix to the *Journals of the House of Representatives*, Session I-10, New Zealand, 1902: 31

[39] *Extension of Commerce Committee*, Appendix to the *Journals of the House of Representatives*, Session I-10a, New Zealand, 1903:19–20.

[40] *Extension of Commerce Committee*, Appendix to the *Journals of the House of Representatives*, Session I-10a, New Zealand, 1903: 2. Similar opposition to government grading was reported in 1908. *Trade between New Zealand and the West-Coast Ports of the United Kingdom*, Appendix to the *Journals of the House of Representatives*, New Zealand, 1908: 36.

[41] Chandler, *Scale and Scope*, 65, 166.

[42] J. B. Jefferys, *Retail Trading in Britain, 1850–1950* (Cambridge: Cambridge University Press, 1954), 187; *The Meat Trades' Journal and Cattle Salesman's Gazette* (hereafter, *Meat Trades Journal*), 8 July 1897, 189.

meant US firms had substantial control of the supply chain, which reduced the likelihood that their beef would be misrepresented. In contrast, the operations of Australasian producers appear insignificant: 'None of the Australian or New Zealand firms could match the United States firms in Britain for coordinated wholesaling and retailing operations.'[43] The New Zealand authorities were alert to the benefits of retailing their lamb and mutton directly to British consumers, but attempts to initiate this failed. As late as 1908, almost twenty years after Eastman's Ltd. was formed, appeals were being made for the establishment of New Zealand government shops.[44] Unsurprisingly, therefore, Australasian meat exports were more vulnerable to misrepresentation.

In the meat trade state intervention was limited to ensuring that meat products were 'safe'. In New Zealand, legislation enacted in 1900 and 1908 provided that a 'meat export certificate' would only be issued if meat destined for export was certified free of disease and fit for human consumption and that, at the time of shipment, the meat was in good condition and had been properly graded, branded, and properly preserved. However, these regulations did not specify the form of brand or mark to be used. In fact, only tinned meat had to be marked 'New Zealand'.[45] Exportation of meat from Australia was prohibited unless certified as 'approved for export' or 'passed for export' by an inspector. These marks could only be stamped if the meat was free from disease and fit for human consumption.[46] Later scholars have suggested that in the pre-1914 period no attempt was made in Australia to grade meat for quality because it was too difficult.[47] Canadian legislation mandated that 'Canada Approved' could only be applied to meat 'passed as fit for food'.[48] Much the same was true of the United States, where legislation in the 1890s required that all types of meat

---

[43] R. Perren, *Taste, Trade and Technology: The Development of the International Meat Industry since 1840* (Aldershot: Ashgate, 2006), 72.

[44] *Trade between New Zealand and the West-Coast Ports of the United Kingdom* Appendix to the *Journals of the House of Representatives*, New Zealand, 1908: 35–36.

[45] New Zealand, The Slaughtering and Inspection Act, 1900, 64 Vict, No. 38; New Zealand, The Slaughtering and Inspection Act, 1908, No. 181.

[46] Such marks were provided for by the Commerce (Trade Descriptions) Act, 1905. Commonwealth of Australia: *Report of the Royal Commission on the Meat Export Trade of Australia*. P.P. 46. Cd.7896 (1915).

[47] T. Henzell, *Australian Agriculture: Its History and Challenges* (Victoria: CSIRO Publishing, 2007), 132.

[48] Canada, An Act Respecting the Inspection of Meats and Canned Foods, 6–7 Edward VII, Chap. 27, 1907; 'Regulations Governing the Inspection of Meats, 1907', in *Report of the Minister of Agriculture for the Dominion of Canada for the Year ended 31 March, 1908*: 130–138.

destined for export had to be inspected to establish that it was 'wholesome, sound, and fit for human food'; subsequent legislation required 'Inspected and Passed' or 'Inspected and Condemned' labelling.[49] Overall, it is difficult to view these marks as indications of origin: they only specified that the meat was fit for human consumption, not that it was of a specified quality – for example – aged for a specified duration, or obtained exclusively from pedigree cattle. It appears that no attempt was made to 'sell fresh beef as a national name-brand product, attracting consumer loyalty to a specific label and product image'.[50]

BRANDING, QUALITY, AND THE BUTTER INDUSTRY

Butter shared some of the key characteristics of the international meat trade. For example, penetration of the British butter market was dominated by a few leading exporters, principally Australasia, Canada, Denmark, Ireland, and the United States. Another similarity was that the butter trade was subject to origin misrepresentation. The US Department of Agriculture (USDA) claimed that, '[o]nce in the hands of the trade, our butter was repeatedly sold as English, Canadian, or Australian, and special efforts were required to get any of it into the hands of consumers, under its true name'.[51] Similarly, New Zealand butter was passed-off in Hong Kong as 'Australian' and 'Finnish' while Dutch and Siberian butter were misrepresented as 'Danish'.[52] A common feature of this fraud was misuse of empty butter tubs. Danish butter tubs were the medium by which Finnish and Russian butter was foisted on the public as 'Danish', and foreign butter was imported to Ireland, repacked into Irish firkins, and reshipped from Ireland as genuine Irish produce.[53]

---

[49] US, 51st Congress, Sess. I., CHAP 839 (1890); US, 51st Congress, Sess. II., CHAP 555; US, 59th Congress, Sess. I., CH. 3913, 674–679. For a reappraisal of this legislation, see G. D. Libecap, 'The Rise of the Chicago Packers and the Origins of Meat Inspection and AntiTrust', *Economic Inquiry*, 30 (1992): 242–262.

[50] I. MacLachlan, *Kill and Chill: Restructuring Canada's Beef Commodity Chain* (Toronto: University of Toronto Press, 2001), 300.

[51] *Yearbook of the USDA* (1897), 15.

[52] *Second Annual Report of the Department of Industries and Commerce by James McGowan*. Appendix to the *Journals of the House of Representatives*, Session I, H-17, New Zealand, 1903: 7; *The Grocer*, 25 January 1908, 247–249; *The Grocer*, 21 January 1899, 185–186; *The Grocer*, 21 March 1903, 930.

[53] *Times*, 3 September 1903, 8 *The Grocer*, 4 April 1903, 1077.

However, unlike meat, greater emphasis was placed on country of origin and quality assurance in the butter industry – which went far beyond guarantees that it was safe for consumption. The USDA, which began overseeing experimental exports of high-quality butter to London in 1897, complained:

The combined efforts of the Government and of commercial enterprise may succeed in the early establishment of a high reputation for American butter in desirable foreign markets. But as soon as accomplished, this becomes liable to be destroyed by the cupidity of those who, trading on this reputation, flood the same market with butter of low grade, yet still entitled to export and sale as 'produce of the United States'.[54]

Henry Cameron took every opportunity to proclaim that stringent grading and branding explained the rapid growth in the reputation of New Zealand butter. Cameron recognised that grading and official inspection would eradicate variations in quality by identifying weaknesses among individual producers and raise the overall standard of New Zealand butter. Between 1892 and 1908, New Zealand introduced numerous Dairy Industry Acts specifying: government inspection of butter factories and creameries; grading of butter exports which had to be marked either 'New Zealand dairy', or 'New Zealand factory', or 'New Zealand creamery', to indicate its composition; registration of butter producers; the output of each producer had to bear its own brand or trademark, and the maximum water content was specified at 16 per cent.[55]

Other countries also used indications of origin when their butter satisfied various requirements. In Sweden, use of the Rune brand, introduced in 1905, was conditional on firms submitting their butter to the Swedish Butter Tests, which specified a maximum water content of 16 per cent. It was claimed that this brand was simultaneously a mark of origin and quality because only the best butter could be so branded.[56] The Finnish government established a similar indication for their butter in 1912 and the regulations governing its use included compulsory examination of butter destined for export, and state-subsidised steamship companies were prohibited from exporting Finnish butter unless it was distributed

---

[54] *Yearbook of the USDA* (1898), 16.
[55] See, for example, 56 Vict., 1892, No. 30: An Act to Regulate the Manufacture of Butter and Cheese for Export, and to Provide for the Purity of the Milk Used in such Manufacture; 58 Vict., 1894, No. 48: An Act to Regulate the Manufacture of Butter and Cheese, and to Provide for the Purity of Milk; 7 Edw. VII, 1907, No. 37: An Act to Regulate the Export of Butter.
[56] *The Grocer*, 11 November 1905, 1230–1231; 16 December 1905, 1629–1630.

in casks indicating Finnish origin. To protect against quality debasement, Finnish regulations stated: 'butter bearing the national brand must not contain more per cent. of water than is allowed in the country to which it is imported'.[57] Likewise, in Denmark, creameries were subject to inspection and their butter could be branded with the 'Lur Brand'.[58] Growing international competition in the genuine butter trade also affected the Dutch response,[59] while in Canada, use of the terms 'Canadian' or 'Canada' was restricted to butter containing a maximum of 16 per cent moisture.[60]

However, the relationship between indication of origin and quality grading was not universal. The Australian butter industry provides a telling example of the problems encountered when trying to establish this link. In 1898 legislation was enacted which provided for the inspection of butter and its branding with a legend consisting of a crown and the words 'Approved for Export' and 'Victoria'.[61] But this legislation did not specify a minimum quality level. Earlier efforts had been made to classify and score butter at the state level, for example, in New South Wales,[62] but there was no state provision linking 'Victoria' to butter quality. The 1898 Act contained other weaknesses. First, butter factories sold different qualities of butter under a variety of brands. Second, British buyers devoted more attention to company brands than indication of origin. But even this practice was suspect because merchants and agents substituted their own brands for those used by the producers. One of the biggest agents, Bartram & Co., owned more than fifty brands, which made it impossible to identify factory-based weaknesses. Because the Australian indication of origin was embossed on butter irrespective of its quality – including butter which was 'absolutely unfit for table use' – it became

[57] *The Grocer*, 8 March 1913, 732.

[58] Denmark: Agricultural Produce Marks Act, 1906; Royal Decree under the Preceding Act, 1907; Departmental Committee on the Irish Butter Industry: 406.

[59] Between 1899 and 1913, the Dutch enacted legislation affecting butter exports and use of government control marks on butter and cheese. J. Bielman, *Five Centuries of Farming: A Short History of Dutch Agriculture, 1500–2000* (Netherlands: Wageningen Academic Publishers, 2010), 163.

[60] Regulations made under the Dairy Products Act, 56 Victoria, Chap. 37 (1893); *The Grocer*, 7 October 1905, 898; *Butter Act*, 3 Edward VII chap 6., s.3.

[61] 62 Vict., No. 1591 (1898): An Act to Provide for Inspection of Live Stock, Meat, Dairy Produce, Fruit and Other Products Intended for Export and to Regulate the Exportation Thereof, Victoria, No. 1591, 1898, s. 8.

[62] A. G. Lloyd, 'The Marketing of Dairy Produce in Australia', *Review of Marketing and Agricultural Economics*, 18 (1950): 16.

worthless. It was even claimed large quantities of exported butter had not been inspected.[63]

Australian butter experts recognised the benefits that grading bestowed on New Zealand butter and they initiated a voluntary scheme involving a sample of butter factories. But even this limited response was undermined precisely because the bulk of Australian butter exports was ungraded.[64] The Commission acknowledged the unfavourable comparison that had been made between Australia and New Zealand and concluded:

The grading of butter is, in our opinion, one of the first steps that should be taken by all exporters of butter. The marked success that has attended the dairy industry in New Zealand since the introduction of grading is a powerful illustration of the soundness of the system.[65]

This recommendation was subsequently enacted by the Commerce (Trade Descriptions) Act, 1905, which specified that butter packages be marked with 'Australia' and the name of the state. Butter was to be graded first, second, and third class, according to the number of points awarded for flavour, aroma, texture, and condition, and the export of butter which failed to meet these standards was prohibited unless marked 'Below standard'.[66] But the saga did not end there. Opposition to grading continued after 1906 for many of the reasons discussed earlier and culminated in a High Court decision in 1912, that grade-marking of butter was unenforceable under the 1905 Act.[67] The renewed Australian resistance to butter grading was gleefully received in New Zealand: 'the New Zealand grading system has been an unqualified success, as instanced by the fact that our prices always exceed the Australian'.[68]

The link between branding and compulsory grading also proved elusive in Ireland and Denmark – both heavily engaged in the supply of butter to Britain.[69] In the former, a Departmental Committee was established in

---

[63] Royal Commission on the Butter Industry. Victoria (1905): Q. 184; QQ. 209–215; QQ. 3817–3818; QQ. 4318–4320; QQ. 6234–6236; QQ. 8455–8458; QQ. 8483–8498; Q. 9455; Q. 13068; QQ. 16896–16901; Q. 20646; Q. 20787.

[64] Royal Commission on the Butter Industry. Q.1873. Later evidence suggested that about 30 per cent of Victorian butter factories supported grading. QQ. 27315–27319.

[65] Royal Commission on the Butter Industry. iv.

[66] Australia, Commerce (Trade Descriptions) Act, No. 16, 1905. This Act came into force on 1 October 1906. *The Grocer*, 29 September 1906, 746.

[67] *The Argus* (Melbourne), 21 August 1912, 6.

[68] *The Sydney Morning Herald*, 4 March 1910, 8.

[69] K. H. O'Rourke, 'Late 19th Century Denmark in an Irish Mirror: Land Tenure, Homogeneity and the Roots of Danish Success', in J. L. Campbell, J. A. Hall, and

1909 to examine the use of false or misleading trade descriptions on different grades of butter and their injurious effects on the Irish butter trade. The Committee reported in favour of the use of the legend 'Irish Creamery Butter' and endorsed the use of a government brand. However, grading was rejected on expense grounds, because its ability to affect the price of Irish butter was 'dubious', and because it would interfere with the trade. Some argued that country of origin could be used independently of quality, while others claimed that British retailers refused to sell Irish butter because it threatened their trade.[70] At the other extreme, Harald Faber claimed that Denmark did not need compulsory grading because its butter was so uniform that it would be impossible to grade it and sell it at different prices in Britain: 'At present every creamery almost receives the same price for the butter ... there is hardly any variation ... and variation in price is not in relation to the quality ... I don't think our butter varies sufficiently in quality for [grading].'[71]

ORIGIN VERSUS COMPOSITION IN THE BUTTER TRADE

A further significant difference between butter and meat was that the former was also affected by fraudulent practices involving composition. US beef was misrepresented as 'Scotch', but it was not passed-off as lamb. However, the origin and composition of butter were misrepresented. Competition from margarine was particularly invidious. Whereas origin misrepresentation affected a particular country, the sale of margarine as butter affected all butter producers. Additionally, passing-off margarine as butter was a total fraud because butter is created from cream, not vegetable oil which has been chemically extracted and refined. Concerns were raised that this practice threatened to undermine the reputation and price of butter. Giving evidence before a Departmental Committee on the Irish butter industry, Harald Faber argued that 'the people in Denmark

O. K. Pedersen (eds.), *The State of Denmark: Small States, Corporatism and the Varieties of Capitalism* (McGill: Queen's University Press, 2006), 159–196; I. Henriksen and K. O'Rourke, 'Incentives, Technology and the Shift to Year-Round Dairying in Late-Nineteenth Century Denmark', *Economic History Review*, 58 (2005): 520–554.

[70] Department of Agriculture and Technical Instruction for Ireland: *Report of the Departmental Committee on the Irish Butter Industry*. P.P. VIII.1. Dublin: HMSO (1910): 14, 16–17; *Report of the Departmental Committee on the Irish Butter Industry. Minutes of Evidence*. P.P. VIII.1 (1910): Q. 2504; *The Grocer*, 12 November 1904, 1194.

[71] *Report of the Departmental Committee on the Irish Butter Industry. Minutes of Evidence*: Q. 16861, Q. 16866.

have realised that the sale of margarine as Danish butter would lower Danish butter generally in the market'.[72] The Canadians recognised that 'butterine' was a strong competitor with their inferior butter. Similar sentiments were expressed in the Australian butter industry: 'growing competition of butter substitutes is an additional argument in correcting our present neglect in attaining the highest standards for our export butter'.[73] Even expert butter buyers were deceived into buying margarine because it could be a perfect imitation of butter.[74] Nationally, the misrepresentation of margarine resulted in a battery of legislative measures to restrict the growth of this industry. For example, margarine was totally prohibited in Canada between 1886 and 1914, and in the United States a variety of taxes were imposed on margarine, subsequently replaced by restrictions on colouring.[75]

Despite these regulations, misrepresentation continued in the international butter trade.[76] For example, margarine was sold as 'Irish butter' and as 'French produce, guaranteed pure butter'.[77] Denmark was particularly susceptible to this fraud because its butter had an unrivalled reputation in Britain. In the 1890s, Harald Faber instigated a series of legal actions against retailers operating as Danish Dairy Co., Denmark Dairy Co., and Danish Butter Co., all of whom were selling margarine as 'Guaranteed Pure Butter' and 'Butter imported direct from the farmhouses of Denmark'. Heavy fines were imposed and Faber issued the following statement: 'not one single shop bearing a similar name is owned by a Danish firm, or by Danish butter producers. Denmark disclaims any relationship to the Company in Gloucester and similar companies in other

---

[72] *Report of the Departmental Committee on the Irish Butter Industry. Minutes of Evidence*: Q. 16676.

[73] *Report of the Minister of Agriculture for the Dominion of Canada, for the Calendar Year 1887*. 51 Victoria, Sessional papers No. 4: 271; *The Grocer*, 11 June 1910, 1732.

[74] *Report from the Select Committee on Food Products Adulteration.* P.P. X.73 (1895): Q. 796.

[75] R. Dupré, '"If It's Yellow, It Must be Butter": Margarine Regulation in North America Since 1886'. *Journal of Economic History*, 59 (1999): 353–371; W. Heick, *A Propensity to Protect: Butter, Margarine and the Rise of Urban Culture in Canada* (Ontario: Wilfrid Laurier University Press, 1991); W. R. Pabst, *Butter and Oleomargarine: An Analysis of Competing Commodities* (New York: AMS Press, 1968), 31–33.

[76] Different legislation applied depending on whether fraud was based on composition or origin. In Britain, for example, false composition was unlawful under the Food and Drugs Acts, whereas misleading indications of origin were covered by the Merchandise Marks Acts.

[77] Numerous cases exist. See, for example, *The Grocer*, 30 March 1907, 867; 20 April 1907, 1032, 1055; 28 March 1908, 910; 16 May 1903, 1517–1518; 30 March 1907, 867.

towns or cities in this country.'[78] Similar examples involving Danish butter occurred in 1905 and 1906, and in each case the maximum penalty was imposed: twelve months' hard labour in the former case and a fine of £20 with £30 costs in the latter.[79]

A further problem affecting the butter industry was 'faking', by which genuine butter was blended with coconut oil and/or milk to increase its weight – sometimes by as much as 25 per cent. The profits earned from this trade were substantial. The New Zealand Minister for Industries and Commerce estimated that 'blenders' daily produced 200 tons of 'water-logged' butter which realised a profit of £12 per ton, equivalent to £14,000 per week.[80] This practice came to prominence in 1905 – the 'Fakers' year' – because new Dutch technology and the scarcity of low-priced butters encouraged the substitution of blended butter. Australian and New Zealand producers were especially vulnerable to this fraud because their butters had comparatively low levels of moisture.[81]

Faking had two adverse consequences for the Australasian butter industry. First, exporters and merchants in the genuine trade were never certain if prevailing prices 'cleared the market' because the blended product increased the total supply of butter. Although, to the extent that blending consumed surplus butter, it helped to stabilise market prices.[82] Second, it was claimed by Charles Lance, Commercial Agent for the Government of New South Wales, that blending undermined government and industry efforts to sell their butter on its merits and weakened the incentive to produce a higher-quality product.[83] Unilateral action could not be taken to solve this problem because although butter was truthfully marked at the time of export, this was not the case after importation. The British government was subjected to considerable lobbying to legislate against 'faking', but the Butter and Food Act of 1907 permitted the production of milk-blended butter subject to a maximum water content of 24 per cent. Unsurprisingly, therefore, expressions of discontent continued.[84]

---

[78] *The Grocer*, 21 November 1891, 987; 9 April 1892, 775; 26 March 1892, 645–646; 17 December 1892, 1192–1193; 3 November 1894, 924.
[79] *The Grocer*, 14 January 1905, 119–120; 3 March 1906, 622–624.
[80] New Zealand, *Industries and Commerce Report*, 28 August 1906: 7.
[81] New Zealand, *Industries and Commerce Report*, 28 August 1906: 3; *The Grocer*, 22 April 1905, 1144.
[82] *Trade between New Zealand and the West-Coast Ports of the United Kingdom*, Appendix to the *Journals of the House of Representatives*, New Zealand, 1908: 20.
[83] *The Grocer*, 3 June 1905, 1538.
[84] French and Phillips, *Cheated not Poisoned?*, 62–63; *The Grocer*, 15 February 1913, 549.

The final component of the geographical origin versus composition theme was the ambiguous and sometimes fraudulent use of trade terms, especially in the Irish butter industry. This misrepresentation was subtle because the descriptions applied to the genuine article referred to its method of production. Three descriptions were available to Irish butter: 'Creamery', which meant 'unblended butter made from cream separated by centrifugal force from the commingled supplies of a number of cowkeepers, in premises adapted for the manufacture of butter in commercial quantities'; 'Dairy' was butter made by farmers on their own premises from whole milk, hand-skimmed cream, or cream extracted from a separator, while 'Factory' was butter which had been blended, reworked, or subjected to other treatment but not to the extent that it 'ceased to be butter'.[85]

Concerned about the fraudulent use of these terms, the Irish Department of Agriculture and Technical Instruction (IDATI), prosecuted traders who misrepresented factory butter as 'Silver Rose Creamery' and 'Castle Dairies Creamery'.[86] Butter descriptions were used interchangeably with the deliberate or unintended effect of misleading consumers. Farmers sold their 'dairy' butter as 'Farmers Creamery', 'Choicest Creams', or 'Creams' in an attempt to represent their butter as superior to 'Creamery'. Similar confusion was apparent when trying to differentiate 'creamery' from 'factory': if 'Irish butter' was applied only to 'creamery', this contradicted 'Guaranteed Irish Butter' or 'Guaranteed Irish Good Butter', embossed on 'factory' butter.[87] Existing trade customs only exacerbated the problem. Some claimed that 'creamery' could be applied to any superior-quality butter, irrespective of its origin; others thought that all butter made from centrifugally separated cream was entitled to the legend 'creamery'. Another question that remained unanswered was the validity of blending two or more creamery butters and branding the combined product as 'creamery'.[88]

In its final report the IDATI indicated that use of 'creamery' on butter produced by alternative methods was erroneous because it conflated quality with method of manufacture. Consequently, the application of 'creamery' was restricted to genuine creamery butter:

---

[85] *Report of the Departmental Committee on the Irish Butter Industry*: 5–8.

[86] *The Grocer*, 25 November 1905, 1443–1444; 3 February 1906, 311; 11 January 1908, 95–96; 4 July 1908, 45–46.

[87] *Report of the Departmental Committee on the Irish Butter Industry. Minutes of Evidence*: Q. 68; QQ. 208–211; QQ. 7023–7024; Q. 12189; Q. 12222.

[88] *Report of the Departmental Committee on the Irish Butter Industry*: 6–8.

The term 'creamery' has acquired a commercial value as indicating the best Irish butter . . . creamery butter has attained such an undisputed position on the markets as the best butter . . . that a demand for other classes of butter in the highest class wholesale trade is practically non existent. Consequently, creamery butter, and it alone, must be relied on to raise the reputation of Irish butter to the first position.[89]

MISREPRESENTATION IN THE BRITISH MARKET

There was a broad consensus that misrepresentation of foodstuffs according to geographical origin was widespread in the late nineteenth and early twentieth centuries. A British Select Committee in 1893 castigated the action of butchers:

That misrepresentation exists the Committee have no doubt . . . It does not appear that retail butchers habitually inform their customers of the source of origin of their meat. The usual practice is to supply such quality of meat as is likely to meet with the approval of the customer without giving any actual guarantee of origin.[90]

Other retailers were subjected to similar criticism. The Federation of Grocers' Associations was concerned that, without intent to defraud, its members were being entrapped into 'technical offences' and it warned the Bacon Curers' Association:

[We] regret that you should . . . enter upon a crusade of harassing respectable members of the retail trade with whom you have such an extensive business . . . if the Bacon Curers' Association persist in their worrying proceedings, it will be necessary for the 11,000 members belonging to the Federation to seriously consider what steps they shall take to protect themselves from the harassing action of those firms who now appeal to them to buy their produce.[91]

However, these British complaints received only qualified support from foreign experts. Hulme Black, who acted for the Queensland government, and Henry Cameron were adamant that passing-off Queensland beef and New Zealand mutton as 'English' was extensive.[92] Other specialists doubted that fraud could be practised to any appreciable extent. William Weddel, representing the Queensland Meat Export and Agency

---

[89] *Report of the Departmental Committee on the Irish Butter Industry*: 6, 24.
[90] *Report from the Select Committee on the Marking of Foreign Meat.* P.P. XII.341, (1893): ix.
[91] *The Grocer*, 30 October 1897, 1056.
[92] *Report from the Select Committee on the Marking of Foreign Meat*: Q. 1274; *Report and Special Report from the Select Committee on the Agricultural Produce (Marks) Bill*, P.P. VIII.227 (1897): Q. 3702.

Co., William Cook of the Sansinena Frozen Meat Co., and Montague Nelson, whose firm had extensive retailing operations in Britain, claimed that frozen meat was easily differentiated from its fresh, British counterpart.[93]

One way to assess the accuracy of these competing claims is to consider the number of prosecutions that occurred in Britain. The Merchandise Marks Act, 1887, criminalised misleading trade descriptions which referred to the 'place or country in which any goods were made or produced'. Subsequently, the Merchandise Marks Act, 1894, empowered the Board of Agriculture to instigate action against the misrepresentation of agricultural products. Before discussing these prosecutions a number of caveats need to be made. First, most of the relevant litigation was unreported, which potentially underestimates the true number of cases. Second, the volume of litigation is potentially an ambiguous indicator of the effectiveness of the Merchandise Marks Acts: numerous prosecutions may indicate that individual traders and officials reacted vigorously to fraud and sought to detect and report all violations; conversely, fewer successful prosecutions, resulting in the imposition of maximum penalties, might have been a powerful deterrent. Finally, as with all legislation, even if a case was proven, judges and magistrates had considerable discretion in the penalties they imposed, and this too may have influenced the scale of litigation.

Prosecutions involving the misrepresentation of foodstuffs by geographical origin between 1893 and 1910 were compiled from the *Grocer* and the *Meat Trade Journal and Cattle Salesman's Gazette*, supplemented with cases reported in the Board of Agriculture and Fisheries *Annual Report of Proceedings*, and secondary literature. Surprisingly, despite the number of claims that American and Canadian beef were passed-off as 'British', no *reported* cases can be detected in these publications. Between 1900 and 1910, for example, the Board of Agriculture and Fisheries investigated only two complaints that live animals imported to Britain were slaughtered at the port of debarkation and described as 'English', but in both cases it decided not to proceed because there was insufficient evidence and because of legal technicalities: 'As a general rule butchers do not "apply" within the meaning of the ... Acts any description whatever to their meat, and if they did it would still be very difficult to obtain evidence.'[94]

---

[93] *Report from the Select Committee on the Marking of Foreign Meat*: Q. 1653; QQ. 2440–2441; QQ. 3886–3887.

[94] Board of Agriculture and Fisheries, *Annual Report of the Intelligence Division* (1909): 32; Board of Agriculture and Fisheries, *Annual Report of the Intelligence Division*

Similarly, complaints that Australian and River Plate mutton were passed-off as 'New Zealand' resulted in just a handful of high-profile prosecutions, most of which occurred in 1901. In the aforementioned cases, a fine of £10 and approximately £7 costs was awarded against each defendant.[95] However, the misrepresentation of Welsh mutton as 'New Zealand' mutton incurred higher penalties. In the 'Welsh' mutton case (1899), the London Chamber of Commerce brought a successful action against the English Farmers Association Limited, which received the maximum fine of £20 on each summons; including costs, total damages were £44, four shillings.[96] A general feature of these and later cases was the role of Henry Cameron.[97]

Unsurprisingly, litigation by foreign governments and their agents extended beyond the meat trade. Harald Faber was an active litigant when defending the reputation of Danish butter and eggs, which were passed-off as 'Dutch' and 'Finnish'. Sir Horace Tozer, Queensland's Agent General in London, prosecuted traders passing-off Queensland butter as 'Russian'. The Irish Department of Agriculture was equally aggressive, particularly when foreign eggs were misrepresented as 'Irish', for example, 'Pat Murphy, Castle Murphy'.[98] The Jamaican government recognised that inferior and spurious imitations of their rum were being misrepresented as 'Jamaican' in the British market, and a specific statute was enacted in 1904 for the Governor to appoint a 'properly qualified person' to institute proceedings under the Merchandise Marks Acts. Finance for these prosecutions was provided by 'The Jamaica Rum Protection Account', which imposed an export duty of ten pence on every puncheon of rum produced and exported from Jamaica. In 1909, this legislation was strengthened by the appointment of a salaried official.[99] Evidence given against the landlord of the Dirty Dick public

(1914): 18. For a broader analysis of the misrepresentation of US beef in Britain, see D. M. Higgins and D. Gangjee, '"Trick or Treat?" The Misrepresentation of American Beef Exports during the Late Nineteenth Century', *Enterprise and Society*, 11 (2010): 203–241.

[95] These cases involved three separate Liverpool-based butchers: MacSymons Stores, Bergle & Co, and John Hull & Co. The figure for costs is an approximation because it was in guineas. *Meat Trades Journal*, 30 May 1901: 105.

[96] *Meat Trades Journal*, 4 May 1899: 15–16.

[97] See, for example, *Meat Trades Journal*, 3 April 1902: 534; J. T. Critchell and J. Raymond, *A History of the Frozen Meat Trade* (London: Constable and Company, 1912), 270–271.

[98] *The Grocer*, 21 January 1899, 185–186; 21 March 1903; 15 July 1905; 24 February 1906, 556; 17 November 1906, 1299–1300; 27 February 1909, 655.

[99] The Jamaica Rum Protection Law. Law 26 of 1904; A Law to Continue and Amend the Jamaica Rum Protection Law, 1904. Law 13 of 1909. West Indian rum was mixed with

house in London in 1906 revealed that the number of distilleries in Jamaica had declined from 150 to 108. In this case the landlord was fined just five shillings (sixty pence), but substantial costs, exceeding £18, were imposed.[100]

Within the grocery trade, bacon and ham were particularly susceptible to misrepresentation. From a total of eighty-four reported actions in the *Grocer* between 1893 and 1912,[101] I estimate that nineteen and forty-two actions involved bacon and ham, respectively. For these commodities the most common form of misrepresentation involved the sale of US or Canadian bacon and hams as 'Irish', or with some indication that they were produced in Britain, for example, 'real Wiltshire', 'Cumberland', 'Choice Home-Fed'.[102] A notable feature of litigation involving these products was the involvement of the British government, via the Treasury, the Board of Agriculture, and British trade bodies, especially the Bacon Curers' Association. Of the sixty-one cases involving bacon or ham which were reported in the *Grocer* during this period, thirty-seven were either instituted by this Association or it gave expert evidence for the plaintiff.[103]

A related theme is the severity of fines imposed under the Merchandise Marks Act, 1887. Under this Act, the maximum penalty that could be imposed ranged from imprisonment for four months with hard labour, or a fine of £20, if the defendant was found guilty by a magistrate, to two years' imprisonment with hard labour, or a fine, or both, if the sentence was imposed by a Crown Court. Successful prosecutions would have exercised little deterrence if only nominal fines were imposed. Although the scale of fines levied has a key limitation – payment of costs could be far higher – they do provide some insight into the operation of this Act. Between 1893 and 1912, only small fines (defined as one quarter of the maximum) were imposed in forty-two cases.[104] Maximum fines were inflicted only in the most flagrant cases, often involving repeat offenders.

---

neutral spirit in Germany and the composite rum was then exported to Britain. Because customs could not distinguish between genuine West Indian and composite rum, it was often imported without detention. *Report from the Select Committee on Merchandise Marks Act, 1887*. P.P. 15. 334 (1890): QQ. 147–154.

[100]   *The Grocer*, 13 January 1906, 111.
[101]   I cannot find any prosecutions involving bacon and ham in 1913.
[102]   *The Grocer*, 15 April 1893, 874–875; 21 March 1896, 744; 12 April 1902, 1045–1046.
[103]   *Meat Trades Journal*, 2 April 1896, 980; *The Grocer*, 1 May 1897, 1113; 22 March 1902, 864–865.
[104]   See, for example, the cases involving Underhill and Maitland, Metropolitan and Provincial Stores, Draycon and Diplock, and David Cunningham reported respectively

For example, Van Straughton & Zoon Ltd. were fined £50 on each of two summonses for misrepresenting Finnish butter as 'Danish', and Melia & Co. were fined £50 for passing-off US roll bacon as 'English roll'.[105]

Other cases involved generic terms for which the Courts had to determine whether their use was 'calculated to deceive'. In the bacon trade considerable use was made of 'Wiltshire' or 'Wiltshire Cut'. Originally, these terms referred to a particular cut of bacon produced in Wiltshire, but by the late nineteenth century they had become generic, denoting a style of cutting. The use of generic terms explains why some cases resulted only in nominal fines or were dismissed altogether. For example, an action brought against H. & T. Jones revealed that 'Pale Wiltshire' had been used in the trade for more than thirty years to denote a particular cut and quality of bacon. Expert witnesses claimed this term could be applied to bacon originating from Ireland, Denmark, or Hamburg, but not the United States because its bacon was judged inferior. This company were fined £2 without costs.[106] Perhaps the most famous case was *Morris v. Royle* (1896) in which the defendant was charged and acquitted of misrepresenting US bacon as 'Finest Wiltshire cut'. The Bacon Curers' Association, which instigated this action, were aggrieved. In their view the learned judges based their decision on the ground that the bacon *was* cut in the Wiltshire style – not whether use of 'Wiltshire' was 'calculated to deceive'. This case appeared to make a mockery of the Merchandise Marks Act: retailers believed they were immune from prosecution if they sold foreign bacon as 'Wiltshire cut'.[107]

An alternative way to assess the scale of misrepresentation is to consider the financial incentive to misrepresent. Table 3.1 shows the profits that could be earned from misrepresenting the geographical origin of ham, which was subject to the greatest litigation.[108] In general terms, a premium of approximately 40 per cent could be obtained by passing-off US ham as 'British' or 'Irish'. These gains far exceed those reported for other foodstuffs during this period.[109] Another observation from Table 3.1 is that handsome gains were

---

in *The Grocer*, 29 February 1896, 527–528; 17 July 1897, 169; 29 March 1902, 930–931; 3 December 1910, 1539–1541.
[105] *The Grocer*, 21 March 1903, 930; *Meat Trades Journal*, 2 April 1896, 980.
[106] *The Grocer*, 3 March 1894, 532–535.   [107] *The Grocer*, 7 August 1897, 308.
[108] For an explanation of how premia were calculated, see Table 3.1. Data limitations mean that Table 3.1 covers the period 1896–1910.
[109] A study of passing-off US beef as 'English' or 'Scotch' between 1894 and 1911 reported average premiums of 12.8, 32.4, and 9.1 per cent. Higgins and Gangjee, 'Trick or Treat', 225. Similarly, between 1897 and 1913, misrepresentation of Danish butter as 'Russian'

TABLE 3.1 *Price premiums[1] (%) from passing-off American ham as 'Irish' and 'English', and Canadian as 'US', 1896–1910[2]*

	Belfast versus	Limerick versus	Irish versus	Cumberl- and versus	Wiltshire versus	Canada versus
	US	US	US	US	US	US[3]
1896	41.3	50.0	n.a.	44.6	n.a.	n.a.
1897	49.1	57.5	n.a.	55.2	n.a.	n.a.
1898	55.0	59.2	n.a.	58.0	n.a.	n.a.
1899	44.4	52.7	n.a.	49.0	n.a.	n.a.
1900	32.2	43.3	n.a.	39.8	n.a.	n.a.
1901	35.5	45.1	n.a.	n.a.	n.a.	n.a.
1902	41.2	47.6	n.a.	n.a.	n.a.	n.a.
1903	26.3	37.6	n.a.	33.6[4]	n.a.	n.a.
1904	37.0	47.2	n.a.	41.7	45.4	7.0
1905	41.8	49.7	n.a.	47.2	48.0	10.5
1906	37.3	45.0	n.a.	41.2	43.4[5]	12.8
1907	29.9	48.7	n.a.	36.1	n.a.	10.9
1908[6]	n.a.	n.a.	42.7	44.0	n.a.	16.4
1909	n.a.	n.a.	38.3	39.7	n.a.	17.8
1910	n.a.	n.a.	27.8	28.5	n.a.	7.7
Average:	39.3	48.6	36.3	43.0	45.6	11.9

(1) The premium is calculated as $(Pa-Pb)/Pa*100$. This equation determines the incentive to pass-off produce from country B as that of country A, and the premium is expressed as a percentage of A's price.
(2) Prices are per hundredweight.
(3) The Canadian series runs from late March 1904–December 1910.
(4) From August 1903, prices refer to Cumberland *and* York.
(5) The Wiltshire series ends in mid-September 1906.
(6) From 1908, a single 'Irish' price is reported.
Source: Calculated from *The Grocer*, various issues

obtainable from passing-off Canadian ham as 'US'. Between 1904 and 1910, the average gain from this misrepresentation was almost 12.0 per cent, and in 1909 this figure peaked at a 17.8 per cent. I can find no reported cases of this type of fraud – possibly because it was much more difficult to detect compared to passing-off US ham as 'Irish' or 'British'.

yielded an average premium of 25 per cent. Higgins and Mordhorst, 'Reputation and Export Performance', 190.

CONCLUSIONS

The rapid growth and development of the international food supply chain from the late nineteenth century was a boon to countries heavily dependent on the export of foodstuffs. But the acceleration of this trade, which was heavily centred on Britain, the world's biggest import market and entrepôt, generated a number of conflicts involving indications of origin and the quality and price signals they conveyed.

Some degree of conflict was inevitable. The Paris Convention for the Protection of Industrial Property, 1883,[110] prohibited the use of false indications of origin and this was subsequently enshrined in the British Merchandise Marks Act, 1887. However, there could never be a perfect translation between the stipulations of an international treaty and its domestic enforcement. In Britain the 1887 Act was not always successfully implemented. One problem was determining whether a trade description was generic. A further problem was that the 1887 Act specified that anybody who *applied* a false trade description was guilty of a criminal offence. This immediately raised difficulties, for example, what if the vendor had only given a verbal assurance of origin – was this sufficient to convict? Henry Cameron thought not. In his view, very few prosecutions were initiated when New Zealand and River Plate mutton were passed-off as 'English' or 'New Zealand', respectively, because most vendors did not specify origin on the invoice. Consequently, even if the plaintiff could prove that the mutton was River Plate, 'you cannot convict him of a fraudulent sale because the invoice is not marked with any trade description indicative of the source of origin'.[111] Exacerbating matters, it was recognised that many consumers did not enquire about geographical origin when purchasing meat.[112] In many cases, organisations such as the Bacon Curers' Association could obtain prosecutions only by entrapment: cajoling the vendor to mark a false indication of origin after the sale had been completed.[113]

---

[110] This Convention is discussed in Chapters 6 and 7.

[111] Appendix to the *Journals of the House of Representatives, Report of the Extension of Commerce Committee on the Frozen Meat Trade*, New Zealand, 1903: 39–40. Cameron thought this weakness was sufficient to justify the need for branding.

[112] *Report from the Select Committee on the Marking of Foreign Meat*: Q. 2468.

[113] See, for example, *Coppen v. Moore, The Grocer*, 5 April 1902, 984–985.

For most of the nineteenth century, substantial price differences existed between foodstuffs according to their provenance. But to what extent was this variation a function of geographical origin? This question is important because it differentiates the experience of the 'regions of recent settlement' from their 'old world' counterparts, especially France. In the latter, appellations in the wine trade played a crucial role in linking 'quality' with location. Consequently, the unique characteristics of each appellation could not be delocalised. But for the major commodities examined in this chapter, the French experience seems less important, even irrelevant. One explanation for this is that statutory marking schemes involving meat simply indicated that it was free from disease. This is a vital characteristic of any foodstuff, irrespective of its origin. Second, farmers in Denmark and the 'new world' understood 'quality' to mean the uniform and consistent supply of particular grades which commanded the highest price in the British market. Particular emphasis was placed on the supply of produce which was consistent in its attributes, such as texture, leanness, moisture, and taste. In other words, the agricultural produce of these regions had less variation in their characteristics compared to GI products.

Although Britain was by far the biggest market for produce, the contrast between it and major food-exporting nations could not have been more marked. Britain became overly dependent on imported produce and her agricultural sector did not perceive the need to initiate marketing campaigns based on a 'British' indication of origin. Indeed, the assumption in the domestic market was that food was British unless its marking indicated foreign origin.[114] In contrast, in the decades preceding 1914, Australasia, Canada, and Denmark pioneered the use of country of origin to promote their exports of foodstuffs. These initiatives provided powerful 'first-mover' advantages which became pronounced during the interwar period.

---

[114] Personal communication with Professor John Chartres, Leeds University.

4

Cooperation, Country of Origin, and Agricultural Trade during the Interwar Period

The Danish cooperatives have been selling in large markets which to a considerable degree are competitive, and a high price for high quality products has been the goal towards which the cooperatives were striving . . . By setting up a system of premiums for the quality demanded by the markets consumer preferences have been transmitted clear back to producers.

E. Jensen, *Danish Agriculture* (Copenhagen: J. H. Schultz Forlag, 1937), 331–336

If you are missing the trade through lack of precise marking, do what thousands of progressive grocers are now doing – *sell* New Zealand butter – *label* it 'New Zealand' and watch the improvement. The name 'New Zealand' inspires confidence. Customers instinctively associate it with the best and it is, therefore, a magnificent 'sale maker' for the grocer . . . It's quite amazing what the reputation of 'New Zealand' butter is worth when translated into terms of quick sales and continuous profit.

The Grocer, 3 February 1934, 64

The international trading environment during the interwar years differed markedly from that which existed before 1914. John Maynard Keynes summed this up when he wrote: 'What an extraordinary episode in the economic progress of man that age was which came to an end in August, 1914! . . . this state of affairs [was regarded] as normal, certain, and permanent, except in the direction of further improvement, and any deviation from it as aberrant, scandalous, and avoidable.'[1] In broad terms, the key differences between these two periods included the collapse of the gold

---

[1] J. M. Keynes, *The Economic Consequences of the Peace* (London: Macmillan, 1920), 9–10.

standard and fixed exchange rates, violent currency speculation, 'beggar my neighbour' policies, and, from the early 1930s, the general collapse of world trade.[2] For example, total world exports of merchandise, at constant prices, increased by 35 per cent between 1913 and 1929, but declined by 10 per cent in the 1930s.[3]

International trade in foodstuffs was not immune from this disruption. In volume terms, food exports increased by 36 per cent between 1913 and 1929, but declined by approximately 2 per cent between 1929 and 1937. Marked differences in the fortunes of particular foods can be identified. For example, between 1913 and 1929, world exports of cereals, livestock products, and sugar increased in volume by 7, 35, and 85 per cent, respectively, whereas between 1929 and 1937, they declined in volume by 8, 12.6, and 17.8 per cent, respectively.[4] The imposition of tariff barriers restricted international trade and distorted global trading patterns in foodstuffs. Higher US tariffs on Canadian milk and cream increased the manufacture of butter in Canada to such an extent that, despite an absence of four years, Canada recommenced export of butter to Britain.[5] New Zealand's efforts to diversify its butter exports backfired when Canada increased its tariffs. Similarly, British exercise of imperial preference after 1932 helped ensure that Australasian meat exports grew at the expense of Argentina and Uruguay, and facilitated New Zealand's rise to ascendancy to become Britain's biggest supplier of butter in 1934.[6]

Nonetheless, one feature of the pre-1914 trade in foodstuffs remained: the continued dominance of the British market. In 1913, Britain accounted for 25.2 per cent of world imports of foodstuffs. By 1953, this figure was largely unchanged at 22.4 per cent. Within this broad category, Britain's dominance was greatest in livestock products being 48.6 and 44.8 per cent of world imports in 1913 and 1953, respectively.[7]

---

[2] See, for example, B. Eichengreen, *Golden Fetters: The Gold Standard and the Great Depression, 1919–1939* (Oxford: Oxford University Press, 1995); C. P. Kindleberger, *The World in Depression, 1929–1939* (California: California University Press, 1976).

[3] Calculated from P. L. Yates, *Forty Years of Foreign Trade* (London: George Allen & Unwin, 1959), table A.17, 225.

[4] Calculated from Yates, *Forty Years of Foreign Trade*, table 4, 63.

[5] *Report of the Minister of Agriculture for the Dominion of Canada for the Year Ending 31 March 1931*: 45; *Report of the Minister of Agriculture for the Dominion of Canada for the Year Ending 31 March 1934*: 31; *Report of the Minister of Agriculture for the Dominion of Canada for the Year Ending 31 March 1935*: 32–33.

[6] Kenwood and Lougheed, *The Growth of the International Economy*, 215; T. Rooth, *British Protectionism and the International Economy: Overseas Commercial Policy in the 1930s* (Cambridge: Cambridge University Press, 1992), 234.

[7] This category includes all types of dairy produce.

The former figure was almost equal to the combined shares of continental Europe, the United States and Canada, and the 'rest of the world'; the latter figure exceeded the combined imports of continental Europe. As far as meat was concerned, Britain absorbed 80 and 67 per cent of world exports in 1913 and 1953, respectively.[8] Britain's pivotal role in the global food trade during the interwar years was unique:

Reviewing as a whole the trade in meat and dairy produce ... It is strongly orientated towards the United Kingdom market ... No other advanced countries depend ... on foreign sources for any significant proportion of their requirements ... and there is therefore no great prospect for expansion of trade.[9]

Effectively, the rate of growth of world food exports and the British market became interdependent. Chapter 3 indicated that in the pre-1914 period Australasia and Denmark were heavily dependent on the British market and this continued throughout the interwar period. For example, on average, between 1925 and 1938, Australia exported 89.5 and 92.0 per cent of its butter and cheese, respectively, to the British market. The relevant figures for New Zealand exports of butter and cheese were 93 and 98 per cent, respectively, between 1923 and 1938.[10]

This chapter discusses foreign competition in the British market for agricultural produce during the interwar period. A prominent feature of this contest was the importance attached to cooperative organisation. Contemporaries recognised that this structure created advantages for Danish bacon and butter which were communicated by the 'Lur Brand' and 'Denmark'. However, Britain was no longer a passive recipient of food imports: it sought to emulate the Danish experience by promoting agricultural cooperatives and encouraging them to sell their produce using an indication of British origin. However, I show that British initiatives were largely unsuccessful. In contrast, Australia and New Zealand successfully imitated the Danish cooperative model and they were able to launch an aggressive marketing campaign involving country of origin and brands which became synonymous with origin, for example, the Australian Kangaroo and New Zealand's Fernleaf and Anchor.[11]

---

[8] Yates, *Forty Years of Foreign Trade*, table 36, 66, 79.

[9] Yates, *Forty Years of Foreign Trade*, 84–85.

[10] Calculated from Commonwealth of Australia, *Annual Reports of the Dairy Produce Control Board*, various issues, and the New Zealand Dairy Produce Control Board, *Annual Reports*, various issues.

[11] These brands are not IGOs because they do not indicate geographical area.

COOPERATION, STANDARDISATION, AND MARKETING

During the interwar period competition in national and international markets for agricultural products increasingly depended on collective associations. The principal explanation for their growth is that the market for produce was more volatile, which exacerbated the marketing problems confronting farmers. Thus, in the United States, the rapid advance of input and output prices during the First World War and their subsequent collapse generated substantial declines in agricultural revenue. For example, at current prices, total agricultural output in 1920 was $3 billion less than in 1919.[12] In Britain the economic dislocation between 1914 and 1918 meant that 'the spread between producers' and consumers' prices was unjustifiably wide'.[13]

To survive in this environment it was thought imperative that farmers combined in collective or cooperative associations to improve the marketing of their produce. During the interwar period there was a plethora of legislation governing the establishment and operation of cooperatives across the globe.[14] One explanation for this movement was that individualistic attitudes to the marketing of agricultural produce – often characterised by haphazard attention to branding, grading, and quality – were inappropriate if agriculturalists wished to sell their produce at the national, rather than the local or regional level. In Britain, these issues were endorsed by the Linlithgow Committee which reported that better knowledge of marketing and distributive processes was vital to British farmers, that standardisation was 'the essential foundation of advertisement', and that cooperatives were particularly suited to ensure standardisation.[15] Similarly, the USDA recognised that the distribution of farm products through cooperative organisations afforded an important opportunity for farmers to properly grade and market their products in commercial quantities at the state and national levels.[16] A second explanation for the growth of large-scale cooperatives was that they were integral to national efforts to promote exports of agricultural produce. In this regard, Australia and New Zealand were untiring in their

[12] *Yearbook of the USDA* (1920), 17.
[13] Ministry of Agriculture and Fisheries (hereafter, MAF), Departmental Committee on Distribution and Prices of Agricultural Produce. *Final Report.* P.P. VII.1 (1924): 13–14.
[14] M. Digby, *Digest of Co-operative Law at Home and Abroad* (London: P. S. King & Son, 1933).
[15] MAF, *Departmental Committee on Distribution and Prices of Agricultural Produce. Final Report:* 13–14.
[16] *Yearbook of the USDA* (1920), 22–23.

insistence on the production of uniformly high-quality butter, cheese, and lamb, and their marketing of this produce using country of origin and related brands.

Broadly defined, marketing encompasses a number of related activities such as distribution, market research, storage, and advertising, but one activity received particular emphasis by contemporaries: grading and standardisation. Grading is the process by which the output of many farmers is classified according to a particular characteristic, such as weight, size, appearance, or quality. In butter production the last characteristic was often determined by experts' assessment of colour, smell, and taste, as well as more objective standards such as the percentage of butter fat. Standardisation ensures that the produce of multiple farmers receiving the same grade is identical. This, in turn, permits the sale of large volumes of produce under a common brand. Obviously, it is uneconomic to process and market large numbers of small lots. Indeed, the separate sale of the produce of individual farmers would destroy the system of grading and marketing under a common brand. Additionally, rigorous testing and quality control removes the free-rider problem. Instead of producers obtaining a price based on the average quality of all grades submitted, they received a payment based on the particular quality supplied. Consequently, standardisation also increases consumer confidence in particular brands, which permits large-scale advertising. Grading, standardisation, and diligent quality control are the essential features of the large-scale cooperative because they are inseparably connected with quality pools without which large-scale marketing would be impossible.[17] According to Harald Faber, cooperative dairies automatically ensured high and uniform levels of quality for produce because the farmers who delivered their milk or pigs to the cooperative dairies and slaughterhouses were genuinely interested in the final result. This provided them with a strong incentive to achieve the highest quality, and to ensure their neighbours did the same. Consequently, the average quality of Danish produce increased and became remarkably uniform.[18] Effectively, the Danish model of cooperation integrated production and marketing activities:

The cooperatives are in a better position to get producers to adapt their production processes to market demands, and a number of cooperatives working together

---

[17] R. B. Forrester, *Report upon Large Scale Co-operative Marketing in the United States of America*, Ministry of Agriculture and Fisheries, Economic Series No. 9 (London: HMSO, 1925), 123.
[18] Faber, *Cooperation in Danish Agriculture*, 38–39.

may more easily adopt standard practices ... The cooperatives have pushed for branding and universal quality control, and the marking of date of manufacture in order to place the regularly produced Danish goods on the market as fresh as possible.[19]

Contemporaries acknowledged that the success of Danish agriculture during the nineteenth and early twentieth centuries fully depended on the cooperative system,[20] which was based on the following principles: members were contractually bound, for a minimum period, to sell their produce only to the cooperative, trade with those outside the organisation was forbidden, and there was careful testing of inputs and outputs at each stage of the supply chain.[21] The Danish experience vividly demonstrated that it was possible to develop a major agricultural sector which was fully responsive to the demands of its consumers. It is no exaggeration to state that the excellence of Danish bacon provided the foundation for the British bacon-eating habit and allowed Denmark to maintain a pre-eminent position as Britain's biggest foreign supplier of bacon during the interwar period.[22] But how easy was it to replicate the Danish model and thereby achieve its associated benefits? One approach is to consider the extent to which indigenous farmers could use the cooperative system to exploit the possibilities offered by their domestic market. In this context, the United States and Britain offer contrasting experiences. An alternative line of enquiry is to discuss the extent to which Australia and New Zealand were successful in using indications of origin to promote their agricultural exports. Each is considered in turn.

Cooperatives were well established in the United States by the interwar period, and some can be traced to the early 1800s. At the turn of the twentieth century cooperative organisations had emerged in milk, butter, walnuts, and, perhaps most famously, citrus fruits and raisins. The California Fruit Growers' Exchange, formed in 1905, built on the foundation of the Orange Growers' Protective Union established in the

[19] Jensen, *Danish Agriculture*, 350–351.
[20] Agricultural Tribunal of Investigation, *Final Report*. P.P. VII.45 (1924): 68–69; MAF, *Departmental Committee on Distribution and Prices of Agricultural Produce. Final Report*: 14; Fay, *Co-operation at Home and Abroad*, 464–471.
[21] There were also political and financial stipulations. For example, decisions were reached democratically, and the net surplus of the cooperative was distributed among its members according to their contribution. Jensen, *Danish Agriculture*.
[22] D. M. Higgins and M. Mordhorst, 'Bringing Home the "Danish" Bacon: Food Chains, National Branding and Danish Supremacy over the British Bacon Market, c. 1900–c. 1938'. *Enterprise & Society*, 16 (2015): 141–185.

1880s. The Exchange was built on many of the cooperative principles detailed earlier and the quality of its produce was conveyed by its Sunkist and Red Ball brands, which were only applied to 'fancy', 'extra choice', and 'choice' grades of lemons and oranges. Although based in California, extensive advertising in the 1920s – amounting to $900,000 in 1924, and including 53 million full-colour pages in magazines and 175 million insertions in daily newspapers – resulted in these brands achieving national celebrity: 'By national advertising, and by helping retailers display the fruit, the California Fruit Growers' Exchange has been able to make the orange about as common, about as much in demand, and about as cheap as the apple.'[23] Similarly, the Californian Associated Raisin Co., formed in 1912, was built on similar cooperative principles to the Exchange. Its Sun-Maid brand became so famous that the company changed its name to Sun-Maid Growers in 1922. A marketing survey of Boston housewives conducted in 1921 reported that 71.5 per cent were familiar with Sun-Maid raisins and that 58 per cent bought this product. The same study reported that 42.5 per cent had bought the Sun-Maid brand because of advertising, and concluded: 'The feature in the advertising most fully impressed on the minds of housewives is the picture of the Sun-Maid (girl with bonnet and basket).'[24] During the interwar years, other cooperatives were formed, the products of which also achieved national celebrity. For example, in 1921, more than 300 cooperative creameries formed the Minnesota Cooperative Creameries Association, one of the most successful cooperative organisations in the United States. This company had 'materially increased the production of high-grade, sweet-cream butter, which is sold under the trademark [*Land O'Lakes*] of the cooperative and has created an extensive market for butter of this quality'. By 1927, this company's turnover exceeded $46 million.[25] Although Sunkist and Sun-Maid were not IGOs, because they did not refer to geographical location, their popularity in the United States indicated that the cooperative organisation facilitated the large-scale marketing of produce under a single brand

---

[23] N. Comish, *Cooperative Marketing of Agricultural Products* (London: D. Appleton and Company, 1929), 22–28.

[24] D. Starch, *Principles of Advertising* (London: A. W. Shaw & Company, 1926), 151, 192–195. The rigid inspection, grading, and standardisation of citrus fruits in the Pacific Coast states had generated such positive results that these grades were enshrined in state law. *Yearbook of the USDA* (1920), 359.

[25] The trademark was established in 1924 and the company was subsequently renamed as Land O'Lakes Creameries Inc. *Yearbook of the USDA* (1928), 40.

TABLE 4.1   *Cooperative associations/farmers' buying and selling associations in the United States (selected years), 1915–1934*

	1915	1923–1924	1928	1930	1931	1932	1933	1934
Dairy Products	1,708	1,966	2,479	2,458	2,391	2,392	2,293	2,286
Fruits and Vegetables	871	1,232	1,269	1,384	1,386	1,347	1,268	1,194
Grain	1,637	3,134	3,455	3,448	3,448	3,500	3,131	3,178
Livestock	96	1,598	2,012	2,153	2,014	1,885	1,575	1,371
Nuts	Na	51	40	44	71	70	65	57
Poultry/Poultry Products	Na	56	90	157	160	172	154	147
Total	4,312	8,037	9,345	9,644	9,470	9,366	8,486	8,233

Sources: 1915 and 1923–1924, from Forrester, *Report upon Large Scale Co-operative Marketing in the United States of America*: 15. Years 1928–1934, *Yearbook of the USDA* (1935), 738.

The rapid growth of the California Fruit Growers' Exchange, the Californian Associated Raisin Co., and the Minnesota Cooperative Creameries Association during the First World War and into the 1920s was part of a much bigger expansion of cooperatives in the United States during this period. Table 4.1 shows the rapid growth in the number of cooperative or collective marketing associations in the principal food groups. Between 1915 and 1923–1924, and 1923–1924 and 1930, the number of food cooperatives increased by 86 per cent and 20 per cent, respectively (Table 4.1). The USDA emphasised the benefits provided by grading and standardisation. Thus, it was difficult to sell mixed lots of produce composed of different varieties and grades because a prospective consumer was likely to object to at least one or more of the constituents. This, in turn, directly affected the prices received by producers. For example, in the absence of recognised grade standards, buyers would only pay a 'flat' rate based on the average value of the consignment.[26] It was also recognised that dissemination of current prices in different regional markets within the United States was of little value unless these prices reflected quality differences. The USDA believed that cooperatives

[26] *Yearbook of the USDA* (1920), 353–355; *Yearbook of the USDA* (1922), 19–20; *Yearbook of the USDA* (1923), 31–32; *Yearbook of the USDA* (1925), 628, 642–644.

were the appropriate solution to these difficulties: 'The need for strong cooperative marketing associations cannot be overemphasized. They are absolutely necessary to bring about efficient and economical marketing and standardization' and '[c]oncerted community effort will gradually be put forth to obtain the results which come from marketing farm products on a graded or quality basis'.[27]

The USDA supported cooperatives in other ways. It provided for butter inspections in New York, Chicago, Philadelphia, and Boston. This federal inspection applied the same standards to these markets with the expectation that they would be adopted in all markets. In 1921, the USDA recommended market grades and standards for thirteen major perishable foodstuffs, which increased to thirty by 1924. Although their use was not compulsory, these grades became widely adopted and received legal backing in many states. Inspection and quality grading for fruits and vegetables began in 1922. Similarly, in meat, the Better Beef Association and the National Livestock & Meat Board began stamping 'prime' and 'choice' on the higher grades of beef, and in 1927 the government inaugurated a beef grading and stamping service. This support provided a guarantee of quality to the consumers, encouraged consumers to pay higher prices for genuinely higher-quality cuts, and benefitted livestock producers because it eliminated quality misrepresentation.[28]

These activities were strengthened by federal legislation. In 1913 Congress approved the formation of a Federal Bureau of Markets tasked with providing a range of marketing information to producers, as well as promulgating market grades, implementing standardisation, and encouraging cooperation.[29] Landmark legislation was enacted in 1922 by the Capper-Volstead Act, which authorised agriculturalists to form associations for the collective processing and marketing of produce for interstate and foreign commerce.[30] Four years later, the Secretary of Agriculture was empowered to establish a division of cooperative marketing within the USDA to 'promote the knowledge of cooperative principles and practices and to cooperate, in promoting such knowledge, with

---

[27] *Yearbook of the USDA* (1924), 44, 444–448; USDA, *Yearbook of the USDA* (1925), 17–19, 627; USDA, *Yearbook of the USDA* (1926), 196.
[28] *Yearbook of the USDA* (1922), 374; *Yearbook of the USDA* (1924), 34–35; *Yearbook of the USDA* (1927), 41; Yearbook of the USDA (1928), 144–146.
[29] *Yearbook of the USDA* (1913), 27–31.
[30] US, 67th Congress, Session II, Chap. 57, An Act to Authorise Association of Producers of Agricultural Products. Prior to this Act there were concerns that the formation of cooperatives was 'in restraint of trade'.

educational and marketing agencies, cooperative associations, and others', and to 'make such special studies in the United States and foreign countries, and to acquire and disseminate such information and findings as may be useful in the development and practice of cooperation'.[31] A Federal Farm Board was created in 1929 to encourage the organisation of producers into effective associations 'under their own control for greater unity of effort in marketing and by promoting the establishment and financing of a farm marketing system of producer-owned and producer-controlled cooperative associations'. Additionally, the Board was 'authorized and directed to promote education in the principles and practices of cooperative marketing of agricultural commodities and food products [and] to encourage the organization, improvement in methods, and development of effective cooperative associations'.[32]

THE LIMITED BRITISH RESPONSE

Britain's heavy reliance on imported produce during the interwar years was a consequence of its pre-1914 development. During the interwar period, successive governments and agriculturalists made greater efforts to increase the share of the home market supplied by domestic farmers. Many factors explain this change in approach; for example, the First World War increased concerns about national self-sufficiency. Additionally, it was recognised that dependence on imported produce exacerbated the balance of payments, particularly when invisible earnings were much lower in the 1920s and 1930s compared to pre-1914.

Indications of origin featured prominently in British attempts to claw back a bigger share of the domestic market. Attempts were made to promote standardisation schemes under the Agricultural Produce (Grading and Marking) Act, 1928.[33] This statute enabled the Minister of Agriculture to authorise the application of a common trademark – the National Mark (NM) – to standard grades of domestic produce. It was

[31] US, 69th Congress, Session I, Chap. 725, An Act to Create a Division of Cooperative Marketing', Sec. 3 (6) and (7).
[32] US, 71st Congress, Session I, Chap. 24, Agricultural Marketing Act, Sec. 1 (3); Sec. 5 (1) and (2). Similar trends in the Canadian production of eggs and poultry were also becoming apparent at the same time. Imperial Economic Committee. *Report of the Imperial Economic Committee on Marketing and Preparing for Market of Foodstuffs Produced within the Empire. Fourth Report – Dairy Produce.* P.P. XII.281 (1926): 29–30.
[33] 18 & 19 Geo. 5. Ch. 19. This Act was extended to fish products and products manufactured wholly or mainly from agricultural produce, for example jam. 21 & 22 Geo.5., Ch. 40, Agricultural Produce (Grading and Marking) Amendment Act, 1931.

envisaged that the NM would denote that the products to which it was affixed had a defined standard of quality, which would improve the competitiveness of British produce. Use of the NM can be viewed as a positive attempt to promote the competitiveness of British agriculture. An alternative approach was much more defensive and involved interested parties requesting the Board of Agriculture to make an Order in Council that produce be marked with an indication of origin at the time of importation and/or when sold wholesale or retail.[34] This scheme was predicated on the belief that the scale of misrepresentation was such that British consumers were unable to purchase domestic produce. Each approach is considered in what follows.

The Agricultural (Grading and Marketing) Act of 1928, and the rules governing its implementation, specified that the Minister of Agriculture could prescribe 'grade designation marks' to indicate that produce had reached a particular standard of quality. For example, strawberries could receive the grade designation marks 'Extra Selected' or 'Selected' if each berry weighed not less than a half or one quarter of an ounce, respectively.[35] The regulations governing the implementation of this Act also specified that the Minister could establish a Committee to authorise use of a certification mark which comprised the words 'National Mark', 'Empire Buying begins at Home', and a circular image of the Union Jack set on a map of England and Wales.[36] This mark was registered in trade-mark classes 4 (raw or partly prepared vegetables, animal and mineral substances), 37 (leather skins), 42 (substances used as food) 43 (fermented liqueurs), and 46 (seeds). Effectively, the NM was designed to be a visible warranty that produce bearing this mark was supplied by British farmers and had reached a minimum quality standard.

However, it is difficult to determine the extent to which the 1928 Act was a success. Between 1929 and 1938, just over fifty such designations were approved, but 60 per cent of these applied to horticultural produce – potatoes, gooseberries, cabbages, rhubarb – in which Britain had considerable strength. Market gardeners in Wisbech and the Vale of Evesham, for example, were renowned for their produce. Other products

---

[34] This marking was enshrined in the Merchandise Marks Act, 1926 (16 & 17 Geo. 5, c. 53).

[35] TNA, MAF 195/1, Agricultural Produce (Grading & Marking) Acts, 1928–1931, Statutory Rues and Orders, 1930, No. 340. These berries had to be blemish free, smooth, and packaged to ensure they would be ripe at the time of sale.

[36] TNA, MAF 195/31, Use of the 'National Mark' and Revival of the National Mark Committee: Registration of National Mark and Pre-War Machinery of Operation (undated).

FIGURE 4.1 'The National Mark scheme was launched to help British farmers regain a bigger share of the domestic market.'
Permission/acknowledgement: MAF 34/469. By permission of The National Archives

for which Britain was heavily import-dependent, such as bacon and lamb, were absent from this scheme. Some products, such as honey, poultry, and tomatoes, were also subject to Marking Orders obtained via the Merchandise Marks Act, 1926.[37] For the latter, the beneficial effects of using the NM might have been enhanced because domestic consumers were more confident exercising a voluntary preference for domestic produce: Marking Orders reduced the likelihood of misrepresentation and '[t]he National Mark is the symbol of home origin and national standards of quality – Government controlled'.[38] Conversely, regional cheeses such as Cheshire, Stilton, and Wensleydale participated in the NM scheme but did not seek Marking Orders. Considerable publicity was generated for the NM which involved the production of films by the Ministry of Agriculture and Fisheries (MAF) and displays of domestic produce at agricultural shows. Famous firms such as Schweppes and Smedley's began to use the NM with their brands.[39] It seems that the scheme had the biggest effect on canned fruits and vegetables: between 1930 and 1937, the number of factories processing NM produce increased from twenty to fifty-four.[40]

The NM scheme encountered numerous problems. Sectional interests threatened to undermine its introduction to the egg and beef industries. In the former, conflict emerged between wholesalers belonging to the National Mark Egg Central Ltd., who were tasked with supplying NM eggs to the retail trade at lowest cost, and independent wholesalers who did not participate in the scheme. In 1930, unregistered dealers at Smithfield were handling NM eggs at a loss to prevent the trade going to registered agents who were then unable to secure sufficient supplies to fully utilise the growing demand for NM eggs.[41] The operation of the NM in beef was even more problematic. MAF introduced an experimental scheme in London and Birmingham in 1929 which, if successful, would operate on a permanent basis. Similar trials were instigated in Bradford, Leeds, and Edinburgh. However, opposition quickly developed. The NM scheme was boycotted in Birmingham and was vehemently opposed by the Edinburgh Master Butchers Association and the Lancashire Council of Meat Traders. Butchers argued that the beef they bought was best suited to their trade and that grading and marking made no difference to this decision. They claimed that NM beef was so expensive that the majority of

---

[37] 16 & 17 Geo. 5. Merchandize Marks Act, 1926.   [38] *Times*, 3 March 1936, 46.
[39] *Times*, 5 June 1931, 6; 3 March 1936, 32.
[40] *Times*, 4 October 1932, 7; 16 September 1935, 14; 24 September 1937, 9.
[41] *Meat Trades Journal*, 1 May 1930, 747.

the population were unable to afford it, which made the public appear unpatriotic.[42] A MAF investigation reported that use of the NM had not eradicated misrepresentation in Birmingham and London because many purchasers did not look for it which reinforced the view that imported, not domestic beef, should be marked.[43] A subsequent report recommended the introduction of compulsory grading and marking 'to prevent the Scheme being deprived, as it is at present, of much of its effect by the opposition of trade interests that are not primarily concerned with the sale of home-killed beef of gradable quality'.[44]

The NM scheme had other weaknesses. Producers with reputable brands had little incentive to participate, especially if their own grading standards exceeded those specified by the NM. The 'Select Creamery' grade applied to butter, for example, did not specify a maximum water content – unlike the stringent regulations governing Danish and New Zealand butter.[45] Scottish farmers ceased sending their beef for grading and marking at Smithfield, preferring to use their private brands instead because 'each consignor will thereby be enabled to more effectively safeguard the interest of the public and the reputation of Scots beef'.[46] Additionally, grade designations could be applied by any farmer whose produce attained the required standard, but they were not compelled to apply the NM. More familiar issues appeared involving ambiguous signage or sharp practice. For example, if the term 'National' was used as part of a trademark before the NM was introduced, the owners of the trademark could legitimately continue using it. This occurred with National Sovereign Brand kippers. Similarly, butchers who only retailed imported beef continued to use private tickets with the legend 'National Mark Beef', because this was a valid indication of origin (recall that exporters marked their beef to indicate it was free from disease).[47] Unsurprisingly, it was reported that:

---

[42] *Meat Trades Journal*, 5 November 1931, 325; 21 April 1932, 179.

[43] MAF, *Report of an Interdepartmental Committee on the Grading and Marking of Beef*. P.P. VIII.167. London: HMSO (1930): 27.

[44] MAF, *Report of the Second Interdepartmental Committee on the Grading and Marking of Beef*. P.P. VI.141. London: HMSO, (1932): 7.

[45] TNA, MAF, 195/1, Agricultural Produce (Grading and Marking) Acts, 1928–1931, List of Pre-War S R-Os Issued: Statutory Rules and Orders, 1935 No. 72, 'Creamery Butter Regulations'.

[46] *Meat Trades Journal*, 18 June 1931, 667.

[47] TNA, MAF, 34/474, Agricultural Produce (Grading and Marking) Acts, 1928 and 1931, Use of Words 'National or National Mark', 2 October 1936; Fitzpatrick & Co. to MAF, 8 November 1937; Extract from Mr Anderson's Report, 3 April 1935.

The progress of the 'National Mark' movement was on the whole disappointing. A few producers tried it out and found it a commercial disadvantage, but the great majority held to their traditional ways and left the market for highly standardised, attractively presented and well-advertised bulk lines of produce, mostly sold under a brand name, to be still further exploited by their overseas competitors.[48]

A related problem was that the NM barely featured in schemes to effect large-scale reorganisation in agriculture along cooperative lines, even though British commentators recognised that the facility with which Denmark and New Zealand penetrated the British market was a function of cooperative organisation and the bulk production of high-quality standardised produce advertised with country of origin.[49] In Britain, the Agricultural Marketing Acts of 1931 and 1933 facilitated cooperation by permitting a representative body of producers (not less than two-thirds of the total number of registered producers) to establish a scheme to regulate the marketing of their produce. Producer-elected boards could be established to control all sales of a particular product and imports could be restricted by quotas.[50]

However, only eight such schemes operated during the 1930s. Four involved milk, in which domestic farmers enjoyed a virtual monopoly. Hops was also covered by the scheme, but its producers were barely affected by imports because they benefitted from agreements with indigenous brewers. Domestic farmers also supplied the bulk of British potato requirements and after 1934, imports were controlled by licence when domestic supplies were plentiful.[51] Although pig farmers and bacon producers also participated in these schemes, Britain was heavily dependent on bacon imports, which accounted for approximately 25 per cent of total consumption in the 1920s and early 1930s. Recent scholarship suggests that British bacon producers did obtain some benefit from the Agricultural Marketing Acts of 1931 and 1933 but, by

---

[48] MAF, Report of the Committee Appointed to Review the Working of the Agricultural Marketing Acts, London: HMSO (1947): 4.

[49] MAF, *Report of the Marketing of Dairy Produce in England and Wales: Part II, Butter and Cream*. London: HMSO (1932): 36–61. Similar points were raised for beef and cheese. MAF, *Report on the Marketing of Cattle and Beef in England and Wales*, London: HMSO (1929): 138–141; MAF, *Report on the Marketing of Dairy Produce in England and Wales, Part I, Cheese*. London: HMSO (1930): 103–107.

[50] 21 & 22 Geo. V. c. 42, Agricultural Marketing Act, 1931; 23 & 24 Geo.V. c. 31, Agricultural Marketing Act, 1933.

[51] P. Self and H. Storing, *The State and the Farmer* (Berkeley: University of California Press, 1963), 89.

1939, imports still accounted for a large proportion of total bacon supplies.[52]

Participation in the above schemes was limited because those involved were largely immune from imports. Effectively, there was little alignment between the standardisation policy encouraged by the 1928 Act and reorganisation enshrined in the Acts of 1931 and 1933. An official enquiry into the operation of the Agricultural Marketing Acts claimed that marketing failures were the most prominent explanation for the depressed condition of British agriculture between the wars. This report castigated British farmers because they 'disliked co-operation', they were only prepared to participate in marketing schemes if their prices were protected, and they failed to regard marketing boards as an 'instrument for the improvement of . . . productive and marketing technique'.[53] Because cooperative marketing had made little progress in the early 1930s, concerns were raised that the rapid extension of producer control over marketing would be impossible without a 'catastrophic disruption of existing agencies' – who might be operating efficiently.[54] Later commentary has been slightly more favourable to British farmers during the interwar years. Although individualistic attitudes were still subject to criticism, it has been claimed that statutory marketing boards might not have been the best method of improving the 'marketing sense' of farmers.[55]

Finally, it can be argued that the NM scheme was overshadowed by the activities of the Empire Marketing Board (EMB), established in 1926. It was envisaged that the publicity campaigns launched by this Board would encourage British consumers to exercise a 'voluntary' or 'non-tariff' preference for empire produce.[56] The EMB's remit also included the promotion of domestic produce to British consumers.[57] Indeed, when suggesting the formation of the EMB, the Imperial Economic Committee (IEC) recommended that when supplying the British market, domestic producers had priority over empire producers and they, in turn, took

---

[52] Higgins and Mordhorst, 'Bringing Home the "Danish" Bacon'.
[53] MAF, *Report of the Committee Appointed to Review the Working of the Agricultural Marketing Acts*, London, HMSO (1947): 3, 13.
[54] H. Wadleigh, 'The British Agricultural Marketing Act', *Journal of Farm Economics*, 14 (1932): 561.
[55] Self and Storing, *The State and the Farmer*, 106–107.
[56] R. Self, 'Treasury Control and the Empire Marketing Board', *20th Century British History*, 5 (1994): 159–161; Trentmann, *Free Trade Nation*, 238.
[57] Constantine, 'Bringing the Empire Alive', 215–216.

precedence over non-empire suppliers.[58] Although the precise impact of
the Board's campaigns are difficult to quantify because British imports of
empire produce increased markedly before the Board's existence, and
a large part of the population could not afford to let ideological considerations affect their consumption decisions,[59] it is apparent that the Board
was active in promoting British produce only in the later years of its
existence. In 1930, the British government made a supplementary grant
of £55,000 to the EMB to provide publicity for the NM, which included
NM weeks in eighteen provincial towns, circular letters to more than
150,000 housewives in Birmingham and London, and the distribution of
more than 4 million publicity booklets and leaflets. The same grant was
also made in the year ending June 1932.[60]

Viewed from another perspective, it is not clear that the activities of the
EMB *did* ensure that British producers had first call on the domestic
market. For example, the EMB reported in 1931 that British imports of
frozen lamb from New Zealand and Australia exceeded their previous
record levels of 1930 and 1922, respectively. Similarly, imports of butter
from New Zealand and Australia surpassed their highest levels achieved in
1930 and 1925, respectively. For the EMB, this evidence '[affords] a clear
proof of the way in which numerous foods from the *overseas* Empire are
establishing themselves in the dietary of the people of Great Britain'.[61]
Similar concerns were expressed in later historiography.[62] Although the
EMB was disbanded in 1932, MAF officials recognised that use of
the term 'Empire Begins at Home' was doing more harm than good to
the British farmer.[63] The failure of the MAF to issue publicity material
correctly depicting the NM created the bizarre possibility that it would be

---

[58] Imperial Economic Committee, *Report of the Imperial Economic Committee on Marketing and Preparing for Market of Foodstuffs Produced in the Overseas Parts of the Empire. First Report.* P.P. XIII.799. London: HMSO (1925): 4.
[59] Constantine, 'Bringing the Empire Alive', 221–224.
[60] Empire Marketing Board (hereafter, EMB), *Annual Report for May 1930 to May 1931.* London, HMSO (1931): 35–36; EMB, *Annual Report for May 1931 to May 1932.* London: HMSO (1932): 80.
[61] Empire Marketing Board, *Annual Report for May 1931 to May 1932.* London: HMSO (1932): 5. Emphasis added.
[62] A. Cooper, *British Agricultural Policy, 1912–36* (Manchester: Manchester University Press, 1989), 86.
[63] TNA, MAF, 34/474, Agricultural Produce (Grading and Marking) Acts, 1928 and 1931, Use of words 'National or National Mark', Minute sheet, 2 August 1939. These concerns were raised when the NM was being drafted. TNA, MAF, 34/469, *Case in Support of the Application of the Ministry of Agriculture and Fisheries for the Registration of a Nation Mark under Section 62 of the Trade Marks Acts 1905–1919* (undated).

unable to instigate prosecutions against those not entitled to use this indication of origin.[64]

If Britain was unable to replicate the Danish and antipodean models of large-scale cooperative activity and the bulk production of standardised, high-quality, branded produce, what other alternatives existed to enable British farmers to regain a larger share of the domestic market? Campaigns for compulsory indications of origin on imported produce date to the late nineteenth century when Britain became the world's biggest importer of produce. These efforts reignited after the First World War when British agriculture was again exposed to international competition. Unlike the pre-1914 period, major legislation was enacted in the 1920s to make these indications compulsory. For example, The Sale of Food Order, 1921, stipulated that when offered for sale, imported meat had to be accompanied with 'imported' or the country of origin. Similar requirements applied to eggs if their description included 'Fresh' or 'New Laid'.[65] Nonetheless, this legislation soon proved ineffective: it was almost impossible for an expert to distinguish home-killed beef from chilled imported beef, particularly when the former was chilled in storage. Identical problems occurred in the egg trade: retailers could sell Danish eggs as 'Fresh' or 'New Laid'. Successful prosecutions involving eggs occurred 'only in cases where the sellers were very stupid or very careless'.[66]

The Sale of Food Order was revoked following The Merchandise Marks Act, 1926, and subsequent Orders in Council requiring origin marking on eggs and meat in 1929 and 1935, respectively.[67] As a result of the 1926 Act, a Standing Committee was appointed to enquire into the marking of produce from the agricultural, horticultural, and fishing industries. Those who desired indications of origin on foodstuffs frequently

[64] TNA, MAF, 34/474, Agricultural Produce (Grading and Marking) Acts, 1928 and 1931, Use of words 'National or National Mark', 'Misuse of National Mark Show Cards', 5 June 1939.

[65] This legislation should not be confused with various Orders introduced between 1914 and 1919, requiring indication of origin but primarily designed to establish maximum wholesale prices for foodstuffs such as bacon, bread, jam, and lard.

[66] TNA, MAF 36/20, Merchandise Marks Bill, 1922: Haygarth Brown to Dobson, 16 March 1922; MAF, Departmental Committee Distribution and Prices of Agricultural Produce: *Interim Report on Meat, Poultry and Eggs*. P.P. IX.297. London: HMSO (1923): 32, 73–75, 122; *First Report of the Royal Commission on Food Prices*, Volume I. P.P. XIII.1. London: HMSO (1925): 98–100.

[67] TNA, MAF 36/208, Revocation of Sale of Food Order, 1921, Marking Imported Eggs, Press Notice, 25 April 1929; Reardon to Monro, 18 January 1934; Carlill to Ministry of Agriculture and Fisheries, 28 November 1934.

justified their case by claiming that British consumers preferred domestic and Empire produce, but the absence of marking made it impossible for them to translate this preference into effective demand.[68] Concerns were also raised that misrepresentation meant consumers paid 'unjustifiably high' prices and working-class consumers were priced out of the market.[69] Exacerbating matters, ambiguous wording was often used to convey the impression that foreign produce was British, for example, marking foreign grapes 'hothouse', and labelling imported chickens 'Beautiful country chickens' and 'Fresh delivery of country-fed chickens'.[70] Similarly, allegations were made that it was the custom of some firms to cure imported pork and sell it as British.[71]

Between 1926 and 1938, nineteen marking applications were submitted, of which two were rejected outright (tea and grapes);[72] one was only partially successful (applicants in the salt industry failed to secure an import Order but secured a sale Order), and in the case of oats and oat products, only the latter received a sale Order. The application for egg marking (eggs in shell) failed on its first attempt in 1927, but was wholly successful in 1928. From one perspective, these Orders were defensive: they were predicated on the belief that British consumers wished to buy domestic produce but the absence of origin marking, and deliberate misrepresentation, prevented this. Such Orders were not designed to extol the benefits of British produce. To avoid the debacle which followed the Merchandise Marks Act, 1887, Standing Committees were required to reject applications if British trade would be affected. This stipulation was necessary precisely because there was a real possibility that marking foreign produce with an indication of origin would confirm its relative superiority, thereby reducing demand for British produce. The first application to secure egg marking in 1927 was rejected because:

An Order for the marking on importation would certainly, in our opinion, stimulate the efforts of exporting countries to make their own produce supreme

---

[68] Merchandise Marks Act, 1926. *Report of the Standing Committee* (hereafter, RSC) *on Butter.* P.P. XV.843. London: HMSO (1931): 5; *RSC on Meat.* P.P.XIV.167. London: HMSO (1933): 7.

[69] *RSC on Frozen or Chilled Salmon and Trout.* P.P. XV.785. London: HMSO (1930): 4.

[70] *RSC on Grapes.* P.P. XIII.953. London: HMSO (1936): 3. *RSC on Poultry.* P.P. XIV.887. London: HMSO (1933): 5.

[71] *The Grocer*, 6 May 1933, 53.

[72] Marking Orders (Orders in Council) could apply at the time of import (import Order) and/or at the time of sale by wholesale and/or retail (sale Order). An application was made for rose trees, but this has been ignored because they are not edible.

in the British market and might well result in a blow to the home industry from which it would take a long time to recover ... we are of [the] opinion that the 'best' imported eggs would derive more advantage than home produced eggs from a Marking Order under this Act, *unless a substantial improvement were first effected in home methods of grading and marketing.*[73]

The effects of requiring imported produce to bear an indication of origin were ambiguous. These indications were not considered protectionist in the sense of increasing the relative price of domestic produce – which would occur only if it was good enough to command a higher price and if it was no longer deprecated by domestic consumers because inferior imported produce was sold under the NM. Conversely, it was claimed that misrepresentation should be permitted because otherwise the public would have to pay the higher prices that genuine produce commanded.[74] Misrepresentation had other advantages. For example, egg traders claimed that mixing first-quality imported eggs with domestic supplies, for sale as 'British', improved the reputation of domestic eggs. The seasonality of home-killed lamb meant butchers could not maintain a consistent supply throughout the year if they relied solely on domestic sources. Indeed, misrepresentation meant consumers often preferred imported meat because of uncertainty about what would be supplied at the higher prices commanded by domestic produce. Finally, use of imported butter by blending factories helped increase the uniformity of domestically produced butter.[75]

An alternative interpretation is that marking imports with an indication of origin and the NM was complementary. If foreign produce was so marked, British advertising campaigns using the NM were unlikely to be undermined by misrepresentation and free-riding. To the extent that an Order facilitated the adoption of the NM, it can be argued that British farmers had an incentive to improve quality. This interpretation was given prominence by the interdepartmental committee on the grading and marketing of beef: origin marking prevented the substitution of imported for domestic beef, thereby increasing the need for the NM. Because imports were already quality graded, any requirement that they be origin marked would give them an advantage unless the NM enabled consumers to

---

[73] *RSC on Eggs.* P.P. XI.175. London: HMSO (1927): 5–6. Emphasis added.
[74] TNA, MAF 36/20, Merchandise Marks Bill, 1922, Memorandum by Sir Daniel Hall (undated).
[75] MAF, *Report on the Marketing of Dairy Produce in England and Wales, Part II, Butter and Cream*, London: HMSO (1932): 43; MAF, *Report on Egg Marketing in England and Wales*, London: HMSO (1926): 23; MAF, *Report on the Marketing of Sheep, Mutton and Lamb in England and Wales*, London: HMSO (1931): 128–129.

distinguish between superior and inferior qualities of domestic beef.[76] However, only two of the nineteen Standing Committee reports pertaining to foodstuffs considered the relationship between the NM and Marking Orders. The earliest, dealing with meat, stated that 'National Mark beef has made good a certain market position and attracts custom.' The second, which investigated the grape industry, rejected a sale or import Order to enable consumers to distinguish domestic and imported produce because 'this objective could be substantially achieved if the growers themselves were to utilise the existing scheme for the grading and marking of home-grown grapes under the National Mark'.[77]

The 1926 Act stipulated that Marking Orders could be refused if they damaged 'the trade generally of other parts of His Majesty's dominions'. Examination of the decisions made by the Standing Committees indicates that it was rarely necessary to take account of this requirement. Australia, Canada, New Zealand, and South Africa supported the use of indications of origin on apples, butter, currants and sultanas, grapes, and tea, but Australia and New Zealand opposed meat marking because they feared it would create prejudice and undermine the prospects of their lamb and mutton industry. The enquiry into meat marking rejected these concerns on two grounds. First, experience in the United States indicated that it was possible to mark meat without prejudicing consumer perception and without undermining efficiency. Indeed, the marking of US beef had been beneficial in advertising the better cuts of beef. Second, changes in domestic demand for meat meant it was imperative that action was taken to prevent misrepresentation:

There is ... a large and growing demand for home-killed and Empire meat in preference to foreign meat, and, quite definitely, a growing desire on the part of purchasers ... that they will not be misled in regard to the origin of their purchases ... substitution of this kind does take place to a substantial extent ... we are of [the] opinion ... that some form of marking of imported meat with an indication of origin is desirable in the public interest.[78]

THE INTERNATIONAL MARKETING CAMPAIGN BY AUSTRALIA AND NEW ZEALAND

Chapter 3 indicated that by 1914, antipodean agriculture was heavily dependent on the British market. Table 4.2 shows that this trend

---

[76] MAF and Scottish Office, *Report of an Interdepartmental Committee on the Grading and Marking of Beef.* P.P. VIII.167. London: HMSO (1930): 36–37.
[77] *RSC on Meat*: 12; *RSC on Grapes*: 7.   [78] *RSC on Meat*: 8–9, 12–15.

TABLE 4.2 *The importance of the British market to Australian and New Zealand exports of butter and cheese (by volume) during the interwar period*

	Butter	Cheese
Australia		
British imports as a percentage of total Australian exports, 1925/6	85.7	93.0
British imports as a percentage of total Australian exports, 1925–1938	89.5	92.0
New Zealand		
British imports as a percentage of total New Zealand exports, 1923	96.7	97.8
British imports as a percentage of total New Zealand exports, 1923–1938	93.1	97.7

Sources: calculated from Commonwealth of Australia, *Annual Reports of the Dairy Produce Control Board*, various issues, and The New Zealand Dairy Produce Control Board, *Annual Reports* (various issues).

continued throughout the interwar period. In broad terms, Britain accounted for 89 and 93 per cent of the butter exports of Australia and New Zealand, respectively, between the early 1920s and the late 1930s, and 92 and 97 per cent, respectively, of cheese exports. Exports of lamb were also highly concentrated: over the same period, Britain absorbed 97 per cent of New Zealand lamb exports. This dependency was vulnerable to competition. Relative newcomers, such as Siberia, sought to increase their exports of butter and longer-established producers, such as Argentina and Canada, were keen to enhance their share of the British market for beef and lamb, and cheese, respectively.

Prior to 1914 government involvement in Australian and New Zealand exports of butter, cheese, lamb, and mutton was focused on quality control along the supply chain and included, for example, mandatory inspection, testing and grading of produce, and controlled use of 'Australia' and 'New Zealand'. During the interwar period state intervention increased. It was recognised that agricultural exports were an important component of total exports and therefore national prosperity. By the late 1930s, exports of total dairy produce (butter, cheese, and processed milk products) accounted for 10.4 per cent, by value, of all Australian exports. The relevant figures for New Zealand were substantially higher: in 1935, butter exports and total dairy exports accounted for 30.2 and 40.7 per cent, respectively, of total export earnings.[79] After 1919, official intervention extended beyond quality control and culminated in the formation of Dairy Produce Control Boards in Australia (ADPCB) and New Zealand (NZDPCB) in 1925 and 1924, respectively, and the New Zealand Meat Producers Board (NZMPB), established in 1922. These Boards were the culmination of cooperative activity established in the nineteenth century and they possessed similar features. For example, government officials were represented on the boards and because Britain was the most important export market, the Boards established a London agency which relayed information about prevailing market conditions. The activities of each Board were financed by a levy on exports, and they were empowered to take control of all exported produce. Finally, the Boards had a broader remit which included advertising and the marketing of produce using indications of origin and related brands.[80]

To promote their advertising campaigns the ADPCB and NZDPCB adopted the Kangaroo and Fernleaf brands, respectively. The former was adopted as the Australian brand for butter and cheese in 1924. It was a Commonwealth standardisation trademark and could only be applied to these products if they achieved a grade mark of ninety-two points or higher. Strangely, it appears that Kangaroo was never registered as a trademark in Britain. Australian officials sought legal advice on whether the Kangaroo brand was protected in Britain and they received the opinion that similar marks were already registered for butter and butter products by McAlister & Co., of Liverpool. The opinion stated that attempts to secure registration were likely to be opposed because Kangaroo conflicted with McAlister's trademarks. The possibility of initiating legal action under the British Merchandise Marks Acts was not considered and the opinion concluded, erroneously, that 'the registration of the brand as a trade mark in Australia does not in any way afford protection in England or any other country outside Australia to the proprietor of the brand. The only means by which protection can be obtained in England or elsewhere is by registration.'[81] In contrast, the

---

[79] Calculated from N. Drane and H. Edwards. *The Australian Dairy Industry* (Melbourne: F. W. Cheshire, 1961), 9; Steel, 'New Zealand is Butterland', 6.

[80] Australia, Dairy Produce Export Control Act, 1923, No. 38. The Australian Meat Board, which was responsible for meat exports, was not established until 1936. New Zealand, 12 Geo.V, 1922, Meat Export Control Act, and 14 Geo V., 1923, Dairy Produce Export Control Act.

[81] A search of the UK Patent Office database confirms that 'Kangaroo' was never registered by the ADPCB. Legal opinions of the Australian Government Solicitor, No. 1364,

NZDPCB succeeded in registering Fernleaf in Britain as a certification trademark in 1925. Again, this trademark was only to be applied to the finest butter. In the case of meat, the NZMPB do not appear to have registered New Zealand as a trademark in Britain. Nonetheless, as discussed later, this Board launched a series of successful prosecutions using the Merchandise Marks Acts.

The Kangaroo and Fernleaf brands imitated Danish experience: they were designed to identify Australian and New Zealand butter and to indicate superlative quality. The need for such brands was recognised in debates preceding the formation of the control boards. In New Zealand, the merits of the Danish model were acknowledged. For example, use of a brand indicating origin and quality encouraged all producers to improve their standards, and that it was pointless to imitate the Danes unless a single brand was used.[82] From their inception and throughout the interwar period, the ADPCB, NZDPCB, and NZMPB recognised that the success of their marketing campaigns depended on guaranteeing high and consistent levels of quality. In 1924, the Australian Minister of Trade and Customs reported:

[T]he 'KANGAROO' brand on Australian butter had already established itself for reliability on the London market ... Other reports showed that adoption of the 'KANGAROO' brand had ... stimulated butter manufacturers to greater efforts, and this was manifested in the larger percentage of choicest butter coming forward for export, and the improved methods of manufacture being adopted. With proper recognition in the way of better prices the quality of Australian butter under the influence of the 'KANGAROO' brand would improve rapidly, so that nothing but the best would be available for export.[83]

Similarly, in 1936, the NZMPB stated:

New Zealand can ill afford to lose sight of the fact that her reputation has been built and maintained on quality, and it cannot be stressed too much that we must

3 December 1924. Accessed from http://legalopinions.ags.gov.au/legalopinion/opinion-1364. This opinion was erroneous: it was possible to prevent misuse of the ADPCB's mark by bringing a passing-off action under the Merchandise Marks Acts.

82 Agricultural and Pastoral Industries and Stock Committee: Dairy Produce Export Control Bill (Together with Minutes of Evidence). New Zealand (1923): 24, 27, 53, 67–72.

83 *The Age*, 5 December 1924, 11. See also *The Grocer*, 8 November 1924, 53; Commonwealth of Australia, *4th Annual Report of the Dairy Produce Control Board* (1929), 4, 9; Commonwealth of Australia, *6th Annual Report of the Dairy Produce Control Board* (1931), 7.

maintain that quality at all costs, and thereby hold our supremacy in the lamb and mutton trade of the world.[84]

Quality improvements in dairy products were achieved in a number of ways. For example, in response to British regulations prohibiting the use of boric acid as a preservative, both the ADPCB and the NZDPCB abolished the use of this ingredient in their butter exports from 1928. The NZDPCB claimed that complying with this regulation would 'frustrate the attempts that have on occasions been made to create a prejudice against Colonial butter because of its use'.[85] These boards also devoted considerable attention to shipping and the cold storage of their dairy produce when it arrived in Britain. The ADPCB required that all butter shipped to Britain had to be consigned by licensed firms.[86] Similarly, the need for more scientific input to solve technical problems in dairying was also recognised. In 1927 a Dairy Research Committee was established comprising representatives of the NZDPCB, Massey College, and the Department of Agriculture. The committee was established 'for the purpose of promoting investigations into the problems affecting the dairy industry and for associating these investigations as closely as possible with the industry itself'. Similar views were expressed by the ADPCB, which noted that the largest cooperative dairying companies in Victoria had established laboratories to conduct research into the dairy industry.[87]

For mutton and lamb, the NZMPB was equally active in promoting quality. Rigorous grading of lamb and mutton ensured that the reputation of New Zealand meat was not besmirched. Fully qualified supervising graders made regular visits to factories and rejected poor-quality lambs. The NZMPB assumed responsibility for the grading of all meat exported from the dominion and it standardised all grade marks. This was crucial to ensure easier handling of meat exports on arrival in London and to project a national image. The confusion which existed before the Board standardised grade marks is evidenced by a single example: one ship had 150,000 carcasses on board differentiated by 915 different marks and numbers.[88]

---

[84] NZMPB, *14th Annual Report and Statement of Accounts* (1936), 7. Similar concerns were expressed for butter by the NZDPCB: *4th Annual Report and Statement of Accounts* (1928), 6; *8th Annual Report and Statement of Accounts* (1932), 12.

[85] NZDPCB, *First Annual Report* (1925), 10.

[86] NZDPCB, *Third Annual Report* (1927), 8; *Fourth Annual Report* (1928), 7; ADPCB, *Fifth Annual Report* (1930), 4; *Sixth Annual Report* (1931), 4.

[87] NZDPCB, *Fourth Annual Report* (1928), 9; ADPCB, *Fifth Annual Report* (1930), 4.

[88] D. Hayward, *Golden Jubilee: The Story of the Meat Producers Board, 1922–1972* (Wellington: Universal Printers Ltd., 1972), 48.

Inspectors were appointed to London to supervise the handling of New Zealand meat.[89] In 1931, the NZMPB prohibited the export of lamb which failed to reach the second class standard because this would 'seriously jeopardise our present valuable premium in price over our competitors'.[90] Elimination of lower-grade lamb automatically raised the percentage of higher grades in exports and increased quality uniformity. Other factors which improved the quality of New Zealand meat exports included: research and experimental work on freezing meat conducted with the British National Physical Laboratory and the Cambridge Low Temperature Research Station; encouraging the greater adoption of Down-Cross lambs which produced 'the ideal butchers' meat for the British market', and Annual District Fat Lamb Competitions, designed to improve the breed and quality of exported lambs.[91] As a result of these initiatives, the NZMPB claimed in 1937 that 'the attention which has been given to the grading by the Board is evidenced by the fact that quality claims are to-day rarely heard of. The efficiency of our grading system must inspire confidence in buyers.'[92]

Both the ADPCB and the NZDPCB realised that marketing campaigns extoling the quality of their exports would be compromised if low-quality produce was exported as Australian or New Zealand. The NZDPCB stated that 'they had clear and conclusive evidence that the good name of the Dominion's finest and first grade creamery butter was being detrimentally affected by the sale of these lower grade butters over the retail counter'. This practice was particularly acute in the early 1930s and the response of both boards was identical and rigorous: second-quality butter could be exported to a single agent in London provided it was not subsequently retailed as Australian or New Zealand. This policy was justified on the grounds that both countries sold a large proportion of their second-grade butters to British blenders and manufacturers who sold the final product with their own brands. Subsequently, the NZDPCB advised its London agents to ensure that second-quality butter was not even sold as 'Empire'.[93]

---

[89] NZMPB, *Second Annual Report* (1924), 4, 6.
[90] NZMPB, *Ninth Annual Report* (1931), 7.
[91] NZMPB, *Eighth Annual Report* (1930),13; *Ninth Annual Report* (1931), 9; *Eleventh Annual Report* (1933), 6, 11; *Twelfth Annual Report* (1934), 4–5.
[92] NZMPB, *Fifteenth Annual Report* (1937), 4–5.
[93] NZDPCB, *Eighth Annual Report* (1932), 12; *Ninth Annual Report* (1933), 11; *Tenth Annual Report* (1934), 14. Commonwealth of Australia, *Tenth Annual Report* (1935), 7. Similar restrictions were applied to the use of skimmed milk in the production of 'New Zealand' cheese. NZDPCB, *Seventh Annual Report* (1931), 10.

As noted earlier, the NZMPB also sought to improve the quality of exported lamb, but its efforts were undermined by the sale of low-quality foreign meat – often Argentinian – as 'New Zealand'. Exacerbating matters was the limited geographical knowledge possessed by British consumers who were 'surprisingly ill-informed regarding the origin of the meat they buy ... many of the housewives of London, in buying Canterbury lamb, still imagine they are buying lamb of Kentish origin'.[94] This ignorance facilitated the misrepresentation of New Zealand lamb. A further problem was that some British butchers believed 'Canterbury' was a generic term synonymous with *all* imported lamb and mutton, irrespective of its geographical origin, and that consumers preferred to use 'Canterbury' because it concealed the fact that they were buying frozen meat.[95] The NZMPB was vigilant in its defence of the brands New Zealand and Canterbury, fully realising that misuse of these indications of origin undermined the reputation of its produce and advertising campaigns:

BE IT KNOWN that the New Zealand Meat Producers' Board will take immediate legal action against any butcher (or butchers) discovered selling other imported meat as 'New Zealand'.

NEW ZEALAND MEAT has earned a national 'quality' reputation which must not be tampered with, and the Board take a very serious view of this wrongful selling. This is ... done ... to provide effective and fair protection for that big body of bona-fide retailers of NEW ZEALAND MEAT who may sometimes come up against this unfair competition.[96]

The NZMPB was most litigious in the early 1930s. In 1930 it instituted thirty-one successful prosecutions throughout Britain.[97] Many of these actions involved mislabelling and imitation of 'get-up'. For example, contractors sold Argentinian lamb to the Greenwich and Deptford Board of Guardians in wrapping indicating the Canterbury Meat Company and bearing its Eclipse brand. The maximum fine of £20 was imposed on the defendants. Window displays advertised 'Canterbury' and 'New Zealand' lamb when only South American lamb was stocked. In other cases, tickets on butchers' hooks indicated New Zealand origin when the lamb was South American.[98]

---

[94] MAF, *Report on the Marketing of Sheep, Mutton and Lamb*: 129.
[95] *Meat Trades Journal*, 2 October 1930, 9; 18 September 1930, 650.
[96] *Meat Trades Journal*, 21 February 1929, 303; *Meat Trades Journal*, 23 January 1930, 138.
[97] NZMPB, *Ninth Annual Report* (1931), 8.
[98] *Meat Trades Journal*, 8 August 1929, 216; 26 February 1931, 520; 29 October 1931, 277; 15 November 1934, 429.

The merits of Australian and New Zealand produce were communicated to British consumers in a blitz of advertising and publicity. One
prominent feature of these marketing drives was the extensive use of show
cards, window displays, and posters on hoardings. The ADPCB reported
that it used these media on 'hundreds of positions throughout London and
suburbs [and that] Show cards were displayed in thousands of retail
shops'. It stated that at one time it had 18,000 complete window displays
showcasing Australian produce and by 1935, this Board noted that over
the previous eight years, 2.8 million Kangaroo Cookery Books and almost
1 million pamphlets on Australian butter had been distributed throughout
Britain.[99] The NZDPCB used a number of temporary shops to display its
produce and ensured that A.B.C. and Associated Restaurants used only
New Zealand butter and cheese in their restaurants. It estimated that
3 million people 'pass through these restaurants weekly'.[100] London
figured prominently in the advertising campaigns of the NZDPCB: it
secured the rights to display 'New Zealand' at prominent locations,
including Piccadilly Circus, Aldwych, and the Strand, as well as in prominent positions in 1,500 shopping centres throughout the metropolis, and
on 300 buses on routes passing busy shopping localities. The NZDPCB
claimed:

The combined effect of these features is such as to make it next to impossible for
anyone living in London to go through his or her normal course of life without
seeing something about New Zealand butter and cheese several times a week.
Advertisements are giving the reasons why, posters are furnishing the
reminders.[101]

The NZMPB was equally prolific in its use of advertising media.
Between 1923 and 1924 the Board instituted the 'presents of lamb' scheme
by which a single carcass of lamb would be delivered to any address in
Britain for £1 13s. By 1931, almost 20,000 carcasses had been distributed
under this scheme. In 1932, the Board arranged for the distribution, from
retailers to consumers, of 3.5 million picture postcards bearing the legend
'The Home of the Finest Lamb in the World'. In the same year the Board's
advertisements appeared in 8 million stamp books issued by the Post
Office. By 1933, the Board reported that its advertising material was
being displayed daily in 12,000 butchers' shops throughout Britain.
A year later, more than 6 million shopping lists, booklets, and pamphlets

[99] ADPCB, *Third Annual Report* (1928), 4; *Tenth Annual Report* (1935), 6.
[100] NZDPCB, *Fifth Annual Report*, 1929: 6–7.
[101] NZDPCB, *Tenth Annual Report* (1934), 29.

had been issued; between 1936 and 1937, the Board issued more than 15 million discs, price tickets, message pads, and New Zealand lamb booklets. The Board also recognised that its advertising campaigns would have more impact if it targeted women, who were 'the actual shoppers'. As early as 1933, the Board estimated that its advertisements were appearing continuously in 14 million editions of women's magazines. To minimise the opportunity that unprincipled retailers used its advertising material to pass-off foreign lamb as 'New Zealand', the Board required that commercial applicants for this material obtained the countersignature of their wholesaler certifying that they were regular stockists of New Zealand lamb.[102]

The importance the control boards attached to marketing is shown in Table 4.3. In broad terms, advertising accounted for around 40 per cent of the total expenditure of each Board throughout the interwar period. Comparing the 1920s with the 1930s, it is also apparent that advertising's share of total expenditure increased. This is particularly pronounced for the NZMPB and the ADPCB. From the mid-1920s, advertising was comfortably the biggest single item of expenditure for all control boards. The heavy advertising expenditures of the Boards – both in absolute and in relative terms – represented defensive and aggressive strategies. They were defensive in the sense that they helped the Boards protect their market share in butter from Russia and Siberia. In the case of mutton and lamb, by the late 1930s, the NZMPB was expressing concern at the annual advertising expenditure of £50,000 incurred by the Argentine Meat Board, and stated, 'it is therefore imperative for New Zealand to maintain and broaden the publicity for her meat products if she is to retain her present position in the British market ... increasing supplies and the keen competition of our rivals in the Home market gave them no other alternative'.[103] Conversely, the advertising expenditures of the control boards were aggressive: the NZDPCB was particularly keen to overtake Danish dominance in the British market and earn higher premia for its butter.

The overriding aim of the advertising campaigns launched by the ADPCB, the NZDPCB, and the NZMPB was to establish and then increase public awareness of 'Australia' and 'New Zealand'. But two developments in the 1920s threated to obfuscate consumer recognition

[102] NZDPCB, *Ninth Annual Report* (1933), 9; *Tenth Annual Report* (1934), 8–9; *Eleventh Annual Report* (1934), 8–9; *Twelfth Annual Report* (1934), 6; *Fifteenth Annual Report* (1937), 6. Australia had a similar 'XMAS' gift scheme.
[103] NZMPB, *16th Annual Report* (1938), 8.

TABLE 4.3 *Advertising expenditure by value, and as a percentage of total expenditure, for the NZDPCB[1], NZMPB, and the ADPCB[2], ca. 1925–1938*

Year	NZDPCB (£)	NZDPCB (%)	NZMPB (£)	NZMPB (%)	ADPCB (£)	ADPCB (%)
1924	n.a.	n.a.	94	0.4	n.a.	n.a.
1925	n.a.	n.a.	329	1.7	n.a.	n.a.
1926	n.a.	n.a.	3,104	13.4	4,000	27.3
1927	n.a.	n.a.	1,054	5.0	8,500	38.1
1928	19,979	34.7	3,753	15.1	11,000	47.7
1929	16,788	35.0	5,913	22.9	5,000	29.4
1930	18,704	36.4	13,049	38.3	10,000	47.2
1931	40,015	82.5	13,963	36.8	7,500	40.0
1932	18,799	34.6	17,397	44.8	7,750	37.6
1933	12,624	23.0	21,357	46.1	20,215	62.5
1934	34,017	49.4	23,515	45.1	n.a.	n.a.
1935	43,349	51.4	22,780	42.2	20,000	61.8
1936	37,636	43.8	18,470	39.3	n.a.	n.a.
1937	n.a.	n.a.	26,581	45.7	n.a.	n.a.
1938	n.a.	n.a.	32,526	48.2	n.a.	n.a.

Notes:
1. Clearly defined advertising expenditure for the NZDPCB only becomes available from 1928. After 1936, separate treatment of advertising expenditure is not reported in the annual reports of the NZDPCB. In these accounts, advertising expenditure was funded from accumulated reserves which represent the build-up of surplus income minus expenditure, from all previous years. They therefore constitute a fund, either for specific projects, or for return to the subscribers. I am grateful to Steve Toms for explaining this latter point.
2. The annual reports of the ADPCB are only available for the period 1926–1935. I have been unable to locate the annual report for 1934.
Sources: Annual Reports and Statement of Accounts, New Zealand Dairy Produce Control Board, 1928–1936; Annual Reports and Statement of Accounts, New Zealand Meat Producers Board, 1924–1938; Commonwealth of Australia, Annual Reports of the Dairy Produce Control Board, 1926–1935.

of these indications of origin. The first threat was that the IEC and the EMB sought to promote 'Empire' produce. The former body recognised individual countries wished to retain exclusive rights to the goodwill attached to their products – and that this should be conveyed by indications of origin. However, the IEC indicated that this preference was a secondary consideration:

We are unanimous in the view that at the time of sale the simple words 'Empire produce' or 'foreign produce', as the case may be, should be attached to the goods. But in order to satisfy the anxiety of those countries within the Empire which desire to maintain the goodwill already attaching to the name of their country we would also provide that where the indication of origin at the time of importation has taken the form of 'a statement as to the country in which the goods were produced' the retailer shall exhibit that statement below the more general indication 'Empire produce'.[104]

A second threat to the advertising campaigns of the Australian and New Zealand Control Boards were the Standing Committees established by the British Merchandise Marks Act, 1926, to determine origin marking for butter and meat. Both Committees recommended that 'indication of origin' meant that the person applying the indication had the discretion to mark the product as 'foreign' or 'empire' or 'with a definite indication of the country in which the goods were ... produced'.[105] For frozen mutton and lamb, the Committee recommended that the principal parts of the carcase – leg, saddle, and shoulder – should be marked with an indication of origin, and that it was sufficient for any joint or cut not bearing this indication to have a ticket stating 'imported meat of Empire origin' or 'imported meat of foreign origin'.[106]

The threats posed by the IEC, the EMB, and the Standing Committees appointed under the Merchandise Marks Act, 1926, to the identity of 'Australia' and 'New Zealand' were acknowledged by the antipodean control boards. In its first annual report published in 1926, the ADPCB was categorical that one of its principal policies was 'to take action to establish and maintain the identity of Australian dairy produce in the retail shops and among consumers', and that the duties of its London agency involved taking 'such action as may be directed by the Board to retain the identity of Australian dairy produce'.[107] The New Zealand Control Boards were even more emphatic in their desire to promote 'New Zealand' rather than 'Empire'. The NZDPCB was not content to freeride on the marketing campaigns promoting 'Empire' produce conducted by the EMB. Instead,

---

[104] *Report of the Imperial Economic Committee on Marketing and Preparing for Market of Foodstuffs Produced in Overseas Parts of the Empire. First Report*: 9.

[105] *RSC on Butter*: 13; *RSC on Meat*: 19; 16 & 17 Geo. 5. Ch. 53, s. 10 (1). Merchandise Marks Act, 1926.

[106] *RSC on Meat*: 20. In the case of cheese, many retailers did not distinguish between 'New Zealand' and 'Canadian' cheddar, and often used the term 'Colonial' or 'Empire' or simply 'Cheddar'. Empire Marketing Board, *The Demand for Cheese in London* (London: HMSO, 1929), 14.

[107] ADPCB, *First Annual Report* (1926), 6.

it was determined to take 'every possible step to assure that any customer . . . would not have far to look before discovering a retail shop where New Zealand Butter and Cheese could be purchased', and 'we contend that, in the retailers' interest, as well as ours, New Zealand butter, as the finest Empire product, can be sold to better advantage under its own name'. Particular emphasis was placed on the use of price tickets and butter 'dummies' because they were, 'in every way consistent with our continual objective – to get more and more New Zealand butter and cheese sold under their exact description'.[108] Following the Meat Marking Order of 1934, the NZMPB altered its marketing strategy to emphasise that 'all New Zealand meat is branded New Zealand and that NO New Zealand meat would be branded Empire'; consumers were actively encouraged to 'look for the mark "New Zealand"'.[109]

ASSESSING THE SUCCESS OF THE CONTROL BOARDS

The antipodean control boards were in the vanguard of international marketing strategies involving the export of produce embossed with indications of origin, national legislation controlling quality along the supply chain, and state authorisation for the imposition of export levies which generated the funds to finance advertising campaigns. But how successful were the ADPCB, the NZDPCB, and the NZMPB?

Success can be measured in a number of ways. Throughout the interwar period, the volume of exports from the antipodes to Britain increased significantly. Between 1925 and 1938, butter exports by weight increased by a factor of 2.6 for Australia and New Zealand. Between 1923 and the mid-1930s, New Zealand's exports of meat, and Australian exports of lamb and mutton to Britain, increased by about 140 and 200 per cent, by weight, respectively.[110] However, it might be objected that the export performance of Australia and New Zealand was artificially enhanced by the introduction of imperial preference. One consequence of the Ottawa Conference of 1932 was that Britain imposed quantitative restrictions on non-empire meat supplies; free entry was given to dominion butter and

---

[108] NZDPCB, *Eighth Annual Report* (1932), 18; *Tenth Annual Report* (1934), 24; *Eleventh Annual Report* (1935), 26.
[109] NZMPB, *Thirteenth Annual Report* (1935), 8; *Fifteenth Annual Report* (1937), 6.
[110] Calculated from the annual reports of the ADPCB, the NZDPCB, and the NZMPB. Australian exports of beef were small and showed little growth during this period. Henzell, *Australian Agriculture*, 119.

cheese for three years and a tariff was imposed on foreign supplies of these products.[111]

The critical benchmark for determining the success of the control boards is the extent to which Australian and New Zealand butter prices exceeded those obtained by Denmark. This was a fundamental objective of the ADPCB and the NZDPCB. The NZDPCB stated, '[c]an New Zealand do anything to bring the prices of her butter into line with those of Denmark?' and '[i]t is urged that we want the same price as the Danish ... receive for their butter, and that the [Dairy Produce Export Control Bill] will enable us to get that'.[112] To examine the extent to which antipodean and Danish butter prices converged, I constructed a price series based on British wholesale prices of butter.[113] The results show that over the period 1926 to 1938, inclusive, the average premium commanded by Danish butter over Australian and New Zealand butter was 12.8 and 11.1 per cent, respectively. For the same period, New Zealand butter traded at a slight premium of two percentage points compared to Australian butter. Another observation is that the Danish premium over Australian and New Zealand butter was much greater in the early-mid 1930s than during the 1920s. Thus, it appears that New Zealand's satisfaction at achieving higher butter prices compared to Australia was tempered only by its failure to achieve parity with Denmark.

It is debatable whether achieving parity with Danish prices was a realistic objective during the interwar period. One problem is that in northern English markets Danish butter was already firmly established as the market leader. Heavy advertising by the ADPCB and the NZDPCB was not sufficient to overcome Danish first-mover advantage. An EMB investigation of the retailing of foreign and empire butters reported that in the North and Midlands, 'Danish' was 'considerably dearer' than New Zealand butter and was 'stocked in many more shops'.[114]

---

[111] Routh, *British Protectionism*, 93–94.

[112] NZDPCB, *Eighth Annual Report* (1932), 10. See also ADPCB, *Third Annual Report* (1928), 11; *Fourth Annual Report* (1929), 4; *Fifth Annual Report* (1930), 10; NZDPCB, *Fifth Annual Report* (1929), 5; *Seventh Annual Report* (1931), 10; *Twelfth Annual Report* (1926), 11; New Zealand, *Dairy Industry Commission* (1934): 19.

[113] MAF, *Agricultural Statistics*, Part II. London: HMSO, various issues. Calculations of these premia are discussed in Chapter 3.

[114] EMB, *The Demand for Empire Butter* (London: HMSO, 1930), 28. Recent scholarship indicates that New Zealand butter prices were higher than Danish in the south of England. F. Barnes and D. M. Higgins, 'Brand Image, Cultural Association and Marketing: New Zealand Butter and Lamb Exports to Britain, c.1920–1938'. *Business History*(forthcoming).

The determination of the NZDPCB to overcome Danish dominance generated experiments to determine whether it was possible to produce 'Danish' butter in New Zealand: 'We thought that all the New Zealand authorities were unanimous that their butter was the finest in the world; now it seems that Danish is finer still, and New Zealand is trying to imitate it, why?'[115] Although Australian and New Zealand butter exports to Britain increased, why were the ADPCB and the NZDPCB unable to achieve parity with Danish butter prices? To address this question I focus on inherent weaknesses in the marketing campaigns of both boards, while recognising that exogenous factors – especially their greater geographical distance from Britain and inability to practice year-round dairying – were also contributory factors.[116]

Danish dominance in the British butter market was based on supplying uniformly high-quality butter marketed with the Lur Brand which was, simultaneously, a mark of origin and quality. There are grounds for believing that the Kangaroo brand did not provide the same guarantee. By the late 1920s, concerns were raised in the Australian press that Kangaroo was being applied to inferior quality butter and/or butters of widely differing quality, and that butter branded Kangaroo before export was subsequently downgraded on arrival in London. This latter practice meant Kangaroo butter was difficult to sell, unlike butter which was only marked 'Australian'. By 1930, producers in New South Wales considered using an alternative mark to indicate their choicest exported butter because of the 'trouble caused the industry by Victoria marketing inferior butter as choicest under the recognised ... brand'. Such problems generated unfavourable comparisons with New Zealand and Denmark. The question 'Why does New Zealand butter on the London market realise higher prices than Australian?' was answered by reference to the higher proportion of low-quality butter exported from Australia compared to New Zealand. It was estimated that for every box of butter lower than first grade exported from New Zealand, three of the same quality were exported from Australia. If Australia was to compete effectively with Denmark, it was equally imperative that there was higher standardisation of butter grading throughout the dominion because '[o]ne of the chief reasons for Danish pre-eminence in Britain was their

[115] *The Grocer*, 16 January 1932, 53–54.
[116] ADPCB, *Eighth Annual Report* (1933), 13–14; Agricultural and Pastoral Industries and Stock Committee. Dairy Produce Export Control Bill (Together with Minutes of Evidence), New Zealand (1923), 19, 24, 39, 99.

care to export only their best butter, which was always uniform and dependable'.[117]

Doubts can also be entertained about the ability of the ADPCB to establish a strong brand identity for Kangaroo. The ADPCB recognised that its marketing propaganda was hampered by the failure to sell Australian 'pat' butter in wrappers indicating Australian origin. Moreover the Kangaroo brand was in competition with numerous Australian brands indicating quality. Brand proliferation was greatest in the 'choicest' grade of butter in which the Kangaroo brand also competed. Thus, in 1926, from a total of 5,323 examined butter consignments, 59, 37.5, and 3.4 per cent belonged to 'choice', 'first' grade, and 'second' grade, respectively. Within each grade category there were, respectively, seventy-one, fifty-one, and eleven brands. By 1935, 364 Australian butter factories had registered 882 brands with the Department of Commerce. In these circumstances it is difficult to envisage how the ADPCB could have launched a British advertising campaign centred on Kangaroo when other Australian butters were entitled to be marked 'Australia'. The ADPCB recognised that Danish butter exports were only marked with the Lur Brand, and that New Zealand had just three brands. To remedy this weakness a national dairy conference was held in April 1935, which recommended that only a few brands should be applied to Australian butter and cheese exports to Britain. For example, a brand comprising an outline of Australia and the legend 'First Grade' was to be used on butter and cheese scoring ninety points and above, while the Kangaroo brand was to be applied only to choicest butter (scoring ninety-two points or above). However, no further action appears to have been taken during the interwar period.[118]

The marketing campaign of the NZDPCB faced comparable problems. Thus, British retailers were passing-off second quality 'New Zealand' butter as 'finest'. There was nothing to prevent this because the class or grade of butter was marked on the box, not when retailed. A further problem was that the NZDPCB advertised its butter using the 'Fernleaf', but the biggest producer of butter in New Zealand – the New Zealand Dairy Cooperative Company (NZDCC) – which accounted for about

---

[117] *The Age*, 19 May 1926, 19; 25 November 1927, 12; *Sydney Morning Herald*, 11 September, 1930, 7; *Sydney Mail*, 1 August 1934, 42.

[118] *The Age*, 19 May 1926, 19; ADPCB, *Fifth Annual Report* (1930), 10; *Tenth Annual Report* (1935), 9–10. This latter report suggests that by the mid-1930s, the Kangaroo brand was being downgraded and the ADPCB was more concerned to sell Australian butter as 'Australian'. ADPCB, *Tenth Annual Report* (1935), 6.

a third of New Zealand's dairy exports, marketed its produce using the Anchor brand. Felicity Barnes argued that it was not until the 1930s that Fernleaf was surpassed by the Anchor brand.[119] Despite the heavy advertising throughout the 1920s and early 1930s, concerns were raised in 1934 that 'there is evidence that customers who ask for "New Zealand" butter are told that "Empire" means the same thing, and it is probable that cheaper Empire butters are sold as New Zealand'.[120] Barnes argued that the marketing campaigns of the EMB may have reduced the opportunities for distinct 'New Zealand' branding.[121] But, with due respect to Barnes, I find this interpretation difficult to reconcile with the point made earlier: the NZDPCB was not content to freeride on EMB publicity but sought, instead, to develop a specific New Zealand brand identity. The extent to which New Zealand butter was sold as 'Empire' depended more on the provisions of the Merchandise Marks Act, 1926, and the recommendations of the Standing Committee on Butter, than the EMB. The decision to sell New Zealand butter as 'New Zealand' or as 'Empire' depended on the retailer, who was lawfully entitled to label genuine New Zealand butter with either term. Both were accepted indications of origin. The NZDPCB recognised that the marking recommendations of the Standing Committee on butter had the potential to damage New Zealand and Australian butter, and acknowledged that it was imperative that its dairy products were marked 'New Zealand', not 'Empire'.[122]

Compared to the ADPCB and the NZDPCB, the marketing campaigns of the NZMPB were an unqualified success. Its publicity succeeded in conveying to the British public the message that New Zealand lamb was 'the best in the world'. In terms of price premia, New Zealand first-quality Canterbury lamb comfortably exceeded first-quality Australian and South American. Between 1923 and 1937, the prices of New Zealand lamb exceeded those of Australia and South America by 7.5 and 11.4 per cent respectively.[123] Barnes argued that the success of the NZMPB rested on its

---

[119] F. Barnes, *New Zealand's London* (Auckland: Auckland University Press, 2012), 170–173.

[120] NZDPCB, *Eighth Annual Report* (1932), 12; New Zealand, *Dairy Industry Commission*, 1934: 35.

[121] Barnes, *New Zealand's London*, 173.

[122] 16 & 17 Geo. 5, Ch. 53, Merchandise Marks Act, s.10 (1); NZDPCB, *Third Annual Report* (1927), 7. There was a suspicion that Danish butter was a trade description synonymous with 'Kiel' or 'cask', which referred to butter produced anywhere in Northern Europe. EMB, *The Demand for Empire Butter*, 14.

[123] Author's calculations based on NZMPB, *Annual Reports*, various issues. For most years, two or three prices are quoted for first quality according to carcass weight.

ability to convey 'Britishness' to British consumers: 'images of whiteness, familiarity and domesticity remained attached to the New Zealand brand'.[124] Other factors can be adduced which complement sociocultural explanations for the success of the NZMPB's marketing campaign. First, the emphasis was always on promoting 'New Zealand'. Second, an important difference existed between passing-off South American lamb as 'New Zealand' and retailing New Zealand butter as 'Empire'. The former practice was unequivocally illegal and the prosecutions instigated by the NZMPB – and the ensuing publicity – reinforced the Board's marketing campaign that New Zealand lamb was always marked 'New Zealand'. In the latter case, as noted earlier, retailers could use their discretion and label butter 'New Zealand' or 'Empire'. A further observation is that New Zealand lamb was acknowledged to be the superlative import:

New Zealand products obtain in the United Kingdom a premium over those of other mutton and lamb exporting countries, due to the fact that her sheep conform closely to the popular English mutton breeds, to the strict grading and to the reputation which her mutton and lamb enjoy.[125]

Viewed from this perspective, the superiority of New Zealand lamb compared to South American lamb, was the mirror image of the failure of New Zealand butter to achieve parity with Danish butter. Powerful reputational effects, supported by aggressive advertising and rigorous control of quality, ensured that New Zealand mutton and lamb always commanded a price premium compared to Australian and South American meat in the British market. What is even more remarkable is that New Zealand lamb and mutton were the most expensive imports and therefore particularly susceptible to competition, especially from South America. Nonetheless, between 1923 and 1932 (the Ottawa year), New Zealand maintained its market share, accounting for approximately 49 per cent of British imports of mutton and lamb, compared to South America's 35.6 per cent.[126]

CONCLUSIONS

This chapter discussed the growth in standardisation and grading of agricultural produce and the communication of these characteristics via

The data reported here are based on the average of first-quality prices for each country.

[124] Barnes, *New Zealand's London*, 168. See also Barnes and Higgins, 'Brand Image'.
[125] Imperial Economic Committee, *Mutton and Lamb Survey* (London: HMSO, 1935), 7.
[126] Author's calculations based on *NZMPB, Annual Reports*, various issues.

indications of origin and brands, such as Anchor and Kangaroo, which became synonymous with country of origin. A key feature distinguishing the interwar period from the pre-1914 era was greater state involvement in agriculture. For the countries examined in this chapter – primarily Australia, Britain, New Zealand, and the United States – official intervention was designed to increase the collective or cooperative production of foodstuffs. In this regard, the Danish model was the exemplar, characterised by strong and extensive cooperation across the vertical supply chain, rigorous quality control, the production of uniformly high-quality bacon and butter, and the marketing of these products using the 'Lur Brand' and 'Denmark'.

The British and US governments enacted considerable legislation to encourage the cooperative production and marketing of foodstuffs, but with markedly different results. In the former, government intervention was ineffective in developing a national agricultural policy based on the Danish model, despite the recommendations of official reports on butter, bacon, cheese, lamb, and mutton. One contemporary argued, '[t]he English agricultural marketing schemes date from 1933 and their first effect was to check voluntary cooperative effort', while others castigated British farmers for their 'ingrained individualism'.[127] In contrast, official intervention in the United States was built on stronger foundations. Cooperative organisations, well established by the 1900s, produced a range of produce which was marketed on a national basis using IGOs such as 'California', and the Sunkist and Sun-Maid brands. The success of these early cooperatives and their continued expansion during the 1920s was facilitated by federal legislation and the promotional work of the USDA (Table 4.1).

British efforts to recover a larger share of the domestic market contained positive and negative elements. The former was characterised by promotion of the NM and legislation encouraging large-scale reorganisation and greater collective effort. The latter, by contrast, played on long-established fears that British farmers suffered from the misrepresentation of foreign produce as 'British', and it was this unfair competition which militated against an effective domestic response. However, possibly the biggest disadvantage facing British agriculture was that attempts to promote British produce using a 'British' or 'Empire'

---

[127] Fay, *Co-operation at Home and Abroad*, 486–487; MAF, *Report of the Committee Appointed to Review the Working of the Agricultural Marketing Acts*: 5.

indication of origin were simply too late. Denmark, for example, had established its dominance in the British butter market by the late nineteenth century. In any event, it can be argued that it was undesirable for British agriculture to have responded more successfully to the Agricultural Marketing Acts: this would have reduced British food imports from the Empire and thereby curtailed British exports of manufactures.

Australia and New Zealand began following the Danish cooperative model from the late nineteenth century. Their imitation of Danish agricultural development accelerated during the interwar period and was communicated by aggressive advertising of 'Australia' and 'New Zealand', together with the Anchor, Fernleaf, and Kangaroo brands. A key objective of the NZDPCB was to secure parity with Danish butter prices. The evidence indicates that, as far as the British market as a whole is concerned, the NZDPCB failed. However, two important caveats need to be made. First, it may be argued that the focus on price parity was misplaced: New Zealand's dependence on the British market required only that highly remunerative prices were obtained.[128] Second, the interwar success of the NZMPB and the NZDPCB ensured that New Zealand lamb and Anchor butter remained powerful brands after 1945.[129]

---

[128] New Zealand Meat Producers Board. *The Case for Closer Trade with Britain: Being Evidence Submitted to the Customs Tariff Commission by the New Zealand Meat Producers Board.* Wellington: New Zealand Meat Producers Board (1933) 16.

[129] R. Clemens and B. Babcock. 'Country of Origin as a Brand: The Case of New Zealand Lamb.' MATRIC Briefing Paper 04-MBP 9, November 2004.

5

'Unfair Competition' and the British Merchandise Marks Act, 1926

Where does the rubbish in every country come from? Germany! This sign was displayed at the Volker stall of the Gas Exhibition at Earl's Court in 1904. At that time we were forced by the agitation (not to mention stale buns and bad tomatoes) of German Importers to remove it, but in season and out of season we have tried to show the MENACE to British Industry of the CHEAP GERMAN GOODS, which, dumped here, bring nothing but discredit on the traders who sell them.

The Grocer, 6 September 1919, 39

A matter that must be faced if voluntary protection for British goods is to be made fully effective is the difficulty of distinguishing between goods that are of British production ... and those that masquerade as such although, in fact, they are of foreign origin.

The Times, 19 December 1925, 13

For much of the period covered in previous chapters, British law on indications of origin was governed by the Merchandise Marks Act, 1887.[1] This Act provided specific conditions under which imports had to bear an indication of origin; otherwise they could be imported 'blank'. The Merchandise Marks Act, 1926, ensured that products could no longer be imported 'blank': an industry or trade association could secure an Order in Council and unmarked products would have to bear an indication of origin before import and/or before sale in Britain. Introduction of the 1926 Act was the culmination of more than forty years of campaigning. In Britain, demands that indications 'origin' be applied to imports was hardened by substantial public hostility towards Germany and Austria

---

[1] 50 & 51 Vict. C. 28. *Merchandise Marks Act, 1887*.

during and after the First World War, and by official concerns about how British industry would revert to peacetime production. Government support for compulsory indications of origin – often directed against German imports – can be observed during the First World War and was closely allied to the incipient campaign to safeguard key British industries. Safeguarding legislation and the Merchandise Marks Act, 1926, shared one major objective: the prevention of 'unfair competition'. However, the former defined unfair competition in terms of depreciation of currency, subsidies, and inferior working conditions, whereas the latter was based on the premise that consumers had a right to know the true geographical origin of the products they purchased.

The campaign to secure compulsory indications of origin overlapped with the increasingly protectionist stance against imports taken by successive interwar governments.[2] To be effective, the imposition of tariffs and other forms of quantitative restriction requires that imports bear an unambiguous indication of origin. The extent to which these indications may have operated as a protectionist measure was officially recognised. For example, between November 1924 and October 1927, The Balfour Committee on Industry and Trade heard evidence from 240 witnesses on the factors affecting British industry and commerce. Unfair competition, especially the misrepresentation of foreign products as 'British', was identified as an adverse influence on industrial competitiveness.[3] The Balfour Committee recognised that use of the Merchandise Marks Act, 1926, as 'a method of veiled protection' violated the spirit of the International Convention on Import and Export Prohibitions, but concluded that if it *was* the case that British consumers preferred British goods, 'This was a perfectly legitimate and desirable result, and has nothing in common with attempts to exclude imports by imposing vexatious conditions on their importation or sale.'[4]

The requirement that imported goods bear an indication of origin has close parallels with the 'Buy British' campaign and the activities of the EMB during the interwar period. Both schemes were based on the belief that British consumers wished to exercise a voluntary preference in favour

---

[2] There is a substantial academic debate on the effectiveness of British tariffs. See, for example, M. Kitson and S. Solomou, *Protectionism and Economic Revival: The Interwar British Economy* (Cambridge: Cambridge University Press, 1990).

[3] Committee on Industry and Trade, *Minutes of Evidence*, Volume 1: 100, 316, 324, 435–36, 454, 656–667; Volume 2: 734, 736, 758, 844, 1123.

[4] *Final Report of the Committee on Industry and Trade*. P.P. VII.413. London, HMSO (1929): 294.

of domestic and empire products. But, in the absence of legally enforceable and unambiguous origin marking, how could consumers accurately exercise their preferences? In any event, what did 'Made in Britain' mean? It was recognised that in many consumer goods industries it was the practice to import foreign components, assemble them, and stamp the finished article 'British'. In the London briar pipe trade it was the custom to stamp 'London made' on pipes which had been fitted and finished in Britain, provided at least 25 per cent of the total cost of labour or material used in their manufacture was British. Where such pipes had been made and fitted abroad, but finished in Britain, they were still entitled to be stamped 'British Finished' or 'London Finished', provided the cost of the finished pipe contained at least 25 per cent British labour or material. Similarly, 'British made' was applied to a variety of children's toys and related products, such as Christmas crackers, even when their component parts were foreign.[5] Concerns were also expressed that the acquisition of British trademarks by foreign companies and their subsequent use on foreign products was misleading.[6] In other words, it was possible that company trademarks erroneously indicated country of origin.

This chapter re-examines the 'Buy British' campaign during the inter-war period. I emphasise the importance of the 1926 Merchandise Marks Act which empowered the Board of Trade to impose compulsory indications of origin on products at import, and/or sale in Britain. Although there was a substantial response to this Act, it proved difficult to implement and the volume of prosecutions it engendered appear insubstantial.

THE EMPIRE MARKETING BOARD AND 'BUY BRITISH' CAMPAIGNS

Indications of origin can be used to promote domestic goods by influencing consumer choices in favour of domestic products.[7] As discussed in previous chapters, prior to 1914, the most significant attempt to introduce

---

[5] Guildhall Library, London (hereafter, Guildhall), MS. 1659. *Briar Pipe Trade Sub-Section*: 20 February 1924; 24 March 1925; 6 May 1925; 17 June 1925; 2 July 1926. Similar issues were raised by the toy manufacturers' association. Guildhall. MS. 16775. *Minutes of the British Toy Manufacturers Association*: 24 February 1931; 14 December 1931.

[6] Modern Records Centre, University of Warwick (hereafter, MRC), Federation of British Industries (FBI). MSS.200/F1/1/1/155. *Minutes of the Committee on Trade Marks and Merchandise Marks and Others, 1919–1926*: 5 February 1920.

[7] See, for example, W. Olins, 'Branding the Nation – the Historical Context', *Brand Management*, 9 (2002); Papadopoulos and Heslop, 'Country Equity and Country

a British national trademark was initiated by the British Empire Trade Marks Association (BETMA), which was concerned that foreign manufactures were being passed-off as 'British'. It believed that adoption of a national mark would undermine this practice and stimulate global demand for British products. It also recognised that adoption of a British indication of origin would protect the preferential treatment given to British exports to the colonies.[8] Despite the advantages claimed for this indication of origin, many of Britain's most famous manufacturers raised serious objections. Concerns were voiced about the likely damage to the goodwill embodied in company trademarks. There was a belief that a national mark used in conjunction with private trademarks would generate confusion and, finally, fears were expressed that an indication of origin would become a badge of inferiority damaging private trademarks and the general reputation of British manufacturers.[9]

After 1919, campaigns to secure a 'British' or 'Empire' indication of origin reignited but ultimately failed. Among trade bodies the Federation of British Industries (FBI) was unflinching in its opposition.[10] It argued that in less sophisticated foreign markets such an indication prevented consumers differentiating high- and low-quality products, and might create the impression that all products were equal. Further, the establishment of a 'British' mark reduced the value of private trademarks registered in foreign countries and, because it was impossible to guarantee the quality of goods bearing this mark, national prestige would be damaged.[11] The Trade Mark, Patents & Design Federation was established to consolidate opposition to a British Empire mark. This body, incorporated in 1920, was composed of firms which owned highly esteemed trademarks and it had opposed similar initiatives before Select

Branding'. The importance of origin marking to the success of 'Buy British' campaigns has been acknowledged. Trentmann, *Free Trade Nation*, 238–239.

[8] Dominions Royal Commission. *Royal Commission on the Natural Resources, Trade and Legislation of Certain Portions of His Majesty's Dominions. Minutes of Evidence Taken in London during October and November, 1912. Part II*, P.P. XVI.393. London: HMSO (1912): Q. 2874, Q. 2918–2919, Q. 2217; QQ. 2243–2246; Merchandise Marks Committee, 1919–1920, *Minutes of Evidence*: QQ. 4543–4545.

[9] D. M. Higgins, '"Made in Britain?" National Trade Marks and Merchandise Marks: The British Experience from the Late Nineteenth Century to the 1920s', *Journal of Industrial History*, 5 (2002): 50–70.

[10] MRC/FBI, MSS.200/F1/1/1/155. *Minutes of the Committee on Trade Marks and Merchandise Marks and Others, 1919–1926*: 5 January 1920; 5 February 1920; 10 June 1925.

[11] MRC/FBI, MSS.200/F/4/2/8. *Ninth Annual Report, 1925*: 15–16.

Committees in the pre-1914 era.[12] The National Union of Manufacturers (NUM) believed adoption of a national or empire mark could be beneficial, but it also recognised that considerable obstacles had to be overcome if private firms were to be convinced of its merits.[13]

Many of these concerns were repeated by witnesses giving evidence before the Select Committee on Merchandise Marks which sat between 1919 and 1920. Addressing the question of national or empire indications of origin, the Committee concluded, 'in the absence of agreement among the bulk of traders . . . we see grave objections to the institution of a British national or Empire mark'.[14] The EMB expressed similar views. It was believed the EMB would overcome the political difficulties to establishing imperial tariff preference, and that by promoting the sale of empire foodstuffs in Britain, it would generate a corresponding increase in demand for British manufactures. The EMB was a distinctly non-tariff solution to the problem of fostering closer commercial ties between Britain and its empire. Steven Constantine argued that 'the EMB was identified as a propaganda organisation . . . it sought to influence consumer choice not by financial means – tariff barriers – but by propaganda'.[15] However, even at the inception of the EMB, it was acknowledged that:

We are unanimously of the opinion that a trade mark is not what is required for the purposes we have in view . . . it would be extremely difficult to find a pictorial symbol, equally appropriate to all classes of goods, which would not be confused with trademarks registered within the United Kingdom or elsewhere.[16]

Without a suitable indication of origin it is difficult to believe that a 'Buy British' campaign would succeed. One problem was the ever-present danger that foreign imports were passed-off as 'British' or 'Empire',[17] or that empire and British products would be misrepresented as foreign.[18] The absence of support for these indications is anomalous

---

[12] *The Times*, 20 June 1921, 16.

[13] *The United Manufacturers' Journal*, 4 February 1918, 49–50.

[14] *Report to the Board of Trade of the Merchandise Marks Committee*: x.

[15] Constantine, 'Bringing the Empire Alive', 200. For a recent survey of the links between this campaign and imperial consumerism, see Trentmann, *Free Trade Nation*, 230–240.

[16] Imperial Economic Committee. *Report of the Imperial Economic Committee on Marketing and Preparing for Market of Foodstuffs Produced in the Overseas Parts of the Empire. First Report*. P.P. XIII.799. London: HMSO (1925): 9.

[17] None of the provisions of the marking requirements stipulated by the Merchandise Marks Act, 1887, applied to products imported 'blank'.

[18] The FBI opposed a mark of origin on empire products, believing they were detrimental to the interests of trademark owners. MRC/FBI, MSS.200/F/4/2/1. Federation of British Industries. *Second Annual Report*, 1918: 15.

because there was both a private and public perception that, *ceteris paribus*, the British public had an innate preference for British products. The FBI believed that '[t]here are surely no Britons who would desire to look elsewhere for their requirements, provided these can be met'.[19] If this perception was accurate, why were many British manufacturers reluctant to champion 'Made in Britain'? Requiring that imports be marked with an indication of origin partly negated the opportunity to promote 'British' goods.

Moreover, even on its own terms, the EMB appears ineffectual. The potential importance of the EMB was recognised by contemporaries and it received government support,[20] but doubts have been expressed about its effectiveness. The EMB was under-funded and did not spend all its available resources; considerable doubts remain about its role in fostering intra-imperial trade because differential movements in empire and foreign prices favoured the former. Additionally, in some cases, the British market was already practically satiated with empire supplies of particular foodstuffs. Unsurprisingly, therefore, it has been claimed that the EMB had 'a modest, limited effect because the message conflicted with the realities of supply and price'.[21]

'Buy British' campaigns were launched at various times in the 1920s and 1930s. Encouraged by the success of an international advertising campaign at Wembley, the FBI attempted to launch a 'Buy British' campaign in 1924.[22] Leading advertising agencies and the FBI's membership were approached to determine prospective support for the campaign. However, it became apparent that the timing of such a campaign was inopportune, and the matter was dropped.[23] By the early 1930s, there was a growing sense of urgency about the need to promote a 'Buy British' campaign. Part of the explanation for this change was unease about promoting empire products in the British market without reciprocal efforts by the empire. This point was made in a powerfully argued

---

[19] MRC/FBI, MSS.200 F/3/D2/2/1. *Correspondence re: 'Buy British Campaign'*: 18 May 1933. Some manufacturers asserted that British consumers would pay a premium of 75 per cent to secure British products. Committee on Industry and Trade. *Minutes of Evidence*, Vol. III: Q. 20, 243.

[20] Constantine, 'Bringing the Empire Alive'; Statement by Sir Philip Cunliffe-Lister, *The Times*, Wednesday 16 December 1925, 11.

[21] J. M. Drummond, *British Economic Policy and the Empire, 1919–1939* (London: Allen & Unwin, 1972), 66; Constantine, 'Bringing the Empire Alive', 224.

[22] *The Times*, 12 June 1925, 13; 20 November 1925, 9.

[23] MRC/FBI, MSS.200/F/1/1/175. *Minutes of Various Committees*. Meeting of the 'Buy British Goods' Committee: 27 March 1924.

letter sent by twelve MPs to *The Times* in 1929;[24] it was reinforced by the decision of the IEC that the EMB's remit should be extended to include the marketing of British produce in the empire which helped pave the way for a dedicated 'Buy British' campaign.[25] Sir John Corcoran, president of the NUM, stated, 'the country is more than ready ... it is anxious ... to Buy British.' He urged British consumers to 'insist on getting a definite indication of British origin', and claimed that a 'Buy British' campaign would improve the balance of trade, secure employment for British workers, and improve revenues and profits for British firms.[26]

Under the auspices of the EMB, the 'Buy British' campaign was launched by the Prince of Wales in November 1931. The campaign attracted widespread publicity. More than 4 million posters were distributed throughout Britain, and the BBC gave prominence to the campaign in its news bulletins. A 'Buy British' film was shown in more than 1,000 cinemas to a total audience in excess of 12 million, and a large illuminated sign proclaiming 'Buy British' was erected in Trafalgar Square.[27] In addition to the support of local councils and other, locally based organisations, such as the Beckenham 'Buy British' Movement, special pageants were held promoting 'Buy British'. The campaign was welcomed by the Trades Union Council, a special 'Buy British' train was run by the Great Western Railway, and exhibitions were launched by, for example, the lace industry.[28]

Determining the extent to which the 'Buy British' campaign was successful is problematic, if not impossible. One obstacle is how to distinguish the impact of the advertising campaign from other variables, for example, changes in the relative price of domestic and foreign manufactures. Just two months after its launch, the Secretary for the Dominions stated that the campaign 'had effectively brought home to the country its duty of buying in the first place home products', while conceding that the campaign had incurred expenditure which was 'so

[24] 'Buy British', *The Times*, 15 March 1929, 17.
[25] Though no action was taken on this. Imperial Committee on Economic Consultation and Cooperation: *Report*: P.P. 11. Cmd.4335. London: HMSO (1933): 51.
[26] MRC/FBI, MSS.200/F/3/D2/2/1. *Correspondence re: 'Buy British Campaign'*. Statement by Sir John Corcoran, Director of the National Union of Manufactures. Undated.
[27] Empire Marketing Board, *Note on the Work and Finance of the Board* ...: 16–17.
[28] Constantine, 'The Buy British Campaign of 1931', 44–59; *The Times*, 13 November 1931, 11; 22 November 1931, 7; 24 November 1931, 11; 17 December 1931, 9; 21 November 1932, 9; 31 May 1932, 11.

FIGURE 5.1 'Buy British, and Protect Your Job'.
Permission/acknowledgement: MSS-200-F-3-D2-2–1. Modern Records Centre,
University of Warwick, UK

large and diversified as to render useless the professional standards by
which they were accustomed to measure advertising campaigns'.[29] Even
the anecdotal evidence is equivocal. Constantine noted that initial enthu-
siasm for 'Buy British' subsequently waned.[30] Despite its public support
for the campaign, the FBI faced internal divisions. It canvassed its membership to determine their support for financing 'Buy British' advertising
material, but the response was weak. The Raleigh Cycle Co. responded,

[29] *Hansard*, 8 December 1931.
[30] Constantine, 'The Buy British Campaign of 1931', 57.

'it would be quite impossible for us to commit ourselves for any further expense in this direction'; Dunlop simply did not wish to participate in the scheme.[31] Replies sent to the FBI during the campaign were also unenthusiastic. Neill & Co. and Pegler Bros., manufacturers of saws and razor blades and of engineers' brass work, respectively, reported that their reliance on dealers and merchants who held substantial stocks made it impossible for them to assess the impact of the campaign.[32] Price differentials between British and foreign products were identified as a key inhibitor of success: 'The very pronounced craze for cheapness ... is, however, ... very strongly resistant to the Buy British Campaign and it usually wins when there is much disparity in price between the British and the foreign article.'[33]

THE CAMPAIGN FOR COMPULSORY INDICATIONS OF ORIGIN

Given the problems confronting the implementation of a 'British' or an 'Empire' indication of origin, the only way forward was to require that imports indicate their country of origin. Such a course was not without risk. To the extent that foreign products were cheaper than British, only the most patriotic of consumers would buy the latter and there was always the danger that a pro-British campaign would advertise the relative expense of British products. Viewed from this perspective it was immaterial whether country of origin was applied to British or foreign products. However, because of widespread concerns that foreign products were imported blank and passed-off as 'British', marking imports with an indication of origin would protect British consumers in two ways: it would ensure that they could accurately exercise their preference for British products and it would prevent them paying a premium for imports in the belief that they were 'British'.

Indications of origin are vital to the success of national marketing schemes since otherwise it is difficult, if not impossible, for consumers to

---

[31] MRC/FBI, MSS.200/F/3/D2/2/1. *Correspondence re: 'Buy British Campaign'*. Raleigh Cycle Co. Ltd. and Dunlop Rubber Co., Ltd., to FBI. 24 November 1931.

[32] MRC/FBI, MSS.200/F/3/D2/2/1. *Correspondence re: 'Buy British Campaign'*. Neill & Co. and Pegler Bros. Ltd. to FBI. 12 December 1931.

[33] MRC/FBI, MSS.200/F/3/D2/2/1. *Correspondence re: 'Buy British Campaign'*. Premier Electric Heaters Ltd. to FBI. 31 December 1931. The 'Buy British' campaign was itself subject to misrepresentation. Ibid.: Luke & Spencer to FBI, 14 March 1932; Nottingham branch of FBI to FBI, 14 May 1932.

distinguish domestic from foreign products. A skilled merchant or manufacturer might be able to differentiate products by origin because they possess expert trade knowledge of the characteristics of particular products. Nonetheless, in the absence of indications of origin, a national marketing scheme promoting domestic products might benefit foreign producers. Additionally, the requirement that products be marked prior to importation imposed costs on foreign manufacturers, thereby reducing some of the price differential between domestic and imported products.

One issue which irritated the British public after the Merchandise Marks Act, 1887, was the German practice of conscientiously applying the indication 'Made in Germany', even when it was not required, because the products did not bear any resemblance to British trademarks, the names of British manufacturers, or the names of British towns and cities. By default it appeared that Britain had scored an astonishing own goal: legislation designed to ensure that British consumers were not misled into buying foreign products in the belief they were British was being used by German manufacturers to promote their exports to Britain. Giving evidence before the Select Committee of 1897, one witness argued, '[t]he "Made in Germany" which it was intended should vilify German goods in foreign lands has become a mark of honour for the same in the furthest markets'.[34] Growing Anglo–German trade rivalry during the late nineteenth century and the ubiquity of the mark 'Made in Germany' were inflamed by Ernest Williams.[35]

Despite growing agitation that it should be compulsory for imported products to bear an indication of origin, Select Committees appointed to review the operation of the Merchandise Marks Act, 1887, were generally unwilling to succumb to this pressure. The Select Committee of 1890 refused to entertain the proposal that imports should bear a 'definite indication of origin', believing such a scheme would damage Britain's entrepôt trade and encourage retaliation. The Select Committee of 1897 thought it should remain lawful for British traders to mark imported products with their own name without an indication of origin.[36]

The First World War galvanised official response to imports from enemy countries. This was manifested by a variety of complex licensing

---

[34] *Report from the Select Committee on Merchandise Marks.* P.P. XI.29. London: HMSO (1897): Q. 3434.
[35] E. E. Williams, *Made in Germany* (London: Heinemann, 1896).
[36] *Report from the Select Committee on Merchandise Marks Act, 1887,* P.P. XV.19. (1890): iv; *Report from the Select Committee on Merchandise Marks* (1897): iv.

schemes.[37] A close overlap emerged between demands for indications of origin and the protection of British industry. Unlike the nineteenth century, when official support for compulsory indications of origin was absent, the Board of Trade was beginning to recommend them, especially when applied to imports from Germany. In 1916 the Board established a committee to investigate the prospects for British trade after the war. The majority of witnesses giving evidence stated that merchandise mark legislation should be strengthened by providing for compulsory indications of origin. Many believed that products of enemy origin should be marked distinctly with the name of the country of manufacture, not obscure indications such as 'Foreign made' or 'Not British'. For products emanating from the German Empire, it was suggested that 'Made in Saxony' and 'Made in Bavaria' should be replaced by 'Made in Germany'. One committee recognised that whereas indications of origin had inadvertently promoted German manufactures prior to 1914, 'there appeared to be a consensus of opinion that for some considerable time it would have the opposite effect in the British market'.[38]

Parallels between indications of origin and the protection of British industry can be observed in the context of 'safeguarding'. The Safeguarding of Industries Act, 1925, made general provision for 'unfair competition' which included 'inferior conditions of employment of labour' and 'any special circumstances by reason of which ... industry in the United Kingdom is placed at a serious relative disadvantage'.[39] One aspect of this competition which received particular attention was the practice of importing 'blank' products. If foreign products competed 'unfairly' by currency depreciation or subsidies, and if British consumers were buying foreign products in the belief they were buying British, it was necessary simultaneously to remove the artificial price disparity (by imposing a tariff) and to ensure that British consumers could not be misled

---

[37] Committee on Industrial and Commercial Policy: *Interim Report on the Importation of Goods from the Present Enemy Countries after the War.* P.P. XIII.221. London: HMSO (1918): 3; *Conditions under Which Trading is Possible since the Raising of the Blockade.* P.P. XLV.723. London: HMSO (1919): 2.

[38] British Trade after the War. *Report of a Sub-Committee of the Advisory Committee to the Board of Trade on Commercial Intelligence with Respect to Measures for Securing the Position, after the War, of Certain Branches of British Industry.* P.P. XV.591. London: HMSO (1916) 14; British Trade after the War (2). *Summaries of the Evidence Taken by a Sub-Committee of the Advisory Committee to the Board of Trade ...* P.P. XV.611. London: HMSO (1916) 4, 16.

[39] 15 & 16 Geo. V. Safeguarding of Industries (Customs Duties) Act, 1925; *Safeguarding of Industries: Procedures and Enquiries.* P.P. XV.573. London: HMSO, (1925): 3.

(by requiring imports bear a clear indication of origin). The committee investigating the glove industry stated, 'gloves coming into this country should bear a stamp conspicuously placed indicating the country of origin, irrespective of whether such gloves bear the name of an English firm or not'.[40] Perhaps the strongest endorsement of this view was made by the committee dealing with the cutlery industry: 'we wish to suggest for your earnest consideration the desirability of extending the law to compel the indelible marking of all articles of imported cutlery with a clear indication that they are of foreign origin'.[41]

THE MERCHANDISE MARKS COMMITTEE, 1919–1920

The introduction of the Merchandise Marks Act, 1926, represented the culmination of a series of efforts to ensure that domestic or empire products were differentiated from those of foreign origin. In 1919, the government appointed the Merchandise Marks Committee. Its terms of reference were threefold: to consider whether existing merchandise marks legislation needed to be extended or amended; to assess the utility of national trademarks, and to determine the extent to which further international action was required to prevent the false marking of goods. The Committee sat between December 1919 and March 1920 and it heard evidence from manufacturers, chambers of commerce, and employers' federations.

Like the Select Committee Reports of 1890 and 1897, a clear dichotomy of views emerged between manufacturers and merchants.[42] This was most apparent with the Committee's first term of reference which addressed compulsory indications of origin.[43] In its final report the committee summarised the evidence on compulsory indications of origin. Arguments in favour included the desirability of informing consumers of the origin of products (predicated on the belief that domestic consumers preferred British to foreign products, especially those exported from

[40] Board of Trade, Safeguarding of Industries: *Report of the Committee on Leather Gloves, Fabric Gloves, and Glove Fabric.* P.P. XV.573. London: HMSO (1925): 11–12.

[41] Board of Trade, Safeguarding of Industries: *Report of the Committee on Cutlery.* P.P. XV.663. London: HMSO (1925):13.

[42] Merchandise Marks Committee. *Minutes of Evidence:* 1919–1920: Q. 2461; Q. 2541, QQ. 3386–3391; Q. 2860, Q. 3483, Q. 3546, QQ. 4012–4014, Q. 4073, QQ. 4209–4302. Opposition by merchants is evidenced at Q. 1876; QQ. 2773–2774; Q. 3092; Q. 3272; Q. 3742; Q. 3898.

[43] *Report to the Board of Trade of the Merchandise Marks Committee.* P.P. XXI.615. London: HMSO (1920): v.

former enemy countries), and the need to distinguish products emanating from countries in which inferior labour conditions existed or unfair methods of competition were practised. Conversely, it was recognised that compulsory indications of origin gave a 'gratuitous advertisement' to foreign products and that any disclosure of the sources from which a merchant obtained supplies was unfair and would result in the loss of a considerable entrepôt trade. Nonetheless, the Committee recognised that a consensus did exist in some industries that the marking of imported products was advantageous. Consequently, it concluded:

> [W]e recommend that, when it has been established that it is in the public interest that the local origin of the goods should be indicated, in the case of any particular class or description of imported goods, the Board of Trade shall have powers to deal with the question by Order.[44]

Despite this recommendation, legislation providing for compulsory indications of origin on imports was not introduced until 1926, primarily because of substantial differences in opinion within and between the various bodies representing commercial and manufacturing interests. The Board of Trade had proposed a bill in 1923 to effect the recommendations of the aforementioned Committee. Subsequently, a confidential draft was circulated in 1925 which formed the basis of a bill introduced to the House of Commons by the President of the Board of Trade, Sir Philip Cunliffe-Lister.[45] The complexity of these bills meant disagreements and changes in opinion were inevitable, for example: who had power to make the Marking Order – the Board of Trade, or the tribunal established to hear evidence? Was it desirable that Marking Orders were presented before Parliament? Delay between presenting and approving a Marking Order might accelerate the importation of unmarked goods. What form should origin marking take? The FBI and the Board of Trade disagreed over the use of indelible marking; other parties thought the tribunal should determine the form of indication of origin because this enabled it to respond to the individual needs of different industries. Was an indication of origin only to be applied to products, or should it apply to advertising matter, such as trade catalogues and periodicals?

---

[44] *Report to the Board of Trade of the Merchandise Marks Committee* (1920): v.
[45] MRC/FBI, MSS.200/F1/1/1/155. *Minutes of the Committee on Trade Marks and Merchandise Marks and Others, 1919–1926*: Meeting of Merchandise Marks Committee, 17 April 1923; Nugent to Chapman, 19 April 1923; Meeting of Merchandise Marks Committee, 17 February 1925. The Merchandise Marks (Imported Goods) Bill 49 (1926) became, after amendment by standing committee, Bill 180 (1926).

Moreover, was the Board of Trade or an industry to be responsible for instigating prosecutions under the proposed legislation? If the latter, there was a risk that a disproportionately heavy financial burden would be imposed on industries composed of small firms.[46] The China and Glassware section of the London Chamber of Commerce (LCC) initially supported the view that products should be marked with their country of origin, but subsequently indicated that existing legislation was sufficient.[47] Other sections of the LCC argued that the interests of British trade were best served by British manufacturers indicating that their products were 'British made': 'in so far as a desire exists to secure that home manufactured goods shall be identified as such, our British manufacturers can mark their own products'. This point was especially pertinent: because many British manufacturers did not mark their products with an indication of origin, it was thought undesirable to request that imports be so marked.[48]

However, the main conflict to be resolved was between the FBI, merchant interests, and the Board of Trade. The FBI recognised the link between the need to alter merchandise mark legislation and the success of any 'Buy British' campaign, arguing:

The Federation of British Industries have had under further consideration the question of the marking of foreign goods with an indication of their origin … In the opinion of this Federation, there can be no serious argument against the desirability of enabling the British public to distinguish goods of foreign manufacture, and thus giving them the opportunity of buying British.[49]

The FBI's principal objective was to ensure that all foreign products were compulsorily marked with their country of origin prior to importation. In situations where this was not possible it was only prepared to concede that the Board should be empowered to give exemption to particular products.[50] These proposals were anathema to the Associated

---

[46] MRC/FBI, MSS.200/F1/1/1/155. *Minutes of the Committee on Trade Marks and Merchandise Marks and Others, 1919–1926*: Report of the Merchandise Marks Committee, 17 April 1923.

[47] Guildhall. MS. 16459/8. The London Chamber of Commerce. *Minutes of Meeting of Council*: 11 March 1920; MS. 16459/10: 13 November 1924.

[48] Guildhall. MS. 16459/10. The London Chamber of Commerce. *Minutes of Meeting of Council*: 12 March 1925; 11 February 1926; 8 April 1926.

[49] MRC/FBI, MSS.200/F/1/1/10. *Minutes of the FBI Executive Committee, 1924–1927*: Nugent to the President of the Board of Trade, 3 December 1924.

[50] MRC/FBI, MSS. 200/F1/1/1/155. *Minutes of the Committee on Trade Marks and Merchandise Marks and Others, 1919–1926*: 17 February 1925; 16 April 1926.

Chamber of Commerce. It was prepared to support the principle that imports from non-empire countries should bear a general indication of origin, such as 'Foreign Manufacture', but it was totally opposed to any requirement that the country of origin be disclosed.[51] The most serious opposition to the FBI was provided by the fancy goods, paper, silk, and textile trades sections of the LCC, all of whom opined that country-of-origin marking would be detrimental to Britain's export and re-export trade.[52] In general, the LCC supported the view that country-of-origin marking was undesirable, but it was not unanimous on the question of whether non-empire imports should be marked 'foreign'.[53]

The Board of Trade was sympathetic to the claim that compulsory indications of origin would damage Britain's re-export trade. In April 1926, the FBI sent a deputation to this Board urging compulsory marking, but it was rebuffed. Some industries did not want compulsory origin marking and thought that it would still be necessary to hear applications for exemption. The Board of Trade argued that use of country-of-origin marking was not necessary if the purpose of the bill was to permit British consumers to distinguish domestic from foreign products. Moreover, because the bill would apply to British dominions and foreign countries, it was thought politically impracticable to impose the same marking requirements on imports from empire and non-empire countries.[54]

Later in 1926, the Board of Trade indicated to the British Federation of Traders' Associations that: 'The President has been consistently opposed to a request that all goods should be marked before importation having regard particularly to the requirements of the entrepôt trade'.[55] Cunliffe-Lister's opposition to the FBI's proposals was re-asserted before the

---

[51] Guildhall. MS. 14476. Associated Chambers of Commerce. *Meeting of the Executive Council*: 1 October 1924; 3 December 1924; 6 May 1925; 3 February 1926; 66th Annual General Meeting of the Association of British Chambers of Commerce, 22–23 April 1926.

[52] Guildhall, London Chamber of Commerce. MS. 16459/10. London Chamber of Commerce. *Minutes of Meeting of Council*: 8 June 1922; 13 July 1922; 8 November 1923; 10 July 1924; 14 May 1925; 11 February 1926; 8 April 1926.

[53] Guildhall, London Chamber of Commerce. MS. 16459/10. *Minutes of Meeting of Council*: 9 April 1925; 14 January 1926.

[54] MRC/FBI. MS. 200 F1/1/1/155. *Minutes of the Committee on Trade Marks and Merchandise Marks and Others, 1919–1926*: Report of deputation to the Board of Trade on the Merchandise Marks Bill, 16 April 1926. Similarly, use of the term 'imported' was disliked because it did not distinguish between empire and foreign products. Cunliffe-Lister, Merchandise Marks (Imported Goods) Bill, Standing Committee, B, 22 June 1926: 642–644.

[55] Guildhall. MS. 16781. British Federation of Traders' Associations. *Minute Book*: Brown to Lloyd, 16 July 1926.

Standing Committee established to consider the Merchandise Marks (Imported Goods) Bill in 1926: 'It is important to consider the interests of the entrepôt trade, because that involves more than a certain number of merchants; it carries an enormous amount of shipping with it.'[56] He explained that his opposition to compulsory marking of indication of origin was not based on anti-protectionist motives; rather, it was necessary to recognise that many industries had a large export and re-export trade.[57] Not only was Cunliffe-Lister responsible for introducing the Merchandise Marks Bill but he also introduced a safeguard specifically to protect the re-export trade.[58]

BRITISH INDUSTRY AND THE MERCHANDISE MARKS ACT, 1926

Legislation enacting one of the recommendations of the Merchandise Marks Committee of 1919–1920 was eventually provided by the Merchandise Marks Act, 1926.[59] A key feature of this Act was that products which were imported blank could be required to bear an indication of origin. This represented a radical departure from previous legislation which defined precise criteria governing the imposition of marks of origin. The 1926 Act contained a number of provisions governing operation, type of marking, and safeguards. Two standing committees were established to approve Marking Orders. The first committee, under the auspices of the Ministry of Agriculture and Fisheries and the Secretaries of State for the Home Department and Scotland, dealt with agricultural and horticultural produce and the produce of any fishing industry. The second committee, which reported to the Board of Trade, was responsible for manufactures. Application for a Marking Order had to satisfy the following criteria: it would only be referred to a Standing Committee if it 'substantially represents the interests of either manufacturers, producers, dealers, traders, users, or consumers, or of any body of wage earners'. Second, the Standing Committee had to be satisfied that

---

[56] Cunliffe-Lister, Merchandise Marks (Imported Goods) Bill, Standing Committee, B, 22 June 1926: 623–624, 698.

[57] Cunliffe-Lister, Merchandise Marks (Imported Goods) Bill, Standing Committee, B, 22 June 1926: 690.

[58] This was to be achieved by importers paying a bond to customs which would be returned once the goods were re-exported. Cunliffe-Lister, Merchandise Marks (Imported Goods) Bill, Standing Committee, B, 22 June 1926: 759.

[59] 16 & 17 Geo. 5 Ch. 53, Merchandise Marks Act, 1926.

British trade, including trade with the empire and the re-export trade, were not adversely affected by a Marking Order. Standing Committees had a range of options available when deciding the type of marking required: foreign goods could be marked prior to importation and/or they could be marked prior to sale within Britain (by retail, wholesale, or both). Provision was also made that marking would not include 'exposure for sale wholesale by a person being a wholesale dealer'. Exemptions were introduced to provide for unforeseen consequences of the Act. For example, a Standing Committee could grant exemptions if it was satisfied that those with a 'substantial interest' would be adversely affected by an Order. Similarly, Standing Committees were authorised to amend existing Orders (for example, changing a sale Order to an import Order).[60]

Between 1927 and 1939, the Standing Committees heard evidence from witnesses representing a diverse range of consumer products including boots, shoes and slippers, briar pipes and bowls, clocks, corsets, fountain pens and propelling pencils, hosiery, knitted products and women's and girls' garments, granite grave monuments, and mowing machines. Intermediate products also figured prominently, for example, chucks for lathes, electric wire and cable, electricity meters, enamel zinc sheets, mill bobbins, Portland cement, and sheet lead and lead pipes. Between 1927 and 1939, the Standing Committees heard 113 applications for marking, of which nine were for import Orders only, thirty were for sales Orders only, and seventy-four were for both import and sales Orders.[61] The fundamental difference between an import and a sales Order was that the former operated at the port of entry and was enforced by customs, whereas the latter did not operate until the goods were sold or exposed for sale in Britain.[62]

Success and failure rates of these applications are shown in Table 5.1, from which a number of observations can be made. Approximately 40 per cent of applications for import Orders were successful, compared

---

[60] 16 & 17 Geo. 5 Ch. 53, Merchandise Marks Act, 1926, s.2, (1), (3), (5); s.10, (4) (b); s.3 (1); s.7 (2).

[61] This figure excludes applications for amendments to existing Orders and applications for exemptions.

[62] Board of Trade, Merchandise Marks Act, 1926: *Report of the Standing Committee* (hereafter, RSC) *on Iron and Steel*. P.P. XI.113. London: HMSO (1927): 5. Where an applicant desired a sale Order this would normally be granted unless there were overriding reasons to the contrary and the onus of proof was on the *objectors* rather than the applicants. For import Orders the onus of proof was on the *applicants*. TNA, BT 63/2/1. *Merchandise Marks. Pumps. Report of the Standing Committee*: Marker to Bremner, 25 October 1927.

TABLE 5.1 *Success and failure of applications for Orders in Council, 1927–1939*[1]

	Number	%
Marking: Importation Orders[2]		
Applications	82	100
Rejections	51	62.2
Approved	31	37.8
Marking: Sale Orders[3]		
Applications	104	100
Rejections	3	n.a.
Approved	110	n.a.

Source: Calculated from: Board of Trade, Merchandise Marks Act, 1926: *Report of the Standing Committee* (all applications)
Notes
(1) The data in Table 5.1 do not include exemption or amendment Orders (e.g., converting an existing sales Order into an import Order).
(2) This figure excludes four applications for import Orders which were withdrawn during the enquiry.
(3) Three applications for sale Orders were rejected. In addition, six applications for an import Order were refused, but granted a sales Order instead.
(4) Data do not include three foodstuffs – tea, maize/maize starch, and salt, which were referred to the Board of Trade instead of the Board of Agriculture.

to a success rate in excess of 100 per cent for sales Orders. The explanation for this latter observation is that six applications for import Orders only were rejected and awarded sales Orders instead.[63] A second observation is that almost all applications for sales Orders were successful, although much depended on whether the Order was to apply to a single product, or a range of related products within a single application. For example, single product applications such as folding coat hangers, mill bobbins, and school rules were granted in their entirety, but this was not the case for multi-part or multi-product applications. Thus, sales Orders for marking on cutlery and pottery did not apply, respectively, to blanks, handles, and

---

[63] These were: cast iron enamel baths, chucks for lathes and machine tools, radio goods, roofing slates, rubber tyres and tubes, and strap butts. In a few other applications it is not entirely clear whether an application was, in fact, made for a sales Order.

safety razors, or to electrical ware and door fittings. In only three cases – boxes and cartons, cased tubes, and sheet lead and pipes – were applications for a sale Order totally rejected.

The primary objective of all Marking Orders was to ensure that British consumers were not confused about the origin of the products they wished to purchase. Even when goods were imported blank, their 'get-up' often suggested British provenance. In the furniture and grave monument industries, foreign firms copied British designs so closely that it was difficult even for experts to differentiate geographical origin.[64] Use of 'Wilton', 'Warranted best steel', 'Pocket balance', 'Hand forged', 'Unbreakable', and 'English cut glass' confused consumers purchasing carpets, cutlery, spring balances, tools, hair combs, and flint glass products, while misleading advertisements in catalogues created bewilderment for those buying asbestos cement products, domestic and fancy glassware, and measuring tapes.[65] To be successful, all applications had to overcome a number of obstacles which included satisfying the Standing Committee that the products in the proposed Order were free from definitional ambiguity. Additionally, to secure an import Order applicants had to prove that this would not damage the re-export trade or be unduly onerous for customs authorities. Each of these obstacles is discussed in what follows.

The first obstacle involved more than semantics: any ambiguity in definition or interpretation could nullify the effectiveness of an Order. Applicants in the firearms industry sought the marking of imported gun parts, not including smooth bore tubes. Such a stance clearly conflicted with the fundamental aim of the Merchandise Marks Act, 1926, and Board of Trade officials opined that the Standing Committee might take the view that 'if it were necessary for the purchaser of a rifle to know that the trigger was imported, it was equally necessary for him to know that the

---

[64] RSC, *Respecting Furniture and Cabinet Ware*, P.P. XI.199. London: HMSO (1927): 4; RSC, *Respecting Granite Monuments and Enclosures and Parts*. P.P. VIII.555. London: HMSO (1928): 4.

[65] RSC, *Respecting Carpets, Rugs and Mats*. P.P. VIII.537. London: HMSO (1928):4; RSC, *Respecting Cutlery*. P.P. VIII.475. London: HMSO (1928): 4; RSC, *Respecting Spring Balances*. P.P. VIII.561. London: HMSO (1929): 3; RSC, *Respecting Tools*. P.P. XVI.51. London: HMSO (1929): 4; RSC, *Respecting Hair Combs and Blanks Therefor*. P.P. XIV.227. London: HMSO (1934):4; Committee on Industry and Trade, *Minutes of Evidence*, Volume 1 (1931): 1297; RSC, *Respecting Asbestos Cement Products*. P.P. XVI.35. London: HMSO (1929):4; RSC, *Respecting Domestic, etc., Glassware and Glass Bottles*. P.P. XVI.13. London: HMSO (1929): 4; RSC, *Respecting Measuring Tapes Made of Cotton or Linen*. P.P. X.805. London: HMSO (1933): 3.

tube was imported'.[66] Responding to the application for marking in the toy industry, officials at the Board of Trade consulted four dictionaries and became confounded with questions such as: was there a difference between 'games' and 'things for playing games with'? Similarly, '[p]lay-things perhaps suggests the exclusion of any game which is played by rule; but could not we say "requisites for games other than sports"?'[67] Finally, even after an Order had been granted, there was uncertainty within the Board of Trade about which foreign articles needed to be marked. For example, while dental aprons, enemas, and nasal syringes had to be marked with an indication of origin, atomisers, throat sprays, and bed pans were 'in the Board's view probably not covered'. The secretary to this Standing Committee stated, 'I am not clear what is meant by a throat spray. I should have thought that [it] would either be the same as an atomiser, or a syringe. If an atomiser it is out; if a syringe it is in.'[68]

Import Orders were particularly valued because the onus for marking was placed on foreign manufacturers, but, as Table 5.1 indicates, these Orders were more difficult to secure. One of the principal reasons why import Orders were refused was the excessive burden they imposed on customs. Referring to the application by the air-compressor industry, an official stated, 'a certain amount of technical knowledge, which [customs] officers would not, normally, possess, is essential in order to identify the goods in question, and further that most of the parts specified are indistinguishable from similar parts intended for use with other machines or appliances'.[69]

If successful, the application for an import Order by firms in the box and carton industry would have paralysed customs with its operational complexity. A key feature of this application was whether an indication of origin embossed on boxes and containers also pertained to their contents. Thus, British products packed in foreign boxes required an indication of origin on the box, but this did not apply to British products packed in British boxes. Similarly, foreign products packed in British boxes did not

---

[66] TNA, BT 63/3/6. *Merchandise Marks. Firearms. Report of Standing Committee*: Reardon to Marker, 24 May 1928.

[67] TNA, BT 63/6/2. *Merchandise Marks. Toys, Imported, Indication of Origin*: Minute 8 April 1930.

[68] TNA, BT 63/3/10. *Merchandise Marks. Certain Rubber or Part Rubber Articles. Application of Surgical Instruments Order*: Carlill to North & Co. Ltd., 12 July 1929; Minute by Reardon, 12 April 1929.

[69] TNA, BT 63/8/6. *Merchandise Marks Act. Air and Gas Compressors, Pneumatic Tools. Report of Standing Committee*: Letter to Fennelly, 8 July 1930.

require an indication of origin on the box, but foreign products *packed in Britain* in foreign boxes did require an indication of origin on the box. Finally, foreign products imported in foreign boxes and sold in the same box did not require an indication of origin on the box. With classic understatement, worthy of *Yes Minister's* Sir Humphrey Appleby, it was suggested that the wording proposed in the application 'might possibly cause some confusion'.[70] Other examples were application for an import Order was refused because of the burden imposed on customs included: gold and silver leaf (difficulty in distinguishing between gold leaf and imitation gold leaf, and between silver leaf and aluminium leaf), cast iron enamel baths (impracticable for customs to identify baths of cast iron from those of other material such as pressed steel, and to decide whether the material with which the bath was coated was porcelain enamel), as well as 'Portland' cement (how to differentiate this cement from other cements?).[71]

An important argument applicants used to secure an import Order was that the extra duties imposed on customs were negligible because the products were already subject to customs inspection. Discussing the cutlery application, the Standing Committee stated, 'as the Customs already examine these goods for purposes of duty, an Importation Order would not add substantially to their work ... Moreover, the category of goods to be comprised within the proposed Order are already defined for purposes of Customs duty.' Similar considerations applied to ball and roller bearings, electric incandescent lamps, hollowware, pottery, and scientific glassware.[72] Another equally important argument, deployed by manufacturers of clocks, picture and greeting postcards, and solid-headed pins, was that the re-export trade was minimal.[73]

---

[70] TNA, BT 63/6/4. *Merchandise Marks. Imported Boxes, Cartons, Cases and other Containers Made of Cardboard, etc. Report of Standing Committee*: Minute by Marker, 26 March 1929.

[71] RSC, *Respecting Gold and Silver Leaf*. P.P. XI.107. London: HMSO (1927): 4; RSC, *Respecting Cast Iron Enamel Baths* P.P. XI.611. London: HMSO (1928): 4; RSC, *Respecting Portland Cement*. P.P. XVI.59. London: HMSO (1929): 5–6.

[72] RSC, *Respecting Cutlery*: 6; RSC, *Respecting Electric Incandescent Lamps*. P.P. XI.625. London: HMSO (1928): 4; RSC, *Respecting Sanitary Ware of Pottery*. P.P. XIII.721. London: HMSO (1938): 7; RSC, *Respecting Scientific Glassware*. P.P. XVI.27. London: HMSO (1929): 4.

[73] RSC, *Respecting Clocks, Movements, Escapements, and Synchronous Motors*. P.P. XIV.877. London: HMSO (1933): 7; RSC, *Respecting Picture and Greeting Postcards*. P.P. XI.565. London: HMSO (1937): 5; RSC, *Respecting Solid Headed Pins of Brass, Iron or Steel*. P.P. XIII.699. London: HMSO (1938): 4.

In practice, considerable overlap existed between import and sales Orders. For example, opposition to the application for an import and sales Order by the boot and shoe industry was based on the claim that marking would advertise foreign goods to the detriment of the domestic industry, even though this advertisement would have occurred with either type of Order. Applicants for import Orders believed that sales Orders *alone* were ineffective, largely because of the difficulty in determining whether certain products were British or foreign.[74] Consequently, in situations where a sales Order was being contravened, there was no guarantee that a plaintiff could adduce evidence which would satisfy the courts.[75] In this situation, unsuccessful litigation generated further uncertainty and might have encouraged greater evasion of an Order. For example, in 1931, the Brass Founders Employers' Association informed the Board of Trade that a British firm was selling German shower bath fittings without an indication of origin. Faced with the reluctance of the complainants to provide an expert witness, the Board of Trade explained, 'I am afraid you may think us a little tricky over this prosecution but the difficulty is that we must be absolutely sure of our case before we go into Court. We feel it would have a very bad effect if we took a merchandise marks prosecution and lost it even on a technicality', before adding, '[m]erchandise marks proceedings are by way of being quasi-criminal proceedings, and the Courts are rather particular as to the evidence'.[76]

The 1926 Act encouraged rival firms to inform the Board of Trade of actual or perceived transgressions. But this did not always guarantee a successful outcome. In a tiresome and circuitous complaint, begun in May 1928 and concluded in April 1929, British Castors informed the Board of Trade that foreign castors were being imported and sold without

---

[74] For example, RSC, *Respecting Insulated Electric Cables and Wires*. P.P. XI.575. London: HMSO (1928): 9; RSC, *Respecting Machinery Belting*. P.P. XVI.83. London: HMSO (1930): 6; RSC, *Respecting Electricity Meters and Parts Thereof*. P.P. XV.807. London: HMSO (1931): 4–5; RSC, *Respecting Printing Blocks*. P.P. XIV.791. London: HMSO (1933): 4.

[75] RSC, *Respecting Spectacle Frames, Fronts, Slides, and Bridges; And Eyeglass Frames and Bridges*. P.P.V.1. London: HMSO (1939):4; RSC, *Respecting Watch Straps, etc.* P.P. XIII.707. London: HMSO (1938):4; RSC, *Hair Combs and Blanks Therefor*: 5.

[76] TNA, BT 63/9/14. *Merchandise Marks. Shaving Brushes Assembled from Imported Materials not 'British Made'*. Letter to the Brass Founders Association, 10 November 1931; 13 November 1931. A successful prosecution was eventually brought against the defendant, H. H. Williams, who was fined fifty shillings and ordered to pay costs of £ 5–5–0 to the prosecution. Ibid.

an indication of origin. However, despite entreaties by this Board, the company was initially unwilling to divulge this information, believing it would be obvious they were the informants – which would damage their business relations with the suspect company. When they subsequently identified the transgressor as J. & J. Taunton, they had the 'strongest objection' to the Board of Trade taking any action, reiterating the damage this would do to their business. Unsurprisingly, this exasperated officials:

[T]hese people are so stupid that we can make no progress. They make a serious allegation against Messrs. Taunton which they wish to be treated as strictly confidential! What is the good of it? ... One feels tempted to reply that we strongly deprecate the making of allegations which the firm are apparently loathe to substantiate.[77]

The Board of Trade were tempted to inform British Castors that unless they supplied more evidence, further proceedings would be abandoned. Such a gambit was not without risk: it might appear that the Board were unsympathetic to the genuine complaints of manufacturers and unwilling to instigate action even when justified. Fortunately, the Board's solicitor devised an ingenious solution to this problem. At a subsequent meeting British Castors were informed that, without more evidence, the Board was unwilling to take any further action; if this course was disagreeable, they were free to seek an import Order. However, as the solicitor explained:

I felt sure that the [Standing] [C]ommittee would first of all ask whether any attempt had been made to enforce the Order, and the applicants would then have to admit that they had refused on business grounds to assist the Board in the matter of obtaining the necessary evidence. In these circumstances it was impossible to say that the matter had been tested in the Courts and that the Order had been found as a result to be unenforceable.[78]

In other cases, successful prosecutions were instigated by either the Board of Trade or the relevant trade association. The Board was empowered to instigate prosecutions in cases which appeared to affect 'the general interests of the country, or of a section of the community, or of a trade'. Trade associations were similarly empowered by regulations made by the Board for the enforcement of the 1926 Act.[79] To secure

---

[77] TNA, BT 63/3/11. *Merchandise Marks. Furniture Castors. Application of Marking Order*: Minute by Marker, 17 August 1928; Owen to Board of Trade, 24 August 1928.
[78] TNA, BT 63/3/11. *Merchandise Marks. Furniture Castors. Application of Marking Order*: Minute 8 March 1929.
[79] 54 Vict. Ch. 15. Merchandise Marks Act, 1891, s.2; Merchandise Marks (Imported Goods) Order, 1927.

convincing evidence that would justify litigation, clandestine methods, often involving agents, were used. In an action brought against the Surgical Manufacturing Company, separate purchases by a specialist instrument maker and a nurse were sufficient to secure a conviction.[80] The prosecution of a furniture retailer required a visit by a member of the London Cabinet and Upholstery Trades Federation during which it was noted:

A certain person ... visited the shop in question this afternoon. There was only a boy there but our representative said that he had come in to look at the suites shown in the window. There were no marks at all on those in sight and he said to the boy 'I suppose those are English bedroom suites?' The reply was 'No they are Italian and we have removed the marks.'[81]

DIFFERENT PERSPECTIVES ON THE MERCHANDISE
MARKS ACT, 1926

The fundamental aim of the 1926 Act was to prevent consumer confusion about the geographical origin of products. Consequently, the Act provided that an application which 'substantially represents the interests of ... consumers'[82] was eligible for consideration by a Standing Committee. However, in *no* case were the views of consumers included in applications for Marking Orders. A related question is: how accurate was the belief that consumers genuinely preferred British products but were unable to exercise this preference because of misrepresentation? Examination of the evidence used by applicants seeking import and/or sales Orders suggests that consumer preference for British products was limited to boots, shoes, and slippers, rubber manufactures, firearms and parts, wall and ceiling papers, brooms and brushes, and spectacles.[83]

    In other industries, it was reported that architects and public authorities often specified 'British made' in contracts governing the supply of sheet lead and lead pipes, enamel zinc sheets, carbon papers, copper

---

[80] 'Sale of surgical goods', *The Times*, 11 December 1930, 18.
[81] TNA, BT 63/6/1. *Merchandise Marks. Furniture Imported without an Indication of Origin. Prosecution*: Taylor to Board of Trade, 21 February 1930.
[82] Merchandise Marks Act, 1926, 16 & 17 Geo, Ch. 53, s 2 (3).
[83] RSC, *Respecting Boots, Shoes and Slippers (other than Rubber ...* P.P. XI.543. London: HMSO (1928): 4; RSC, *Respecting Rubber Manufactures.* P.P. VIII.575. London: HMSO (1929): 4; RSC, *Respecting Firearms and Parts Thereof.* P.P. VIII.601. London: HMSO (1929): 4; RSC, *Respecting Wall Papers, Ceiling Papers, etc.* P.P. XVI.109. London: HMSO (1930): 4; RSC, *Respecting Spectacle Frames, Fronts, Slides, and Bridges*: 4.

plates, and Portland cement. British advertising firms preferred British printing blocks. In response to customer demand, the Cased Tube Association instructed its members to mark their products 'British made'.[84] Finally, the scientific community and British hospitals specified British-made scientific glassware and crepe bandages, respectively; in surgical, medical, dental, and veterinary products it was stated, 'no surgeon or doctor would use instruments permanently marked with an indication of their foreign origin'.[85] From a total of 114 applications, only 22, or 19.4 per cent, made any direct reference to whether consumers demanded or preferred British goods, or bought foreign goods under the impression they were buying British. Overall, while demands for origin-marking schemes were motivated by a desire for 'honest trade' and the protection of the British consumer, it appears that British manufacturers used consumer preference as a pretext to secure origin marking.

Was it the case that applications for Marking Orders were motivated by protectionist desires? One way to address this question is to consider how much overlap existed between industries applying for origin marking and those that secured protection via safeguarding legislation. In the post-1925 period the answer is generally negative. Between 1927 and 1939, more than 100 sale Orders were approved. In contrast, in the post-1925 period, just sixteen applications were made for safeguarding, not all of which were successful.[86] Viewed from this perspective it is hard to believe that industries that failed to secure safeguarding sought origin marking as an alternative form of protection. Moreover, if misrepresentation was prevalent, origin marking ensured consumers could exercise their preferences for domestic *and* foreign products. It may be argued that the scale of misrepresentation was negligible in those industries not deemed important enough to warrant safeguarding. For example, the application for a Marking Order for school rulers was made on behalf of an industry which employed fewer than 100 workers producing an annual output which did not exceed £25,000.[87] With the possible exceptions of electric

---

[84] RSC, *Respecting Cased Tubes*. P.P. XIII.253. London: HMSO (1939): 3.

[85] RSC, *Respecting Surgical, Medical, Dental and Veterinary Instruments and Appliances* ... P.P. VIII.467. London: HMSO (1928): 6.

[86] Marrison, *British Business*, 443–446. The figure quoted does not double-count industries making more than one application, for example, hosiery. The successful applicants included cutlery, pottery, and gas mantles. Board of Trade, Safeguarding of Industries: *Report of the Committee on Cutlery*: 17; Board of Trade, Safeguarding of Industries: *Report of the Committee on Gas Mantles*: 13.

[87] TNA, BT 63/2/10. *Merchandise Marks. Wood Rulers as Used in Schools. Report of Standing Committee*: Minute by Marker, 17 March 1928.

cables and wires, iron and steel, and scientific glassware, it is difficult to believe that the other industries which applied for Marking Orders were of strategic importance to the British economy.

Moreover, the efficacy of marking as a form of protection was undermined by well-documented evasion, partly attributable to weaknesses in the 1926 Act. For example, foreign products which were 'substantially changed' after import were not required to be marked with an indication of origin.[88] The NUM alleged that this loophole enabled ready-made clothing containing foreign material to be sold in Britain to people who assumed it was British. This organisation identified other loopholes. For example, product samples did not have to be marked if their origin was communicated in writing. If a sale was made verbally, it was not until the products were delivered that their foreign origin needed to be revealed on the invoice.[89] The FBI complained that other loopholes in the Act meant that foreign bicycle bells and lamps were 'being freely advertised without the necessity for it to be stated that they were of foreign origin. The Act was not affording the protection originally hoped for'.[90] Producers of sanitary ware of pottery claimed that the marking prescribed by the import and sales Order awarded to them in 1928 was not very effective: 'a mark which was accepted as conspicuous by customs at the time of importation, nevertheless proved to be valueless at the time of exposure for sale'.[91] Cyril Salmon, representing the wooden tobacco pipe and bowl trade, claimed that their sale Order, granted in 1929, 'had proved so difficult to enforce as to be virtually ineffective. In their view it was possible to evade the existing Order with impunity'.[92]

Nonetheless, weaknesses in the design and implementation of the 1926 Act helped set in motion broader concerns about misrepresentation, especially the use of trade descriptions such as 'British made' by domestic manufacturers – the mirror image of requiring foreign origin to be marked on British imports. For example, should statutory provision for trade descriptions be restricted to mode of manufacture and

---

[88] 16 &17 Geo, Ch. 23. *Merchandise Marks Act*, 1926 s.10 (1).
[89] *The Times*, 18 February 1935, 19.
[90] MRC/FBI/ MSS 200/F/1/1/15, Minutes of executive committee, 18 November 1936. The loophole identified was contained in Section 5(2) of the Merchandise Marks Act, 1926: it was only an offence to advertise foreign products subject to a Marking Order if they were embossed with a particular brand or designation.
[91] RSC, *Respecting Sanitary Ware of Pottery*: 3.
[92] RSC, *Respecting Wooden Tobacco Pipes and Bowls therefor.* P.P. XIV. 871. London: HMSO (1933): 2.

materials, or should it be extended to geographical indications? If the former, how would 'British made' be meaningfully defined when it covered an extensive range of products? If the latter, consider the inequity of rejecting trade descriptions which included a geographical name. Referring to the general misuse of the term 'British made', the Board of Trade lamented: 'It is a matter of common knowledge that this word is used with different meanings in different connections. The Board have no authority to define the limits within which the word may be used or to decide whether its use in a particular context is legitimate or not.'[93]

Concern about misrepresentation affected foreign companies operating in Britain. Many studies have documented the growth of American and European foreign direct investment in Britain during the interwar years.[94] Following the 1926 Act, the issue of whether products made in Britain by foreign companies needed be marked with an indication of origin, became a source of concern to MNCs, and was reflected in their opposition to Marking Orders. For example, the Goodyear Tyre and Rubber Co., the Firestone Tyre and Rubber Co., and the Michelin Tyre Co., Ltd. argued that to impose a Marking Order on rubber tyres would 'be tantamount to a prohibition on advertising'; the application for a Marking Order on surgical and medical products was opposed by the leading German and American optical manufacturers, Carl Zeiss, Emil Busch Optical Co., Ltd., and the American Optical Company, respectively, on the grounds that customs examination at the port of entry would damage delicate equipment.[95]

Ford Motor Company was concerned about the adverse effects of marking 'Made in the USA' on their British-made motor cars. This was a particularly sensitive issue in 1927 because Ford intended to cease production at Trafford Park, Manchester, in order to re-tool for a new car. To avoid disruption to their sales campaign, Ford sought an exemption from the 1926 Act which would allow them to import 'blank' a large

---

[93] TNA, BT 63/11/8. *Merchandise Marks. 'British'. Use of Description on 'Empire' Goods. Summary of Board of Trade Replies*. Minute by Reardon, 24 February 1932.

[94] F. Bostock and G. Jones, 'Foreign Multinationals in British Manufacturing, 1850–1962', *Business History*, 36 (1994): 89–126; G. Jones and F. Bostock. 'U.S. Multinationals in British Manufacturing before 1962', *Business History Review*, 70 (1996): 207–256; S. R. Fletcher and A. Godley, 'Foreign Direct Investment in British Retailing, 1850–1962', *Business History*, 42 (2000): 43–62. A. Godley, 'Foreign Multinationals and Innovation in British Retailing, 1850–1962', *Business History*, 45 (2003): 80–100.

[95] RSC, *Respecting Rubber Tyres and Tubes*. P.P. XI.167. London: HMSO (1927): 5; RSC, *Respecting Surgical, Medical, Dental and Veterinary Instruments* . . .: 5.

part of the new model from the United States while the Manchester factory was being re-fitted. To support their claim, Ford argued:

[A] tremendous amount of money, time and efforts have been expended on publicity ... to live down the tradition that the 'Ford' in this country was an American Car. Our efforts in this direction, however, will be discounted to a very great extent if ... it is necessary to import a large percentage of the car and if these have to be run about the country, marked 'Made in the USA' on the Radiator and other prominent place owing to the fact that such parts are branded 'Ford'.[96]

During the transition phase, estimated at three months, 65 per cent of the prime cost of the new car would be imported from the United States. This conflicted with the views of the British Association of Motor Manufacturers and Traders, which argued that a car could only be described as 'British' if at least 75 per cent of the value of the chassis was made in Britain. Nonetheless, the Board of Trade thought that 'no useful purpose would be served by requiring qualification of the word "Ford" on imported parts'.[97] The Board based its decision on the following criteria. First, doubts were raised about whether the assembled car needed an indication of origin since 'the car is something different from the parts which go to compose it'. There was a risk that an indication of origin would lead British consumers to think the car was foreign, when, after the transition phase, it could rightly be described as 'British'. The Board also recognised that even if an exemption was granted there was no question that it would mislead the public because the car had generated substantial public interest and 'everybody interested knows that, at any rate to begin with, it will largely be produced in the U.S.'. Finally, the Board was satisfied that the parts imported by Ford would be used in the assembly of Ford cars and would not be sold separately to British dealers in motor car parts.[98]

Phillips & Co. (electrical product manufacturers based in Holland) and the Yale and Towne Manufacturing Co. (manufacturers of locks, keys,

---

[96] TNA, BT 64/40. *Merchandise Marks Act. Motor-Cars, Motor-Cycles and Pedal Cycles Made from foreign Components and Assembled in ...*: Ford Motor Company (England) to Customs and Excise, 29 August 1927.

[97] TNA, BT 64/40. *Merchandise Marks Act. Motor-Cars, Motor-Cycles and Pedal Cycles Made from foreign Components and Assembled in ...*: Minute dated 2 August 1927; Fountain to Customs and Excise, 21 September 1927; Minute to Fountain, 15 September 1927.

[98] TNA, BT 64/40. *Merchandise Marks Act. Motor-Cars, Motor-Cycles and Pedal Cycles Made from foreign Components and Assembled in ...*: Minute by Marker, 15 March 1927; Minute to Marker, 2 August 1927; Minute to Fountain, 15 September 1927.

and safe equipment, located in Connecticut, USA) confronted different, but equally challenging problems. These companies were based in Holland and the United States, respectively, and both had subsidiary companies located in Britain. Were these subsidiaries permitted to import products from their parent companies and sell them in Britain without an indication of origin? If the answer was affirmative, the Board of Trade recognised that foreign firms would easily circumvent the 1926 Act by establishing subsidiary companies in Britain. Much depended on the perceptions of British consumers. For example, '[n]o one purchasing these lamps from Phillips Lamps Limited would imagine that they were not the product of the English company'. As regards Yale, the Board stated: 'For many years the only name on the goods has been that of the Manufacturing Company and probably very few of the public know of any other Company at all … it seems to me absurd that the Company's own name can "purport to be" the name of some other trader.'[99] Despite these observations, the Law Officers determined that exports from Phillips & Co. and the Yale and Towne Manufacturing Co. to their British subsidiaries had to bear an indication of origin.[100]

Determining whether the 1926 Act was a success is difficult because no statute is ever totally observed or fully enforced. Use of quantitative measures such as imports is potentially treacherous: the definition of products in Marking Orders does not always match exactly the definitions used in official trade returns. Some products which were subject to Marking Orders – watchstraps, mill bobbins, screw bottle stoppers, Portland cement – were not individually enumerated in the Board of Trade returns. Applications involving wire netting and woven wire and iron and steel encompassed a broader range of products than those specified in the trade returns, while other products such as medical, surgical, dental, and veterinary instruments were reported in terms of value, not quantity, and therefore varied with fluctuations in the sterling exchange rate. In any case, trends in import quantities are ambiguous: a fall in imports post-Order might indicate that consumers were free to accurately exercise their patriotic preferences, but the evidence shows that

---

[99] TNA, BT 63/1/3. *Merchandise Marks. Electric Lamps. Marking of Origin:* In the Matter of the N.V. Phillips Metaal-Gloeilampenfabriek and the Phillips Lamps Ltd. Case for the Opinion of the Law Officers; In the Matter of the Yale and Towne Manufacturing Co., and the Yale & Towne Co. Case for the Opinion of the Law Officers.

[100] TNA, BT 63/1/3. *Merchandise Marks. Electric Lamps. Marking of Origin:* Cook to Messrs. Gisborne & Co., 13 August 1928; Cook to Messrs. Janson, Cobb, Pearson & Co., 13 August 1928.

the *general* trend of imports declined sharply between 1930 and 1933 (because of the depression and the imposition of tariffs), but grew thereafter. Conversely, a rise in imports might indicate that Marking Orders had backfired because consumers preferred to purchase foreign products. Determining whether consumer preference was based on price – and therefore subject to exchange rate fluctuation – or a perception that foreign products represented better value for money is an intractable issue. Moreover, some industries did not apply for Marking Orders until the late 1930s, so it is difficult, if not impossible, to determine the effects of their applications, especially if they were affected by war preparations.[101]

The number of prosecutions instigated by the Board of Trade is an alternative measure by which to judge the effectiveness of the 1926 Act. Although this yardstick is subject to obvious caveats – the Board was not solely responsible for instigating actions and not all cases were reported – it does provide some indication of the scale of misrepresentation and the level of official involvement in its eradication. Judging by the number of prosecutions instituted by the Board of Trade, it is hard to believe they were swamped by cases of misrepresentation. The number of prosecutions instituted by the Board under *all* Merchandise Marks Acts was forty-six over the period 1923–1942.[102] If we focus solely on prosecutions brought under the 1926 Act, the level of official involvement was relatively low: between 1928 and 1933, the Board instituted nineteen prosecutions.[103] However, the volume of official prosecutions is potentially ambiguous. One interpretation is that British business wholeheartedly obeyed the Act, but this rests uneasily with claims of substantial evasion. A further interpretation is that prosecutions under the 1926 Act are surprisingly small because the penalties for disregarding this Act were paltry. The Board of Agriculture complained that '[d]issatisfaction has been expressed by magistrates, local authorities, etc. from time to time with the alleged inadequacy of the penalties under Section 5 of the Merchandise Marks Act 1926'.[104]

---

[101] The picture and greeting postcard industry urged compulsory marks of origin in the 1880s, but did not apply for a Marking Order until 1937.

[102] TNA, BT 258/957. Committee on Consumer Protection: Board of Trade Submission on Merchandise Marks Acts: Minute 29 June 1961. The data are reported as quinquennial averages and relate to all types of mis-description.

[103] TNA, BT 64/39. *Merchandise Marks. Prosecutions by the Board of Trade, 1936–1938*.

[104] TNA, BT 63/9/4. *Merchandise Marks. Eggs. Inadequate Penalties for Fraudulent Removal of Marks*. 14 March 1931.

A final observation is that the drink and food industries, which were among the most visible in the British economy, do not feature in applications for Marking Orders. It may be argued that because the products of these industries were sufficiently differentiated by branding there could be no consumer confusion about their geographical origin. Thus, Cadbury's, and Rowntrees in chocolate confectionery, Lever Bros. in toiletries, and Bass and Guinness in brewing had expended considerable sums protecting and advertising their trademarks during the nineteenth and early twentieth centuries. Consequently, by the inter-war period, their products were quintessentially 'British'. Subsequently, these companies were joined in the interwar period by American producers owning equally famous brands – Kelloggs, Mars, Quaker Oats, and Shredded Wheat.[105] Another explanation why such companies were not involved in Marking Orders was that the processing of their inputs in Britain represented a 'substantial transformation' which removed the need for origin marking. Whichever explanation is preferred, it may be that use of private trademarks indicating trade origin was more valuable to consumers than merchandise marks depicting geographical origin.

CONCLUSIONS

The Merchandise Marks Act of 1926 was introduced to prevent the misrepresentation of foreign products sold in Britain. One of the unusual features of this legislation was that only foreign products were required to be marked with an indication of origin. This regulation was defensive: it was not designed to promote a 'Buy British' campaign by extolling the virtues of British manufactures. Moreover, the Act only applied to products sold in Britain, and therefore it did not benefit British exports. The stipulation that imports had to be marked with an indication of origin alleviated the concerns of domestic manufacturers owning valuable trademarks, and ensured that consumers could continue to exercise a preference for domestic products by rejecting those that were not British.

In one respect the Act was ineffectual. If the objective was to protect manufacturers from unfair competition, why not require that *all* imports be marked? A precedent for this was established in the United States by the McKinley tariff of 1890. Conversely, Argentina and Colombia

[105] Jones and Bostock, 'U.S. Multinationals'.

required that domestic products be marked 'Industria Argentine' and 'Industria Colombiana', respectively. In other countries, mandatory indication of country of origin was required for specific categories of products. In France, imports of wine, fish, and vegetables were prohibited unless they were marked with country of origin.[106] From another perspective, it can be argued that the 1926 Act was unnecessary: the Merchandise Marks Act, 1887, remained the principal statute governing misrepresentation of indications of origin. However, the 1926 Act did have one advantage over its 1887 predecessor: it could be applied to foreign 'blanks' at the time of their importation and/or sale. Given the clamour for marking, it is surprising that there were so few prosecutions. It may be that the Act was a deterrent, but this observation does not explain why some firms were reluctant to inform on rivals. Compared to the country-of-origin requirements of other countries, it appears that the British policy was a hybrid.

Perhaps the major explanation for Britain's failure to pursue a policy similar to the United States' was dissonance between manufacturers and merchants. The FBI was adamant that opposition from merchants was the biggest obstacle it faced when trying to secure the compulsory imposition of marks of origin on all imported products.[107] As noted earlier, merchant opposition to compulsory marks of origin on imports was long-standing and explains why the Select Committees of 1890 and 1897 were unwilling to adopt such a policy, and why the Committee of 1919–1920 recommended a compromise. Conflict between manufacturers and merchants is an enduring feature of British business and economic history. On the specific topic of 'Made in', it appears that the views of the 'gentleman capitalists' outweighed those of manufacturers.[108]

A final observation relates to marketing strategy. The majority of British manufacturers were unwilling to support legislation requiring that their products be marked with country of origin. This can be interpreted to mean that they perceived no gain from use of 'Made in Britain' or 'British made'. Consequently, despite the cause celebre of 'Made in Germany' in the 1880s, British manufacturers were unwilling to promote

---

[106] League of Nations. Economic and Financial Section. International Economic Conference. *Marks of Origin.* Document C.E.I. 20: 7, 25, 32.
[107] MRC/FBI. MSS.200/F1/1/1/155. *Minutes of the Committee on Trade Marks and Merchandise Marks and Others, 1919–1926:* 11 March 1926.
[108] P. J. Cain and A. G. Hopkins, *British Imperialism: Innovation and Expansion, 1688–1914* (London: Longman, 1993), 25.

'British' and thereby obtain the benefits that have been claimed for country of origin marking in the marketing literature. A related point is that historical debates on what constituted 'foreign' or 'British' anticipated current debates – discussed in Chapter 9 – about legitimate use of 'Swiss made' or 'Made in the USA'.

6

From Paris to London

The International Legal Framework for the Protection of IGOs, ca. 1880–1945

If it is to the interest of Sheffield to protect its good name, equally it is to the interests of any rising manufacturing place abroad to take care that a reputation being slowly built shall at all times be protected from fraudulent manufactures elsewhere.

Papers Relative to the Recent Conference at Rome on the Subject of Industrial Property, London: HMSO,(1886): 11

Vineyards took their shapes, their names, and their value from their soils, their slopes, and their shelter from bad weather; all the factors that go to make up their individual terroir … [but] Terroir was held by modernists to be French hocus-pocus, essentially meaning old French vineyards.

H. Johnson and J. Robinson, *The World Atlas of Wine*, 5th edition (London: Octopus Publishing Group, 2001), 6

The use of IGOs is an ancient custom. In the fourth century BC they were used on Corinthian wines, Sicilian honey, Naxos almonds, Paros marble, and Thasos wine. During Roman times they were applied to Egyptian dates, Brindisi oysters, and Iberian hams.[1] The rapid growth of international trade during the nineteenth century provided a fertile environment for the misuse of IGOs which necessitated efforts to provide for their international protection. The need for international, as opposed to national, or even bilateral safeguarding, coincided with growing recognition of '[t]he uncertainty, incompleteness, and inadequacy of the protection of foreigners' rights of industrial property afforded by the

---

[1] Devlétian, 'The Protection of Appellations and Indications of Origin', 9; V. Mantrov, *EU Law on Indications of Geographical Origin* (London: Springer, 2014), 33.

municipal law of ... various countries'.[2] Industrial or intellectual property, which includes patents, designs, trademarks, and copyright, has been defined as 'any potentially valuable human product (broadly "information") that has an existence separable from a unique physical embodiment'.[3]

This chapter begins with a discussion of the establishment of the Paris Convention for the Protection of Industrial Property in 1883 (hereafter, Paris Convention). This convention was the first attempt to develop international protocols for the protection of intellectual property, and it provided a framework which continues today. Particular attention is devoted to the higher protection afforded wine appellations compared to other products. In the third section of this chapter the broader problem of unfair competition is discussed. The penultimate section examines product-specific initiatives to combat unfair competition in the international egg trade and conclusions are drawn in the fifth section.

BUILDING AN INTERNATIONAL FRAMEWORK

Throughout the period covered by this chapter the most important multilateral agreement for the protection of IGOs was established by the Paris Convention and the Madrid Agreement for the Repression of False or Deceptive Indications of Source on Goods (hereafter, Madrid Agreement) which was signed in 1890.[4] The former developed from the Vienna Congress of 1873, and from earlier meetings in Paris, in 1878 and 1880, which sought international agreement on a broader range of intellectual property,[5] whereas the latter was solely concerned with false indications of origin. The Paris Convention and its successors (Table 6.1) were built on the fundamental premise that each Member State must apply to nationals of other Members 'the same treatment as it gives to its own nationals, without being allowed to require reciprocity'.[6] This Convention also established a broad set of protocols for its revision as

---

[2] Ladas, *Patents, Trademarks, and Related Rights*, 59.
[3] Landes and Posner, *The Economic Structure*, 1.
[4] The provisions of the Paris Convention provided the basis for subsequent multilateral agreements on the protection of trade names and IGOs involving North and South America. S. P. Ladas, 'Pan American Conventions on Industrial Property', *American Journal of International Law*, 22 (1928): 810.
[5] Ladas, *Patents, Trademarks and Related Rights*, 59–68.
[6] G. Bodenhausen, *Guide to the Application of the Paris Convention for the Protection of Industrial Property* (Geneva: United International Bureau for the Protection of Intellectual Property, 1969; reprinted by the World Intellectual Property Organization, 1991), 12.

TABLE 6.1 *Overview of the Paris Convention for the Protection of Industrial Property, 1883–1934*

1883	Paris Convention for the Protection of Industrial Property
	Article II requires that each contracting state must grant the same protection to citizens of other contracting states that it grants to its own citizens.
	Article IX provides for the seizure of imported goods illegally bearing a trademark or trade name if they are protected in the importing country.
	Article X extends Article IX to products falsely bearing the name of any locality as an indication of the place of origin when it is associated with a trade name of fictitious character, or assumed with fraudulent intent.
1886	First Conference of Revision, Rome
	No substantive changes to the Paris Convention.
1890–1891	Second Conference of Revision, Madrid
	No substantive changes to the Paris Convention.
1891	Madrid Agreement for the Repression of False or Deceptive Indications of Source on Goods
	This was a 'special' or 'restricted' union of members belonging to the Paris Convention.
	Article I stipulates that all goods bearing a false or deceptive indication of source by which one of the contracting states, or a place therein, is directly or indirectly indicated as being the country or place of origin must be seized on importation.
	Article IV empowered the courts in each member state to determine which appellations were generic, excluding 'products of the vine'.
1897	Third Conference of Revision, Brussels
	No substantive changes were made to the Paris Convention or the Madrid Agreement.
	Article X was amended to include 'dishonest competition'.
1911	Fourth Conference of Revision, Washington
	No substantive changes were made to the Paris Convention or the Madrid Agreement.
	Article X was amended to include 'unfair competition'.
1925	Fifth Conference of Revision, The Hague
	No substantive changes were made to the Paris Convention or the Madrid Agreement.
	'Unfair competition' was defined for the first time.
1934	Sixth Conference of Revision, London
	No substantive changes were made to the Paris Convention or the Madrid Agreement.

Note: This table only refers to IGOs.

well as rights of priority in the registration of intellectual property and the establishment, in Berne, of the International Office of the Union for the Protection of Industrial Property.

Of particular relevance to this book are Articles IX and X of the Paris Convention. The former stated:

All goods illegally bearing a trade-mark or trade name may be seized on importation into those States of the Union where this mark or name has the right to legal protection.

The seizure shall be effected at the request of either the proper Public department or of the interested party, pursuant to the internal legislation of each country.

Article X stipulated that:

The provisions of the preceding Article shall apply to all goods falsely bearing the name of any locality as indication of the place of origin, when such indication is associated with a trade name of a fictitious character or assumed with a fraudulent intention.

Any manufacturer of, or trader in, such goods, established in the locality falsely designated as the place of origin, shall be deemed an interested party.[7]

A crucial weakness in Article X was that it did not protect the name of a place: it applied only when it was joined to a fictitious business name or assumed with fraudulent intent. Effectively, the Paris Convention was implicitly authorising deception when false indications of origin alone were applied to products.[8] Further weaknesses in Article X became apparent. It was deemed inapplicable when products were embossed with the fictitious name of a locality or a fictitious trade name. Consider the indication 'Kenty-on-Trent'. Although the Trent is an English river, and many riverside towns use the term 'on Trent' – for example, Stoke-on Trent – 'Kenty' is not a town. Similarly, non-British products bearing the marks 'Smith and Fox, London' and 'Ingland Originale' escaped seizure because it was ruled that the invention of a fictitious name was not illegal.[9] By imposing restrictions on the operation of Article X, the Paris Convention ensured that only the most flagrant misuse of IGOs was

---

[7] *International Convention for the Protection of Industrial Property*. P.P. 87. C.4043, (1884): 7–8. At a previous conference it was proposed that there should be an absolute prohibition on false indications of origin. Ladas, *Patents, Trademarks and Related Rights*, 843.

[8] *Actes de la Conférence de la Haye*: 251.

[9] *Actes de la Conférence Réunie à Londres*: 196; TNA, BT 209/793: *False Indications and Appellations of Origin*: International Union for the Protection of Industrial Property, Lisbon Conference, Preliminary Documents: 3.

prohibited: 'Cases of ... compound fraud were indeed rare because they were so obvious that manufacturers or traders could not possibly get away with them.'[10]

This deficiency particularly aggrieved Sheffield's cutlery manufacturers. The Cutlers' Company was at the forefront of British efforts to alter Article X so that unqualified use of false IGOs was prohibited. The Company was not the only employers' body to complain of the misuse of IGOs,[11] but the reasons for Sheffield's importance in the British campaign to amend Article X are not difficult to discern. Two of Sheffield's MPs, Anthony Mundella and Howard Vincent, sat on various Select Committee hearings on merchandise marks in the later nineteenth century and introduced bills on this subject. Many of Sheffield's leading manufacturers gave evidence before these Committees, and the law clerk to the Cutlers' Company and secretary to the Sheffield chamber of commerce, Herbert Hughes, was a recognised authority in this area and a technical advisor to British delegations attending meetings of the Paris Convention held at Rome (1886), Madrid (1890), Brussels (1897–1900), and Washington (1911).

In urging the Foreign Office to seek an amendment to Article X, the Cutlers' Company argued it was protecting Sheffield from two adverse consequences of misrepresentation: the direct loss of sales when foreign manufacturers, especially those located in France and Germany, passed off their products as 'Sheffield', and the insidious reputational consequences when 'Sheffield' was applied to low-quality articles.[12] The campaigns launched by the Cutlers' Company coincided with growing Anglo–German trade rivalry. For example, it has been estimated that Germany's share of total British imports of 'miscellaneous manufactures' increased from 30 per cent in 1880 to 37 per cent in 1896. For particular product categories – such as toys and chinaware – Germany's share of total British imports was much higher, at 77 per cent and 54 per cent, respectively.[13]

[10] Ladas, *Patents, Trademarks and Related Rights*, 1580.
[11] Similar concerns were raised by the Redditch Needle & Fishhook Association. *Correspondence Relative to the Protection of Industrial Property*. P.P. 98. C. 5521 (1888): 22.
[12] *Papers Relative to the Recent Conference at Rome on the Subject of Industrial Property; and Correspondence Relating to the Fraudulent use of Trade Marks*. P.P. 60. C. 4837 (1886): 10, 19.
[13] C. Buchheim, 'Aspects of XIXth Century Anglo–German Trade Rivalry Reconsidered', *Journal of European Economic History*, X (1981): 285–286.

The Cutlers' Company faced two principal obstacles in trying to amend Article X. First, it needed to demonstrate that it had 'clean hands'. Second, it needed to prove that 'Sheffield' had not become a generic term. To make a convincing case that it was acting in the interests of a community, it was imperative that the Company demonstrated that Sheffield cutlers were beyond reproach – that they did not impress misleading IGOs on their products. On this point some caution is required because Sheffield manufacturers *did* impress their products with false IGOs. The Sheffield Trades Enquiry Report concluded that: 'the practice of putting labels on goods manufactured in Germany intimating that the same are from or manufactured by Sheffield firms exists to a large extent ... and, as such goods are generally of inferior workmanship, the practice has a natural tendency to bring Sheffield wares into disrepute'.[14] Exacerbating matters, this inquiry and evidence given before a Royal Commission revealed that Sheffield manufacturers conflated origin and quality. For example, a variety of products were stamped 'Cast Steel, Sheffield' but comprised low-grade Bessemer steel.[15] The date on which this evidence was published, 1886, was hardly propitious because it coincided with the Rome meeting of the Paris Convention.

A related problem, outside the control of the Cutlers' Company, was that British manufacturers embossed their products with foreign IGOs. 'Nouveanté de Paris', 'Articles de Paris', or 'Paris' were frequently applied to boots made in England, and porcelain made in Staffordshire was sold as 'Dresden China'.[16] Such practices constrained the bargaining power of the Cutlers' Company: because it was imperative that the reputations of *all* communities were protected, the Company could not focus on Sheffield alone; why should 'Sheffield' be protected if other regions were not? Conversely, foreign diplomats argued that the Company's defence of 'Sheffield' was undermined by the malpractice of some of its own manufacturers. Count Berchem, an official in the German foreign office, argued that these practices suited British manufacturers:

It was ... those countries, which had attained a higher development in industrial and commercial respects, which instigated the stamping of German goods ... by

[14] 'Borough of Sheffield. Trades Enquiry Committee: Report'. TNA, FO 83/1074, *Industrial Property Convention*, Vol. 1.
[15] *Second Report of the Royal Commission Appointed to Inquire into the Depression of Trade and Industry*. P.P. XXI. 231. C. 4715 (1886): QQ. 1143–1148; Q. 1214.
[16] *Second Report of the Royal Commission Appointed to Inquire into the Depression of Trade and Industry*, Q. 2964.

making use of the cheaper rates of wages, to give orders in Germany ... and then bringing them into the world market as their own manufacture without allowing the producer to have any notion of their foreign origin.[17]

These practices were contrasted with German efforts to prevent the use of false IGOs on domestic manufactures, including hats, woollen and jute products, pottery, and sewing machines.[18] In view of these claims, German reluctance to support British requests that Article X should also deal with situations when false indications alone were used seems understandable.

The use of terms such as 'Paris' by British manufacturers was part of a second, more fundamental obstacle to amending Article X and involved international treatment of generic marks. It was well established by the late nineteenth century that 'Eau de Cologne', 'Brussels' carpets, 'Russian' leather, and 'Utrecht' velvet referred to the manufacturing process, not geographical origin. Consequently, though misleading, use of these terms was not illegal.[19] The difficulties surrounding generic names was a major factor behind the Board of Trade's initial refusal to accede to requests by the Cutlers' Company that Article X be amended. Correspondence between the Foreign Office and Herbert Hughes eventually convinced the Board of Trade that 'Sheffield' could not be considered a generic term. Unlike labels such as 'Brussels' carpets, which described a particular kind of article, Sheffield was celebrated for all kinds of products. This diversity meant that it was 'very difficult to see how the word "Sheffield" can ever become a well-recognised name of any particular make or quality of wares'.[20] Consequently, at the Rome Conference in 1886, British delegates suggested a number of changes to Article X, including '[e]very article bearing illegally a false indication of origin may be seized on importation in all the contracting States' and '[t]he tribunals of each country must decide what are the appellations which in virtue of their generic nature do not come within the present regulations'. The British

---

[17] TNA, FO 412/44, *Further Correspondence Respecting the Industrial Property Convention*: 14.

[18] The British government tried to conclude an agreement with Germany which would stop the trade in falsely marked Sheffield products, but this was unsuccessful.

[19] Conférence Internationale Pour la Protection De La Propriété Industrielle. Paris (1880): 88.

[20] *Papers Relative to the Recent Conference at Rome on the Subject of Industrial Property*: 10.

proposal to amend Article X was approved with eight votes in favour, one against, and three abstentions.[21]

However, this proposal did not become operative. Some delegates indicated that legislation in their countries did not recognise customs measures for the repression of false IGOs. Concerns were also raised that the British proposals were not designed to protect industrial property but were motivated by protectionism.[22] At the Madrid conference in 1890, British delegates renewed their efforts to change Article X, and achieved some success. As with previous conferences, it proved impossible to achieve international consensus on the need to change this Article. Nonetheless, it was agreed that countries seeking protection of their IGOs could establish a restricted union and in 1891, Britain, France, Spain, Switzerland, and Tunisia acceded to the Madrid Agreement. Article 1 of this Agreement stated:

All goods bearing a false indication of origin, in which one of the Contracting States, or a place situated therein, shall be directly or indirectly indicated as being the country or place of origin, shall be seized on importation into any of the said States.[23]

The protection offered by this Article was much stronger than that provided by Article X of the Paris Convention: false indications of origin alone were protected; there was no requirement that action could only be taken when a misleading indication was accompanied by the 'trade name of a fictitious character or assumed with a fraudulent intention'. Nonetheless, the Madrid Agreement contained weaknesses. One defect was that few countries became signatories. By 1914, it had been ratified by only eight countries, by 1945, just eighteen, whereas the relevant figures for the Paris Convention were twenty-one and thirty-five countries, respectively.[24] These differences in accession are not, perhaps, surprising. Unlike the Madrid Agreement, the Paris Convention addressed a broader range of industrial property.

A second weakness of the Madrid Agreement was contained in Article IV:

---

[21] *Papers Relative to the Recent Conference at Rome on the Subject of Industrial Property*: 20–21.

[22] TNA, BT 209/793, *False Indications and Appellations of Origin*: 1.

[23] False indication of origin applied to a specific geographical locality and a country's name. Ladas, *Patents, Trademarks, and Related Rights*,: 1586.

[24] Calculated from WIPO, Administered Treaties. www.wipo.int/treaties/en/ShowResults .jsp?treaty_id=2

The Tribunals of each country will decide what appellations, on account of their generic character, do not fall within the provisions of the present Agreement, regional appellations concerning the origin of products of the vine being, however, not comprised in the reserve provided for by the present Article.[25]

This apparently innocuous Article, which appears to have been introduced by the Portuguese delegate, Oliveira Martins, differentiated wine from all other products and discriminated in its favour. Martins argued that, as applied to wine, appellations denoted a specially designated product, the qualities of which depended on natural factors such as climate and terroir, which could not be delocalised. Martins' view was supported by the French delegate, Michel Pelletier: wine was created solely by natural forces and the restriction applied in Article IV facilitated the work of the tribunals because they could focus on 'products that, originally agricultural, are frequently adulterated after being rendered used by industrial handling'.[26]

The argument that wine should be treated as a special category was not universally accepted. Contemporaries and later scholars have commented on the fundamental conflict in the Madrid Agreement between the need to protect 'all goods' contained in Article I and the restrictions applied to wine in Article IV. One Paris-based advocate claimed that the stipulations in Article I were too radical and absolute.[27] A related problem was how to protect wine appellations in countries which did not accede to the Madrid Agreement. It seemed absurd that a wine appellation might be protected in France but treated as generic in an important export market.[28] A vigorous debate ensued about how to determine whether a product was generic. At the forefront of these discussions were members of the Association for the Protection of Industrial Property (AIPPI), which was formed in 1897 and comprised 'the three spiritual families who have an interest in industrial property, jurists, patent attorneys and industrialists'.[29]

[25] Treaty Series No. 13. Arrangement between Great Britain, Spain, France, Switzerland and Tunis for the Prevention of False Indications of Origin on Goods. Signed at Madrid 14 April 1891. London, HMSO: 1892.
[26] Procès-Verbaux de la Conferènce de Madrid de 1890 de l'Union pour la Protection de la Propriété Industrielle (Impr. Jent et Reinart), Berne (1892): 87–88. This view was reiterated at the next meeting of the Convention. Actes de La Conferénce de Bruxelles: 268.
[27] Annuaire De L'Association Internationale Pour La Protection De La Propriété Industrielle (hereafter, Annuaire), 1906: 84; Ladas, *Patents, Trademarks, and Related Rights*, 1587.
[28] TNA, BT 209/785, *Revision at Lisbon: Preparatory Work on the Agenda*: 12.
[29] International Association for the Protection of Industrial Property, *AIPPI and the Development*: 23.

A key problem confronting the AIPPI was comprehending the meaning of 'products of the vine'. In French law Cognac was an appellation, but in Germany it was a generic term which was simply indicative of eau-de-vie. Considerable debate occurred on whether Cognac was indeed generic. German and Austrian advocates were adamant that Cognac was an eau-de-vie and did not denote provenance. German advocates claimed that 'Kognak' derived its qualities from special techniques applied after the distillation of wine. Using 'quality' as a benchmark, it was suggested that the processes used in the manufacture of Cognac were equally as important as the terroir from which the wine was obtained, and that various infusions were used to complement the wine used in the production of Cognac. It was argued that very few Germans knew that Cognac was a town. Complicating matters, how could a consumer distinguish 'Cognac' from 'Kognak' if a German distillery had plants in France and Germany? In any case, did consumers of this wine devote attention to whether it was spelled with 'C' or 'K'? German objections to classifying Cognac as an appellation were sufficiently strong that it could not accede to the Madrid Agreement before 1914 because it would thereby be 'stripped of the names they considered [had] become part of their national heritage'.[30]

One way of overcoming German resistance was to recommend that Cognac or 'Kognak' be accompanied with a clear indication of origin, for example, 'Cognac, Charente'. But this proposal was unacceptable to French delegates: consent to this proposal undermined French attempts to defend Cognac in other countries and might result in the surrender of other wine appellations. A bilateral agreement between France and Germany was one way to solve this impasse. Such an agreement between Austria and Germany ensured that the latter recognised that Tokay was reserved for wines produced within a particular radius of Tokay. But the French rejected this solution because it entailed bilateral agreements with other countries and would have resulted in a multiplicity of treaties which were not necessarily uniform or comprehensive in the protection they afforded.[31]

The favoured treatment offered to wine raised other problems. Could the exemption afforded to wine be extended to other products whose characteristics were determined by nature? Czechoslovakia argued that its Pilsner beers, mineral waters, and hops should not be considered

---

[30] Annuaire, 1902:162–167; Annuaire, 1905: 161–167, 225–240.
[31] Annuaire, 1910: 161–166.

generic because their essential qualities derived from the soil and climate. The French argued that Vichy could not be applied to other mineral waters even if they had the same qualities and chemical composition. Similar concerns were raised for other appellations. For example, it was absurd that Gruyère cheese was generic in France but classed as an appellation in Switzerland. Similarly, Camembert was held to be generic in France, but an appellation in Germany.[32]

For non-comestible natural products, French delegates admitted that the demarcation between generic terms and appellations was nebulous. Thus, Angers slate, Limoges kaolin (an essential ingredient in porcelain), and Vallauris clay were expressions which 'by force of circumstance have ... retained their indication of provenance'. Similar claims were made for Tebessa (Algeria) phosphates, Carrara marble (Italy), and Boulogne Portland cement. However, Fontainbleau, Creil, and Jura stone were generic. According to one interpretation, the facility with which a product could be transported between different regions determined whether it was generic. The corollary of this was whether products with *identical* qualities could be sourced from multiple locations.[33] Differences in the treatment of generic terms threatened to undermine international unity. For example, Russia had little incentive to accede to the Madrid Agreement if 'Russian leather' was considered generic. Article IV permitted members to determine whether non-vine products were generic. But how would this stipulation work in practice if identical place names simultaneously existed in different countries? Which court would then determine whether a product was generic – the country in which litigation occurred or the country from which the product was exported?[34]

Initially, it is difficult to conceive how the quality of industrial products depended on natural factors such as soil or climate. If it was valid that appellations be protected, why make a distinction between wine and other manufactures? It was considered unacceptable that 'Sheffield' or 'Manchester' was applied, respectively, to steel and cotton textiles not produced in these regions. Some manufactures, for example, 'Marseilles soap' and 'Solingen steel', possessed characteristics which did not depend on terroir. Similar considerations applied with equal force to other centres of manufacturing excellence, for example, 'Geneva watches' and 'Zurich

---

[32] Annuaire, 1902: 163; Annuaire, 1910: 164; Annuaire, 1928: 326; Ladas, *Patents, Trademarks and Related Rights*, 1590.
[33] Annuaire, 1906: 87–88. Own translation.   [34] Annuaire, 1897: 190.

silk'. Richard Iklé, a Swiss jurist, urged that Article IV be extended to all products which derived their reputation from the soil. Robert Burrell, a British expert on industrial property, recommended that Article IV be extended to all indications of origin which 'give a product a specific and superior commercial value to similar products'. The AIPPI accepted this proposal, but it was not adopted prior to 1945 in either the Madrid Agreement or the Paris Convention.[35]

Extending the provisions of Article IV to a wider range of products had the advantage of making the Madrid Agreement more attractive to countries not primarily engaged in wine production because they would then be assured that their own products would not be treated as generic. But as more countries joined the Madrid Agreement there was a greater need to align its provisions with those of the Paris Convention. Indeed, British delegates consistently emphasised the need to remove the restrictions in Article X so that false indications alone were prohibited. But acceding to British demands would have rendered superfluous Article I of the Madrid Agreement.[36] Attempts to secure consonance between the Paris Convention and the Madrid Agreement were unsuccessful. One obstacle was the intransigence of wine-producing countries:

[Article IV] provides the wine producing countries with so great an advantage that they refuse to consider the whole problem of indications of origin in a provision of the General Convention if it does not deal expressly with appellations of vine products in the same way as Madrid.[37]

The French consistently opposed the extension of Article IV to other naturally occurring products and any alteration in the Paris Convention which threatened the special treatment of wine.[38] French resistance was based on the belief that countries which sought reciprocal protection for their appellations and indications of origin needed only to accede to the Madrid Agreement. France would only agree to changes in Article X if the Paris Convention made special provision for wine appellations. But if such provision was made, what was the value of the Madrid Agreement?[39] Although Article IV was relevant only to the few countries that acceded to

---

[35] Annuaire, 1925–1926: 131; Annuaire, 1928: 96–98. Own translation.
[36] Actes de la Conférence de Washington: 104; Actes de la Conference de la Haye: 310.
[37] TNA, BT 209/793: *False Indications and Appellations of Origin*: International Union for the Protection of Industrial Property, Lisbon Conference, Preliminary Documents: 3.
[38] Annuaire, 1910: 159; Actes de a Conférence Réunie à Londres: 195.
[39] Actes de la Conférence de Washington: 303; Actes de la Conférence de la Haye: 310–312. French opposition was supported by Cuba, Portugal, and Turkey. *Papers and Correspondence Relative to the Recent Conference of the International Union for the*

this Agreement, it had much wider ramifications: it ensured that attempts to extend Article X to cover unqualified use of false IGOs were unsuccessful. In fact, the only 'concession' to be made was that 'appellations of origin' was inserted into Article I of the Paris Convention following the conference at The Hague.[40]

Another reason why some countries refused to accede to the Madrid Agreement was the primacy given to national courts in determining whether a product was generic. This was particularly true for the United States, which acknowledged that Article I of the Madrid Agreement offered advantages to its agriculture.[41] For example, it was claimed that US butter was comparable to Danish, and was often passed-off as such, whereas inferior butters were misrepresented as 'US'. At state level, 'Omaha' and 'Kansas City' were used for commercial purposes and a congressional committee reported: 'We are of the opinion that the United States should make use of this [Madrid] agreement before the names of certain of her products become generic, as, for example, champagne has become to the great loss of the champagne districts of France.'[42]

If a geographical name had become generic it was not possible to claim that it had been falsely used by a defendant. In *French Republic v. Saratoga Vichy Co.* (1903), the plaintiffs argued that Vichy was being applied to mineral waters drawn from a well in Saratoga, New York. Although Vichy was a well-established appellation in France, the court noted, the plaintiff had failed to enforce their exclusive right to the term 'Vichy'; the defendant had been openly and notoriously bottling and selling its waters under the name of 'Saratoga Vichy' for thirty years without opposition. The volume of sales of 'Saratoga Vichy' was such that indifference or inattention could not explain the delay of the plaintiffs

---

Protection of Industrial Property Held at The Hague, 8 October–6 November, 1925. London: HMSO (1926): 93–94, 100.

[40] British delegates pressed for this revision to address semantic differences when 'indications of source', 'origin', 'indications of provenance', and 'appellations' were translated from French into English. *Actes de la Conférence de la Haye*: 535; *Papers and Correspondence Relative to the Recent Conference of the International Union for the Protection of Industrial Property Held at The Hague*: 96.

[41] M. G. Coerper, 'The Protection of Geographical Indications in the United States of America, with Particular Reference to Certification Marks', *Industrial Property*, 29 (1990): 235.

[42] *Report of the Commissioners Appointed to Revise the Statutes Relating to Patents, Trade and Other Marks, and Trade and Commercial Names* (Washington, DC: Government Printing Office, 1902), 46.

who had 'allowed the name to become generic and indicative of the character of the water'.[43]

In the United States many foreign wine appellations were treated as generic and this was endorsed by federal legislation. In 1936, Californian senators Johnson and McAdoo were instrumental in changing the Federal Alcohol Administration Act of 1935. They proposed that a wide range of appellations – Burgundy, Chablis, Champagne, Chianti, Malaga, Riesling, and Sauterne – could be applied to domestically produced wines provided they were 'of the same type' and were conspicuously 'qualified by the name of the State or other locality in the United States in which the product is produced'.[44] These senators were particularly dismissive of the view that Champagne was a uniquely French appellation:

On what conceivable theory is it to be said that a process which exists in France today shall be the only process by which champagne may be made, or that anybody in this country shall be forbidden making champagne as he sees fit? ... What difference does it make whether a producer in some state shall manufacture a champagne by a specific process of his own, or a process which he may have purchased in France, or which he may have obtained in some other fashion?[45]

Johnson and McAdoo's arguments were challenged. In the United States it was recognised that certain wines were identified with specific geographical locations. There was also the threat of retaliation: how would the United States respond if France or Spain began exporting to the United States oranges and raisins marked Sun Kist or Sun Maid, respectively? The Johnson-McAdoo amendment was subsequently passed, but Champagne was excluded from their original list.[46]

No substantial change was made to Article X until after 1945. Nonetheless, attempts to reconcile the Paris Convention with the Madrid Agreement continued before the Second World War. At its 1936 Berlin conference there was agreement within the AIPPI that these two protocols were fundamentally in conflict. This consensus was acknowledged by the International Chamber of Commerce, which advocated 'an absolute and complete protection of geographical designations of origin known to constitute one of the main factors in the reputation and

---

[43] *The French Republic* v. *Saratoga Vichy Spring Co.* (1903), 191 US: 428, 436–437.
[44] Lenzen, 'Bachus in the Hinterlands', 157.
[45] Lenzen, 'Bachus in the Hinterlands', 158; Ladas, *Patents, Trademarks, and Related Rights,*: 1610.
[46] Lenzen, 'Bachus in the Hinterlands', 158–161.

commercial value of the products'.[47] The only question that needed to be addressed was: how were these differences to be eliminated? The AIPPI grappled with three fundamental issues at its 1938 Prague conference: international registration of appellations; which types of product were suitable for registration; and the role of courts in determining whether an appellation was generic.[48]

It was recognised that decisions on appellations varied considerably between countries; this could weaken international economic relations and distort trade patterns. For example, products recognised as appellations in the exporting country became less valuable if treated as generic by an importing country. There was nothing to stop producers in the importing country using the generic term on their own products because there was no possibility of deceiving indigenous consumers. This problem was the direct result of entrusting to *national* courts the authority to determine whether an appellation was generic. One solution was to ensure greater international uniformity in the treatment of appellations, which would be facilitated by their registration at the International Bureaux of Intellectual Property in Berne. Once registered, an appellation obtained protection in those countries which also registered their appellations with the Bureaux.[49]

A related problem involved determination of which products could be classed as appellations. In 1937, the AIPPI reaffirmed its view that the unique protection afforded 'products of the vine' should be extended to other products which derived their qualities from the soil. Unsurprisingly, Czechoslovakia reiterated the claim that its Pilsner beer should be placed on the same footing as wine. But why stop there? A particular concern of the Czechs was that there was no clear demarcation between 'agricultural' products and 'industrial' products. Thus, beer was an industrial product made using large-scale plants, but it was linked by its use of barley and hops to agriculture. Similarly, it was argued that Article IV was too narrow: product quality depended not only on climate and soil but also on other local circumstances, especially the skill and experience of the local workforce.[50]

The Czech arguments highlighted a major inconsistency in the Madrid Agreement. Article I of this Agreement stated that '*all* goods bearing

---

[47] International Chamber of Commerce, *World Trade*, vol. IX, 1 July 1937, 51.
[48] These debates provided part of the framework for the Lisbon conference in 1958.
[49] Annuaire, 1938: 240, 244–254. French delegates at this conference thought it desirable to restore appellations which had become generic.
[50] Annuaire, 1938: 256, 277–280.

a false indication' were to be detained, but if an indication was deemed generic it was not subject to sanctions. If the Madrid Agreement was to appeal to more countries it was imperative that Article IV provided an unambiguous distinction between 'agricultural' and 'industrial' products: 'For just as there are no reasonable grounds for restricting protection effectively to wine products, there is no reason to stop halfway and not to grant protection to industrial products.'[51] But this perspective was not universally accepted. Belgian jurists claimed that Belgium obtained no advantage from protecting the origin designations of its agricultural products because it did not legally define and control its own produce. Moreover, they claimed that Belgium did not have specialist producers possessing a de facto monopoly in the supply of specific products. Although Belgium did not accede to the Madrid Agreement, it opposed the extension of Article IV to industrial products:

[I]t is true that certain industrial products have acquired fame from their place of manufacture. But, this is most often based on a reputation for making 'good' quality products; the fame does not derive from quality inherent to local natural conditions and climate and terrain.[52]

Finally, establishing the ground rules that would underpin a registration scheme was problematic: which courts determined whether an appellation was generic? French delegates argued that this decision should be entrusted exclusively to the courts of the country in which the appellation was located and that it should be protected in all other countries simply because it was declared protected in that country. The French proposals also raised the possibility that some appellations, including Champagne and Cognac, which had become generic in other countries, could be restored as appellations. These proposals reignited the debate about the sovereignty of national courts and were criticised by Austrian, Dutch, Italian, and Swiss jurists.[53] The British position was that the confusion and deception of consumers was fundamentally wrong and there was no justification preventing the courts from determining the generic-ness of wine. For example, British consumers were not misled by the terms 'Australian Burgundy', 'South African Burgundy', or 'Spanish Sauternes', or the application of 'Wiltshire' and 'Cheddar' to imported ham and cheese, respectively.[54]

---

[51] Annuaire, 1938: 277–278.   [52] Annuaire, 1938: 243.   [53] Annuaire, 1938: 238, 259.
[54] Annuaire, 1938: 262.

At the end of the period covered by this chapter, major fault lines existed in the international treatment of IGOs. This was particularly true for appellations. The Madrid Agreement is considered of minor importance except for certain countries which owned wine appellations.[55] Even so, the protocols established by the Paris Convention and the Madrid Agreement provided the basis for landmark national legislation governing the importation of products bearing false indications of origin. In this regard the British Merchandise Marks Act, 1887, was exemplary.[56] Additionally, these international conventions facilitated global recognition of the need to combat unfair competition.

UNFAIR COMPETITION

Unfair competition refers to any act contrary to honest practice in industrial and commercial matters. It can be divided into two major categories: those that directly affect the goodwill of a business and those that are primarily directed against the public and only indirectly affect goodwill. The first category includes infringement of intellectual property, such as copyright and industrial design, trademarks, and patents, and other practices which have adverse effects on goodwill, for example, disparaging remarks about product quality, resale price maintenance, and exclusive supply relationships. The second category refers to a broad range of acts designed to mislead consumers about the nature, composition, and origin of products.[57]

Unfair competition is a broad doctrine that permits the courts to enjoin practices that do not necessarily infringe property rights. It is particularly relevant to IGOs which do not grant individual rights to the exclusive use of the name of a place; this privilege belongs to the community as a whole.[58] Litigation involving generic terms and IGOs was long recognised as a constituent of unfair competition.[59] Court decisions involving unfair competition took account of consumer interests, not just those of producers. Consequently, in such cases, there was less need for the courts to become embroiled in determining the vested interests of the latter, and more need to decide whether consumers were deceived. Indeed, it was observed that '[v]ery few cases in which competitors are litigants involve

---

[55] Benson, 'Toward a New Theory for the Protection of Geographical Indications', 132.
[56] Annuaire, 1897: 267.   [57] Ladas, *Patents, Trademarks and Related Rights*, 1705.
[58] Ladas, *Patents, Trademarks and Related Rights*, 39.
[59] H. D. Nims, *The Law of Unfair Business Competition* (New York: Baker, Voorhis and Company, 1909), 226–259.

a violation of purely private rights'.[60] When discussing misuse of 'Minneapolis' by manufacturers not based in that city, Harry Nims concluded, '[i]f the private interests involved in this question are great, the public interests are greater, for the public has a right to honest brands'.[61]

Before discussing the development of unfair competition it is necessary to recognise that there is some overlap between customs regulations governing IGOs for tariff purposes and those emanating from intellectual property law. A key feature of the interwar years was the imposition of tariffs. During the 1920s, Belgium, France, Germany, and Italy introduced tariffs for the first time or revised existing tariffs upwards.[62] In the United States, the Fordney-McCumber tariff, introduced in 1922, raised tariffs to a then unprecedented level, and in 1932, Britain entered the protectionist era with the enactment of the Import Duties Act. The purpose of these tariffs was to restrict or close domestic markets to foreign producers. Clearly, accurate indications of origin are necessary if customs are to impose the correct tariff. However, during the interwar period, there was growing recognition that legislation designed to protect consumers from misrepresentation:

> sometimes became an instrument for the protection of national markets ... Of late years, the laws relating to marks of origin have been more and more used for the purpose of closing home markets to foreign goods. This ... causes great disturbance to international trade and often proves more restrictive than protective Customs policies. The promotion of international commerce [requires] that the laws on marks of origin should be applied ... for their original and essential purpose – the repression of unfair competition.[63]

Although there may be some coincidence between the duties of customs and other statutory bodies in relation to IGOs, there are fundamental differences in their operation. For example, both the United States Tariff Commission (USTC) and the Federal Trade Commission (FTC) were empowered to require accurate country-of-origin marking on imports. However, the USTC, which operated under the Tariff Acts, was concerned with marking at the time of importation. In contrast, the FTC had a much broader remit involving interstate commerce and it was empowered to issue 'cease and desist' orders to

---

[60] R. Callmann, 'Unfair Competition with Imported Trademarked Goods', *Virginia Law Review*, 43 (1957): 342; Ladas, *Patents, Trademarks and Related Rights*, 1686–1687.
[61] Nims, *The Law of Unfair Business Competition*, 237.
[62] Kenwood and Lougheed, *The Growth of the International Economy*, 176.
[63] League of Nations, Economic and Financial Section: International Economic Conference, Geneva, May 1927, Part II: 18, 22.

US firms.[64] Similarly, in Britain, customs possessed long-established powers to prohibit the import of foreign products bearing the brands, marks, or names of British manufacturers.[65] These powers were extended by the Merchandise Marks Act, 1887, to false indications of origin alone.[66] Subsequent legislation empowered the Boards of Trade and Agriculture to instigate litigation when the general interests of the nation, or a section of the community, or a trade, were affected by the import of products with misleading IGOs.[67]

Prior to 1900, the Paris Convention did not explicitly recognise unfair competition. Before this date the Convention only afforded protection to defined intellectual property rights – patents, industrial designs, and trademarks. As noted earlier, protection against misuse of IGOs occurred only when they were associated with 'a trade name of a fictitious character or assumed with fraudulent intention'. Contemporaries criticised this omission. For example, unfair competition could be practised without violating defined intellectual property rights, and the adverse effects could be just as damaging. Moreover, some contemporaries claimed that the Paris Convention did not protect against misuse of appellations, even though they were of fundamental importance to international trade.[68] The failure of this Convention to provide an internationally uniform set of guidelines addressing unfair competition before 1900 was attributed to substantial variation in national laws. For example, in Britain and the United States, the common law based on equity determined rulings on unfair competition. France, by contrast, employed the Civil Code, which provided a general system of protection. In other countries, the law governing unfair competition was considered rudimentary. Some experts believed that there was insufficient public concern with this issue while others thought the diversity of practices encompassed by 'concurrence déloyale' meant it was difficult for the Convention to make comprehensive provision.[69]

---

[64] J. T. McCarthy and V. C. Devitt, 'Protection of Geographic Denominations: Domestic and International', *Trade Mark Reporter*, 69 (1979): 222–225; L. Bendekgey and C. Mead, 'International Protection of Appellations of Origin and Other Geographic Indications', *Trade Mark Reporter*, 82 (1992): 778.

[65] 16 & 17 VICTORIAE, c. 106, 107. An Act to Amend and Consolidate the Laws Relating to the Customs of the United Kingdom and of the Isle of Man, and Certain Laws Relating to Trade and Navigation and the British Possessions (1853): s. CLXI.

[66] 50 & 51 Vict., Ch. 28. Merchandise Marks Act (1887): s. 16 (4).

[67] 54 Vict., c. 15. Merchandise Marks Act (1891).

[68] Annuaire, 1897: 284; Annuaire, 1898: 406. The Madrid Agreement remedied this deficiency, but few countries acceded to this protocol.

[69] Annuaire, 1897: 453–454.

By the turn of the twentieth century, the Paris Convention was beginning to make limited provision for unfair competition. At Brussels, in 1900, Article X was endorsed: citizens of the contracting states would 'enjoy in all the States of the Union the protection accorded to nationals against dishonest competition'. This Article ensured domestic and foreign citizens were equally protected against unfair competition, though no obligation was imposed on Member States to provide remedies against such practices. Subsequently, at Washington in 1911, Article X was amended: 'All the contracting countries undertake to assure to those who enjoy the benefits of the Union effective protection against unfair trade competition.'[70] At the Washington conference Britain again attempted to extend Article X to cover any product embossed only with a false indication of origin. But these efforts were in vain: French delegates were adamant that such an extension undermined the Madrid Agreement. From the French perspective, it was not the responsibility of foreign courts to determine whether Champagne or Cognac were generic, and if countries wished to ensure reciprocal protection against the use of unqualified false indications of origin, this could only be achieved by acceding to the Madrid Agreement.[71] The Brussels and Washington conferences did not provide an explicit definition of what acts constituted unfair competition. This omission is explained by the concerns of some delegates that specification of certain acts might be interpreted as excluding others.[72]

The First World War provided a major impetus to the development of legislation on unfair competition.[73] Article 274 of the Peace Treaty of Versailles, 1919, specified that Germany would adopt all necessary measures to protect the products of the Allied powers from all forms of unfair competition, and stipulated that 'Germany undertakes to prohibit and repress ... the importation, exportation, manufacture, distribution, sale ... in its territory of all goods bearing ... any marks, name, devices, or description whatsoever which are calculated to convey ... a false indication of origin, type, nature, or special characteristics of such goods.'[74]

---

[70] Additional Act Modifying the Industrial Property Convention of 20 March 1883, Treaty Series No. 15, 1902, Cd. 1084: 12; International Convention for the Protection of Industrial Property Signed at Washington, 2 June 1911, Treaty Series No. 8, 1913, Cd. 6805: 113.

[71] Actes de la Conférence de Washington: 302–303.

[72] Ladas, *Patents, Trademarks, and Related Rights*, 1679.

[73] W. Notz, 'New Phases of Unfair Competition and Measures for Its Suppression – National and International', *Yale Law Journal*, 30 (1920–1921): 384.

[74] Enforced compliance with Article 274 was not onerous because it was already enshrined in Article X of the Paris Convention. The imposition of even more stringent obligations

Article 275 of the same treaty required Germany to respect the laws of any allied state regarding wine and spirit appellations, provided German appellations received reciprocal recognition. Following the Armistice, Germany acceded to the Madrid Agreement. After 1919 many countries introduced legislation addressing unfair competition in which indications of origin featured prominently. Thus, Australia prohibited the import of products not indicating the place or country of origin; Denmark and Finland made similar provisions where imports were impressed with incorrect indication of origin or marks 'of a nature to convey false indication of the origin of the goods'.[75]

Nonetheless, the League of Nations doubted whether indications of origin were effective in combatting unfair competition. Founded in 1919, the League began a wide-ranging investigation of the factors distorting international trade. The League acknowledged that it was impossible to prevent countries adopting measures enabling their consumers to distinguish domestic from foreign products, but noted that use of indications of origin was problematic on a number of counts. For example, they might be removed in further processing. Misplaced patriotism could encourage consumers to purchase domestic instead of better and cheaper foreign products. Concerns were raised that these indications might be discriminatory, for example, when imposed on some countries but not others. The ludicrous situation emerged in which some countries were unable to benefit from commercial treaties because of the regulations governing indications of origin imposed by others.[76]

The League was also highly critical of Article X. It argued that there was no clear definition of the types of unfair competition prohibited by the Paris Convention, or the types of redress that could be obtained. The League thought it desirable that unqualified 'false and misleading indications of geographical ... origin' should be enumerated within Article X and that it was preferable that more countries acceded to the Madrid Agreement. It appears that the League was trying to reconcile the

---

was rejected. C. Wadlow, 'The International Law of Unfair Competition: The British Origins of Article 10bis of the Paris Convention for the Protection of Industrial Property'. Oxford Intellectual Property Research Centre, 19 November (2002): 12.

[75] League of Nations, Economic and Financial Section: International Economic Conference, Geneva, May 1927, Part II: 19–20; Annex I: 25–37.

[76] Ibid.: 22–23; League of Nations, *Official Journal*, November 1931: 2104–2105. As discussed in Chapter 5, the UK's policy of requiring indications of geographical origin was an unusual hybrid: there was no general stipulation that all imports had to be marked with geographical origin. Instead, such indications could only be imposed if they were judged to be in the 'public interest'.

differences between those countries adhering to the Paris Convention and those belonging to the Madrid Agreement. Attempts at rapprochement required the League to consider solutions to the problem of the varied treatment of generic versus non-generic products, but on this point too difficulties were encountered. For example, there was no agreement on which types of produce could be classed as appellations, or how to demarcate their geographical boundaries. Additionally, there existed 'a natural tendency to exaggerate' the relationship between the qualities of wine and its location – which made it imperative that safeguards were applied to prevent the perpetuation of monopolies which had no 'real natural justification'. In view of these hurdles, the League decided to petition the Paris Convention to consider its views.[77]

At The Hague conference in 1925, unfair competition featured prominently. It was recognised that 'concurrence déloyale' included misleading statements on packaging and in advertisements and brochures; the use of false invoices; obtaining confidential information on competitors; intimidation of competitors' customers; and misleading references to industrial awards, such as diplomas and medals.[78] There was renewed debate on false IGOs and a subtle difference emerged over their definition. The French argued that unfair competition occurred when an IGO was used on a product not originating from that region. Other countries placed more emphasis on whether use of the IGO was deceptive. In any event, the French delegates reiterated their long-established view that amendment of Article X to include unqualified misuse of IGOs undermined the Madrid Agreement.[79] The Hague meeting defined 'unfair competition' as:

[a]ll manner of acts, of such a nature as to create confusion by any means whatsoever with the goods of a competitor; [f]alse allegations, in the course of trade of such a nature as to discredit the goods of a competitor.[80]

Although some minor amendments were made to Article X following the London conference in 1934, the Paris Convention's treatment of misleading

---

[77] League of Nations, *Official Journal*, June 1922: 625–632. Another factor influencing this decision was that Germany and the United States were members of the Paris Convention, but not the League of Nations.

[78] Actes de la Conférence de la Haye: 95–96, 349–350.

[79] Actes de la Conférence de la Haye: 470–471, 578.

[80] Article 1obis, International Convention for the Protection of Industrial Property signed at The Hague, 6 November 1925, Treaty Series No. 16, 1928, Cmd: 3167. Article 1oter permitted industry associations to take court proceedings to repress 'unfair competition'.

IGOs remained unchanged since its inception. On the eve of the Second World War two protocols existed for the international protection of IGOs – the Paris Convention and the Madrid Agreement. Article X of the Paris Convention afforded protection only when an indication of origin was accompanied by a fictitious trade name or assumed with fraudulent intent. Subsequent amendments to this Article, especially its extension to unfair competition, provided the signatories with more latitude in how to deal with misleading IGOs. From its establishment, the Madrid Agreement unconditionally prohibited false IGOs and enshrined the uniqueness of wine appellations. However, this protection was not without cost: the courts of each signatory lost their right to determine whether 'products of the vine' were generic.

The differences between the Paris Convention and the Madrid Agreement meant national variation in the protection of IGOs was pronounced before 1945. The Hague and London conferences were relatively unimportant to countries such as France and Britain. The former had long-established laws addressing unfair competition and the latter had made strong provision via the Merchandise Marks Acts of 1887 and 1926. Although the United States was a signatory to the Paris Convention, the affront to the sovereignty of its national courts implied by Article IV meant it could not accede to the Madrid Agreement. Consequently, before 1945, the United States protected foreign IGOs under trademark law and the doctrine of unfair competition. For example, during the interwar period, the FTC issued 'cease and desist' orders against the use of 'Geneva' and 'Sheffield' on US-made watches and silver plate, respectively; the import of Chinese lace marked 'Irish lace'; 'Paris' and 'France' on domestically produced perfume; and 'Havana' on cigars made in New York from US tobacco.[81] Other countries, such as Japan, acceded only to the Paris Convention before 1945, and did not enact legislation addressing unfair competition until 1934.

ORIGIN, QUALITY, AND THE INTERNATIONAL EGG TRADE

Despite the growth of international protocols on intellectual property, national differences in the treatment of IGOs remained. A case can be

---

[81] FTC, *Annual Report for the Year Ending 1924*: 162; FTC, *Annual Report for the Year Ending 1925*: 39; FTC, *Annual Report for the Year Ending 1929*: 86–87; FTC, *Annual Report for the Year Ending 1930*: 172; FTC, *Annual Report for the Year Ending 1934*: 78.

made that greater alignment between national and international protection of IGOs would have been achieved if the focus centred on particular products. The advantage of obtaining international agreement for specific products is that it avoided the vexed questions of having to determine whether special status applied to 'products of the vine' and which products were generic. The growth in agricultural trade during the interwar period fostered greater interest in international food standards, including the Convention for the Unification of Methods of Cheese Sampling and Analysis in 1934. Another scheme, beginning in 1931, which was not convened under the Paris Convention or the Madrid Agreement, applied to the international egg trade.[82]

The major problem confronting the egg industry was that international storage and distribution blurred the distinction between country of origin and quality marks such as Fresh, New laid, and Cold stored. Unfair competition occurred when cold-stored imported eggs were sold as New laid, which affected domestic producers who were genuinely supplying New laid eggs. National attempts to eradicate this practice were not always successful. Sweden mandated that all cold-stored eggs exported to Britain had to be marked 'Cold-stored Swedish', but this did not prevent the export of fresh eggs which were subsequently cold stored in Britain and sold as Fresh. Strong consumer prejudice against cold-stored eggs meant domestic producers were adversely affected by the fraudulent sale of these eggs. In the Netherlands this prejudice was sufficiently strong that legislation requiring cold-stored eggs be marked as such would have resulted in their export to Germany and Britain, and the Netherlands would have experienced a shortage.[83]

According to Fritz Graevenitz, the impetus to a European agreement on egg marking originated from the British experience.[84] Misrepresentation was pronounced in Britain, the biggest importer of eggs. Between 1909 and 1913, Britain accounted for 32 per cent of global egg imports (by volume). By 1928, this figure was 41 per cent.[85] Contemporaries claimed that stale foreign eggs from China and Egypt were mixed with British eggs

---

[82] International Convention on the marking of eggs in international trade. Signed at Brussels 11 December 1931. League of Nations, *Official Journal*, 1936: 253.

[83] *Report of Proceedings of the 4th World's Poultry Congress*, London: HMSO (1930): 575–576, 662–663.

[84] F. G. von Graevenitz, 'State and Market in Agriculture – France and Germany in the Interwar Period'. Downloaded from www.ebha.org/ebha2007/pdf/vonGraevenitz.pdf.

[85] Calculated from *Report of Proceedings of the 4th World's Poultry Congress*: 675.

and sold as New laid.[86] Strong financial incentives encouraged this fraudulent activity. For example, in the mid-1920s, price data suggest that a 100 per cent profit margin could be obtained by selling Egyptian eggs as British or New laid.[87] Evidence given before a government inquiry, as well as numerous prosecutions, attest to the misuse of New laid and Fresh on imported preserved eggs.[88] The trade press recognised that many European countries preserved their eggs for ultimate disposal in the British market.[89]

The problem generated by the unlawful sale of preserved eggs as New laid was exacerbated because this term could not be satisfactorily defined. Complicating matters, domestic and foreign suppliers withheld eggs until prices improved. In Britain, official measures to undermine the fraudulent sale of eggs were provided by the Merchandise Marks Act, 1926, and the Agricultural Produce (Grading and Marking) (Eggs) Regulations of 1928. As a result of the former Act, a Standing Committee recommended in 1928 that imported eggs had to be marked with an indication of origin. The latter legislation required that 'British' eggs bear an indication showing how they had been preserved.[90] However, the efficacy of these measures in combatting unfair competition has been questioned. Although British regulations governing origin marking resulted in similar legislation being enacted in Belgium and the Netherlands, opportunities for fraud remained. For example, China imported eggs from Belgium to benefit from the Belgian origin mark and subsequently exported them to Britain, leading British consumers to conclude that European eggs were not fresher than Chinese. In other words, British legislation permitted the import of foreign eggs provided they were marked with the country of origin, but no safeguards existed to prevent these foreign eggs being stored and sold as Fresh or New laid. The end result was that the European egg market became a 'jungle of ... marks of origin with different language, type, size, and denomination of quality, which made it difficult for ... producers to ... sell their products'.[91]

---

[86] *The Grocer*, 3 March 1923, 87.   [87] *The Grocer*, 8 March 1924, 70.
[88] *The Grocer*, 9 May 1925, 111; 25 December 1926, 62–63; 9 July 1927, 118; 21 April 1928, 93.
[89] *The Grocer*, 6 February 1926, 126.
[90] In Northern Ireland, the Marketing of Eggs Act, 1923 (effective from 1924), provided that dealers in preserved eggs – preserved either by cold storage or pickling – had to be registered and they had to mark cases of stored eggs with either of these labels.
[91] Graevenitz, 'State and Market'.

Given the chaos generated by such conflicting marking regimes, the World Poultry Congress which assembled in London in 1930 unanimously voted that:

All eggs cold stored in any country should be stamped with an internationally agreed mark, and that steps should be taken for a meeting of authorised representatives of the Governments concerned to be convened as soon as possible in order to arrive at some definite agreement on the subject.[92]

A congress was held in December 1931 to discuss standardisation of egg marks. It was claimed that variation in European marking regimes acted as a barrier to trade which damaged consumers and producers. The requirement that eggs be marked with an indelible indication of origin meant distributors were unable to respond to evolving market conditions. For example, eggs destined for the British market and marked in compliance with British regulations might be refused entry into Germany if prices rose in the latter. Consequently, prices in Germany might rise further – because of restrictions on imports – to the detriment of German consumers. Similarly, producers of these eggs were adversely affected because they were unable to obtain higher prices. This situation encouraged distributors to hold unmarked stocks of eggs for as long as possible until they could be more certain of market trends. The Congress welcomed the increased trade in preserved eggs, recognising that this had dampened the cycle of glut and shortage, leading to more stable prices which benefitted consumers. Another advantage of uniform supply and stable prices was that there was now less incentive for unscrupulous retailers to pass-off stored eggs as 'New laid'.[93]

The principal articles ratified by this Congress involved indications of origin and quality indicia.[94] Article I stipulated the format in which the country of origin was to be indicated, for example, Belgium was to be marked Belgica. Article II specified the marking requirements for fresh and preserved eggs. The former were to be marked in black ink between March and August, and red ink was to be used during the intervening period.[95] Nineteen countries were represented at the

[92] *Report of Proceedings of the 4th World's Poultry Congress*: 663.
[93] Documentation pour la reunion de la conference diplomatique internationale en vue de l'etablissement d'une convention pour le marquage des oefs dans le commerce international. Au Palais Des Academies, Bruxelles, 7 December (1931): 17–19.
[94] See Chapter 3 for similar debates on the international butter trade.
[95] Strangely, Article II also required that preserved eggs had to be marked in black throughout the year. The implication is that, during the spring and summer months, there was no way of differentiating preserved and fresh eggs.

Congress and thirteen became signatories. Of the many international agreements governing food quality during the interwar period, the egg agreement has been judged relatively successful.[96] Greece, Argentina, Brazil, and Egypt subsequently acceded in the 1950s. From 1948, this convention was subsumed within the Food and Agricultural Organisation of the United Nations.[97]

CONCLUSIONS

This chapter has shown that the construction of an effective international protocol for the protection of IGOs was limited prior to 1945. The greatest obstacles to the development of equal protection for all IGOs were the restrictions imposed by Article X of the Paris Convention and the inability to alter Article IV of the Madrid Agreement to include non-vine products. Throughout this period the French were intransigent on both issues. A charitable interpretation of this opposition is that France's internal battles on these issues made it unwilling to revisit them at the international level: acquiescence on Article IV or Article X threatened to undermine domestic consensus. A more critical assessment is that the French put their domestic interests first.

This interpretation is not without merit. France was, indeed, a pioneer in the protection of IGOs. However, the bulk of French wine was consumed domestically. On average, between 1866 and 1913, French wine exports were just 5 per cent of total production.[98] It may be argued that French law was only significant against domestic misrepresentation. Indeed, Paul Duguid has shown that during the nineteenth century French wine producers relied on British law to protect their appellations.[99] This prompts the question: why did France have so much influence on the development of international law governing appellations?

At the international level, a fundamental difference existed between the protection of 'products of the vine' and other products. This difference appears to be unjust: why should wine – the characteristics of which are a function of randomly distributed natural factors – be more deserving of

---

[96] F. Townshend, 'Food Standards: Their Importance, Limitations and Problems with Special Reference to International Work', in S. M. Herschdoerfer, *Quality Control in the Food Industry*, Volume 1 (London: Academic Press, 1967), 324.

[97] US 62 STAT. 1581; Treaties and Other International Acts Series 1719.

[98] Calculated from Simpson, *Creating Wine*, 62, 104. The figure quoted does not include imports.

[99] Duguid, 'Developing the Brand'.

protection than manufactures which relied on human ingenuity, craftsmanship, and entrepreneurship? As noted, the manufacture of cutlery in
Sheffield and Solingen was long established and highly renowned. Viewed
from this perspective it can be argued the French approach ensured that
'monopoly' rents for wine were considered more deserving of protection
than rents based on 'artificial' factors such as craftsmanship.

A related observation is that the focus on terroir ignores the importance
of other interpretations of 'quality' when applied to produce. From the
late nineteenth century, Australia, Canada, Denmark, New Zealand, and
the United States emerged as the leading exporters of butter and bacon,
beef and lamb. The quality of this produce did not depend on terroir, but
on extensive monitoring and supervision. The end result was produce
which was remarkably uniform in all of its characteristics: taste, appearance, and colour. For these agrarian exporters the issues surrounding
appellations were irrelevant because national, not regional or local regulation was crucial.

Perhaps the most critical weaknesses in the Paris Convention and the
Madrid Agreement is that neither defined the meaning of appellations and
indications of source. In common law countries such as Britain and the
United States, 'appellations' were not recognised; certainly, they were not
capable of precise translation into the English language.

7

The Evolving International Framework for the Protection of IGOs after 1945

The problem of the protection of appellations of origin and other indications of source is a delicate one to solve for two main reasons. First, the concepts of indication of source and appellation of origin are not uniformly recognized in all countries. Secondly, the means whereby appellations of origin and other indications of source are protected at the national level tend to differ.

WIPO, 'Present Situation and Possible New Solutions', 28 June 1974 (document TAO/1/2): 3

Although terroir and a claim for a unique communications function for geographical indications is the European Union's public rhetoric ... the European Commission has a simpler goal: control of geographic words for their evocative value in the marketplace. The monopoly rents available from exclusive control of this evocative value drive the EC position in the debates over geographical indications.

J. Hughes, 'Champagne, Feta, and Bourbon: The Spirited Debate about Geographical Indications', *Hastings Law Journal*, 58 (2006): 305

The previous chapter showed that by 1945, international protection of IGOs was provided by the Paris Convention and the Madrid Agreement. The post-1945 period witnessed the continuation of earlier efforts to ensure that the protection of IGOs was more robust and comprehensive (Table 7.1). However, in the post-1945 period, the international framework became more complex. After 1945 a plethora of intergovernmental institutions was established, all of which, to varying degrees, were involved in intellectual property, including the Organisation for European Economic Cooperation (1948), the World Health Organization (1948), and the Council of Europe (1949). Ensuring a high level of consonance among

TABLE 7.1   *The evolution of the multilateral protection of industrial property, 1958–2015*[1]

1958	**Seventh Conference of Revision, Lisbon**
	Article X was amended to prohibit unqualified use of a direct or indirect use of a false indication of the source of goods.
	Establishment of a Special Union for the Protection of Appellations of Origin Registered at the International Bureau
	For the first time, an appellation was defined as:
	'[t]he geographical denomination of a country, region, or locality, which serves to designate a product originating therein, the quality or characteristics of which are due exclusively or essentially to the geographical environment, including natural and human factors'.
	Registered appellations were protected against becoming generic.
	Registered appellations were also protected against imitation or usurpation, even if the true origin of the product is indicated or accompanied by terms such as 'kind', 'type', 'make', or similar.
1967	**Eighth Conference of Revision, Stockholm**
	No substantive changes were made to the Paris Convention.
1994	**Agreement on Trade-Related Aspects of Intellectual Property Rights (TRIPS)**
	This Agreement is binding on all members of the World Trade Organization.
	Geographical indications (GIs) are defined as:
	'indications which identify a good as originating in the territory of a Member, or a region or a locality in that territory, where a given quality, reputation or other characteristic of the good is essentially attributable to its geographical origin'.
	Additional protection was afforded GIs for wines and spirits (Article 23).
2015	**Regulations under the Geneva Act of the Lisbon Agreement on Appellations of Origin and Geographical Indications (as adopted on 20 May 2015)**
	This conference adopted a new Act of the Lisbon Agreement for the Protection of Appellations of Origin and Their International Registration that makes the Lisbon Agreement more attractive for states, while preserving its principles and objectives.
	Primarily, it updates the administrative procedures governing the Lisbon Agreement.

Note: This table only refers to IGOs.

these organisations was important since otherwise tension between the Paris Convention and the Madrid Agreement would have increased. The AIPPI thought it 'essential that there is a close connection between the various ... international organizations ... and the international offices at Berne'.[1]

Another feature of the post-1945 period was the growth of supra-national bodies to promote freer trade, for example, the European Economic Community, formed in 1957, the General Agreement on Trade and Tariffs (GATT), established in 1947, and the World Trade Organization, created in 1995. The post-1945 era differs from earlier periods because IGOs featured prominently in trade negotiations. However, harmonious alignment between the promotion of freer trade and more robust protection of IGOs was not always apparent. Indeed, at times, there was considerable discord between these two objectives. For example, Articles 30–36 of the Treaty of Rome, signed in 1957, required the elimination of quantitative restrictions between Member States to ensure 'the free movement of goods'. But in the *Deserbais* case (1988), the courts had to determine whether German exports of Edam cheese to France was lawful. Similar issues appeared with the marketing of Cambozola cheese in Austria and the extent to which this caused confusion among consumers wishing to purchase Gorgonzola. More recently, the United States complained that the EU scheme for the protection of GIs contravened GATT. The United States argued that the EU scheme accorded less favourable treatment to imported products because they were not eligible for registration as GIs on the same terms as products originating from the EU.[2]

This chapter discusses the development of international protocols to protect IGOs after 1945. Increasingly, the focus was on protecting appellations and this was clearly signalled by the Lisbon Agreement of 1958 and the TRIPS Agreement of 1994. However, I argue that both conventions suffered from major weaknesses. As far as TRIPS is concerned, these faults ignited an acrimonious battle between the United States and the EU which raised broader questions about protectionism and the best way to protect GIs.

---

[1] Actes de la Conference de Lisbonne: 182.
[2] M. Echols, *Geographical Indications for Food Products* (Alphen aan den Rijn: Wolters Kluwer, 2008), 48–52; WTO, *European Communities – Protection of Trademarks and Geographical Indications for Agricultural Products and Foodstuffs, Complaint by the United States, Report of the Panel*, 2005: 61. This issue is discussed later in this chapter.

THE LISBON AGREEMENT

Following the London conference of 1934, there was growing international consensus that the Paris Convention and the Madrid Agreement were not providing appropriate protection of IGOs. In the later 1930s, and especially at the AIPPI's Prague meeting in 1938, much of the debate focused on the feasibility of amending the Madrid Agreement. But significant difficulties involving the registration and protection of appellations remained. By the 1950s, some countries believed there was little hope of amending the Madrid Agreement. German experts considered it retrogressive to abandon the absolute protection afforded wine, even though many countries did not provide this special treatment. Maintaining the status quo, that only national courts were empowered to determine whether a product was generic, failed to address the problem of 'doubtful appellations': Emmental and Eau de Cologne had once been appellations, but, as a result of abuse, they had become generic. Concerns were also raised that judges were neglecting foreign interests in their decisions.[3]

The international registration of appellations was a solution to some of these problems. For example, it would publicise those that were protected in a particular country; it would oblige other countries to note these appellations and, possibly, offer the same protection as provided by the host country. Registration also ensured that appellations could never become generic. However, registration of appellations was potentially risky. It was feared that individual countries would seek to register as many as possible based on current and anticipated needs and that national governments would over-exercise their right to veto applications from other countries. The latter consideration was pertinent for 'doubtful appellations' which were subject to an 'insoluble dilemma'. A country seeking to register such appellations would inevitably face severe opposition, for example, German protests if France sought to register Eau de Cologne. Conversely, failure to obtain registration would confirm that the appellation was generic and therefore incapable of protection.[4]

Further problems carried over from the interwar period included how to define an appellation. Clearly, if they were to be robustly protected by registration, it was imperative that their meaning was fully understood.

---

[3] *Annuaire* (1956, part I): 329, 351; *Annuaire*, 1958: 171.
[4] TNA, BT 209/832, International Union for the Protection of Industrial Property, Lisbon Conference Preliminary Documents: Draft International Agreement, Explanatory Note: E7; *Annuaire* (1958): 172.

There was also the difficulty of determining whether an appellation could be applied to industrial products, and how to distinguish appellations from indications of origin. The Stresa Convention of 1951, established to facilitate international cooperation on the accurate use of appellations applied to cheese, suggested a possible way forward: appellations were restricted to 'cheese manufactured or matured in traditional regions, by virtue of *local, loyal and uninterrupted* usages', whereas denominations applied to cheeses with 'definite characteristics [which] refer mainly to the shape, weight, size, type and colour of the rind and curd, as well as to the fat content of the cheese'.⁵ In this scheme, only appellations signalled origin, whereas denominations communicated non-geographical characteristics. However, the Stresa Convention suffered from two major weaknesses. First, only a handful of countries, all heavily engaged in cheese production – Austria, Denmark, France, Italy, the Netherlands, Norway, Sweden, and Switzerland – became signatories. In other words, like the Madrid Agreement, the Stresa Convention had limited international appeal. The second weakness was that only two cheeses, Roquefort and Peccorino Romano, received appellation status at the Convention. Signatories could request that a cheese be upgraded from 'denomination' to appellation, but to be successful the application had to be supported by 75 per cent of the Permanent Council. This requirement further undermined the general appeal of Stresa: 'It is utopian to believe that a sufficient number of states would give up national sovereignty in the framework of a General Convention on designations of origin.'⁶

Amending the Paris Convention was an alternative means to ensure more effective and comprehensive international protection of IGOs. On the eve of the Lisbon Conference, there were forty-two and twenty-five signatories, respectively, to the Paris Convention and the Madrid Agreement. Of particular significance, only the Paris Convention included Australia, Canada, Denmark (major exporting nations), and the United States (a major importer and exporter).⁷ By the 1950s, there was growing recognition that altering Article X of the Paris Convention was desirable.

---

⁵ A. Peaslee, *International Governmental Organisations: Constitutional Documents* (The Hague: Martinus Nijhoff, 1979), 407. These definitions are comparable to those governing the European Union's Protected Designation of Origin (PDO) and Protected Geographical Indication (PGI) scheme of 1992.

⁶ Annuaire (1958): 172; WIPO, 'Present Situation and Possible New Solutions', 28 June 1974 (document TAO/1/2): 8.

⁷ Calculated from www.wipo.int/export/sites/www/treaties/en/documents/pdf/paris.pdf, and same for Madrid.

Indeed, at its Paris meeting in 1950, the AIPPI had unanimously agreed that the restrictions embodied in Article X be abolished.[8] Following the Lanham Act of 1946, the United States became fully supportive of the need to amend Article X: 'This provision of the Convention should be the most important . . . it aims to protect the public against deception and fraud due to false statements concerning the products offered for sale.'[9] The United States proposed that the limitations stipulated in Article X should be excised and that it should apply to any false description.

Disagreement emerged about the precise wording of the US proposals. Did they apply to indirect indications of origin, for example, Scottish instead of Scotland, and Sauternes rather than Made in Sauternes? Doubts were raised about the extent to which use of fictitious IGOs misled consumers, for example, use of North Pole on bananas. The treatment of generic terms under the US proposal was potentially the biggest source of disagreement. Changing Article X obviated the need to become entangled in determining the genericity of any product, not just wine. Scandinavian countries suggested that if the qualifications governing Article X were removed, so that false indications alone were prohibited, it would be necessary to insert a clause in the Paris Convention permitting the courts to determine whether an appellation was generic and therefore incapable of constituting a false indication. Resolving this issue was crucial since otherwise there was no guarantee that national legislation would prevent misuse of IGOs. For example, Swiss law required products to be truthfully marked with an indication of origin, but this did not apply to generic indications. German courts prevented an appellation from becoming generic if a significant proportion of the public believed the appellation to be accurate. Consequently, use of Pilsner was permissible when accompanied by the name of a German location, for example, Radeberger Pilsner and Gottesberger Pilsner.[10] The United States and Canada were emphatically opposed to the Scandinavian proposals: when a term was recognised as generic, the public could not be deceived into believing that it designated a particular geographic location. Additionally, once a term became generic, public rights to it could not be revoked:

Expressions such as 'New York Champagne', 'Ohio Sauterne' and 'California Burgundy' . . . are intended to identify certain special characteristics of taste,

---

[8] Annuaire (1950): 123–125.
[9] USC 15, Ch. 22. Sections 1124 (42) and 1125 (43) prohibited the importation of products bearing false or misleading indications of origin. Annuaire, 1955: 258.
[10] Annuaire (1956), part I: 334, 336; Annuaire (1957): 207, 310.

quality or kind of wine; they have no other purpose ... There is no way provided by law in the United States prohibiting the use of these expressions ... Any law passed by Congress [in this direction] would be unconstitutional and would not be applied by the Courts. The United States cannot, by means of an international treaty, remove the right of US citizens to use generic names.[11]

The US suggestions were supported by Britain, Germany, Italy, and Scandinavia. Even France, a traditional opponent to changes in Article X, was in favour of the US recommendations – possibly because the proposed alteration to Article X did not affect the absolute protection afforded 'products of the vine' contained in Article IV of the Madrid Agreement.[12]

The net effect of debates between the late 1930s and the mid-1950s was that a much stronger consensus emerged on the need to remove the restrictions governing Article X of the Paris Convention, reassess Article IV of the Madrid Agreement, enshrine a definition of appellation, and provide for their international registration. These discussions coalesced in the Lisbon Agreement, 1958, which represented 'the high water mark in the international protection' of IGOs'.[13] The Lisbon conference followed a similar format to previous meetings. It was entrusted with the task of revising the Paris Convention and the Madrid Agreement. Additionally, and unlike previous conferences, it established an Arrangement for the Protection of Appellations of Origin and their International Registration (Lisbon Agreement). To keep the discussion tractable, each component is discussed in turn.

As noted, by the 1950s, there was a clear consensus that the restrictions embodied in Article X needed to be abolished. At Lisbon, this unanimity was maintained and the revised Article X stated: 'The provisions of the preceding Article shall apply in cases of direct or indirect use of a false indication of the source of the product or the identity of the producer, manufacturer or trader.' Article X now had a much broader remit: the term 'indirect' covered scenarios where the false indication appeared on an invoice, not just the product. Similarly, protection was extended to misleading use of the name of a manufacturer, an issue on which Hungarian delegates were particularly vociferous. The overall effect of changes to Article X was that it was now more closely aligned with the provisions governing unfair competition.[14]

---

[11] *Annuaire* (1957): 315.   [12] *Annuaire* (1956), part I: 329–352.
[13] Gangjee, *Relocating the Law of Geographical Indications*, 127.
[14] *Actes de Lisbonne*: 776–786. The voting for the new Article X was: eighteen in favour, eight abstentions, and none against.

Turning to the Madrid Agreement, its limited attractiveness derived from Article IV: the courts were not entitled to adjudicate on whether 'products of the vine' were generic. At Lisbon, this Article came under renewed scrutiny. Like previous conferences, Czechoslovakian delegates argued that the favourable treatment of wine should be extended to beer and other manufactures. Irish delegates thought that alcoholic spirits would benefit from this extension. British, Italian, Japanese, and Swedish delegates suggested that the exemption given to wine should be removed with the consequence that the revised Article would state: 'The Tribunals of each country will decide what appellations, on account of their generic character, do not fall within the provisions of the present Arrangement.'[15] The advantage of this suggestion was that all products – irrespective of whether their qualities were determined by the natural environment or artisanal skill – were subject to court rulings. However, France maintained its opposition to any change in Article IV:

When an appellation of origin is protected for many years in its country of origin and in many other countries, we do not see how some countries could use the pretext that they ascribe to it a generic meaning. If an appellation of origin is usurped in a country and acquires a so-called generic character it is because the laws of the country [of origin] are not known ... which is contrary to the principle of the Protection of Appellations of Origin laid down in the Paris Convention.[16]

French resistance was based on one of the founding principles of the Paris Convention: 'Persons within the jurisdiction of each of the countries of the Union shall, as regards the protection of industrial property, enjoy in all other countries of the Union the advantages that their respective laws now grant.'[17] In other words, despite the criticisms levelled at Article IV, the French could rightly claim that their appellations deserved protection under the Paris Convention. The French argument appears to have been sufficient to ensure that Article IV remained unchanged.[18]

A unique feature of the Lisbon Agreement was that it provided a definition of appellation and established a framework for their registration. These new features were integral to each other. Prior to Lisbon, the Paris Convention and Madrid Agreement employed different nomenclature without defining the terms used. The former referred to 'indications

---

[15] Actes de Lisbonne: 792–812.   [16] Actes de Lisbonne: 812. Own translation.
[17] Board of Trade: *International Convention for the Protection of Industrial Property*, London: HMSO (1934): 3.
[18] The Lisbon Conference made slight changes to other parts of the Madrid Agreement. For example, Article I was amended to include 'deceptive' indications of origin.

of source or appellations of origin'; the latter used 'false indication of origin', 'appellations', 'regional appellations', and 'generic'. Without a consensus on the meaning of 'appellation' their protection would have depended on national legislation and bilateral treaties. Simultaneously, it was acknowledged that a fundamental objective at Lisbon was to ensure that appellations received international protection which was best secured by global registration.[19]

Establishing a special union for appellations overcame a number of thorny issues which bedevilled previous conferences. For example, Article I of the Paris Convention referred to 'indications of source or appellations of origin'. This implied, inaccurately, that the two terms referred to the same subject matter. At its 1957 meeting in Oslo, the executive committee of the AIPPI differentiated the terms: an indication of source was a direct or indirect indication of the place, country, region, or locality; an appellation (or appellation of origin) was the geographical name of a place in which products derived their qualities from the soil, climate, custom, or technique. This distinction was broadly the same as that proposed at Lisbon.[20] 'Appellation' and 'indications of source' were distinguished in France, Italy, and Spain, but not in Israel, Sweden, Britain, or the United States. Semantic issues aside, 'appellations' and 'indications of source' possessed different legal properties in countries which recognised them to be separate forms of intellectual property. The former gave producers in a specific location an exclusive right to the appellation, whereas the latter was governed by unfair competition and the relationship between buyer and seller.[21] The creation of a 'special union' within the Lisbon Agreement generated another advantage: it benefitted those countries having a special interest in appellations and thereby removed the need to obtain agreement within the Paris Convention.[22]

The main features of the Lisbon Agreement were that appellations 'recognized and protected as such in the country of origin', and registered with the United International Bureaux for the Protection of Intellectual Property (WIPO's predecessor), would be protected by other countries in the union (Article 1). In other words, reciprocal protection of appellations was guaranteed within the special union. Appellations were defined as 'the

---

[19] Actes de Lisbonne: 813–814.
[20] Annuaire (1958): 12. For ontological issues, see, for example, Ladas, *Patents, Trademarks and Related Rights*, 1574; Actes de Lisbonne: 771–773.
[21] Actes de Lisbonne: 773–774, 808, 814.
[22] The Lisbon Agreement created a union of signatories with their own assembly.

geographical name of a country, region or locality which serves to designate a product originating therein, the quality and characteristics of which are due exclusively or essentially to the geographical environment, including natural and human factors' (Article 2.1). Additionally, protection was extended to cases where an appellation was accompanied by terms such as 'kind', 'make', 'type', or 'style'. The advantage of this stipulation was that it addressed the long-standing problem of legends such as 'Spanish Champagne': although consumers might not be misled into thinking that this Champagne was French, there was, nonetheless, a clear attempt to usurp the true origin of the wine.[23] The Lisbon Agreement also contained transitional measures: upon notification from the Bureaux that application to register an appellation had been lodged, countries had one year to raise opposition. Additionally, third parties employing an appellation in another country prior to its international registration had two years in which to abandon its use. Further articles specified an appellation could never become generic once registered and that if an appellation was protected 'as such' in the country of origin, protection would continue even if there was a failure to renew registration.[24]

Did the Lisbon Conference represent a success? From one perspective this question can be answered affirmatively: the restrictions governing Article X were removed. In addition, the well-established tension between the different levels and types of protection offered by the Paris Convention and the Madrid Agreement were eased by the establishment of a special union for appellations. The Lisbon Agreement also advanced the international protection of appellations in other respects. For example, compared to the Paris Convention and the Madrid Agreement, use of qualifying terms such as 'kind' or 'style' was prohibited. Czech producers of beer and mineral waters were likely to have been especially pleased with the Lisbon Agreement: after campaigning for more than fifty years to have their beverages placed on a par with 'products of the vine', Budweiser beer, Budvar, L'eau minerale de Carlsbad, Pils, Pilsen, and Pilsner were among the first appellations recorded in the international register.[25]

Nonetheless, by April 2017, only twenty-eight countries had acceded to the Lisbon Agreement. As may be expected, France, Italy, Spain, and

---

[23] Other problems can arise. For example, it can encourage the use of 'Champagne' as a generic expression. Gangjee, *Relocating the Law of Geographical Indications*, 159–160.

[24] *Records of the Intellectual Property Conference of Stockholm, 11 June–14 July 1967.* WIPO: Geneva, 1971: 66–68.

[25] www.wipo.int/lisbon/en/bulletin/

Portugal were among the signatories. However, many significant economies, including Britain, Germany, Japan, and the United States, did not
accede.[26] A number of general weaknesses in the Lisbon Agreement prevented the accession of more countries. For example, the definition of
'appellation was too narrow', and the Agreement failed to stipulate the
grounds on which registration could be refused.[27] Other problems became
apparent. What if an appellation corresponded to a territory overlapping
many states? Was it possible to register and protect an appellation which,
while not a 'proper' geographic name (a place that actually exists), was
perceived by the public to have a geographical connotation? Austrian
officials argued that 'the reputation of a given product was based not
only on conditions imposed by geographical environment, but also on the
idea which the customer had formed of the quality of the product'.[28]
A further problem was whether other manufactured products could be
classed as appellations. Article 2.1 of the Lisbon Agreement required that
a qualitative link be established between the geographic environment and
the product, but:

This link, which existed at the start of the manufacture of the industrial product,
may subsequently have been stretched to the point that its existence is difficult to
prove, although the name has not become a purely generic term; in other words,
the name gives a certain reputation to the product which bears it, in spite of the
doubt concerning the geographical link.[29]

Signatories to the Lisbon Agreement were required to protect appellations 'as such': protection in the country of origin had to be established by
a specific legislative or judicial act. This meant that counties which protected appellations under unfair competition law were effectively
excluded. The German (FDR) Minister of Justice argued that only a few
of the appellations belonging to his country, for example, Solingen and
wines listed in the Wine Register (Weinbergsrolle), benefitted from special

---

[26] www.wipo.int/export/sites/www/treaties/en/documents/pdf/lisbon.pdf
[27] WIPO, 'Present Situation and Possible New Solutions', 28 June 1974 (document TAO/1/
2): 12–13.
[28] Lisbon Council, 'Problems Arising from the Practical Application of the Lisbon
Agreement', 1 July 1970 (document AO/V/5): 2; Lisbon Council, 'Report of the Fifth
Session', 26 September 1970 (document AO/V/8) 3; WIPO, 'Revision of the Lisbon
Agreement for the Protection of Appellations of Origin and Their International
Registration or the Drafting of a New Treaty', 30 June 1972 (document P/EC/VIII/6,
Annex II): 3. Thus, there is no geographical place called Basmati, although it is strongly
associated with the Punjab region and the rice that is produced there is distinctive
(similarly, Feta is not a place, but this cheese is associated with Greece).
[29] WIPO, 'Present Situation and Possible New Solutions', 10.

protection arising from specific legislation. Consequently, only a few West German appellations were capable of registration under the Lisbon Agreement.[30] Similarly, Argentine officials claimed it was impossible for them to accede to the Lisbon Agreement:

In fact, since our country has for some considerable time been producing a wide variety of articles originally produced elsewhere, it is now a deep-rooted custom, which it would be almost impossible for us to change, to give these articles the same name as the original product; this appellation is moreover necessary and irreplaceable. It follows that it would be impossible for a country such as ours to be obliged to prevent the use of expressions which are indispensable in trade and in common parlance to designate a countless variety of articles, leaving aside, of course, those appellations which are relatively recent and which are not yet in general use.[31]

A major obstacle preventing Britain and the United States acceding to the Lisbon Agreement was that the power of their courts to adjudicate on appellations was nullified.[32] Prior to the Lisbon Conference a thorough review of the relationship between domestic law and appellations was conducted by the British government which admitted that appellations did not receive domestic recognition. The government acknowledged that terms such as 'Spanish Port' and 'Swiss Champagne' provided the basis for giving a generic character to these geographical names. Similarly, the application of Burgundy and Sherry to wines made elsewhere had been in common use for a considerable time and they had become generic. Indeed, post-Lisbon, it was not thought necessary to restrict British sales of 'South African Sherry'. Business interests had a vested interest in protecting the status quo. The British Wine and Spirit Association stated, 'the matter is very delicate, and it would be most difficult, and very controversial, to attempt to draw a line between titles which have become generic and those which should still be restricted to the products of particular regions'.[33]

---

[30] Lisbon Council, 'Territorial Expansion of the Lisbon Union', 25 June 1971 (document AO/VI/4): 3. Moreover, the Agreement made no provision for GIs that were already generic in particular countries. B. O'Connor, *The Law of Geographical Indications* (London: Cameron May, 2004), 39–40.

[31] WIPO, 'Revision of the Lisbon Agreement for the Protection of Appellations of Origin and Their International Registration or the Drafting of a New Treaty', 30 June 1972 (document P/EC/VIII/6, Annex II): 2.

[32] Ladas, *Patents, Trademarks and Related Rights*, 1607.

[33] TNA, BT 209/785. Revision at Lisbon: Preparatory Work on the Agenda: Lisbon Conference, Preliminary Documents: B13–B14; TNA, BT 209/793, False Indications and Appellations of Origin. Wine and Spirit Association of Great Britain to Board of Trade, 7 May 1958; Letter to Ball, 22 August 1958; Draft of Letter to Stephen Miles, Commonwealth Relations Office, 1959.

Despite these conflicting signals, the fundamental position of the British government was that all questions pertaining to appellations, indications of origin, and generic terms were to be decided by British courts.[34] Even though Britain remained a signatory to the Madrid Agreement after the Lisbon Conference, it had never effectively implemented the reserve for 'products of the vine' contained in Article IV, preferring to leave this to the courts. In any event, the British government was adamant that the laws of each country should be sufficient to protect against false or misleading IGOs. However, the 'Spanish Champagne' case presented the government with a dilemma and exposed tensions between the protection offered by national legislation and the exemption afforded 'products of the vine'.[35]

In 1958, the French Comité Interprofessionel du Vin de Champagne and the Institut National des Appellations d'Origine des Vins et Eaux-de-vie brought an action against the Costa Brava Wine Co. Ltd., for importing and selling 'Perelada Spanish Champagne'. The prosecution was based on the Merchandise Marks Acts, which made it an offence to apply to products a description which was 'false or misleading in a material respect'. Two questions were central to this action. First, when used on its own, did Champagne only mean sparkling white wine produced in the Champagne district of France? Second, if 'Spanish' was placed before Champagne did the label as a whole indicate sparkling white wine of *Champagne character*, produced in Spain?[36] This litigation placed the British government in a quandary: 'If the prosecution succeeds, we may have to reconsider our attitude, not only to wines which, not being French, are described as "Champagne of a kind" but to such things as Australian Chablis. If it fails, then we may be in trouble in respect of article 4.'[37]

---

[34] TNA, BT 209/788, Preparatory Work on the Agenda: Preliminary Documents, Propositions and Observations of Other Governments: International Union for the Protection of Industrial Property: Lisbon Conference Preliminary Documents: 171; TNA, 209/790, Proposed Revision of the Arrangement of The Hague 1925 and Madrid Arrangement (Marks) of Origin. Revision of the Madrid Arrangement on False Indications of Origin. Meeting, 4 August 1955; TNA, BT 209/793, False Indications and Appellations of Origin: Meeting, 17 June 1958; Brief for UK Delegates to Lisbon Conference of the International Bureau for the Protection of Industrial Property, 15 August 1958: 6–7.

[35] TNA, BT 209/793, *False Indications and Appellations of Origin*: International Bureau for the Protection of Industrial Property, Lisbon Conference, 1958, u.d., document 19; Note of a meeting held on Wednesday, 27 August, to discuss the brief for the Conference on questions relating to indications of origin.

[36] *Times*, 21 November 1958, 17.

[37] TNA, BT 209/793, False Indications and Appellations of Origin: Letter to Ball, 22 August 1958.

This case highlighted other problems both for the British government and for French Champagne producers. For example, a description which starts as false or misleading and is tolerated and allowed to persist may cease to be misleading and may no longer be 'false' within the meaning of the Merchandise Marks Acts. The failure of French wine producers to bring earlier actions was attributed to 'short-sightedness, over-confidence and apathy'.[38] In a later case involving 'British' and 'South African' Sherry, it was held that they 'had been in use for so long without objection that it was too late to stop them now'.[39]

The jury found for the defendants. This verdict nearly provoked a trade war when Parisian merchants started selling Dutch spirits as Scotch whisky.[40] Subsequently, in 1959, twelve major champagne producers led by Bollinger brought an action against the Costa Brava Wine Company.[41] Again, the court had to address fundamental issues. For example, was Champagne understood by the public to mean wine produced in that region, or did it refer to a particular kind of wine produced by a special process that could be made by producers in other regions? Did use of this term by the defendants constitute 'unlawful trade competition'? Did addition of the word Spanish show that the wine was not produced in France, which meant consumers could not be deceived? Justice Danckwerts agreed with the plaintiffs, stating: '"Champagne" in this country means the product produced in the Champagne district of France ... "Champagne" in this country has not come to mean a type of wine.'[42]

FROM LISBON TO MARRAKECH

By the early 1960s it was becoming apparent that the Lisbon Agreement needed revision. It was amended at Stockholm in 1967, but this did not

---

[38] *Times*, 5 December 1958, 13.
[39] T. Unwin, *Wine and the Vine* (London: Routledge (1991), 320.
[40] *Times*, 22 December 1958, 7.
[41] *J. Bollinger and Others* v. *Costa Brava Wine Co. Ltd.* (1960) Ch. 262–288; *J. Bollinger* v. *Costa Brava Wine Co. Ltd.* (1961) 1 All ER: 561–568. The other plaintiffs were Charles Heidsieck & Co., Krug & Co., Lanson Père & Fils, Louis Roederer, Maison A. Mérand & Co., Maison Moët & Chandon, G. H. Mumm & Co., Perrier Jouët, Pol Roger & Co., and Veuve Clicquot Ponsardin.
[42] *J. Bollinger* v. *Costa Brava Wine Co. Ltd.* (1961) 1 All ER: 564. Misuse of 'Scotch Whiskey' was also successfully prevented in action brought by John Walker and other whisky producers.

affect its substantive provisions.[43] A major factor driving the review was that few countries had acceded to the Agreement. One way to secure territorial expansion of this Agreement was to focus on those countries which were signatories to the Paris Convention and who could be assumed to have a general interest in the protection of appellations.[44] The growth of bilateral treaties involving France, Germany, Italy, and Greece indicated that countries sought to overcome weaknesses in the multilateral framework. Although such treaties increased the diversity of protection available, they possessed a number of advantages over international treaties. First, it was easier for the contacting states to take account of specific circumstances. For example, they accommodated situations where appellations had become generic in the country of origin but not in the importing country. Second, they provided that in the event of dispute, courts in the importing country were required to apply the law of the country of origin.[45]

A WIPO committee of experts issued a questionnaire to numerous countries to determine how best to develop multilateral protection of appellations.[46] The subsequent replies can be roughly divided into two categories. The first category included those that were not interested in the international protection of appellations: Belgium, Finland, the Republic of Ireland, the Netherlands, and South Africa. Second, many countries agreed on the need for greater defence of appellations but differed on how best to achieve this. For example, Danish officials thought greater reliance should be placed on Article X of the Paris Convention, whereas Swedish officials preferred the Madrid Agreement. The desirability of merging the Madrid and Lisbon Agreements was mooted by officials representing Cuba, Hungary, Italy, and Senegal.[47]

The outcome of these debates was that the range of options available to WIPO was limited, though a consensus existed that a new international system had to possess certain desirable features, including the need to protect all kinds of terms and signs referring directly or indirectly to geographical origin. Additionally, protection needed to operate on two

[43] WIPO, 'Present Situation and Possible New Solutions', 28 June 1972 (document TAO/1/2): 8.
[44] Lisbon Council, 'Report of the Sixth Session', 2 October 1971 (document AO/VI/5): 1–2.
[45] WIPO, 'Present Situation and Possible New Solutions', 28 June 1974 (document TAO/1/2): 14–16.
[46] WIPO empowered this committee to prepare a new multilateral treaty for the protection of appellations.
[47] WIPO, 'Revision of the Lisbon Agreement for the Protection of Appellations of Origin and Their International Registration or Drafting of a New Treaty', 30 June 1972 (document P/EC/VIII/6): 3–4.

levels. First, all appellations would be covered against deceptive practices. Second, a dedicated system of protection was to be established including regulations on registration and the provision that the law of the country of origin would govern dispute resolution.[48] A further departure from the Lisbon Agreement was that the provisions for registration and opposition were changed.[49] However, WIPO's proposals were discontinued when diplomatic preparations began on a revision of the Paris Convention.[50] Subsequently, despite occasional attempts to re-engage with this topic, a new treaty was not enacted until 2015.[51]

During the intervening period – between the Lisbon Agreement of 1958 and the Geneva Act of 2015 – two major developments affected the international protection of appellations. First, there was a series of European Commission (EC) initiatives concerning wine and foodstuffs primarily designed to increase quality and to combat the effects of globalisation. The second, launched under the auspices of the WTO and concluded at Marrakech in 1994, represented a concerted effort by all Member States of the WTO to agree to minimum standards for the protection of appellations. Each is considered later in this chapter.

The formation of the EEC in 1957 and the subsequent rapid growth of intra-European trade in wine indicated the need for a Community approach to wine labelling. Until the 1970s, a hotchpotch of national rules and regulations existed which had the potential to generate discord within the Common Market:

Some [M]ember States gave priority to accurate consumer information and to the freedom of action of the trade, while others endeavoured to combine these aspects with the need to protect producers ... against distortions of competition; ... with the aim of reconciling these different approaches ... and of avoiding too divergent interpretations, it was deemed to appropriate lay down fairly comprehensive rules on description.[52]

[48] WIPO, 'Report Adopted by the Committee of Experts', 15 November 1974 (document TAO/1/8): 4–6.
[49] WIPO, 'Draft Treaty on the Protection of Geographical Indications', 25 August 1975 (document TAO/II/2): 2, 8.
[50] WIPO, 'The Need for a New Treaty and Its Possible Contents', 9 April 1990 (document GEO/CE/I/2): 12.
[51] The Geneva Act of the Lisbon Agreement on Appellations of Origin and Geographical Indications came into force in 2015. www.wipo.int/meetings/diplomatic_conferences/2 015/en/. Essentially, this Act strengthened the regulations governing applications for and registration of appellations.
[52] EEC 2392/89: 'Laying Down General Rules for the Description and Presentation of Wines and Grape Musts'. *Official Journal of the EU* (hereafter, *Official Journal*), 9 August (1989): 13.

From the 1970s a battery of regulations was introduced to encourage quality improvements, to punish fraud and misrepresentation, and to facilitate the creation of a single community market for wine.[53] A fundamental objective of EU regulations on the Common wine market was to 'preserve as far as possible the specific characteristics bestowed by its origin on each quality wine psr'.[54] Consequently, the EU stipulated that 'quality wines' produced in specified regions included, for example: Appellation d' origine contrôlée, Appellation contrôlée and Champagne in France, as well as Denominazione di origine controllata (DOC) and Denominazione di origine controllata e garanita (DOCG) in Italy.[55] Further amendments were enacted in 1991 to resolve the conflict between brands which were subsequently recognised as wine-producing regions.[56]

Turning to foodstuffs, in 1992, the EU authorised the use of specific GIs to be applied to food. The two most important were protected designation of origin (PDO) and protected geographical indication (PGI).[57] The specifications governing PDOs and PGIs were thought to be of fundamental importance to consumers because they indicated a link between the quality of produce and its geographical origin. In 1992, the EU also permitted registration of products as Traditional Speciality Guaranteed (TSG), if they used 'traditional raw materials', or were characterised by 'a traditional composition or a mode of production', or were subjected to 'processing reflecting a traditional type of production'. In direct contrast to PDOs and PGIs, products were ineligible for

---

[53] EEC 337/79: 'On the Common Organisation of the Market in Wine'. *Official Journal*, No. L 54. 5 March 1979: 1–4.

[54] Psr is an acronym which refers to wines 'produced in specified regions'.

[55] EEC 338/79: 'Laying Down Special Provisions Relating to Quality Wines Produced in Specific Regions'. *Official Journal*, 5 March 1979: 48, 53. Subsequently, 'quality' and 'table' wines became classified as PDO and PGI, respectively.

[56] EEC Council Regulation 3897/91: amending for the third time Regulation (EEC) No. 2392/ 89 laying down general rules for the description and presentation of wines and grape musts. *Official Journal*, 31 December 1991: 5. The conflict arose because Michael Torres, a Spanish wine producer, was using *TORRES* as a trademark long before the Portuguese government stipulated that TORRES VEDRAS was a recognised wine region in Portugal. L. A. Lindquist, 'Champagne or Champagne? An Examination of U.S. Failure to Comply with the Geographical Provisions of the TRIPS Agreement', *Georgia Journal of International and Comparative Law*, 27 (1999): 320–321.

[57] 'Council Regulation No 2081/92 of 14 July 1992 on the Protection of Geographical Indications and Designations of Origin for Agricultural Products and Foodstuffs', *Official Journal*, L 208, 24 July 1992: 4–5. Amended by Council Regulation 510/2006, *Official Journal*, L 93, 31 March 2006.

registration as TSG if their particular characteristics were due to geographical origin. TSGs, therefore, appear highly anomalous in the EU campaign to link produce quality with origin. Examples of TSG-labelled produce include Kabanos sausage from Poland and a variety of fruit beers from Belgium.

In the same way that French legislation preceded and then informed the protection of appellations at the Paris Convention and the Madrid Agreement, so the wine and food regulations enacted by the EU influenced the TRIPS Agreement. Indeed, it has been claimed that the higher protection afforded wine and spirits in TRIPS was the result of political manoeuvring to guarantee EU participation in the Uruguay Round.[58] One feature of EU wine and PDO/PGI regulations which fed directly into TRIPS was the relationship between trademarks and GIs. In broad terms, the EU schemes stipulated coexistence, a legal regime under which a GI and a trademark can both be used concurrently, even though the use of either infringed the rights conferred on the other.[59] The wine directives stated that owners of brand names which were identical to a geographical unit (designation) could continue to use these names provided they had been employed for more than twenty-five years before the designation was officially recognised. Private brands could not be invoked against the registration of GIs. Some EU regulations allowed wine trademarks with prior authority to be expunged without compensation in favour of GIs if a 'confusingly similar designation was later protected as a geographical indication for wine'. Registered geographical indications such as PDO and PGI obtained similar privileges.[60]

The second initiative to be discussed is the TRIPS Agreement, widely considered one of the most significant international treaties governing intellectual property law. According to Daniel Gervais, '[i]ts scope is . . . much broader than that of any previous international agreement, covering not only all areas already . . . protected under extant agreements, but also giving new life to pre-existing treaties that failed'.[61] Unlike the Paris

---

[58] K. Raustiala and S. R. Munzer, 'The Global Struggle over Geographical Indications', *European Journal of International Law*, 18 (2007): 343. The Uruguay Round was the eighth round of multilateral trade negotiations under the auspices of GATT. It met between 1986 and 1994.
[59] G. E. Evans and M. Blakeney, 'The Protection of Geographical Indications after Doha: Quo Vadis?', *Journal of International Economic Law*, 9 (2006): 599.
[60] EC 3897/91: Article 1.7; EC 2081/92: Articles 13 and 14.
[61] D. Gervais, *The TRIPS Agreement: Drafting History and Analysis* (London: Sweet & Maxwell, 2008), 3; O'Connor, *The Law of Geographical Indications*, 50.

Convention, which became part of WIPO, the TRIPS Agreement evolved under the aegis of GATT. Formed in 1947, GATT was the primary body for determining tariff regimes. Non-tariff barriers first became the subject of debate at the Tokyo Round (1973), but it was not until the Uruguay Round (1986–1994) that intellectual property appeared on the agenda. The Uruguay Round ended with the establishment of the WTO (GATT's successor) and the TRIPS Agreement, which was signed at Marrakech and commenced on 1 January 1995. One of the most important features of TRIPS was that it linked intellectual property to trade: TRIPS is binding on all members of the WTO.[62] The United States played a key role integrating trade and intellectual property by employing 'a coercive trade-based strategy, threatening trade sanctions and the denial of trade benefits for countries whose IP regimes were deemed unacceptably weak'.[63] Other advantages have been claimed for this relationship. For example, it extended the global scope and appeal of the TRIPS Agreement and it allowed states to apply enforcement mechanisms previously used in trade disputes to conflicts involving intellectual property.[64]

Within the TRIPS Agreement three articles addressed GIs. Article 22 defined a standard level of protection available to all products to ensure the public were not deceived and to prevent unfair competition. Article 22.1 defined GIs as 'indications which identify a good as originating in the territory of a Member, or a region or locality in that territory, where a given quality, reputation or other characteristic of the good is essentially attributable to its geographical origin'. This Article also stipulated that a Member could invalidate a registered trademark if it contained or consisted of 'a geographical indication with respect to goods not originating in the territory indicated [or] of such nature as to mislead the public as to true place of origin'. Effectively, Article 22 replicated EU wine and food regulations: GIs had precedence over trademarks. Article 23 provided enhanced protection for wines and spirits: subject to various exceptions, they were protected even if misuse would not cause the public to be misled. Article 23 required each Member State to provide legal means to prevent use of GIs on wines which did not originate from the location shown by

---

[62] TRIPS was adopted at Marrakech on 15 April 1994 as Annex 1 c of the Final Act Embodying the Results of the Uruguay Round of Multilateral Trade Negotiations. Gervais, *The TRIPS Agreement*, 28.
[63] S. Sell, *Private Power, Public Law* (Cambridge: Cambridge University Press, 2003), 13.
[64] J. Braithwaite and P. Drahos, *Global Business Regulation* (Cambridge: Cambridge University Press, 2000), 61.

the indication. This Article applied even when the true indication was accompanied by 'kind', 'style', or 'type' – for example, 'Colorado Cognac' or 'Cognac-style brandy'. It also provided for the establishment of a multilateral system of notification and registration of GIs for wines and spirits eligible for protection in Member States. Article 24 stipulated that Member States agreed to enter into negotiations intended to increase the protection of individual GIs. The 'exceptions' in this Article included a 'grandfather' clause which ensured that a state could not prevent use of a GI applied to wines or spirits in another Member State if the citizens in the latter had 'used that geographical indication in a continuous manner with regard to the same or related goods or services' either for ten years preceding 15 April 1994 (the date on which the TRIPS Agreement was adopted at Marrakech), or in good faith before that date. Additionally, GIs which had become generic were not eligible for protection.[65]

In a number of respects the TRIPS Agreement can be viewed as a major success. Currently, it has a membership of 162 countries com-pared to 28 for the Lisbon Agreement. TRIPS was a major multilateral agreement involving trademarks *and* GIs. The latter were no longer relegated to the periphery to be the subject of 'special' unions but were treated on a par with other forms of intellectual property. The Agreement referred to 'goods', not just food and wine, and so the scope of protection was extended to include traditional textiles and handicrafts, for example, Kolhapuri chappals (sandals) from India and Zhostovo metal trays from Russia. Moreover, there was no longer a requirement that a GI had to be a geographical name. Symbols repre-senting geographical origin, such as the Eiffel Tower or a Swiss chalet, were eligible for protection.[66]

However, it has been argued that the TRIPS Agreement weakened the relationship between product quality and location: 'essentially' in Article 22.1 could be interpreted to mean that production of a specific good may partially take place outside the defined location. Inclusion of 'reputation' in the same Article meant there was no specific requirement that a food be produced, processed, or prepared in a defined locality. In any case, was 'reputation' a purely subjective criterion or was it

---

[65] The full text of these Articles can be obtained from www.wipo.int/wipolex/en/other_trea ties/details.jsp?treaty_id=231.

[66] *Chocosuisse Union Des Fabricants Suisse De Chocolat and Others* v. *Cadbury Ltd.* RPC, 115 (1998): 117–154. The defendants had launched a chocolate bar under the name 'Swiss Chalet' and the confectionery was enclosed in a wrapper embossed with the Matterhorn Mountain.

capable of measurement?[67] Related scepticism has focused on the inter-play between the natural features of a particular region, which are geographically 'fixed', and human or artisanal skills, which are mobile.[68]

TWO TRIBES GO TO WAR?

Despite its unparalleled international appeal, the TRIPS Agreement gener-ated friction. As noted earlier, problems surrounding the protection of GIs permeated international concords ever since the Paris Convention of 1883. By relating trade policy to the protection of intellectual property, the TRIPS Agreement exacerbated relations among Member States, especially between the EU and the United States. The global reach of the TRIPS Agreement brought into conflict systems of GI protection which had pre-viously coexisted independently and in relative harmony. From an abstract perspective this difference appears to be of little consequence. In practice, though, conflict did arise between these different systems. Two events catalysed this discord: first, invocation of the WTO's Dispute Settlement Board by the United States and Australia against the EU's protection of GIs, which began in 1999 and culminated in 2005; second, beginning in 2003, EU efforts to develop TRIPS (TRIPS PLUS) by 'clawing back' GIs which had become generic, and extending the (higher) protection afforded wines and spirits to other products. Each is considered in what follows.

The complaints of the United States and Australia before the Dispute Settlement Board focused primarily on EC Regulation 2081/92.[69] One concern was that this directive was discriminatory because it favoured EU citizens (national treatment claims). It was claimed that the only way non-EU citizens could benefit from this directive was if their government's offered reciprocal and equivalent protection. But this was considered objectionable because it was tantamount to the importation of the EU framework without regard to existing national systems for protection. In the United States, the GIs California raisins, Florida citrus, Idaho potatoes, and Virginia ham were protected as certification or collective trademarks. Even if a product from outside the EU satisfied Regulation 2081/92 it was still ineligible to use the EU logos and it was not protected

---

[67] M. A. Echols, *Geographical Indications for Food Products* (Alphen aan den Rijn: Wolters Kluwer, 2008), 61–65; Gangjee, *Relocating the Law of Geographical Indications*, 223–237; Gervais, *The TRIPS Agreement*, 298.

[68] Raustiala and Munzer, 'The Global Struggle', 356.

[69] This regulation established the PDO and PGI schemes.

from becoming generic. Taken together, the essence of the US–Australian claim was that it was not possible for a GI originating outside the EU to benefit from Regulation 2081/92.[70] Subsequently, the views of 'third-party' countries reinforced the claims of the United States and Australia. For example, cochineal, a dye-producing insect, was originally cultivated in Mexico by the Aztecs. Subsequently, cochineal was farmed on the Canary Islands and registered as a GI within the EU. It was claimed that many of the characteristics of this insect could be attributed 'essentially' to Mexico, but it was not possible to register Mexican cochineal in the EU. Similarly, the protection that TRIPS afforded GIs was different from that in the EU because the former did not specify registration as a prerequisite for protection.[71] The Canadian government raised the temperature in the debate by claiming that the discrimination the EU practised with respect to GIs was tantamount to discrimination according to nationality:

[The EC] ignores the simple and incontestable reality that EC nationals are likely to register for protection of geographical indications originating from within the European Communities, whereas non EC-nationals are likely to register for protection of geographical indications originating from outside of the European Communities.[72]

The Canadian argument appears compelling: by definition, GIs are inextricably linked to a particular location, and, therefore, indigenous producers. It was thought inconceivable that non-EU nationals located within the EU were producing foods eligible for registration under the 2081/92 Regulation.

A further complaint involved coexistence of trademarks and GIs. The previous section indicated that the EU permitted the registration of GIs even when they 'clashed' with registered trademarks. This approach was anathema to the United States, which treats GIs as certification or collective trademarks, for which the governing principle is 'first in time, first in right'.[73] Debate on coexistence focused on alleged dissonance between TRIPS and the 2081/92 Regulation. Consider, for example, the GI Budweiser. The production of beer in the Czech town Budweis dates

---

70 Dispute Settlement Board, 'First Written Submission of the United States', 23 April 2004 (document WT/DS174/R/Add.1 Annex A-2): A17–A20, A30–A31, A40–A41.
71 Dispute Settlement Board, 'Arguments of the Third Parties', 15 March 2005 (document WT/DS174/R/Add.3: Annex C): C 29, C 42.
72 Dispute Settlement Board, 'Arguments of the Third Parties', 15 March 2005 (document WT/DS174/R/Add.3: Annex C): C 13.
73 Dispute Settlement Board, 'First Written Submission of the United States', 23 April 2004 (document WT/DS174/R/Add.1 Annex A-2): A 47–A56.

to the thirteenth century. In 1795 a brewery bearing the name of the town was established. Subsequently, the beer was sold as Budvar and then Budweiser Budvar. The US company Anheuser Busch established in 1876, registered the trademark Budweiser in the United States in 1907.[74] Anheuser Busch was concerned that the accession of the Czech Republic to the EU, and the registration of Budweiser Budvar under Regulation 2081/92, permitted the Czech brewer to sell its beer within the EU using the Budweiser mark. Clearly, this posed a direct marketing threat to Anheuser Busch, whose trademarks had global exposure. The key issue here was that EU regulations prevented owners of prior registered trademarks taking action when similar or identical marks were used as GIs. Even within Europe, the US brewer sold about five times more beer than its Czech counterpart.[75] Additionally, there was a more serious concern: Anheuser Busch could lose the right to sell its beer as Budweiser in the EU. It has been claimed that 'trade mark wars over the competitive European market for beer [have] seen US trademarks "Budweiser" and "Bud" subject to termination in various Member States of the EU because the European law holds "Budweiser" and "Bud" to be GIs for beer from the Czech Republic'.[76]

The EU rejected the US and Australian claims. Of particular interest are the arguments it made in relation to coexistence. The EC admitted that coexistence was not a perfect solution to the problematic relationship between trademarks and GIs. It claimed that the first in time, first in right doctrine could not be used to resolve conflicts between these two types of intellectual property because although trademarks can be acquired almost instantaneously, the creation of GIs requires that a link be established between the indication (place) and its associated product characteristics – which might take several years. Proprietors of GIs could not change the name of the geographical area in which they were located. Moreover, GIs served a public interest which justified additional protection. For example, GIs inform consumers that the product originates in a specific area and therefore possesses unique characteristics linked to that area, whereas a trademark only identifies a particular firm. Finally, because GIs were the common property of all

---

[74] Heath, 'The Budweiser Cases'.
[75] The Status of the World Trade Organization Negotiations on Agriculture. Hearings before the Committee on Agriculture House of Representatives, 108th Congress First Session, Serial No. 108–105, 21 May–22 July. Washington, DC: US Government Printer, 2003: 328–331 (hereafter, Hearings).
[76] Evans and Blakeney, 'The Protection of Geographical Indications after Doha', 23.

FIGURE 7.1 The true 'Budweiser Budvar'
By permission of Budějovický Budvar

producers in a specific area, it was unfair to grant an individual exclusive
rights to a GI simply because they registered the geographic name as
a trademark.[77]

The Dispute Settlement Board made its judgment in 2005. The Board
agreed with the US claim that EU regulations were discriminatory: 'with
respect to the equivalence and reciprocity conditions, as applicable to the
availability of GI protection, the Regulation [EC 2081/92] accords treatment to the nationals of other Members less favourable than that it
accords to the European Communities' own nationals'. However, the
Board reported that EU regulations did take into account the 'legitimate
interests' of trademark owners. Indeed, of more than 600 GIs registered
under the EU scheme at the time of the dispute, the complainants and third

---

[77] Dispute Settlement Board, 'First Written Submission by the European Communities',
25 May 2004 (document WT/DS174/R/Add.2): B75–B79.

parties could identify only four that could be used in such a way that there would be confusion with a prior trademark. Three involved Czech beer brands. For the other exception, Bayerisches Bier, the complainants and third parties were unable to provide an example of 'actual confusion' with the trademark.[78] The judgement of the Dispute Settlement Board provided succour to both sides: 'The EU was able to claim that its GI protection program was not WTO-incompatible as such, and the US could point to the fact that the EU ... violated WTO articles in the way in which it implemented that policy.'[79]

The second area of conflict between the EU and the WTO involved the 'clawback' of GIs which had become generic, extension to other products of the (higher) protection afforded wines and spirits by TRIPS, and the establishment of a multilateral register of GIs. These proposals were interrelated: they represented 'slightly different procedural means to achieve the same policy end'.[80] Additionally, they undermined long-standing efforts to secure comprehensive international agreement on the protection of GIs. The desire to extend protection beyond wines and spirits recalls similar debates over Article IV of the Madrid Agreement. Similarly, determining the best way to develop the Lisbon Agreement so that it attracted more accessions proved irresolvable for almost sixty years. However, the EU's clawback represented a significant change in policy. Previously, generic terms were ineligible for registration because they indicated mode of manufacture, not a specific location. Additionally, negotiations to extend higher protection to products other than wines and spirits was no longer restricted only to intellectual property: they were subsumed within efforts to liberalise international trade under the Doha Development Agenda (2001).[81]

In 2003, the EU issued a list of forty-one GIs being used by producers other than the rights holder. The list was almost equally divided between drinks and foods. The former included Bordeaux, Champagne, Chianti,

---

[78] WTO, 'European Communities – Protection of Trademarks and Geographical Indications for Agricultural Products and Foodstuffs. Complaint by the United States', 15 March 2005 (document WT/DS174/R): 60, 148.

[79] T. E. Josling and S. Tangermann, *Transatlantic Food and Agricultural Trade Policy* (Cheltenham: Edward Elgar, 2015), 190.

[80] Issues Related to the Extension of the Protection of Geographical Indications Provided for in Article 23 of the TRIPS Agreement to Products other than Wines and Spirits. WTO, WT/GC/W/546TN/C/W/25 18 May (2005): 4 (hereafter, WTO, Issues Related).

[81] The Doha Development Round began in 2001. It sought to promote global trade, but the negotiations on LDC access to agricultural markets in the EU and the United States were contentious.

Jerez, and Rioja, while the latter involved Comte, Feta, Mozzarella, Parmigiano Reggiano, and Prosciutto di Parma. These products were already registered within the EU under Regulation 2081/92. They were the subject of clawback because they were either classed as generic or had been registered as trademarks in third countries. The EC claimed that misuse often occurred in major export markets: 'Attention has focused on those third countries where these kinds of abuses have been most frequently observed and which are also the most important markets for these products.'[82]

The dispute over clawback indicated the unparalleled importance of GIs in international trade. A recurring theme in many of the debates on clawback was whether efforts to make international trade freer (by reducing export subsidies and tariffs) conflicted with simultaneous attempts to ensure fair trade was 'fair' – in the sense that GIs were not being used to misrepresent origin. Witnesses before the US House of Representatives Committee on Agriculture claimed that clawback was part of a bargaining strategy in which the EU agreed to progress on agricultural reform only if the forty-one GIs were recognised as such. To pacify European farmers who were concerned about impending subsidy reductions, clawback granted 'market access to the rest of the world for the exclusive use of your products'.[83] It appeared absurd to give EU products global monopoly rights – which undermined the competitiveness of non-European producers – while simultaneously reducing artificial barriers to trade. Lynne Beresford claimed that the EU approach to GIs was fundamentally in conflict with that of the United States: the former treated GIs as an agricultural trade interest that required intergovernmental negotiation, whereas in the latter they were a component of private intellectual property for which the government was responsible for providing appropriate protection.

Attempts to claw back GIs provoked a backlash. Argentina, Brazil, New Zealand, and the United States argued that forfeiture of the right to use the names contained on the list disturbed the balance of rights and obligations contained in TRIPS, and that without acceptance of the continued use of these terms by countries outside the EU, the TRIPS Agreement would not have existed.[84] The United States was adamant that its legislation adequately protected GIs.[85] Examination of the

---

[82] European Commission. Press Release Database, 'WTO Talks: EU Steps Up Bid for Better Protection of Regional Quality Products', IP 03/1178, 28 August 2003.

[83] Hearings: 303, 321, 327.   [84] WTO, Issues Related: 3.

[85] See, for example, S. D. Goldberg, 'Who Will Raise the White Flag? The Battle between the United States and the European Union over the Protection of Geographical Indications', *University of Pennsylvania Journal of International Economic Law*, 22 (2001): 107–151;

evidence given before the US House of Representatives Committee on Agriculture reveals a range of arguments against the EU proposal. Witnesses representing the Grocery Manufacturers Association stated that the reclamation of just one name would cost its members hundreds of millions of dollars in repackaging costs and campaigns educating consumers about rebranding. If these costs were multiplied by the number of WTO members and the number of products on the claw-back list, the total cost of complying with EU demands could amount to billions of dollars.[86] Depriving US companies of the freedom to use names such as Parmesan eradicated the goodwill they had established in their brands:

> In fact, the real value of that term has not come from anything that has been done by the citizens of Parma, Italy, but rather, the millions of dollars spent by cheese processors in the United States, Kraft obviously being the leading one with the issue of parmesan. But there are many other companies that also produce parmesan cheese and put that on the label of the canisters that they produce. They have spent millions of dollars creating a value, which if the European Union were successful in these negotiations in their claw back, that is a very accurate description, they would be clawing back the benefit of those many, many tens or hundreds of millions of dollars that have been used to create the public awareness and support for those particular names.[87]

Many of the GIs subject to claw back were brought to the United States long before any regime for their protection existed. Thomas Suber, representing the US Dairy Export Council, argued that immigrants from Europe laid the foundations of the US dairy industry by bringing with them their expertise and knowledge of local foods. Over time, US citizens became loyal consumers of these products. Effectively, the culinary history of the United States from the mid-nineteenth century was intertwined with mass immigration, as evidenced by the popularity of hamburgers and frankfurters.[88] In any event, treating Parmesan or Mozzarella as generic terms in the United States did not mean a claim was being made that they were identical to the same cheeses produced in Europe: 'American

---

M. K. Kirk, 'Revision of the Paris Convention and Appellations of Origin', *Patent, Trademark and Copyright Law Proceedings*, American Bar Association, (1979): 185–203; Simon, 'Appellations of Origin'.

[86] *Hearings*: 276, 323. [87] *Hearings*: 307.

[88] Similar considerations applied to manufactures. The towns of Paris in the states of Arkansas, Indiana, Texas, and Wisconsin obviously derived their name from their French predecessor. When 'Paris' garters were sold in the United States, consumers did not wear them under the belief that they were from Paris, France, or even from one of the US 'Paris' towns. B. W. Pattishall, 'Geographical Indications of Origin', *Proceedings of the American Bar Association, Patent, Trademark & Copyright Law Section* (1979): 198.

consumers understand the nuanced differences that exist within generic cheese varieties made by different suppliers, whether these suppliers are domestic or foreign.' Related questions included: why had France, Italy, or the EU not taken earlier action to prevent GIs becoming generic? And why was the EU focusing only on a limited range of products which excluded Cheddar, Swiss cheese, and Swiss steak, which were also produced globally?[89]

Thus, the United States remains implacably opposed to clawback.[90] The EU's dealings with Canada were more fruitful despite the fact that the Consorzio Del Prosciutto Di Parma was engaged in a protracted and ultimately unsuccessful legal challenge against the use of Parma by the Canadian company Maple Leaf Foods Inc.[91] The Comprehensive Economic Trade Agreement (CETA) between the EU and Canada was concluded in 2014.[92] It prohibits the manufacture, preparation, labelling, selling, or importing of foods in a manner that is 'false, misleading, or deceptive or is likely to create an erroneous impression regarding its origin'. The Agreement ensured protection for many of the EU's famous food GIs, for example, Morbier and Cantal cheeses, Lübecker Marzipan confectionary, and the meat products Prosciutto di Parma and Prosciutto di San Daniele. However, for other foodstuffs, the EU was less successful. Thus, Canada was not required to prevent use of Asiago, Feta, Gorgonzola, and Munster when applied to cheese made outside the EU. This freedom also applied to the GI Jambon de Bayonne when it was used by a manufacturer for at least ten years before the CETA was concluded.

Greater progress was achieved for wines and spirits. The EU signed numerous bilateral agreements with major wine-producing countries such as Australia and South Africa. Key features of these accords included: reciprocal protection of the name of the country in which the wine originated and of specific wine GIs; enforcement procedures could be implemented when translation of a description was 'misleading as to the

---

[89] *Hearings*: 307, 316–317, 322. Blakeney and Evans, 'The Protection of Geographical Indications after Doha', 17.

[90] At the time of writing, the EU and the United States had not reached an accord on foodstuffs.

[91] *Maple Leaf Foods Inc.* v. *Consorzio Del Prosciutto Di Parma* (2012 FC 416 (April 12 2012).

[92] Downloaded from www.international.gc.ca/trade-agreements-accords-commerciaux/ag r-acc/ceta-aecg/text-texte/22.aspx?lang=eng, Article 7.4 (4); Article 7.6 (1); Article 7.6 (4); Annex I, Part A.

origin, nature or quality of the wine', or when names, inscriptions, illustrations, or advertising material gave 'false or misleading information as to the provenance, origin, nature ... or material qualities of the wine'; and transitional arrangements governing the use of Port and Sherry (in Australia and South Africa) and Burgundy, Chablis, Champagne, and Tokay (in Australia).[93] Between 1970 and 1971, a semi-formal agreement was concluded between France and the United States in which the former agreed to prohibit the internal sale and export of Bourbon and Bourbon Whisky, unless made in the United States or in conformity with American legislation. In return the United States imposed similar restrictions on the GIs Armagnac, Calvados, and Cognac.[94] This accord was subsequently extended to wine products in 2006.[95]

A related source of conflict involved attempts to extend to food products the higher protection afforded wine and spirits embodied in TRIPS Article 23. Proponents of extension included the EU and developing countries. The EU featured prominently in this battle because its PDO and PGI schemes offered greater safeguards than those provided by TRIPS Article 22. Consequently, the basic level of protection provided by this Article was insufficient to ensure global protection of European GIs. As discussed earlier, bilateral treaties did not always provide greater safeguards. For example, CETA permitted the continued use in Canada of Feta and Gorgonzola, even when accompanied by the terms 'like' or 'style'. Exacerbating matters was the difficulty of establishing consumer confusion when a GI was accompanied by a true indication of origin, such as 'Australian Feta'.[96] Other arguments in favour of extension included the need to establish a framework for the protection of GIs not *currently* considered generic (which would obviate the need for claw-back in the

---

[93] 'Agreement between the European Community and the Republic of South Africa on Trade in Wine', *Official Journal*, 30 January 2002: Article 8; Article 9; Article 12; 'Agreement between the European Community and Australia on Trade in Wine', *Official Journal*, 31 March 1994: Article 2; Article 8; 'Agreement between the European Community and Australia on Trade in Wine', *Official Journal*, 31 March 2009: Article 12; Article 15; Article 25.

[94] Ladas, *Patents, Trademarks and Related Rights*, 1611.

[95] 'Agreement between the European Community and the United States of America on Trade in Wine', *Official Journal*, 24 March 2003. This Agreement replicated many of the provisions stipulated in the EU–Australia and EU–South Africa Agreements discussed earlier.

[96] DG AGRI Working Document on International Protection of EU Geographical Indications: Objectives, Outcome and Challenges. Ref. Ares (2012) 669394. Downloaded from: http://ec.europa.eu/agriculture/consultations/advisory-groups/international/2012-06-25/agri-working-doc_en.pdf.

future). It was claimed the preferential treatment of wines and spirits was not based on commercial, economic, or legal logic but was 'the result of historical negotiation and specific circumstances that were particular to the wine sector'. Finally, it was argued that extension would be especially beneficial for small producers because it removed the need to engage in costly procedures involving opinion polls to satisfy the 'misleading the public test' contained in TRIPS Article 22.[97]

But for every argument advanced in favour of extension, equally compelling counterarguments were raised. For example, extension undermined cultural diversity by eradicating the rights of immigrants to use customary terms. Extension created imbalance between the obligations of Member States. For example, some owning a few GIs would be obliged to protect the thousands owned by others. In any event, was it the number of GIs which mattered or their economic importance? Basmati rice generated USD $300 million in exports – a sum which exceeded considerably the value of many other GI products. In common with previous debates, the definition of GI became important. For example, how to deal with non-geographical names such as Basmati, Jasmine rice, or Cava as applied to wine? The claim that extension of TRIPS Article 23 would benefit small and medium-sized enterprises was also questioned. Significant costs were involved in establishing *domestic* rights to a GI which included establishing an association of producers and agreement on the territorial limits within which the essential link to 'quality', 'reputation', or 'other characteristic' of a product applied; then it was necessary to lobby national governments and to defend claims against producers located outside the demarcated boundary. It was argued that these costs represented a substantial obstacle to developing countries in which small and medium-sized enterprises predominated.[98]

Achieving a satisfactory resolution to this problem has proved impossible. Currently, the conflict permeates EU–US negotiations on the establishment of the Transatlantic Trade and Investment Partnership (TTIP), which is designed to facilitate economic cooperation by eliminating trade barriers. Conflict was exacerbated by the EC issuing a list in March 2016 of more than 200 food terms, including Feta, Asiago, and Fontina cheeses, Mortadella Bologna, and Valencia oranges, for which it wanted stronger US protection. Additionally, some EU officials threatened to delay agreements on the TTIP unless the United States acceded to this demand.[99]

---

[97] WTO, Issues Related: 4, 14–16.   [98] WTO, Issues Related: 6–7, 9, 11, 17.
[99] Consortium for Common Food Names, 'Senators Remind Negotiators of Need to Address GI Abuse in TTIP', 1 June 2016, downloaded from www.commonfoodnames

Unsurprisingly, the United States dismissed this ultimatum. Twenty-six senators representing the Senate Committee on Agriculture, Nutrition and Forestry communicated to US Trade Representative Michael Froman that the EU proposals were diametrically opposed to the aims of the TTIP: 'The EU has continued to use Free Trade Agreements (FTAs) with trading partners to impose barriers on U.S. exports under the pretense of negotiating GIs.' Trade in cheese supports the US position: the EU exports nearly $1 billion of cheese to the United States each year, compared to US exports of about $6 million to the EU. These figures suggest that requests for extension are unjustified: EU producers do benefit from US trademark protection.[100] Nonetheless, because of the fundamental differences between the United States and the EU on the best way to protect GIs, it is difficult to envisage how a resolution can ever be obtained, especially because both are major producers of foodstuffs.[101]

CONCLUSIONS

In the post-1945 era, GIs attracted unprecedented global interest. Simultaneously, the economic justification for their protection increased. Defending GIs underpins EU efforts to make its agricultural sector more competitive, while the United States has resisted the clawback of generic terms because, it is alleged, this would cost its food-processing companies billions of dollars. In earlier periods the evolving global architecture on GIs was largely subsumed within debates about unfair competition and the particular concerns of France, Italy, and Spain to protect their famous wine appellations. After 1945, GIs became a defining feature of EU agricultural policy, and after the TRIPS Agreement these indications became central to multilateral efforts to liberalise international trade. Although there is little disagreement on the need to protect GIs, conflict has been generated on how best to achieve this.

On one level, it is tempting to view the ongoing debate in adversarial terms by classifying countries into two groups: those that protect GIs as

---

.com/senators-remind-negotiators-of-need-to-address-gi-abuse-in-ttip/; Ibid., 'TTIP Proposal Reinforces Desire to Block U.S. Food Exports', 1 June 2016, downloaded from www.commonfoodnames.com/eu-ttip-proposal-reinforces-desire-to-block-u-s-fo od-exports/.

[100] Office of the US Representative, *Special 301 Report*, April 2016: 24.
[101] K. William Watson, 'Geographical Indications in TTIP: An Impossible Task', October 2015, downloaded from www.cato.org/publications/cato-online-forum/geogra phical-indications-ttip-impossible-task.

certification or collective marks and those that prefer a separate, sui generis system. But this dichotomy is rough and misleading. For this author, at least, the systems in place for the protection of GIs are stupefying. Daniel Gervais observed 'a lack of uniformity in both definitions and administrative practices'. Some countries rely on trademark protection, others rely on laws relating to business practices (for example, unfair competition), while others rely on sui generis systems. Among the latter, monitoring is entrusted to statutory bodies, government ministries, other public institutions, or administrative authorities, together with producer associations.[102] The TRIPS Agreement itself has added to this complexity by stipulating that 'Members shall be free to determine the appropriate method of implementing the provisions of this Agreement within their own legal system and practice.'[103] It has been argued that one paradoxical result of this freedom is that the protection of certain types of GI was undermined.[104]

Part of the debate on the protection of GIs progressed beyond the well-established conflict between the EU's sui generis system and the trademark system of the United States. Lori Simon argued that EU–US differences can be reduced to a simple dichotomy: the EU is primarily concerned to protect the interests of producers and prevent the improper use of GIs by others. In contrast, the United States has traditionally been more concerned with protecting consumers from deception.[105] Other scholars have emphasised that one of the essential characteristics of the EU's policy on GIs – collective ownership – challenges 'the law, culture and economic logic of American business, orientated as it is towards liberal economic theory based on individual ownership'.[106]

Different approaches to the protection of GIs has also stimulated a broader debate on the nature of market competition. Although consortia are required to focus on quality standards, what safeguards exist to ensure they do not restrict output to increase prices? Justin Hughes has been a prominent advocate of the view that the EU's economic case

---

[102] D. J. Gervais, 'Reinventing Lisbon: The Case for a Protocol to the Lisbon Agreement (Geographical Indications)', *Chicago Journal of International Law*, 11 (2010): 87.

[103] *TRIPS Agreement*, Part I, Article 1:1.

[104] J. R. Renaud, 'Can't Get There from Here: How NAFTA and GATT Have Reduced Protection for Geographical Trademarks', *Brooklyn Journal of International Law*, 26 (2001): 1097–1123.

[105] Simon, 'Appellations of Origin', 134–135, 151–152.

[106] E. Barham, 'Translating Terroir: The Global Challenge of French AOC Labelling', *Journal of Rural Studies*, 19 (2003): 127–138.

for the protection of GIs is fundamentally protectionist. According to Hughes, the debate on how best to protect them is 'an instantiation of the larger debate about government versus markets and about how much decision making is given to government officials and what is left to market signals'. For Hughes, privately held trademarks are superior to certification marks and GIs because they facilitate competitive response, whereas the objective of EU laws on GIs is to safeguard the status quo.[107]

A related observation is that debates on the protection of GIs have concentrated almost exclusively on agricultural produce. This focus is not particularly surprising given the importance of food, wines, and spirits in global trade. Nonetheless, there is no reason why GIs cannot be registered for non-agricultural products. Registrations under the Lisbon Agreement currently include Bohemian Garnett Jewellery, Fine Bohemian China, and Lace of Vamberk (Czechoslovakia). Many of these products are produced by small- to medium-sized enterprises who are unfamiliar with the different types of legal protection available for their GIs, and who may not have sufficient financial resources to protect them outside the EU.[108]

In any case, it appears the EU was labouring under a delusion. To what extent would clawback improve the export prospects of European producers? A study by Michel Vincent suggests this question deserves a negative answer. According to Vincent, the United States and Canada were the most important markets outside the EU for Roquefort, Parmigiano Reggiano, Grana Padano, and hams from Parma and San Daniele. Between 1995 and 2004, exports of these products to the United States and Canada grew considerably. In other words, it is difficult to believe that clawback would significantly alter EU exports to North America.[109] This claim received further support from Raimondo Serra, who noted that in 2010, 60 per cent of all EU products with PDO or PGI status were sold within the Member State, with a further 20 per cent being sold within the EU.[110]

---

[107] Hughes, 'Champagne, Feta, and Bourbon', 331, 336–339.
[108] Insight Consulting. *Study on the Protection of Geographical Indications for Products Other than Wines, Spirits, Agricultural Products or Foodstuffs* (2009): 122–128.
[109] M. Vincent, 'Extending Protection at the WTO to Products Other than Wines and Spirits: Who Will Benefit?', *The Estey Centre Journal of International Law and Trade Policy*, 8 (2007): 60–61.
[110] R. Serra, 'The Protection', European Association of Agricultural Economists, 145th seminar, 14–15 April 2015. Downloaded from: http://purl.umn.edu/206447.

8

EU Policy on Geographical Indications

Ambitious, but Misguided?

There is a growing belief that rural populations should no longer underrate the features which make them unique. Rather, they should at least consider local specialities and resources as potential advantages for development and at the same time as sources of pride ... Changes in consumer tastes and preferences have increased demand for goods ... which are in some way special and out of the ordinary ... The question is how best to exploit these resources for successful rural development.

Niche Markets as a Rural Development Strategy,
Paris: OECD (1995): 13

Image building receives more attention than does accurate information about the production process. In the case of PDO/PGI regulations, no reference is made to the actual quality of products which are eligible for protection ... There is thus an assumption that quality can be directly attributable to, and guaranteed by, the geographic location of production.

B. Ilbery and M. Kneafsey, 'Niche Markets and Regional Speciality Food
Products in Europe: Towards a Research Agenda', *Environment
and Planning A*, 31 (1999): 2211

The year 2018 marks the twenty-fifth anniversary of the EU. This institution evolved from the six nations that formed the European Economic Community in 1957. Currently, the EU has twenty-eight Member States. Despite this growth, it is highly uncertain whether the EU will survive in its current form for another twenty-five years. The financial crises between 2007 and 2009 severely affected Spain, Italy, and Greece and strained the European Central Bank. BREXIT means that Britain will (probably) cease to be a member by 2019. Exacerbating matters, substantial immigration into Europe has raised broader issues about national identity and sovereignty, and the election of Donald Trump raises doubts about the long-term future of the North Atlantic Treaty Organization.

Despite this chaos, it remains true that for many people a powerful relationship exists between rural regions and landscape. An OECD report commented that areas within Member States contained many characteristics traditionally associated with the rural landscape: 'beautiful vineyards, terraced farms ... small patterned fields enclosed by hedgerows or stone walls built over centuries, old growth forests, land reclaimed from the sea, rural commons in and around small towns [and] picturesque fishing villages'. This landscape is both beautiful and of substantial importance to rural areas because it provides a range of cultural, economic, recreational, and social benefits for its inhabitants.[1] Within this broad framework, the relationship between region and produce is especially striking and is exemplified by the Member States belonging to the EU. In France, for example, the Medoc vineyards of Bordeaux were classified in 1855; the first modern French law to combat fraudulently labelled wines was enacted in 1905, and a national committee on appellations d' origine for cheese was established in 1955. In other European countries, producer associations have a similar lineage. For example, in Italy, the Consorzio del formaggio Parmigiano Reggiano (Parmesan cheese) was formed in 1934, while in Britain, the Stilton Cheesemakers Association was established in 1936.[2]

However, in the post-1945 period, the importance of rural areas to the economy and the broader environment was threatened. The decline of the agricultural sector compared to manufacturing and services generated a number of problems for rural regions which included depopulation and the higher incidence of unemployment and poverty. Increasingly it was recognised that traditional policies for supporting agriculture – largely focused on price-support schemes – were not only unviable but

---

[1] *What Future For Our Countryside? A Rural Development Policy* (OECD: Paris, 1993), 30–31.

[2] F. Arfini, 'The Value of Typical Products: The Case of Prosciutto di Parma and Parmigiano Reggiano Cheese', in B. Sylvander, D. Barjolle, and F. Arfini (eds.), *The Socio-Economics of Origin-Labelled Products in Agri-Food Supply Chains: Spatial, Institutional and Co-ordination Aspects.* Vol. 1 (Versailles: European Association of Agricultural Economists, 2000), 84; Hughes, 'Champagne, Feta, and Bourbon', 306–307; B. Ilbery and M. Kneafsey, 'Registering Regional Speciality Food and Drink Products in the UK: The Case of PDOs and PGIs', *Area*, 32 (2000): 317–325.

were the root cause of substantial imbalances between supply and demand: 'boosted by agricultural support policies in OECD countries ... the prospects facing the OECD area continue to point to a situation of structural oversupply and declining real prices. This gives rise to even greater concern since ... it means that, overall, resources in the sector must be reduced.'[3] The OECD emphasised the need for structural adjustment within agriculture and the need for better targeting of support, especially the importance of local initiatives, for example, the formation of 'product specialisation areas' and 'local productive systems'.[4]

This chapter examines the EU's policy to promote the use of GIs on agricultural produce. I show that there was a rapid increase in GI registrations under the EU's PDO and PGI scheme. However, the response among Member States to this initiative varied considerably: France, Italy, Portugal, and Spain dominated registrations. I argue that the EU scheme failed to establish a robust link between 'quality', 'product', and 'terroir'. Consequently, considerable doubts remain about whether the scheme protects the viability of EU farmers and the agricultural sector as a whole.

EU GEOGRAPHICAL INDICATIONS FOR FOODSTUFFS

EU concerns about rural development mirrored many of the issues raised by the OECD and were given further impetus by glaring weaknesses in the Common Agricultural Policy (CAP), established in 1962 to increase productivity, stabilise markets and prices, and secure food supplies. CAP policies were also designed to secure a fair standard of living for the agricultural community and they took account of the socio-economic structure of agriculture, particularly disparities between the various agricultural regions within Europe. However, the pricing and subsidy schemes which underpinned CAP resulted in substantial overproduction and the stockpiling of enormous quantities of produce: milk and wine 'lakes', butter and cheese 'mountains', tomato 'swamps', peach 'mounds', and olive oil 'wells'. These stocks were criticised because they appeared morally

---

[3] OECD, *Agricultural Policies, Markets and Trade: Monitoring and Outlook 1988* (OECD: Paris, 1988), 9.
[4] Product specialisation areas and local productive systems are characterised by small firms competing in the same sector and making the same type of product. The former does not involve cooperation between the firms, whereas in the latter there is strong cooperation and networks. OECD, *Implementing Change: Entrepreneurship and Local Initiative* (Paris: OECD, 1990), 42–43.

unjustifiable when parts of Africa suffered malnutrition. Additionally, food prices in Europe were artificially higher than world prices, and low-cost producers across the globe suffered.[5] Between 1979/1981 and 1986, average subsidies in the EU increased from 37 to 50 per cent, considerably exceeding those of other major food-producing nations. In Australia, New Zealand, and the United States, the equivalent subsidies were 15.3, 31.1, and 35.4 per cent, respectively.[6] By 1990, the situation in the EU had deteriorated in comparison with these three countries.[7] Consequently, the EU recognised that some adjustment between supply and demand was required.

Within the EU, the problem of devising a response to broader changes in the pattern of consumer expenditure towards products for which cultural heritage, artisanal production, and provenance were emphasised and guaranteed was exacerbated by the diversity of foodstuffs and the number of associated brands, logos, and product information. It was imperative, therefore, that any labelling scheme provided clear and succinct information. It was also recognised that some Member States had already introduced 'registered designations of origin' which had 'proved successful with producers who have secured higher incomes in return for a genuine effort to improve quality, and with consumers, who can purchase high quality products with guarantees as to the method of production and origin'. However, the diversity of national practices governing GIs meant community-wide provision was necessary. A further factor influencing the EU's response was the belief that the promotion of products possessing geographically defined characteristics would improve the income of farmers.[8]

---

[5] M. Atkin, *Snouts in the Trough: European Farmers, the Common Agricultural Policy and the Public Purse* (Cambridge: Woodhead, 1993); F. Knox, *The Common Market and World Agriculture* (London: Praeger, 1972), 4; Perren, *Taste, Trade and Technology*, 171–180.

[6] These subsidies are defined as Total Net Producer Subsidy Equivalent and represent the value of output accounted for by assistance. In the EU's case, more than 80 per cent of this assistance was accounted for by supporting market prices. OECD *Agricultural Policies, Marketing and Trade: Monitoring Outlook, 1988*, 12, 46.

[7] OECD, *Agricultural Policies, Markets and Trade: Monitoring Outlook, 1988*, 13, 17, 22, 27.

[8] European Commission (hereafter, EC), 'Council Regulation No. 2081/92 of 14 July 1992 on the Protection of Geographical Indications and Designations of Origin for Agricultural Products and Foodstuffs', *Official Journal*, L 208, 24 July 1992: 4–5. Amended by Council Regulation No. 510/2006, *Official Journal*, L 93, 31, March 2006, and Council Regulation No. 1151/2012, *Official Journal*, L 343, 21 November 2012.

In 1992, the EU introduced regulations governing the use of protected designation of origin (PDO) and protected geographical indication (PGI). Both share a number of essential characteristics: they refer to the 'name of a region, a specific place or, in exceptional cases, a country, used to describe an agricultural product or a foodstuff' originating in that area. Additionally, both had to comply with numerous requirements governing product specification, for example, by providing the name of the agricultural product or foodstuffs, a description of the raw materials used in the product, a definition of the geographical area, and details of inspection procedures. Nonetheless, significant differences exist between PDO and PGI, the most important of which concerns the strength of the product–region relationship. Eligibility to use PDO required that the quality or characteristics of the product are 'essentially or exclusively due to a particular geographic environment with its inherent natural and human factors, and the production, processing and preparation of which take place in the defined geographical area'. Examples of PDOs are French cheese from Cantal, and Munster; dry-cured hams from Teruel, Parma, and San Daniele; as well as Cornish clotted cream, Jersey Royal potatoes, and Orkney beef and lamb. The threshold governing use of PGI was lower, requiring only that a particular characteristic of the product – for example, quality or reputation – was 'attributable to the geographical origin' and specifying that it was sufficient for production, processing, or preparation to occur within the defined geographical area. Typical PGI products include German beers originating from Dortmund, Cologne, and Munich. EU regulations included a third indication: Traditional Speciality Guaranteed (TSG), which simply represents a traditional production process and is not related to origin. TSGs include various Belgian beers, for example, Vieille Gueuze, Vieille Kriek-Lambic, and Vieille Framboise-Lambic.

Although the EU scheme became effective in 1993, no data are available until 1996.[9] The broad trends in total registrations are shown in Table 8.1, which indicates that, after a speedy uptake resulting in more than 300 registrations in 1996, total registrations collapsed thereafter.[10]

---

[9] It took the EC three years to process the huge volume of applications submitted in 1993. Personal communication from europa.eu. 31 May 2012.

[10] The annual data presented in Table 8.1 differ from those in previous studies, which report cumulative registrations over time. See, for example, *Evaluation of the CAP Policy on Protected Designations of Origin (PDO) and Protected Geographical Indications (PGI). Final Report*. London Economics. November (2008): 97.

FIGURES 8.1 AND 8.2 Protected Designation of Origin and Protected
Geographical Indication. These GIs are ubiquitous in the EU.
By permission of the European Commission. DG Agriculture and Rural Development

In fact, it took nine years for the cumulative number of registrations to
exceed the level obtained in 1996. A further observation from Table 8.1 is
that taking the period 1996 to 2016, as a whole, PGIs were numerically
the most important. On average, prior to 2007, PDOs were the dominant
type of registration, but thereafter they were exceeded by PGIs. Finally,
Table 8.1 indicates that TSGs were of practically no importance: taking

TABLE 8.1 *PDOs, PGIs, and TSGs, registered (by number and percentage),*
1996–2016

	Total GI registrations	PDO registrations	Column 3 as % Column 2	PGI registrations	Column 5 as % Column 2	TSG registrations	Column 7 as % Column 2
1996	328	214	65.2	114	34.8	0	0
1997	68	33	48.5	32	47.1	3	4.4
1998	46	15	32.6	28	60.9	3	6.5
1999	23	13	56.5	9	39.1	1	4.4
2000	35	19	54.3	14	40.0	2	5.7
2001	23	12	52.2	10	43.5	1	4.3
2002	29	11	37.9	15	51.7	3	10.4
2003	46	24	52.2	21	45.7	1	2.2
2004	45	13	28.9	31	68.9	1	2.2
2005	27	19	70.4	8	29.6	0	0
2006	7	5	71.4	2	28.6	0	0
2007	66	28	42.4	37	56.1	1	1.5
2008	68	21	30.9	43	63.2	4	5.9
2009	57	18	31.6	38	66.7	1	1.8
2010	99	33	33.3	58	58.6	8	8.1
2011	86	35	40.7	44	51.2	7	8.1
2012	60	21	35.0	38	63.3	1	1.7
2013	83	30	36.2	48	57.8	5	6.0
2014	53	19	35.9	28	52.8	6	11.3
2015	62	15	24.2	43	69.4	4	6.5
2016	69	21	30.4	47	68.1	1	1.5
Total	1,380	619	44.9	708	51.3	53	3.8

Source: Calculated from Europa DOORS database
Notes: Total GI registrations are defined as PDO + PGI + TSG at the date of *first* registration.
For some entries, multiple dates of registration can appear on the database. These later dates
are a result of 'amendment requests'. In some cases, the *original* registration date has been
changed to the 'registration date' of the amendment request. Use of first date at registration
avoids double counting (personal correspondence with Europa). These annual figures differ
from previous work using the same database – such as London Economics, which use
cumulative registrations over time.

The data exclude a Colombian registration for a PGI in 2007; 2010 excludes a Chinese
PGI registration, but includes registrations for German sparkling waters which were
subsequently discontinued.

Percentages may not sum to 100 because of rounding.

TABLE 8.2 *Principal ownership of PDO, PGI, and TSG by European country, 1996–2016, and by vintage, 1996–1997*[1]

	Number	Percentage of total registrations[2]	Registrations between 1996 and 1997	Registrations 1996–1997 as % of country total
France	237	17.2	88	37.1
Germany	84	6.1	12	14.3
Great Britain	59	4.3	19	32.2
Greece	103	7.5	63	61.2
Italy	288	20.9	81	28.1
Portugal	136	9.9	71	52.2
Spain	192	13.9	34	17.7
Total	1,099	79.8	368	n.a.
Average	157	11.4	52.6	33.5

Notes: (1) 1996–1997 refers to date on which first registered. (2) Column 3 uses the figure of 1,380 for the total number of registrations, as given in Table 8.1 (3) n.a. means not applicable

the period as a whole they account for less than 4 per cent of total registrations, exceeding 10 per cent of total registrations in just two years, 2002 and 2014. These trends suggest that GIs with the strongest link to location were the most coveted. In contrast, and not unsurprisingly, TSGs, for which no link with provenance is required, were the least important.

To examine these trends in more detail, Table 8.2 shows the relative importance of individual countries in total registrations. A number of key trends are suggested by this table. One observation is that four countries, France, Italy, Portugal, and Spain, account for more than 60 percent of registrations. It is also clear that there is a pronounced north–south divide within the EU. Four southern European countries, Greece, Italy, Portugal, and Spain, account for more than 50 per cent of total registrations. Excluding France and Germany, the remainder of Europe's northern and central countries – Belgium, Britain, the Czech Republic, the Netherlands, Poland, and Scandinavia – barely figure.[11] A final

[11] EC, *Impact Assessment Report on Geographical Indications: Proposal for a Regulation of the European Parliament and of the Council on Agricultural Product Quality Schemes*, 10 December, 2010: 13.

observation is that there does not appear to be a positive relationship between the volume and vintage of registration: more than 50 per cent of total registrations in Greece and Portugal occurred in 1996 and 1997, compared to approximately a third for France, Britain, and Italy. In contrast, most of Spain's registrations occur at a later date. In other words, countries with the most registrations did not always respond with alacrity to the EU scheme.

Comprehensive analysis of the EC scheme was undertaken by the European Association of Agricultural Economists (EAAE) and published in 2000. Four interrelated themes were central to this publication: consumer expectations and purchasing behaviour, including price premia; spatial economics and rural development; economics of the supply chain, markets, and coordination and their impact on the competitive position of products bearing PDO/PGI indicia; and local and global agreements about quality and origin.[12] Subsequently, the scholars involved in the original publication extended their field of inquiry to include globalisation, the problems confronting less-developed countries, and the broader public policy framework in which GIs are situated.[13] It will become apparent later in this chapter that the research conducted by the EAAE has been influential in determining how 'success' may be measured and the major problems which continue to affect the EU scheme.

Despite the rapid growth of PDO and PGI registrations, an assessment of their effectiveness is problematic. One difficulty is that debates on the relationship between product quality and place have evolved into wider concerns about biodiversity and conservation, which did not feature in PDO and PGI specifications issued in 1992.[14] Another problem concerns the role of GIs as a solution to the surpluses generated by the CAP. By definition, niche products such as PDOs and PGIs, which emphasise their artisanal inputs and cultural heritage and are firmly anchored to particular regions, are characterised by small- not large-scale production, and their products are heterogeneous rather than homogeneous. These factors alone warn against placing too much emphasis on GIs as a solution to the CAP. Moreover, producers who were unable to register

---

[12] Sylvander, Barjolle, and Arfini, *The Socio-Economics of Origin-Labelled Products*, Vol. 1, 7.

[13] E. Barham and B. Sylvander, 'Introduction', in Barham and Sylvander, *Labels of Origin for Food*, ix–xviii.

[14] J. L. Guerra, *Geographical Indications In Situ Conservation and Traditional Knowledge*. International Centre for Trade and Sustainable Development. Policy Brief No. 3, 2010.

their products under the EU scheme could not obtain its associated benefits.

From the perspective of EU agriculture as a whole, the limited data available suggest that PDOs and PGIs are important in absolute, but not relative terms. For example, in France, in 2004, turnover attributable to PGI and PDO products was €2.8 billion, representing 6.3 per cent of total turnover of agricultural production. In 2006, total turnover of German PDOs and PGIs was €4.4 billion, or just 2.2 per cent of the combined production value of agriculture and food processing. As Table 8.3 indicates, there is substantial variation in the importance of PDOs and PGIs used on individual products. Cheese and beer are by far the two most important products covered by the EU scheme, accounting for 33 per cent and 20 per cent of the total value of EU cheese and beer production, respectively.[15] Crucially, these two products also reflect high value–volume ratios, of 2.7 and 3.6, respectively. Later research indicated there was a low correlation between the number of registered products and total sales value, that larger price premia were reported for registered wines and spirits compared to registered food-stuffs, and that gross margins were not always larger for PDO/PGI products.[16] Moreover, the relationship between market share and GI was highly concentrated. In Italy, for example, 82 per cent of the total turnover of Italian PDO/PGI products is accounted for by ten brands.[17] Turning to exports, by 2013, the EC estimated that the total value of external exports of products registered under its scheme was €11.5 billion, which represents about 15 per cent of total EU food and drink exports. Member States' national markets were the most important, accounting for 60 per cent of sales while intra–EU exports accounted for approximately 20 per cent of sales.[18]

---

[15] Calculations from official estimates suggest that cheese and beer together account for 51.3 per cent of EU GI sales under the agricultural products and foodstuffs schemes. European Commission, *Value of Production of Agricultural Products and Foodstuffs, Wines, Aromatised Wines and Spirits Protected by a Geographical Indication (GI)*. Final Report, October (2012): table 39, 77.

[16] T. Chever, 'Geographical Indications (GIs) in the European Union: Economic Aspects', WIPO: Worldwide Symposium on Geographical Indications. 22 October 2015.

[17] M.-L. Katia, 'Are Geographical Indications on EU Food Labels Worth Obtaining?' Downloaded from www.linkedin.com/pulse/geographical-indications-eu-food-labels-worth-obtaining-katia.

[18] European Commission, 'Main Findings in a Nutshell', in *Value of Production*. Final Report.

Further studies revealed that participation in the EU scheme generated other economic advantages which were pronounced at the regional level, for example, adoption of PGI status for Huetor-Tajar Asparagus in Spain and Swabian pork in Germany. To the extent that local populations capitalised on the originality and authenticity of their products, their development prospects improved.[19] In a British context, it was noted that PDOs provided a defence against foreign competition for Gloucester cheesemakers and for cider makers in Gloucestershire, Herefordshire, and Worcestershire.[20] Similarly, the successful bid to secure PGI status for Cornish pasties insulated this industry from British competitors not based in Cornwall and helped preserve local employment. Members of the Cornish Pasty Association (CPA) employ more than 1,800 permanent staff members, and it was estimated that about 13,000 people directly or indirectly benefited from this industry. Unsurprisingly, the CPA claimed 'protection of the Cornish pasty was necessary to safeguard the heritage of the Cornish pasty, the future of the industry and the reputation of the product'.[21] Clearly, PDO/PGI certification is a means of reaffirming the link between locality and produce which affords protection against the global supply of generic produce.

The evidence presented in Table 8.3 is closely aligned to the extent to which adoption of PDO or PGI generated significant price premia for their owners. The role of price premia was fundamental to EC statements on GIs. For example, in 2003, the EC reported that French GI cheeses were sold at a premium of two euros; French Poulet de Bresse had a market value four times greater than regular French chicken; milk used in the production of Comte cheese was paid 10 per cent over the standard milk price, and Italian Toscano oil was sold at a premium of 20 per cent since its registration in 1998. Consequently, it was claimed '[t]here is ample evidence that GIs are positive for consumer protection. According to market surveys, GIs are perceived as origin and quality indicators ... In a recent consumer survey, more than 40% of consumers showed willingness to pay a 10% price premium if the origin of the product was guaranteed.'[22] In 2007, the EC stated, 'The "bottom line" for farmers must be whether

---

[19] Guerra, 'Geographical Indications', 8–9.

[20] Ilbery and Kneafsey, 'Registering Regional Speciality', 322.

[21] www.cornishpartyassociation.co.uk/about.html

[22] EC, Press Release Database, 'Why Do Geographical Indications Matter to Us?', Memo / 03/160, Brussels 30 July 2003. These findings are also reported in London Economics, *Evaluation of the CAP Policy*: 126.

TABLE 8.3 *Importance of PDO and PGI products by product (value and volume), 2009–2010*

	Value (%)[1]	Volume (%)[2]
Beer	20.0	7.35
Bread and Pastries	4.0	n.a.
Butter	n.a.	1.5
Cheese	33.0	9.2
Fresh Meat	6.0	0.05
Fruit and Vegetables	4.0	0.44
Meat Products	1.7	< 3.0
Olive Oil	n.a	1.8

Notes: 1. Defined as percent of total value of production. 2. Defined as percent of volume for cheese, fresh fruit and vegetables, fresh meat and poultry, meat products; per cent of production for beer, butter, and olive oil. With the exception of beer, the basis of reference for all products is EU 27. The importance of beer is measured in comparison with EU 25.

Source: Calculated from European Commission, *Impact Assessment of Geographical Indications* (European Commission, 2010): 14–15

the exclusive right to use a product name leads to a higher price than for similar products in the same food category.'[23]

However, academic studies have provided only qualified support for these claims. A study of Parmigiano-Reggiano (Parmesan) and Parma ham reported that these products commanded premia of 7.2 and 7.5, per cent, respectively, compared to unlabelled cheese and ham products. Galician veal with PGI certification earned a premium of thirty-two pesetas per kilogram, but this premium was more pronounced for expensive steaks and high-quality cuts. A broader investigation revealed that on average, consumers were willing to pay a premium of 18 per cent for PDO or PGI cheese, fruit, ham, lamb, and potatoes, compared to similar regional produce not governed by the EU scheme.[24] Joel Espejel and colleagues

[23] European Commission, *Fact Sheet: European Policy for Quality Agricultural Products,* (January 2007): 12.

[24] Arfini, 'The Value of Typical Products', 88, 94, 218; K. V. Ittersum, M. J. J. M. Candel, and F. Torelli, 'The Market for PDO/PGI Protected Regional Products: Consumers' Attitudes and Behaviour', in Sylvander, Barjolle, and Arfini, *The Socio-Economics of Origin-Labelled Products,* Vol. 1, 218; M. Loureiro and J. J. McCluskey, 'Effectiveness of

reported that the Spanish PDOs Jamón de Teruel (ham) and Olive Oil from Rioja Aragon benefitted from increased monopoly power, greater levels of consumer satisfaction, loyalty, and repeat purchasing.[25] Nonetheless, a detailed investigation of eighteen PDO/PGI products revealed that fourteen producers earned a price premium, but these margins translated into higher profitability for only six producers. The results for eight producers suggested that participation in the EU scheme had zero or limited impact on profitability. For three of these products, Lübecker Marzipan, Spreewälder Gurken, and Mela Val di Non (Italian apples), the effects of PDO/PGI labelling could not be separated from the effects of a strong trademark.[26]

More recent research has confirmed many of these mixed results. A meta-analysis by Oana Deselnicu, Marco Costanigro, Souza-Monteiro, and McFadden reported that the percentage premium for all GI registered products ranged from -36.7 per cent to 181.9 per cent, respectively, for the Italian cheeses Provolone Valpadana and Valle d'Aosta Fromadzo. Their study indicated substantial variation in the premia earned by products in their sample: grain, meat, and fresh produce earned the highest premia, whereas olive oil and wine earned the lowest. Of particular significance, the authors argued that registration was only one determinant of price premia. Other factors included the extent to which products were processed, the length of the supply chain, and whether products were undifferentiated (i.e., did all producers sell their products only with the same GI, or were the products sold with a GI and company brand)?[27]

In any case, there is no guarantee that price premia are caused by the EU scheme. The direction of causation is crucial because if PDO/PGI products

PGI and PDO Labels as a Rural Development Policy', in Sylvander, Barjolle, and Arfini, *The Socio-Economics of Origin-Labelled Products*, Vol. 1, 316–317.

[25] J. Espejel, C. Fandos, and C. Flavián, 'Spanish Air-Cured Ham with Protected Designation of Origin (PDO): A Study of Intrinsic and Extrinsic Attributes' Influence on Consumer Satisfaction and Loyalty', *Journal of International Food & Agribusiness Marketing*, 19 (2007): 5–30; J. Espejel, C. Fandos, and C. Flavián, 'Consumer Satisfaction: A Key Factor of Consumer Loyalty and Buying Intention of a PDO Food Product', *British Food Journal*, 110 (2008): 865–881.

[26] A higher premium is not sufficient because GI products incur higher production, certification, and administrative costs. London Economics, *Evaluation of the CAP Policy*: 145–147.

[27] O. C. Deselnicu, M. Costanigro, D. M. Souza-Monteiro, and D. T. McFadden, 'A Meta-Analysis of Geographical Indication Food Valuation Studies: What Drives the Premium for Origin-Based Labels', *Journal of Agricultural and Resource Economics*, 38, 2013: 204–219.

did not earn higher than average prices, an important justification for the scheme is undermined. Jersey Royal Potatoes is a singular example. This product became a PDO in 1996, but between 1991 and 1995, its price was, on average, more than four times the price of British 'early' potatoes.[28] Related research has indicated that Camembert with a PDO designation received only average consumer ratings compared to the lowest price, national leader, private-label Camembert cheese.[29] Similarly, three other PDO cheeses, Cantal, Noord-Hollandse Edammer (Edam), and West Country Farmhouse Cheddar, were characterised by weak market attractiveness and low competitiveness. Clearly, a range of other factors, not just registration, drive relative market strength and the ability to charge higher prices. Thus, West Country Farmhouse Cheddar experienced strong price competition from American and Canadian cheddars. Similarly, although Noord-Hollandse Edammer possessed a high reputation, it was not sufficiently differentiated from other Edammers to justify a higher price. The explanation advanced for the inability of these last two cheeses to earn a price premia was that they 'are characterized by a strong competition where the price becomes the most important factor in the retailer's and consumer's purchase decision'.[30]

Moreover, it is not clear that products registered under the EU scheme generate a higher premia compared to other brands. Filippo Arfini showed that the small premia earned by PDO Parmigiano-Reggiano cheese and Parma ham was dwarfed by the premia that consumers would pay for cheese and ham bearing the consortia label only:

[H]ow can a consumer be willing to pay a premium price for strengthening quality control, if he/she does not know or knows very little about the label which guarantees such improvement? The situation, then, is even more unbearable, considering the European PDO labels have to compete, in the consumers' minds and age-long experience, with the Consortia labels which ... meet great success and favour with the consumers.[31]

---

[28] Calculated from N. Wilson, K. van Ittersum, and A. Fearne, 'Cooperation and Coordination in the Supply Chain: A Comparison between the Jersey Royal and the Opperdoezer Ronde Potato', in Sylvander, Barjolle, and Arfini, *The Socio-Economics of Origin-Labelled Products*, Vol. 2, 98–99.

[29] G. Giraud, L. Sirieix, and A. Lebecque, 'Consumers' Purchase Behaviour towards Typical Foods in Mass Marketing: The Case of PDO Camembert from Normandy', in Sylvander, Barjolle, and Arfini, *The Socio-Economics of Origin-Labelled Products*, Vol. 1, 122–123.

[30] D. Barjolle, J.-M. Chappuis, and M. Dufour, 'Competitive Position of Some PDO Cheeses on Their Reference Market: Identification of the Key Success Factors', in Sylvander, Barjolle, and Arfini, *The Socio-Economics of Origin-Labelled Products*, Vol. 2, 21.

[31] Arfini, 'The Value of Typical Products', 87.

This finding raises fundamental questions about the desirability of certification schemes which refer only to region and mode of manufacture but fail to specify minimum quality guarantees. For example, how reliable is the EU scheme when quality differences exist between producers using the same GI? A study of Tuscan extra virgin olive oil by Giovanni Belletti indicated that some of the firms eligible to participate in this PGI scheme refused because compliance with certification regulations reduced the value of their product-specific capital. Because olive oil from outside the region was being labelled 'Tuscan', producers in the highly renowned areas of Lucca, Florence, and Siena refused to participate in the scheme, with the effect that 85 per cent of the olive oil classed as PGI originated in provinces with low reputations.[32] Consequently, when high- quality producers do not participate in the scheme, any claim that PDO/PGI registration enhances quality is undermined.

Quality variation between producers is particularly pronounced for San Daniele and Iberico hams. The founding statutes of the Consorzio Prosciutto San Daniele stipulate that it prevents 'internal competition between first quality and lower quality products having the same San Daniele origin'. The requirement that members of the Consorzio must ensure that at least 80 per cent of their pigs qualify for PDO status can generate adverse consequences for this GI: 'The growers ... will sell the unmarked product in secondary market channels using improperly the name of San Daniele; this parallel channel will damage the image of the higher quality product.'[33] The Iberico hams Jamón de Huelva, Jamón de Guijuelo, Dehesa de Extremadura, and Los Pedroches are all PDO certified, but the quality of the resulting ham is based on the *dietary regime* of the pigs. For example, Iberico de bellota o terminado en montanera is from animals fattened on acorns, herbs, and other natural resources from the pasture, the population density of which must not exceed two pigs per hectare. Iberico de recebo o terminado en recebo is obtained from animals fattened to a specified minimum weight, and their diet may be supplemented by fodders of a type specified in the Regulations.[34]

Fundamentally, the EU scheme could only be effective if the tripartite relationship between product, quality, and region were strongly

[32] G. Belletti, 'Origin Labeled Products, Reputation and Heterogeneity of Firms', in Sylvander, Barjolle, and Arfini, *The Socio-Economics of Origin-Labelled Products*, Vol. 1, 245–250.
[33] F. Rosa, 'Total Quality Management of the PDO Prosciutto San Daniele', in Sylvander, Barjolle, and Arfini, *The Socio-Economics of Origin-Labelled Products*, Vol. 2, 42.
[34] I am grateful to Dr Paul Jordan for this information.

cemented. Research by legal scholars on this unholy alliance has revealed a minefield of philosophical and semantic problems, and judgements by the European Court of Justice are byzantine in their complexity.[35] Complementary research by other scholars (see later in this chapter) has indicated that the EU scheme is vulnerable to sustained attack on a number of fronts. Consequently, when the scheme is viewed in its entirety, it is difficult to believe it was a sensible solution to the historic problems confronting EU agriculture. In order to understand the scope and severity of the criticisms levelled at the EC regulations, the discussion that follows is categorised under the following headings: What does quality mean and is it guaranteed by origin? What is the role of other indicators of rural heritage? and, how did the EU respond to identified weaknesses?

QUALITY – WHAT DOES IT MEAN?

Despite the central importance of 'quality' in the PDO/PGI regulations, the EC did not define this term. This omission is understandable because there is no universally accepted definition of quality. Economists, for example, refer to horizontal and vertical product differentiation. The former is where a product has a number of essential characteristics in relation to which consumers' preferences vary. For example, in the case of cheese, some prefer 'soft', while others prefer 'hard'. Consumers also vary in their preferences for strong cheeses, the degree of saltiness, and other attributes, such as whether the cheese is blue-veined. With this type of product differentiation there is no consensus that one type of cheese is superior to another: it is entirely a matter of personal preference. Vertical differentiation, by contrast, is based on quality (or characteristics) about which all consumers agree. With vertical differentiation, low-quality products are sold at lower prices compared to high-quality products. Irrespective of the ability to purchase, most consumers agree with the vertical ranking of products and their associated prices.

Similar problems of definition have been identified by scholars investigating the marketing of agricultural produce. Much depends on whose perspective is adopted – the producers' or the consumers'? For example, the former may be more concerned about the benefits of association with a particular region and certification as well as defining quality from a production perspective in which product differentiation and competitive

---

[35] Gangjee, *Relocating the Law of Geographical Indications*, 223–237.

advantage are supply-side resources. By contrast, there are different determinants of food quality for consumers, such as hygiene (safety), huma-
nistic quality (environmental values), nutritional quality (health),
symbolic quality (cultural), and organoleptic characteristics (aroma,
smell, taste), all of which can be totally independent of food origin.[36]
Because quality is a socially constructed variable, any objective assessment
of its importance, by producers or consumers, is itself socially
determined.[37] Consequently, it can be argued that producers' reliance
on origin as a source of quality may be misaligned with consumers'
perceptions of quality.

Other scholars recognise that quality is a positional characteristic, 'that
which is above the minimum standards . . . producers must relate quality
to the satisfaction of consumer needs and wants'.[38] But how are these
needs and wants determined? Because food is extremely varied in its
quality attributes, and consumer preferences towards food characteristics
are almost infinite, certification of a product by itself cannot guarantee
that it will appeal to consumers: 'The PDO/PGI device is not a quality
mark, and registration does not involve any explicit or *comparative*
quality assessment'(emphasis added).[39] Perhaps the most critical assessment of quality in relation to the EU scheme was provided by the large-
scale, multi-country, Development of Origin Labelled Products:
Humanity, Innovation and Sustainability (DOLPHINS) project:

From a consumer perspective, PDO/PGI designations are intended as guarantees
of product authenticity [but] there is a lack of clarity regarding exactly what is
being authenticated. The designations do not offer explicit guarantees to
consumers. [If] the representations are basically subjective . . . the authenticity
appears quite uneasy to establish . . . In this context . . . 'origin', 'typicity', or
'tradition' are flexible concepts exchanged between different actors (eg

---

[36] A. Prigent-Simonin and C. Hérault-Fournier, 'The Role of Trust in the Perception of the
Quality of Local Food Products: With Particular Reference to Direct Relationships
between Producer and Consumer', *Anthropology of Food*, May (2005): 1–16.

[37] B. Ilbery and M. Kneafsey, 'Producer Constructions of Quality in Regional Speciality
Food Production: A Case Study from South West England', *Journal of Rural Studies*, 16
(2000): 217–230.

[38] P. Leat, F. Williams, and J. Brannigan, 'Rural Competitiveness through Quality and
Imagery across Lagging Regions of the European Union'. Paper presented to European
Policy at the Crossroads, University of Aberdeen (2000): 4. A copy of this document was
supplied by Philip Leat, University of Aberdeen.

[39] N. Parrott, N. Wilson, and J. Murdoch. 'Spatializing Quality: Regional Protection and
the Alternative Geography of Food', *European Urban and Regional Studies*, 93 (2002):
246.

producers and consumers) ... the question is raised of what role a guarantee of authenticity has at all.[40]

The sheer variety and numerical importance of cheese approved for PDO and PGI status suggest that the scheme was not intended to institute vertical quality rankings (for example, a PDO hard cheese is 'better' than a non-PDO hard cheese), but was designed simply to give products another attribute – certified or uncertified – which might influence the purchasing decisions of some consumers. The failure of the EU to provide an explicit definition of quality was a major oversight because the scheme did no more than certify that certain product characteristics had an identifiable geographical location. This omission is even more astonishing because if vertical quality differences were communicated, higher prices would be achieved: 'a quality food and drink is one which is differentiated in a positive manner ... from the standard product, it is recognised as such by the consumer, and can therefore command a market benefit if it is effectively marketed'.[41]

The failure to define quality raises further doubts about whether PDO/ PGI registration can establish a strong relationship between origin and quality. The essential feature of the EU scheme is that the quality of a product is determined by its geography. Applicants seeking PDO/PGI status for their produce must establish the geographical boundaries from which it emanates. For example, the PDO application by East Kent Goldings Growers (hops) stated that their boundary was:

The geographical area of production is adjacent to the old Roman Road now known as the A2 as far as Bishopsbourne. It starts with the parish of Rainham and passes through Hartlip, Tonge, Borden, Lynsted, Norton, Teynham, Buckland, Stone, Ospringe, Faversham, Boughton-under-Blean, Selling, Chartham, Chilham, Harbledown, Canterbury, Bekesbourne, Bridge and Bishopsbourne. From Canterbury the A257 extends the area through Littlebourne, Wingham, Staple, Ash and Woodnesborough.[42]

These boundaries formalise the link between product and place. But is quality synonymous with place? The EU sidestepped this crucial question by making quality dependent on technical definitions of production

---

[40] B. Sylvander, DOLPHINS Working Paper No. 7. *Final Report: Synthesis and Recommendations*, (2004): 67. The DOLPHINS project was a wide-ranging investigation into origin-labelled products (OLPs) involving nine European countries.

[41] Scottish Food Strategy Group. Quoted in Leat, Williams, and Brannigan, 'Rural Competitiveness', 4.

[42] Downloaded from www.defra.gov.uk/food-farm/food/protected-names/protected-names-applications/.

methods and product specifications, while simultaneously failing to recognise that origin is but one component of quality.[43] Consider, for example, the comments of *Guardian* correspondent Lesley Gillilan when Cornish pasties were awarded PGI status in 2011:

> Laying down the law on quality is all very well, but there's a lot of genuinely Cornish pasties out there that couldn't satisfy a single one of the directive's must haves. Steak, yes, but just a solitary chunk lost in a sticky potato stodge; or lots of rather grey meat that looks like it's been boiled, or been through a hot-wash cycle. Add gristle. Add heavy, lardy pastry (pet hate: chomping through a wall of the stuff before you hit the filling). Light seasoning? How many post-pasty hours have I spent looking for pints of water to drown the salt. Personally, I wouldn't touch a Ginsters. Genuinely Cornish, yes, but I've seen and smelt the factory in Callington.[44]

Although PGIs accounted for more than 50 percent of total registrations between 1996 and 2016 (Table 8.1), they suffered from the weakness that processing in a geographical area was sufficient to secure the GI. This further undermined the link between quality and origin because other producers could claim that they make foodstuffs of comparable quality, using traditional methods, even though located outside the designated area. Northern Foods plc, for example, had been applying 'Melton Mowbray' to its pork pies from the 1800s, even though production was based in Trowbridge (Wiltshire). When opposing the application by the Melton Mowbray Pork Pie Association (MMPPA) to obtain PGI status in 2005, Northern Food's company secretary claimed, 'Our pies are very high quality and made to traditional recipes, and we think that is more important than whether or not the factory that makes them is in a completely spurious area of the East Midlands – which is much larger than the immediate area around Melton Mowbray.'[45]

Further doubts have been expressed about the representativeness of the link between quality and origin. A priori, this link should convey the same message independent of location, but this does not appear to be the case. A distinction has been drawn between northern and southern Europe, and it is claimed that institutions in the former focus more on health and

---

[43] Rangnekar, 'The Socio-Economics of Geographical Indications', 5, 24.

[44] www.guardian.co.uk/lifestyle/wordofmouth/2011/feb/22/protected-status-for-cornish-pasty

[45] 'Melton Mowbray Pie Fight Hits the UK's Courts', http://foodproductiondaily.com/Supply-Chain/Melton-Mowbray-pie-fight-hits-the-UK's-courts; D. Gangjee, 'Melton Mowbray and the GI Pie in the Sky: Exploring Cartographies of Protection', *Intellectual Property Quarterly*, 3 (2006): 291–309.

hygiene, whereas in the latter there is more emphasis on terroir and product specificity.[46] The implication of this claim is that quality signals transmitted by PDO/PGI products varied within the EU, raising further difficulties. For example, if PDOs and PGIs failed to convey a consistent message about quality, how certain could consumers be that there was uniform implementation of the EU scheme? The EC suggested: 'it is important to suspend all communication with consumers. Given the varying level of quality and specificity of registered products and their methods of production, the current information being communicated to consumers is misleading.'[47] Moreover, the evidence presented in Table 8.2, which supports the interpretation of a north–south divide, suggests that the benefits of the EU certification scheme would always be unequally distributed.

APPROPRIATION OF 'QUALITY' BY OUTSIDERS

The failure to galvanise the relationship between quality and origin was, perhaps, the most serious weakness in the EU scheme. Nonetheless, closer inspection of PDO/PGI labelling reveals other problems which are equally disquieting. For these GIs to be valid indicators of origin, governance of the supply chain is crucial if authenticity is to be communicated to consumers. But firms in the supply chain, each producing identical intermediate or final products, cooperate and compete with each other. The balance between these forces affects industry organisation. This, in turn, affects consumer perceptions of authenticity and heritage. For example, it is difficult to reconcile consumer perceptions of small-scale, artisanal production of Parmigiano-Reggiano with reports that 76 per cent of producers rely on a single wholesale ripener to sell three-quarters of their output. Similarly, the West Country Farmhouse Cheddar industry also has high levels of concentration and integration. For Melton Mowbray pork pies, the situation was even more extreme: in 2007, two years before the MMPPA secured PGI status, it was claimed that Samworth Brothers produced more than 99 per cent of the pies produced by the MMPPA.[48]

---

[46] EC, *PDO and PGI Products: Market, Supply Chains and Institutions*. Final Report by D. Barjolle and B. Sylvander, June (2000): 26; Parrott, Wilson, and Murdoch, 'Spatializing Quality', 246–248.

[47] EC, *PDO and PGI Products: Market, Supply Chains and Institutions*: 40.

[48] 'Pie Factory Moves in Bid to Keep Melton Mowbray Name', www.foodproductiondaily .com?processing/Pie-factory-moves-in-bid-to-keep-Melton-Mowbray-name. Samworth

Concerns have also been raised about the extent to which 'outsiders', particularly large-scale firms, have appropriated the reputation of designated areas, often with adverse consequences.[49] Belletti noted that the practice of 'milking' the reputation of Tuscan olive oil included abandoning traditional practices in order to keep production costs low and selling oil from other regions as 'Tuscan'. These practices were exacerbated by big bottling firms and supermarket chains coupling their own brand to 'Tuscan'.[50] Kees Roest's study of Parmigiano-Reggiano reported significant changes in the genetics and feeding practices of dairy cattle which adversely affected the composition of milk used in the production of this cheese. The interests of large-scale distributors required greater consistency in milk production and this was partly achieved by mixing milk of *different origin* in single vats. Consequently: 'The main defect [of this practice] is that it is unlikely to produce the very highest quality cheese. The product may well be of good quality, but the main reason for using this method is rather to keep the variability of the cheese produced to a minimum. This clearly tends to be at the expense of the highest quality production.'[51]

MARKETING

The inauguration of the EU policy was similar to campaigns used by firms to introduce new products. Heavy advertising was necessary to inform consumers that new GI foodstuffs were being launched. To be effective it was equally important that consumers understood the messages conveyed by PDO and PGI; otherwise asymmetric information would have created an impasse in which consumers were unable to verify claims made by producers marking their products as GIs. The EC recognised the importance of such a campaign by declaring it would 'take the necessary steps to inform the public of the meaning of the indications "PDO", "PGI", "protected designation of origin" and "protected

---

Brothers are a multi-line food producer who acquired Dickinson & Morris in 1992. The latter are one of the oldest producers of Melton Mowbray Pork Pies and a founding member of the MMPPA.

[49] Ilbery and Kneafsey, 'Niche Markets and Regional Speciality Food Products in Europe', 2211.

[50] Belletti, 'Origin Labeled Products', 244–246.

[51] K. De Roest, 'The Dynamics of the Parmigiano-Reggiano Production System', in Sylvander, Barjolle, and Arfini, *The Socio-Economics of Origin-Labelled Products*, Vol. 1, 278–279.

geographical origin" in the Community languages'.[52] Between 1996 and 1998, the EC launched a campaign targeted at producers, distributors and consumers, across the (then) fifteen Member States on the theme of 'Products with a history'. A variety of media, including conferences, press communications, competitions in each Member State, and a barrage of reports on television were deployed, costing approximately 8.8 million Ecus.[53]

However, one theme which reverberates throughout the literature on the EU scheme is the high level of ignorance shown by consumers towards PDO and PGI labelling. A study conducted in 2007 revealed that only 8 per cent of consumers were able to recognise and distinguish these GIs.[54] Other scholars reported contradictions between consumers' perceptions of authentic and regional products, and products with PDO/PGI status. For example, Wensleydale cheese and Bakewell tart were widely recognised as regional foods possessing tradition and heritage, but neither product initially qualified for PDO or PGI status: the former was not produced exclusively in Wensleydale, and the latter was considered generic.[55] The EC recognised that there was considerable confusion among consumers about what the symbols meant. Only 51 per cent of consumers recognised that PDO and PGI meant the product originated in a specific area; only about one third appreciated that the symbols identified the products being produced according to an established specification or with a quality related to the area in which it was produced. More troubling was that approximately 25 per cent believed that the PDO/PGI symbol referred to products made using traditional ingredients or reflecting a traditional *type* of manufacturing (a characteristic of TSG products) – which need not be produced in a geographically delimited area.[56] These findings had the potential to undermine the entire scheme.

In an attempt to remedy these defects the EC reviewed its policies governing agricultural product quality between 2008 and 2009. This

---

[52] Commission Regulation (EEC) No. 2037/93, *Official Journal*, L 185, 27 July 1993.

[53] EC, *PDO and PGI Products: Market, Supply Chains and Institutions*: 36.

[54] London Economics, *Evaluation of the CAP Policy*: 154; Rangnekar, 'The Socio-Economics of Geographical Indications', 28; Ilbery and Kneafsey, 'Registering Regional Speciality', 322.

[55] A. Tregear, S. Kuznesof, and A. Moxey, 'Policy Initiatives for Regional Foods: Some Insights from Consumer Research', *Food Policy*, 23 (1998): 391. 'Wensleydale' cheese was registered as a PGI in 2013.

[56] EC: *Impact Assessment of Geographical Indications*. 'Proposal for a Regulation of the European Parliament and of the Council on Agricultural Product Quality Schemes': 21.

evaluation was the culmination of several years of work dating to 2004 and involving numerous stakeholders and advisory groups. Part of the review involved a consultation scheme which operated between October and December 2008 and generated 560 responses. France was the biggest participant, accounting for almost one-third of replies. Northern European countries, which owned fewer PDO/PGI registrations, also participated. Belgium, Britain, Germany, and Poland accounted for 29 per cent of responses . In terms of interest groups, the largest class of respondents were organisations and individuals from the farming sector (41 per cent), followed by the general public (18 per cent) and organisations from the food-processing sector (11 per cent). In contrast, national and regional/local authorities provided just 6 and 4 per cent, respectively, of total replies, while representatives of the retail sector accounted for just 1 per cent.[57]

This evidence indicated that consumers were largely ignorant of PDO/PGI indicia. Regulations governing their use was inaugurated in 1992, but the relevant logos and legends were not created until 1993 and thirteen years had to elapse before the EC pronounced it was obligatory for registered products to be labelled 'Protected Designation of Origin' or 'Protected Geographical Indication'. Even then, '[a] reasonable length of time should be allowed for operators to adjust to the obligation'. Consequently, it was not until 2009 – sixteen years after the launch of the scheme – that adoption of these terms was compulsory.[58] Bizarrely, PDO and PGI labels were not differentiated until 2008 (red and yellow for the former, blue and yellow for the latter), and this change was not applicable until 1 May 2010. This last observation is surprising because PDOs earn a higher premium than PGIs.[59] Consequently, unless consumers took the precaution of reading

---

[57] EC, Directorate General for Agriculture and Rural Development: *Conclusions from the Consultation on Agricultural Product Quality* (2009): 4–5.

[58] Council Regulations (EC) 509/2006, 510/2006, of 20 March 2006, 'On the Protection of Geographical Indications and Designations of Origin for Agricultural Products and Foodstuffs': 2, 10, 16. These regulations were repealed by Regulation (EU) 1151/2012 of 21 November 2012. Informal communication with Simon Johnson, who worked at the Department of Environment, Food and Rural Affairs (DEFRA), indicated that considerable differences existed among Member States as to whether any scheme should be compulsory; in very broad terms, it appears that northern European states were less concerned than southern states to make this compulsory.

[59] EC: *Impact Assessment of Geographical Indications*. Proposal for a Regulation of the European Parliament and of the Council on Agricultural Product Quality Schemes: 21, Annex IX: 26–27.

the legend embossed on the label, there was no guarantee the premium they were paying accurately reflected their perception of the different labels. Some consumers might have preferred the lower-priced PGI product without realising that PDO products had much stronger geographical links.

MORE PROBLEMS EMERGE

Even accepting that some level of ignorance was inevitable because it takes time for consumers to recognise and appreciate the messages conveyed by PDO and PGI, it is astonishing that their use was not made compulsory much earlier. Unsurprisingly, therefore, in 2009 the EC was forced to admit that its general marketing policies were 'excessively complex' and 'characterized by inflexibility of compulsory rules that cannot be adapted quickly to changing marketing needs, and substantial burdens on farmers in complying with standards that may not be needed by buyers'.[60] Starting from a base that 8 per cent of consumers recognised PDO/PGI logos in 2007, the EC set itself a series of limited operational objectives designed to increase the recognition rate by 0.5 per cent per annum and to provide for a simpler scheme operating throughout the EU which would ensure that the number of registered PDO and PGIs increased by fifty per annum, reaching a total of 1,250 by the end of 2015.[61]

The EC consultation uncovered further weaknesses in the scheme. One set of problems concerned significant differences in the costs and time involved in registering GIs which affected the receptiveness of producers to the scheme: 'Producers have a limited knowledge about the system as well as low interest in collective initiatives [the] PDO/PGI scheme is perceived as bureaucratic, costly (creation of an applicant group, drafting the specifications, evidence of the use of the name, burdens and cost of certification and controls) and time consuming.' Estimates of the costs involved in securing PDO/PGI registration ranged between €3,000 and €5,000, to €20,000 and €40,000. Although these costs were compensated by the prospect of higher margins, the delay between submitting an application and eligibility to use PDO or PGI was perceived as a deterrent. The absolute minimum time that had to elapse was twenty-

---

[60] EC, *Communication on Agricultural Product Quality Policy: Impact Assessment Report* (version 08–04–09): 21–22.

[61] EC, *Impact Assessment of Geographical Indications: Proposal for a Regulation of the European Parliament and of the Council on Agricultural Product Quality Schemes*: 28.

two months; the average interval was four years, but in 2009, 22 per cent of applications were delayed for more than four years. This variation was affected by national differences in the time allowed for raising objections to registration: one month in Belgium and Italy, compared to five months in the Czech Republic. Clearly, if producers were reluctant to participate in the scheme this would increase consumers' ignorance and a classic coordination problem would develop. It was also recognised that cost and time delays differentially affected firms according to their size. The opportunity to participate in the scheme was greater for larger firms, which potentially undermined the range of agricultural products submitted for registration.[62]

A further problem, apparently not understood when the scheme was inaugurated, was how to deal with raw materials 'imported' into a defined region for processing into a PGI product. This problem was particularly acute because it had a direct bearing on consumers' perceptions of the relationship between product and origin; there was also the risk that consumers were being misled:

The issue of non-information on raw material origin used in PGI products is complex. The impact of such lack of information depends entirely on whether the consumer subjectively believes that all the ingredients in a PGI are from the area named in the product's name because either some of the ingredients can or are actually sourced in the region or is actually aware of the fact [that] ingredients from outside the region can be used.[63]

Opportunities to address this weakness were missed and by 2009, sixteen years after the launch of the scheme, a clear consensus did not exist on how consumers comprehended the PDO and PGI scheme.[64] The EC claimed that consumers did not raise concerns about the origin of raw materials used in PGI products. Plausible explanations for this allegation included consumers' generally limited knowledge about these products and/or the possibility that they simply could not conceive that raw materials were sourced from outside the defined area. Nationally, the picture was more complex. In Italy, some firms producing the PGI product Bresaola della Valtellini used meat obtained from Brazil. Similar concerns

---

[62] EC: *Impact Assessment of Geographical Indications: Proposal for a Regulation of the European Parliament and of the Council on Agricultural Product Quality Schemes*: 9–10, 13, 22–23.
[63] *Agricultural Product Quality Policy: Impact Assessment Part B* (version 8, April 2009), Annex B: Geographical Indications: 40.
[64] For example, I cannot find information on this issue in Regulation (EC) 510/2006 of 20 March 2006.

were raised about Mortadella di Bologna. Contradictory views on PGIs were expressed by the German Consumers Association. This body claimed that there was no evidence that consumers were confused about the specification of origin on Spreewälder Gherkins or Lübecker Marzipan: German nationals knew that almonds did not grow in Germany. But for other German specialities with PGI status the association was more critical. For example, the PGI suggested regional origin even though the ingredients used to process the foodstuff were imported from outside the defined area.[65] Similarly, consider Grimsby Traditionally Smoked Fish, which has PGI status. Do British consumers really believe that this fish is obtained from the Lincolnshire coastline as opposed, for example, to the fishing grounds near Scotland?

Before discussing the response to these problems it is important to introduce a caveat: impact assessment of the PDO/PGI scheme was part of a more substantial review of the marketing of all 'quality' agricultural products. The EU's agricultural product quality criteria were built on minimum standards demanded by society which were to be officially enforced, for example, hygiene and safety requirements, animal welfare, and environmental compliance. These were complemented by EU marketing and product quality schemes. The former refer to directives defining agricultural product identity while the latter include GIs. These two broad categories contain overlapping subcategories. Thus, differentiation schemes include PDO and PGI, which require official certification, whereas 'extra virgin' olive oil, 'free range' eggs, and 'skimmed' milk rely on the declarations of producers, with only limited official involvement. Exacerbating matters, EU schemes were in competition with a variety of national and/or private certification schemes which also communicated minimum criteria, for example, 'assured farm produce', and differentiation criteria, for example, 'fair trade' and 'label rouge'.[66]

Reform of the EU scheme was based on a number of criteria including the need to provide clearer information about the link between a product's specific characteristics and geographical origin, and the importance of

---

[65] EC, *Agricultural Product Quality Policy. Impact Assessment: Annex B: Geographical Indications*: 38.

[66] EC, *Communication on Agricultural Product Quality Policy: Impact Assessment Report* (version 08–04–09): 5–10. France's 'label rouge' can only be applied to poultry certified as free range by the National Institute for Origin and Quality. Additionally, poultry bearing this label must be superior to 'standard' poultry.

simplifying its GI policy.[67] The first criteria was the subject of question nine in the Green Paper consultation exercise: 'What are the advantages and disadvantages of identifying the origin of raw materials in cases where they come from somewhere else than the location of the geographical indication?'[68] In broad terms, consumers and farmers preferred the identification of raw materials because this aided transparency and traceability, but there was disagreement about how best to effect this: should it only be applied to principal ingredients, or those obtained from outside the EU? Processors were strongly against identification, claiming it would confuse consumers and possibly generate a negative reaction to all GIs. It was alleged the existing scheme added nothing to the 'quality concept' and many PGI holders suggested it was impossible to obtain the required inputs from within the demarcated region. In any event, proposed changes in labelling and packaging increased costs. The EC was firmly on the side of consumers, stating: 'The bottom line is that the non-information on raw material origin used in PGI may, in some cases, be a source of confusion for consumers.' However, devising a robust solution to this problem threatened to negate other objectives. For example, comprehensive market research for each PGI would identify the degree to which consumers were misled, but it was costly and time-consuming. In view of these competing requirements, the EC could only suggest that it would be necessary to issue further guidelines.[69]

Interestingly, one proposal to simplify the scheme involved merging PDO with PGI, which would have necessitated the abolition of PDO registrations.[70] Had this suggestion been effected, the demands for simplicity, clarity, and streamlining would have undermined the intensity of the link between product and geographical origin. It was acknowledged that PDO proprietors might prefer to use alternative brands rather than accept demotion to PGI status. But consumers' associations wanted greater differentiation between GIs, not the abolition of PDO. Finally, the proposed merger required that those entitled to use PDO write-off

---

[67] EC, *Agricultural Product Quality Policy. Impact Assessment: Annex B: Geographical Indications*: 30.

[68] EC, *Green Paper on Agricultural Product Quality: Product Standards, Farming Requirements and Quality Schemes. Com* (2008), Brussels, 15 October (2008): 15.

[69] *Impact Assessment Annex B*: 41–42; EC, *Green Paper: Communication from the Commission to the European Parliament, the Council, the European Economic and Social Committee and the Committee of the Regions, on Agricultural Product Quality Policy*, 28 May 2009: 11.

[70] For this proposal to be effective it was necessary to lower the criteria linking product to region.

substantial investments in communication and marketing. For example, between 2007 and 2010, the French dairy organisation Centre National Interprofessionnel de l'Economie Laitière incurred expenditures of €3.595 million promoting its PDO (though 50 per cent was financed by the EU). Fortunately – depending on your point of view – the EC does not appear to have responded to the merger proposal with any vigour, indicating only that a 'possible recast of the geographical indications legislation' would follow.[71]

CONCLUSIONS

The EU scheme represents an ambitious attempt to use GIs to solve a number of problems which confronted agriculture and rural communities. Since its inauguration in 1992, there were, at the end of 2016, almost 1,400 PDO, PGI, and TSG registrations. This figure appears to show that the scheme was successful, particularly so because many of Europe's most famous GI food products are included in this total. However, as demonstrated, it is difficult to understand why so many producers sought PDO/PGI status when the benefits from registration are uncertain and ambiguous. Thus, only some PDO/PGI products obtained a price premia compared to related products not covered by the scheme. This immediately raises difficult questions about how the EU should develop GI registration in the future. For example, what happens if products labelled PDO or PGI do not achieve a premia? Should these products be withdrawn because they might jeopardise 'successful' PDO/PGI products, or should they continue to be promoted in the hope that future consumers will value them?[72] Viewed from another perspective, was EC policy a blunt instrument to differentiate 'winners' and 'losers'? If so, why should producers with relatively 'unsuccessful' GI products continue to bear the costs of registration and monitoring, and how can this be reconciled with the EU's aim to safeguard rural communities?

[71] *Impact Assessment of Geographical Indications*: 41; *Impact Assessment, Annex B*: 64; *Impact Assessment: Product Quality Policy*: 48; EC, *Green Paper: Communication from the Commission to the European Parliament, the Council, the European Economic and Social Committee and the Committee of the Regions, on Agricultural Product Quality Policy*, 28 May 2009: 10. Current EU policy on GIs for foodstuffs is provided in Regulation (EU) 1151/2012 of 21 November 2012, which reaffirms the EU's commitment to PDOs, PGIs, and TSGs.
[72] Loureiro and McCluskey, 'Effectiveness of PGI and PDO', 161.

Such questions are especially pertinent in view of BREXIT, which has raised concerns about the extent to which the British government will replace EU subsidies. Currently, British farmers receive approximately £3.5 billion per annum from the Common Agricultural Policy, which equates to 55 per cent of their income.[73] A related theme is whether British food producers will continue to derive any benefit from applying PDO and PGI indicia to their products after BREXIT. In theory, British products which meet the requirements of the PDO/PGI scheme will continue to be eligible to use these logos. Indeed, countries which do not belong to the EU have succeeded in obtaining registration for their produce. For example, Darjeeling and Café de Valdesia were registered by India and the Dominican Republic, in 2011 and 2016, respectively. However, the divorce from the EU may raise tariffs and weaken the competitiveness of British food exports, irrespective of their PDO/PGI status.

The theme of 'winners' and 'losers' is clearly revealed by analysis of countries which responded energetically to the EU initiative. As Table 8.2 indicates, more than 60 per cent of total registrations between 1996 and 2016 were accounted for by four countries: France, Italy, Spain, and Portugal. In addition, between 1995 and 2005, agriculture as a proportion of national income in these four countries comfortably exceeded the average for EU-25 countries, and was particularly pronounced in relation to the northern European countries of Belgium and Britain[74] This trend has continued.[75] Even allowing for the fact that agriculture as a proportion of national income has declined in all EU Member States, a fair generalisation is that those in which agriculture remains *relatively* important have engaged most strongly with the EU scheme.[76]

Perhaps the strongest explanation for the previous observation is that the concepts of 'artisanal', 'heritage', 'original', and 'traditional' which underpin the EU scheme, are most strongly embedded in only a few

---

[73] 'The anguish of Britain's farmers', *Financial Times*, 5 January 2017.

[74] Calculated from Eurostat, *Agricultural Statistics*, 1995–2005, EC Luxembourg, 2007: table 1.2, 14; *Agriculture in the EU: Statistical and Economic Information, Report 2010*, EC Luxembourg, 2011: table 2.0.1.2, 43; *Agriculture in the European Union Statistical and Economic Information*, 2011, EC, Luxembourg, 2012: table 2.0.1.3, 50.

[75] The data refer to value added in agriculture as a percentage of GDP. Calculated from World Bank: http://data.worldbank.org/indicator/NV.AGR.TOTL.ZS.

[76] There are exceptions. Agriculture is a much bigger share of national income in newcomers to the EU, such as the Czech and Slovak Republics and Poland, compared to France, Italy, Spain, and Portugal, but the former are negligible in terms of PDO/PGI registrations.

European countries. For example, France's *appellation d' origine contrôlée* (AOC) is the oldest in the EU, closely paralleled by Italy's *Denominazione di origine controllata* (DOC). A substantial volume of sociological and cultural literature has emerged which explains this embeddedness in terms of preserving local knowledge against the destructive effects of globalisation while simultaneously permitting the valorisation of local food.[77] Other scholars in this tradition emphasise that the transmission of this knowledge through time helps generate a collective memory which differentiates provenance from origin: 'the difference between merely coming from a place that does not attribute the least particularity to it, from belonging to a place that involves a relationship with a special meaning'.[78] In contrast, it is claimed that rapid industrialisation in some countries destroyed the link between produce and origin: 'the regional distinctiveness of products and consumption habits in the UK were pulverized during the Industrial Revolution into a "placeless foodscape"'.[79]

Looking to the future, this literature suggests that heritage-based quality initiatives can generate the seeds of their own destruction. For example, the participation of extra-local agents may generate conflict if they do not value the culture and traditions of local actors; formal codification of rules and regulations can stifle diversity, contributing to 'standardisation' and homogenisation, leading ultimately to 'Disneyfication'.[80] This potential problem can originate from another source which is the exact antithesis of the PDO/PGI scheme: biotechnical research. If scientific inquiry can successfully identify and accurately replicate the factors that give a product its 'typicity', these characteristics can be delocalised and their imitation may become legitimate.[81]

Two particular weaknesses in the EU scheme were given prominence: the ambiguous link between quality and origin, and the failure of the EU to market successfully PDO and PGI products. Because these problems are interrelated, their joint solution remains problematic. Thus, the

---

[77] M. Fonte, 'Knowledge, Food and Place: A Way of Producing, a Way of Knowing', *Sociologia Ruralis*, 48 (2008): 200–222.

[78] L. Bérard and P. Marcheny, 'Local Products and Geographical Indications: Taking Account of Local Knowledge and Biodiversity', *International Social Science Journal*, 58 (2006): 110.

[79] Ilbery and Kneafsey, 'Registering Regional Speciality', 319.

[80] S. Bowen and K. De Master, 'New Rural Livelihoods or Museums of Production? Quality Food Initiatives in Practice', *Journal of Rural Studies*, 27 (2011): 77.

[81] Sylvander, DOLPHINS Working Paper 7, *Final Report: Synthesis and Recommendations*, 2004: 8–9.

participation of major supermarket groups can help local, small-scale producers of GI products to increase their market share and ensure their long-term survival. But if the major retailers become increasingly power-ful and integrate backwards into the supply chain, they might undermine authenticity and the related values associated with PDO and PGI. Similarly, although large retailing chains provide an opportunity for such products to reach distant markets, retailers' own brands might displace GIs as the primary means to communicate a product's authenticity.[82]

In the final reckoning, the EU scheme attempted to build an enduring and visible relationship between product, place, and quality. The link between product and place is comprehensible even if, historically, it was the subject of substantial litigation. However, establishing a clear, unam-biguous link between place and quality has proved contentious – perhaps elusive. From a consumer's perspective, the only statement that can be made with any confidence is that the relationship between product quality and geographical origin, is complex, dynamic, and multi-layered. Ultimately, therefore, the old adage that 'beauty is in the eye of the beholder' appears to be true.

---

[82] Rangnekar, 'The Socio-Economics of Geographical Indications', 30–32; A. Gracia and L. M. Albisu, 'Food Consumption in the European Union: Main Determinants and Country Differences', *Agribusiness*, 17 (2001): 482–486.

9

'Made in' and Country of Origin in the Post-1945 Period

[Country of origin] effect is no longer a major issue for international marketing operations: multinational production, global branding, and the decline of origin labelling in WTO rules tend to blur the [country of origin] issue and to lessen its relevance ... many consumers are unaware of the manufacturing origin (made-in) of the goods they buy and, if aware, tend to use the origin information in conjunction with ... price, brand, retail store image.

Usunier, 'Relevance in Business Research', 61

What Switzerland is suffering from, oddly enough, is the good name of Swiss watches. Watches incorporating Swiss workings and made abroad for sale under a 'Swiss Made' mark are in definite competition with products exported directly from Switzerland.

Financial Times, 4 January 1967, 5

This chapter focuses on country of origin, or 'Made in'. There can be little doubt that this indication can exert positive effects on consumer expectations. For the twentieth century, David Head argued that 'Made in Germany' became a powerful symbol of 'German commerce and industry'.[1] 'Made in Italy' conjures images of exquisite quality and design, and products bearing 'Made in Japan' eventually became 'commonly regarded as high quality' because of that country's reputation as a leading manufacturer and exporter.[2] Turning to Scandinavia, Per Hansen argued

[1] D. Head, Made in Germany: The Corporate Identity of a Nation (London: Hodder and Stoughton, 1992), 6.
[2] P. Kotler and D. Gertner, 'Country as Brand, Product, and Beyond: A Place Marketing and Brand Management Perspective', Journal of Brand Management, 9 (2002): 250.

that the association between Denmark and Danish Modern furniture enabled Denmark to establish a strong national image in the United States with respect to design. In the 1960s it was claimed that Danish merchandise was 'outstandingly tasteful and handsomely designed'.[3]

Nonetheless, there are grounds for believing that 'Made in' is a misleading indication of origin when applied to manufactures. In the post-1945 period, manufactures became an increasingly important component in global trade: their share of world trade in merchandise exports increased from 45 to 65 per cent between 1955 and 2011. In contrast, the share of agriculture declined from 35 to 9 per cent during the same period.[4] However, in contrast to produce, the location of manufacturing is largely independent of the natural environment. The WTO reported that 'virtually all manufactured products available in markets today are produced in more than one country'.[5] According to Richard Baldwin, a key feature of this fragmentation was the 'second unbundling' of production from consumption in the early 1980s, which 'made it easy for rich-nation firms to combine the high technology they developed at home with low-wage workers abroad'.[6] The US International Trade Commission stated:

For the consumer, the globalisation of production ... may result in increasingly complex purchasing decisions ... many consumers will continue to seek products that are made domestically or by domestic companies ... In this context, a company gains a competitive advantage if it can mark its products 'Made in the USA.' ... However, the growing use of foreign inputs or manufacturing facilities by companies with brand names perceived by consumers as representing domestic firms increasingly blurs distinctions based on country of origin.[7]

Provided all materials, assembly, and finishing are located in a single country, use of 'Made in' provides a clear and unambiguous indication of origin. However, the acceleration of globalisation during the later twentieth century, and the associated fragmentation of global supply chains – sometimes referred to as 'off-shore assembly' or 'outsourcing' – meant that 'Made in' is no longer an unambiguous indication of origin.

[3] P. H. Hansen, 'Cobranding Product and Nation: Danish Modern Furniture and Denmark in the United States, 1940–1970', in Silva Lopes and Duguid, *Trademarks, Brands and Competitiveness*, 77.

[4] WTO, *World Trade Report* for 2013: 54.   [5] WTO, *World Trade Report* for 2013: 78.

[6] R. Baldwin, 'Trade and Industrialisation after Globalisation's 2nd Unbundling: How Building and Joining a Supply Chain Are Different and Why It Matters', *National Bureau of Economic Research*, Working Paper 17716 (2011): 13.

[7] US International Trade Commission: *Country-of-Origin Marking: Review of Laws, Regulations and Practices*. Publication 2975, Washington, DC, 1996: 4.2.

Again, and in contrast to GIs, 'Made in' can be de-localised. In the case of 'Made in Italy', for example, it was reported in the late 1990s that many leading design houses began outsourcing production to firms in other countries. Specifically, manufacturers sent production designs and fabrics to 'cut-make-trim' (CMT) firms to assemble the garments. By 1997, it was estimated that approximately 20 per cent of all Italian clothing was produced by foreign CMT firms.[8]

Determining the country of origin is particularly problematic for manufactures for two interrelated reasons which involve customs policy on imports and the use of country names to promote exports. First, Rules of Origin became especially important following the growth of preferential trading regimes, for example, the North American Free Trade Association. Rules of Origin are primarily used to determine the nationality of a product for customs purposes including the imposition of tariffs and quotas. The Rules are also used for statistical purposes, such as the collection of data on trade flows and the balance of payments.[9] From a customs perspective, country of origin is defined as the last country in which a product underwent 'substantial transformation'.[10] However, the Rules applied to determine origin vary between countries. Attempts to achieve global harmony in the application of Rules of Origin have been evolving for more than seventy years. The GATT in 1947 and the Kyoto Conventions of 1973 and 1977 failed to achieve global alignment. The Uruguay Round, which concluded in 1994, established a Harmonisation Work Programme to align the various Rules of Origin. However, no agreement has yet been reached. Ironically, one obstacle to progress was the belief that many products were '"made in the world", so the concept of country of origin lost its importance'.[11]

---

[8] S. Forden, 'Pride versus Profits: Italian Makers Confront Offshore Production', quoted in D. Besanko, D. Dranove, and M. Shanley, *Economics of Strategy* (London: Wiley, 2000), 133.

[9] Customs are sometimes deployed to enforce labelling requirements for the purposes of informing domestic consumers about the origin of their imports.

[10] Substantial transformation may be assessed by an *ad valorem* percentage rule (e.g., to qualify for the label 'Made in the USA', there must be a minimum component of US labour and/or value added), a change in tariff classification, and a technical test (prescribing production or sourcing processes that confer originating status). See, for example, E. Vermulst, P. Waer, and J. Bourgeois, *Rules of Origin in International Trade: A Comparative Study* (Ann Arbor: University of Michigan Press, 1994); N. A. Zaimis, *EC Rules of Origin* (London: Chancery Law Publishing, 1992).

[11] WTO, *Report of the Committee on Rules of Origin to the Council for Trade in Goods*: G/L/1047, 10 October 2013.

Second, a recurring theme in the literature on country of origin is that MNCs place less emphasis on national origin and more emphasis on private brands because their global sourcing is partly based on low-cost countries which possess weak quality images.[12] A related issue is that conflicts emerge between country of origin and brand origin. For example, Louis Vuitton is a quintessential French brand, even though much of its production occurs in China. Similarly, New Balance markets its sports shoes with labels proclaiming 'Made in the USA', notwithstanding that the outer soles used in their construction are Chinese.[13]

Exacerbating matters, differences exist in the legal protection afforded country names and trademarks. Historically, country names were ineligible for registration as trademarks because they are geographically descriptive, misleading, or false. Recent discussions within the WTO have reaffirmed this position.[14] However, country names may be registered as GIs. Recall from Chapter 7 that TRIPS Article 22.1 defined GIs as 'indications which identify a good as originating in the territory of a Member, or a region or locality in that territory, where a given quality, reputation or other characteristic of the good is essentially attributable to its geographical origin'. Generally, the name of any locality, irrespective of its geographical area, can qualify as a GI. For this to occur it is necessary to establish a relationship between a product's quality, reputation, or other characteristic, and its geographical origin. Consequently, some country names have been registered as GIs, for example: Luxembourg for meat products, Guyane rum, Irish whisky, and Danish Aquavit. However, establishing this relationship for manufactures has proved more difficult. Nonetheless, in Europe, GIs as applied to non-agricultural products include Bordado da Madeira (embroidery produced in the Madeira Islands), Cuero de Ubrique (leather products from Ubrique in Cádiz), Couteaux de Thiers (hand-made knives made in Thiers, France), and Fine Bohemian China.[15] However, only Switzerland has succeeded in registering its name as a GI for a non-agricultural product: 'Swiss made' as applied to watches.

---

[12] Usunier, 'Relevance in Business Research', 64.

[13] Samiee, 'Resolving the Impasse'; www.wsj.com/articles/new-balance-shoe-materials-arent-all-u-s-made-1412109111.

[14] WIPO, *Study on the Protection of Country Names*, SCT/29/5 Rev, 8 July 2013; WIPO, *The Protection of Country Names against Registration and Use as Trademarks*, Strad/INF/7, 23 November 2015.

[15] See, for example, Insight Consulting, *Study on the Protection of Geographical Indications for Products Other than Wines, Spirits, Agricultural Products or Foodstuffs.* November 2009. Obtained from: http://trade.ec.europa.eu/doclib/docs/201 1/may/tradoc_147926.pdf.

This chapter is organised as follows. In the next section I discuss the campaign which re-established the link between production, quality, and country of origin in the Swiss watch industry. The third section examines the problems that confronted the Federal Trade Commission (FTC) in its attempts to establish an unambiguous definition of 'Made in the USA' during the 1990s. I then explain why the EU failed to introduce a mandatory 'Made in the EU' indication. Conclusions are presented in the fifth section.

'SWISS-MADE' WATCHES

'Swiss made' and watches are synonymous.[16] Although famous watch brands are based in other countries, for example, Ingersoll and Timex in the United States, and Seiko in Japan, Switzerland is the established home of most of the world's leading watch brands, including Breitling, Jaeger-LeCoultre, Omega, Patek Phillippe, and Rolex. Of course, many countries own famous brands and it is possible that the brand becomes more valuable than the country of origin. For example, Nike is a famous US brand, even though Nike shoes are not entitled to be labelled 'Made in the USA'. However, 'Swiss made' accompanies famous Swiss watch brands. In other words, the country of origin effect and the brand are complementary. According to the Federation of the Swiss Watch Industry:

> The intrinsic value of the 'Swiss made' label ... is the result of considerable efforts on the part of watchmaking companies, who are ultimately responsible for maintaining its reputation. Whilst prestigious brand names have thrived, they have never relegated the 'Swiss made' label to a secondary place. The brand names and 'Swiss made' have always worked together in an alliance that provides the consumer with the best of guarantees.[17]

It has been estimated that the value added by 'Swiss made' is 20 per cent of the sales price of standard watches, rising to 50 per cent for some mechanical watches.[18] An academic study compared the International Watch

---

[16] This section is not concerned with 'Swiss-ness' legislation, which is related to nation branding. See, for example, R. J. Breidling, *Swiss Made* (London: Profile Books, 2013).

[17] Federation of the Swiss Watch Industry: https://web.archive.org/web/20140115202807/ http://www.fhs.ch/en/swissm.php#juridique.

[18] 'Révision de l'ordonnance réglant l'utilisation du nom "Suisse" pour les montres: rapport rendant compte des résultats de la consultation 2016'. Downloaded from: www.ipi.ch/fr/ ip4all/indications-de-provenance/swissness/ordonnances-de-branche/revision-de-lordon nance-reglant-lutilisation-du-nom-suisse-pour-les-montres/consultation-2015.html? type=oskqislp.

Company (IWC) – which can legally apply 'Swiss made' to its watches – with Casio, and reported that some IWC watches obtained prices which were 1,000 times those of Casio. The authors of this study concluded, 'the single greatest determinant of a watch's value is its country of origin'.[19] However, this association was not always harmonious: chablonnage – the export of unassembled parts of a watch movement for assembly and sale abroad – was beneficial to individual firms but threatened the renown of 'Swiss made'.

Outsourcing the manufacture of Swiss watches has been dated to the eighteenth century when the transfer of technology from Switzerland facilitated the emergence of cheap watch production in the Vallée de l'Arve (south-east France), where subcontracting for Geneva-based watch manufacturers was widespread. Subsequently, the scale of chablonnage increased rapidly. The export of chablons increased from 3.9 to 7.4 million between 1935 and 1950, and then to 10.8 million by 1960.[20] These exports accelerated the manufacturing capabilities of foreign watchmaking industries and directly affected the global competitiveness of the Swiss watch industry.

During the twentieth century the Swiss watch industry and the Swiss government introduced a series of regulations to ensure that the manufacture of watch movements and their assembly into finished watches occurred within Switzerland.[21] The primary purpose of these regulations was to restrict chablonnage. Such initiatives included a 1928 agreement between the Federation of the Swiss Watch Industry, Ebauches S.A., and L'Union des Branches Annexes de l'Horlogerie, representing manufacturers and assemblers of watches, ebauches, and watch-component parts, respectively. Subsequently, in 1931, a major holding company – the Societe Generale de l'Horlogerie de Suisse, S.A. – was established to ensure greater control over the watch industry. The 1928 agreement formed the basis of the Collective Convention which tried to ensure that the trade in watch parts was restricted to its members. Such gentlemen's agreements were reinforced by statutes enacted in 1934, 1951, 1961, and 1962. The statute of 1961 was particularly significant because it instituted

---

[19] A. Goodman, F. Maro, R. Molander, J. Ojeda, and O. Tompkins, 'The Swiss Watch Cluster'. Harvard Business School: The Microeconomics of Competitiveness, 6 May (2010): 16.

[20] P. Y. Donze, *History of the Swiss Watch Industry: From Jacques David to Nicolas Hayek* (Bern: Peter Lang AG, 2012), 22–23, 105.

[21] Movement (or calibre) refers to the watch's working mechanism which is protected by the case.

a system of technical control sanctioned by public law.[22] The Swiss government argued that the need to protect the reputation of Swiss watches necessitated government intervention:

Because important standards of quality of a watch ... were not ascertainable by buyers at the time of purchase and because watches without trade names (in the sale of which some importance may be attached to the origin of the watch) represented a considerable share of the overall production of the Swiss watchmaking industry, the Council felt that the competitive position of the Swiss watch ... could be maintained only if its reputation was retained.[23]

Essentially, these agreements and statutes were designed to use monopolistic powers to control supply and quality. In theory, such a strategy could reassure consumers that watches marked 'Swiss made' were fully manufactured from domestic components and finished in Switzerland. However, the assumption that monopoly power obviated the need for a legal definition of 'Swiss made' can be rejected. The statutes enacted in the 1930s permitted watch assemblers to purchase parts from non-Swiss manufacturers provided their prices were more than 20 per cent below Swiss prices. Intense price competition during the 1960s and 1970s encouraged some Swiss watch companies to establish assembly operations for electronic watches in Hong Kong.[24] Such practices improved the competitiveness of Swiss watchmakers, but also carried risks: there was no guarantee that foreign components possessed the same level of craftsmanship as Swiss components. Additionally, growing reliance on foreign suppliers created dissonance between private brands and country of origin. Some observers commented that it was 'not the indication of the country of origin but the creation, promotion and care of watch brands [which] is decisive for the success of the industry as demonstrated by the competitors from the USA and Japan'.[25]

One way to achieve greater alignment between private brands and country of origin was to enact legislation governing the use of 'Swiss made'. It was recognised that application of 'Swiss made' to watches represented, 'a particular national interest' which would promote the

---

[22] US Tariff Commission: *Watches, Watch Movements and Watch Parts. Report to the President on Investigation* No. 337–19. Washington, DC (1966): 19–30, 47–51.

[23] US Tariff Commission: *Watches, Watch Movements and Watch Parts*: 57–58; I. S. Campo and P. Aerni, *When Corporatism Leads to Corporate Governance Failure: The Case of the Swiss Watch Industry* (Cambridge: Banson, 2016), 20.

[24] By including Swiss movements in their watches, many Hong Kong manufacturers sold their watches as 'Swiss'. A. Glasmeier, *Manufacturing Time* (New York: Guildford Press, 2000), 151, 225, 251.

[25] Campo and Aerni, *When Corporatism Leads to Corporate Governance Failure*, 25.

reputation of *all* Swiss products.[26] Instead of restricting supply to control quality, which only benefitted the watch industry, a new type of corporatism developed which sought to promote the reputation of Swiss products in the public interest.[27] The legal basis for 'Swiss made' applied to watches differed from 'Made in Switzerland' or 'Produce of Switzerland'. The latter are indications of origin, not GIs.

The application of 'Swiss made' to watches was enacted in 1971 by an ordinance 'governing the use of the appellation "Switzerland" or "Swiss"' for watches. According to this legislation, a watch was defined as 'Swiss' if the movement, its encasement, and final inspection by the manufacturer were conducted in Switzerland. It was further stipulated that at least 50 per cent of the value of the movement had to be obtained from components made in Switzerland. Appellations containing the words 'Swiss' or 'Swiss quality' were reserved exclusively for Swiss watches or watch movements. Other articles governed the marking of movements, watch cases, and watch dials.[28]

Nonetheless, a major weakness in this ordinance was that Swiss watchmakers still had considerable scope to outsource their production *and* comply with the 'Swiss made' regulations. According to Pierre Donze, the 1971 legislation was a pragmatic gesture to retain employment in Switzerland and to strengthen the Swiss watch industry by permitting relocation of low-value-added manufacturing to Asia.[29] In fact, growing competition from cheaper Chinese watch parts enabled Swiss watch firms to source offshore and remain compliant with the 1971 ordinance. The net result was that only an 'extremely small fraction' of the value of many Swiss watches originated in Switzerland. Offshoring was particularly appealing to manufacturers competing in the low-mid-price market who wished to benefit from the cachet of 'Swiss made'.[30] Concerns were also raised that 'Swiss made' created a 'moral hazard': the major watch conglomerates expended significant sums in the global promotion of Swiss watches while many smaller Swiss watchmakers failed to devote any resources to marketing, relying solely on 'Swiss made'.[31] Exacerbating matters, the brands of

---

[26] See, for example, Breidling, *Swiss Made*.
[27] Campo and Aerni, *When Corporatism Leads to Corporate Governance Failure*, 23–24.
[28] Downloaded from www.fhs.swiss/file/8/ordonnance_swiss_made_1971_En.pdf.
[29] Donze, *History of the Swiss Watch Industry*, 122.
[30] 'Swiss Made' to Mean a Whole Lot More for Watches in 2017'. Downloaded from www .ablogtowatch.com/swiss-made-mean-whole-lot-more-watches-2017/.
[31] A second-round effect of freeriding was the risk that expenditure on innovation would decline and more firms would sell their watches under the 'Swiss made' brand. In other

luxury and designer clothiers, for example, Donna Karan and Tommy Hilfiger, were being applied to watches. This practice was a further threat to the repute of 'Swiss made': consumers might assume that watches branded Donna Karan were comparable to 'Swiss-made' watches, even though the former had no experience of watch manufacture. In fact, Donna Karan watches were almost exclusively assembled in Hong Kong. Moreover, sales of designer-label watches depended on the company brand, not the appellation 'Swiss made'. Similar trends have been observed when the production of big brand watches was relocated to Thailand.[32] When owners of designer brands such as Louis Vuitton Möet Hennessy and Gucci conducted their design and marketing functions abroad, Switzerland risked losing control of its main source of value creation because '[t]he cost of components and movement assembly for a typical Swiss luxury watch is only 6% of its retail price [and] the bulk of the value creation happens in the consumer's mind through branding and functions such as design and marketing'.[33]

It can be argued that revisions to the 1971 ordinance further weakened the reputation of 'Swiss made'. In 1995, the Swiss Federal Council permitted the application of 'Swiss made' to foreign watchcases and dials that were to be used in the manufacture of Swiss watches. From 1995 Swiss manufacturers of parts destined for foreign watches were authorised to visibly indicate that they originated in Switzerland. These innovations were designed to increase the transparency of the geographical origin of watch parts. [34] The revision was not intended to reduce the protection afforded 'Swiss made', but it is clear that opportunities existed for foreign manufacturers to engage in ambiguous marketing practices, for example, using the indication 'Made in China, from Swiss parts'.

Accelerating globalisation and rapid developments in watch manufacture meant that the 1971 and 1995 ordinances were becoming increasingly unreliable indicators of provenance. The Swiss watch industry also had to contend with the growing trade in counterfeit watches.

words, competitive quality debasement nullified the benefit of the appellation. Goodman, Maro et al., 'The Swiss Watch Cluster', 28.

[32] Glasmeier, *Manufacturing Time*, 250; www.credit-suisse.com/media/production/pb/doc s/unternehmen/kmugrossunternehmen/uhrenstudie-en.pdf: 32. Accessed September 2016. It has been suggested that some Swiss firms eschew the 'Swiss made' indicia because their own brands are more important. L. Trueb, *The World of Watches* (New York: Ebner Publishing International, 2005), 362–363.

[33] Goodman and Maro, et al., 'The Swiss Watch Cluster', 21, 27.

[34] Federal Department of Justice and Police, Information and Press Service, 29 March 1995.

FIGURE 9.1 Rolex and 'Swiss-made' watches.
Model shown 'Air_King_116900_16th_006 Oyster Perpetual Air King'. By permission of Rolex. © Rolex/Thomas Hensinger

The Federation of the Swiss Watch Industry reported continuously on seizures of contraband watches, the scale of which was astonishing. For example, the Federation was instrumental in the destruction of 400,000 counterfeit watches in Dubai in 2003. In 2009, it estimated that more than 40 million fake Swiss watches were made per annum, compared to genuine exports of just 26 million, and that this illicit trade generated net profits of approximately $1 billion.[35] This fraud 'included not only counterfeit brands and copies of well-known models, but also neutral watches bearing fake Swiss geographical markings (Swiss made, Geneva)'.[36]

Growing concerns about the reliability of 'Swiss made' watches coincided with similar worries about misuse of 'Switzerland', 'Swiss', and the Swiss red cross on a diverse range of products. The Hutter and Fetz postulates of 2006 mandated the Swiss government to examine measures which would better protect 'Swiss' designations.[37] In 2013 the

---

[35] www.fhs.swiss/eng/2009-02-06_680.html. Accessed September 2016.
[36] The Swiss Watch Industry, 'Fake Swiss Watches – Spectacular Destruction'. www.fhs .swiss/eng/2004-08-25_324.html. Accessed September 2016.
[37] Anita Fetz and Jasmin Hutter were members of the Swiss Federal Parliament. Report of the Federal Council, 'Protecting "Made in Switzerland" Designations and the Swiss Cross'. Downloaded from www.ige.ch/fileadmin/user_upload/Juristische_Infos/e/j1080 2e.pdf. Accessed September 2016.

Federal Act on the Protection of Trade Marks and Indications of Source ('Swiss-ness' Bill) was enacted, stipulating that food products were only permitted to use designations of Swiss origin if a minimum of 80 per cent of the ingredients used to make the product originated in Switzerland. For other products, at least 60 per cent of manufacturing costs had to be incurred in Switzerland.[38]

Contemporaneously, the Federation of the Swiss Watch Industry sought to tighten the regulations governing use of 'Swiss made' on watches and proposed the following changes: mechanical watches in which a minimum of 80 per cent of the production costs originated within Switzerland were eligible to use this appellation; the same percentage was to apply to movements used in mechanical watches, but for electronic watches, the relevant proportion was 60 per cent. The Federation also required that technical construction and prototype development occur in Switzerland.[39]

However, the Federation's proposals were not welcomed by all Swiss watch manufacturers. It was claimed that the Federation only represented the interests of the luxury watchmakers, for example, the Swatch group, which owns Omega and Tissot, Patek Philippe, and Rolex, all of whom had a particular interest in the cachet and premia generated by 'Swiss made'. Small and medium-sized companies were more reliant on global supply chains, and they established the 'IG Swiss Made' group to fight the Federation's plans. This opposition focused on two fundamental issues: what was the minimum content requirement, and how was this to be determined? The group argued that existing cantonal law stipulated that to qualify as 'Swiss made', only 50 per cent of production costs had to be incurred in Switzerland. Moreover, in other countries, use of country of origin varied substantially. Some specified a minimum content of 50 per cent, while others did not impose any percentage. Moreover, what grounds existed for believing that a lower national content requirement constituted 'unfair competition'?[40]

Further consultation in 2015 involving representatives of the Swiss watch industry resulted in a revised ordinance which specified the following conditions for use of 'Swiss made': at least 60 per cent of the costs of

[38] www.ige.ch/fileadmin/user_upload/Swissness/e/TmPA_Amendments_of_21_June_2013_EN.pdf. Accessed September 2016.
[39] The Swiss Watch Industry, 'Swiss Made Proposed Reinforcement'. www.fhs.swiss/eng/2007-03-21_540.html. Accessed September 2016.
[40] Letter to Federal Council. Downloaded from https://translate.google.co.uk/translate?hl=en&sl=de&u=https://www.ige.ch/fileadmin/user_upload/Juristische_Infos/swissness_vl/10802046.pdf&prev=search. Accessed September 2016.

manufacturing a complete watch (as an end product) had to be generated in Switzerland,[41] and at least 50 per cent of the value of the movement had to consist of components made in Switzerland. Additionally, technical developments involving 'Swiss Made' watches and 'Swiss Made' movements were also required to occur in Switzerland. Recent technological advances required that the regulations apply to 'smart' watches.[42] Watch casings and glass can be excluded from the calculation of manufacturing costs until 31 December 2018 (provided they were already in stock at the time this 'Swiss made' ordinance came into force). This ensures that producers have sufficient time to reduce all stock legitimately accumulated. The revised ordinance for 'Swiss-made' watches entered into force on 1 January 2017.[43]

This discussion on 'Swiss-made' watches indicated tension between luxury and mid-range watch manufacturers, which partly reflected differences in the extent to which they were integrated into global supply chains. Growing competition in the international watch industry raised fundamental questions about what 'Swiss made' actually meant to producers and consumers, and whether use of cheaper imported components was compatible with the traditional image conveyed by 'Swiss made'. In any event, *irrespective* of the domestic content requirements of 'Swiss made', counterfeiting remains a serious challenge. But, how relevant is the 'Swiss made' example to other countries which also possess a strong country of origin image?

'MADE IN THE USA'?

In some respects the issues affecting protection of 'Made in the USA' were fundamentally different from 'Swiss made'. Thus, the United States possesses a more diverse manufacturing base than Switzerland and it is home to more famous brands.[44] Consequently, the United States faced bigger

---

[41] Previously, this rule applied only to the watch movement itself.
[42] Revision of the ordinance governing use of the name 'Swiss' for watches. Downloaded from www.ige.ch/fr/indications-de-provenance/swissness/ordonnances-de-branche/revi sion-de-lordonnance-reglant-lutilisation-du-nom-suisse-pour-les-montres/consultation-2015.html. Accessed September 2016.
[43] Downloaded from www.ige.ch/en/indications-of-source/swissness/industry-ordinances/ revision-of-the-ordinance-on-the-use-of-swiss-for-watches.html. Accessed September 2016.
[44] Seven of the top ten global brands in 2016 were American. Interbrand: Best Global Brands 2016. http://interbrand.com/best-brands/best-global-brands/2016/ranking. Accessed September 2016.

obstacles to achieving national consensus on the criteria that allowed a product to be branded 'Made in the USA'. Another difference is that the United States is much less dependent on international trade. In 1960, trade as a percentage of GDP was 25, 39, and 9 per cent, respectively, for the world, the EU, and the United States. In 2010, the relevant figures were 92, 82, and 28 per cent, respectively.[45] This insularity meant that 'Made in the USA' was more relevant to domestic consumers. As discussed later in this chapter, much of the evidence presented to the FTC focused on US consumers' understanding of 'Made in the USA'. Little, if any, consideration was given to the misrepresentation of this indication of origin in foreign markets.

Nonetheless, a major similarity between all industrial economies is that country of origin was undermined by globalisation. This, in turn, affected companies' marketing decisions. For example, should they rely solely on their brands, or would a combination of brand and country of origin be more effective? Such issues were particularly pertinent to US manufacturers. Many, such as Ford and Nike, owned renowned brands but they were unable to satisfy the criteria governing lawful use of 'Made in the USA'.

In the United States, the FTC oversees 'Made in the USA' claims. Legislation establishing the FTC required it to 'prevent unfair methods of competition in commerce'.[46] During the interwar period, the Wheeler-Lea Act extended the remit of the FTC to include 'unfair or deceptive acts or practices in commerce'.[47] This amendment was significant because it recognised the importance of consumer protection: there was no longer a presumption that the FTC could act only if unfair competition diverted custom from one trader to another.[48] This Act was subsequently amended

---

[45] http://data.worldbank.org/indicator/NE.TRD.GNFS.ZS?end=2015&start=1960&year_low_desc=false. In contrast, the trade–GDP ratio for Switzerland in 2010 was 118 per cent. This ratio measures the total value of trade (imports and exports) in relation to national income and indicates the 'openness' of an economy. It is usually high for small economies and low for large economies.

[46] 1 FTC Act P.L. 63–203 38 Stat. September 26 1914 717 1914: s.5.

[47] FTC Act Amendments of 1938 (Wheeler-Lea Act): Public Law 75–447: 21 March 1938: 52 U.S. Statutes at Large 111.

[48] M. L. Lindahl, 'The Federal Trade Commission Act as Amended in 1938, *Journal of Political Economy*, 47 (1939): 497–525; D. A. Rice, 'Consumer Unfairness at the FTC: Misadventures in Law and Economics', *George Washington Law Review*, 52 (1983–1984): 16. It was not until 1983 that the FTC issued a policy statement defining the three key requirements of deceptive practices: there must be a representation, omission, or practice that is likely to mislead the consumer; the practice is examined from the perspective of a consumer while acting reasonably in the circumstances; and the

by legislation in 1994 which retained the clause on 'unfair or deceptive acts or practices' and made special provision for labels: 'To the extent any person introduces, delivers for introduction, sells, advertises, or offers for sale in commerce a product with a "Made in U.S.A." or "Made in America" label, or the equivalent thereof, in order to represent that such product was in whole or substantial part of domestic origin, such label shall be consistent with decisions and orders of the Federal Trade Commission issued pursuant to section 45 of this title.'[49]

The Vulcan Lamp Works Inc. complaint in 1940 is apparently the earliest 'Made in the USA' case involving the FTC. Vulcan purchased incandescent light bulbs and their fittings and assembled them into finished incandescent lights, automobile, and flashlight bulbs. Some of the bulbs were imported from Japan with 'Made in Japan' marked on the neck. However, during assembly, the latter were inserted into US-made bases which concealed the Japanese origin of the bulbs and the entire product was sold as 'Made in the USA'. The FTC reported that the public had a strong preference for products manufactured in the United States and that Vulcan's activities had the capacity to 'mislead and deceive a substantial portion of the purchasing public with the erroneous and mistaken belief that such lamps are *wholly* of domestic origin or manufacture'. The FTC ordered Vulcan to 'cease and desist' from representing that its lamps were 'Made in the USA' when such lamps, 'or the basic parts thereof', were manufactured abroad.[50]

During the 1960s, the FTC investigated ambiguously marked American products. These inquiries highlighted a number of key themes. First, US consumers were willing to pay a premia of between 50 and 100 per cent for US watch bands compared to those made in Hong Kong or Japan. Further, if the foreign components of a product were not conspicuously marked, US consumers presumed that the *entire* product was 'wholly of domestic origin'. Sometimes indirect suggestions were used to deceive consumers, for example, 'Windsor Pen Corp., Printed in USA'. In such cases the FTC issued 'cease and desist' orders requiring that companies refrain from selling products *wholly* or

---

representation or omission must be 'material' – would consumers have chosen differently without the deception? *FTC Policy Statement on Deception.* Appended to Cliffdale Associates, Inc., 103 F.T.C. 110, 174 (1984).

[49] FTC Act Amendments of 1994. 15 USC, 45; 15 USC 45a.

[50] Emphasis added. *Complaint in the Matter of Vulcan Lamp Works, Inc.*, FTC Decisions, 32 (1940): 11–12.

substantially composed of foreign parts unless their foreign origin was affirmatively or conspicuously disclosed.[51]

Subsequently, the FTC acknowledged that it did not bring enforcement actions against those using 'Made in the USA' claims, preferring, instead, to issue 'numerous public advisory opinions stating that a manufacturer could claim that a product was Made in USA only if the product was comprised wholly of domestic parts and labour'.[52] Thus, it advised the NTN Bearing Corporation of America that its packaged bearings could not be marked 'Made in the USA' because 'such marking would constitute an affirmative representation that the finished product was made in its *entirety* in the United States, which is contrary to fact'.[53] Examination of the FTC's Annual Reports during the 1970s and 1980s suggests there was little need for a substantial 'Made in the USA' enforcement policy. Moreover, given the FTC's focus on other policy matters and the hostile political climate within which it operated during the 1970s, as well as funding constraints, it is debatable whether it could have devoted more attention to deceptive 'Made in the USA' claims.[54] Finally, use of this indication of origin was voluntary, not compulsory: domestic manufacturers were at liberty to use 'Made in the USA' provided *only* that this marking was not deceptive.[55]

Nonetheless, in 1995, the FTC investigated two leading US sport shoe manufacturers. Unlike previous inquiries where issue of a 'cease and desist' order was sufficient to prevent further misrepresentation, the actions brought against New Balance Athletic Shoe, Inc. and Hyde Athletic Industries, Inc. – that they falsely represented that all of their athletic shoes were made in the United States[56] – triggered a backlash.

[51] Emphasis added. *Baldwin Bracelet Corp. et al.*, FTC Decisions, 61 (1962): 1345–1378; *Manco Watch Strap Co., Inc.*, FTC Decisions, 60 (1962): 495–523; *Rieser Co., Inc., et al.*, FTC Decisions, 61 (1962): 1378–1389; *Spiegel Brothers Corporation et al.*, FTC Decisions, 63 (July–December, 1963): 2190; *Windsor Pen Corp. et al.*, FTC Decisions, 64 (1964): 454–461.

[52] *Federal Register*, 60, no. 201, 18 October 1995: 53923, 53928.

[53] Emphasis added. FTC Decisions, 77 (1970): 1760.

[54] Rice, 'Consumer Unfairness at the FTC'.

[55] Textiles, wool products, and automobiles are exceptions. Products covered by the Textile Fiber Product Identification Act (1958) and the Wool Products Labelling Act (1939) must be labelled to identify the country in which they were manufactured. The American Automobile Labelling Act (1992) requires that automobiles manufactured for sale in the United States indicate where the car was assembled, the percentage of equipment that originated in the United States or Canada, and the country of origin of the engine and transmission.

[56] *In the Matter of Hyde Athletic Industries Inc.*, FTC File No. 922–3236, 1996; *In the Matter of New Balance Athletic Shoe Inc.*, FTC File No. 921–0050, 1996.

New Balance led a campaign involving congressmen and manufacturers of bicycles, furniture, and luggage to relax the criteria governing 'Made in the USA'.[57] In response, the FTC announced in 1995 that it would solicit public opinion. This was followed by a two-day workshop between 26 and 27 March 1996, and a further announcement that the record would remain open for post-workshop comments until June 1996. The FTC also ordered studies examining consumer understanding of US origin claims.

The FTC received evidence from a range of prominent US companies including Abercrombie, Brother International, Caterpillar, Compaq, ITT Industries, and major industry and trade union organisations, such as the American Hand Tool Coalition, the Crafted with Pride Council, the National Electrical Manufacturers Association, and the International Brotherhood of Teamsters and United Auto Workers. Evidence was also submitted by the National Consumers League, the US Customs Service and the Department of Commerce. The FTC sought to address the fundamental question: should the 'all or virtually all' threshold for use of 'Made in the USA' be maintained?[58] This question generated a series of further queries: what importance did consumers attach to 'Made in the USA'? What did the US public understand by such marking? If the FTC decided to alter its criteria for 'Made in the USA', where should the 'bright line' be drawn? Each is considered in what follows.

Although there has been significant growth in country-of-origin studies, there was a paucity of academic research on what 'Made in the USA' actually meant to US consumers at the time the FTC began its investigations. According to Robert Maronick, 'Few authors have examined what "made in USA" means to consumers ... Furthermore, no study has examined consumers' perceptions of the amount of "American" parts and/or labour that is implied by a "Made in USA" claim.'[59] The FTC needed to determine the extent to which consumers valued 'Made in the USA' and then assess how sensitive this appreciation was to other factors, for example, minimum domestic content and US assembly operations.

<hr />

[57] M. Bales, 'Implications and Effects of the FTC's Decision to Retain the "All or Virtually All" Standard', *University of Miami Law School Institutional Repository*, 30 (1999): 734.
[58] Following the New Balance and Hyde Athletic cases, the FTC refined its traditional criteria for 'Made in the USA', from 'wholly' to 'all, or virtually all'. *Federal Register*, 60, no. 201, 18 October 1995: 53923.
[59] T. J. Maronick, 'An Empirical Investigation of Consumer Perceptions of "Made in USA" Claims', *International Marketing Review*, 12 (1995): 15. This study was published in May 1995 and seems to have been unaware that the FTC had conducted surveys of consumer opinion on 'Made in the USA' in 1991 and 1995.

FIGURE 9.2 'Proudly Made in the USA'
Permission/acknowledgement: Callahan/shutterstock.com

In broad terms, the survey evidence indicated qualified support for 'Made in the USA' as a determinant of US consumers' purchasing decisions. A test to determine advertising effectiveness conducted by the FTC in 1991 using Smith-Corona typewriters and Huffy bicycles reported that 52 and 33 per cent, respectively, of each sample thought 'Made in the USA' important. In 1995, a similar test conducted by the FTC asked: 'When you are considering buying a [product] how important is it to you that the item be made in the USA?' Using a scale of 0–10, where zero meant not important, and ten indicated highly significant, 39, 39, and 22 per cent of respondents, respectively, answered in the range 8–10, 3–7, and 0–2. Simultaneously, in response to an Attitude Survey to assess the importance of 'Made in the USA' on pens and stereos, respondents indicated that US origin was much more important for pens than stereos.[60]

Similar mixed results were reported in unofficial surveys. A study for the American Handtool Coalition revealed that 'a "Made in USA" label was as important as price in buying handtools, and significantly more important than brand name or reputation of the store'. A Gallup poll commissioned by the International Mass Retail Association reported that, '[o]verall, most Americans say they prefer American products to

[60] FTC, *Proposed Guides for the Use of U.S. Origin Claims*, May 1997: 43.

those produced overseas'. This poll indicated that 84 per cent exhibited strong or moderate preferences for buying US products, while 19 per cent were firmly of the opinion that they would buy a US product even if it was 10 per cent more expensive than the comparable imported product. However, the poll also reported that slightly more than 50 per cent favoured imports because they provided US consumers with a greater variety of products and moderated the increase in US prices.[61] Jerry Wind, who conducted a consumer survey on behalf of New Balance while it was being investigated by the FTC, stated, 'The country of origin, U.S. or other ... is of no importance [or] relevance in consumers' decision to buy athletic shoes.' Wind's study showed that comfort, fit, and durability were substantially more important determinants of consumers' purchases than country of origin. Similar views were reported by Frank Schapiro representing Crafted with Pride: the 'fit', 'fashion', and 'value' of textile products were important, and where respondents claimed 'satisfaction' with their purchases it was because they devoted particular attention to the United States as the country of origin.[62]

A survey conducted by the US International Trade Commission indicated similar division amongst manufacturers. Overall, this commission found that 93 per cent of US companies in its sample responded affirmatively to the question: did they mark their products 'Made in the USA'? But this aggregate response concealed significant variation between industries. Excluding the chemical industry, it is apparent from Table 9.1 that consumer preference, averaging 47.3 per cent, was the main reason companies used 'Made in the USA'.[63] However, it is also apparent from Table 9.1 that such preferences did not translate into 'hard' economic benefits: 10 per cent or less of respondents in the metal and metal products, machinery, electronics, and textile industries believed 'Made in the USA' increased unit sales; only 6 per cent or less thought it increased unit prices. This evidence indicated that although consumers expressed an interest in or preference for US manufactures, this was not always reflected in their purchases.[64]

---

[61] FTC, 'Made in the USA'. *Official Transcript: Proceedings before Federal Trade Commission*, 26 March 1996: 49, 78. Hereafter, FTC, 'Made in the USA'.

[62] FTC, 'Made in the USA': 56–57, 67–73.

[63] This figure is obtained by combining retail and wholesale customer preferences for each industry.

[64] 'It is not sensible to expect consumers to buy shoes that do not fit ... simply because those products are labelled "Made in USA".' FTC, Proposed Guides for the Use of U.S. Origin Claims. *Federal Register Notice*, May 1997: 46.

TABLE 9.1 *Benefits received by companies using 'Made in USA' labelling (% response)*

Benefit	Chemicals	Metals and metal products	Machinery	Electronics	Textiles
Preference by retail customer	0	17	25	31	25
Preference by wholesale customer	0	17	29	25	20
Brand loyalty for domestic products	0	17	17	3	16
Designates superior quality	33	14	4	14	5
Increased unit sales	0	10	8	6	4
Easier to meet 'Buy America' policy	0	11	13	0	7
Increased unit prices	0	6	4	6	4
Other benefits	67	3	0	6	15
None – no benefits	0	6	0	0	4
Total responses	3	175	24	36	55

Note: The agricultural sector provided responses to the survey, which are not included in this table. This sector is defined as fruit and vegetables, live animals, lumber, plants, seeds, and other edible products. Consequently, there are doubts about how relevant 'Made in the USA' is for these products.

Source: US International Trade Commission, *Country-of-Origin Marking: Review of Laws, Regulations, and Practices.* Publication 2975 (July 1996): section 4, page 21

Consumer preference for US products was not simply a function of their comparative quality, but reflected broader concerns about protecting domestic jobs and the economy. This view was expressed most forcibly by Robin Lanier of the International Mass Retail Association: 'It seems to me that the issue here for American consumers is not some notion of value … in many cases, I don't think that's what's going on here. I think what they value, okay, is American jobs … that's the most important thing, that we protect a maximum number of U.S. jobs.'[65] The investigation by the US International Trade Commission also reported that patriotism was

---

[65] FTC, 'Made in the USA': 580, 594.

a key determinant of consumers' purchasing decisions, especially with regard to handmade tools. Some companies indicated that although 'Made in the USA' was not directly beneficial to them, it helped transmit 'information to the company's labor union that [it] is supporting the domestic economy and preserving domestic jobs'. Moreover, this study indicated that consumers rejected imports from countries perceived to harbour values contrary to their beliefs, for example, employment of child labour and unsafe working conditions.[66]

A related issue requiring the FTC's attention was public understanding of 'Made in the USA'. There was a strong prima facie case for the FTC to relax or ignore its 'all or virtually all' threshold if consumers were indifferent about the domestic content of US manufactures. At the very least, the FTC's mandate to prevent deceptive advertising became less important the more apathetic consumers became towards 'Made in the USA': only consumers who wished to buy US products were adversely affected by false US-origin claims.[67] Accelerating globalisation and rapid import penetration in particular sectors also had a bearing on this issue. As consumers recognised that US companies were becoming more reliant on foreign components, their perception of what constituted 'Made in the USA' fell below the FTC's traditional standard. Consequently, consumers could not be deceived if 'Made in the USA' was applied to US products containing foreign components. Conversely, import penetration and the plethora of foreign labels on products sold in the United States meant high US content became more, not less important, if 'Made in the USA' was to help US employment.[68]

Inquiries into consumer understanding of 'Made in the USA' were hindered by two interrelated obstacles. First, the FTC never adequately defined its 'all or virtually all' standard.[69] Second, during the course of its workshop, concerns were raised by Gail Cumins, representing the American Association of Exporters and Importers, that the FTC had reached a verdict on 'Made in the USA' without defining the term – which

---

[66] US International Trade Commission, *Country-of-Origin Marking: Review of Laws, Regulations and Practices*: 4–17, 4–18, 5–11.

[67] FTC, 'Made in the USA': 90–91.

[68] FTC, 'Made in the USA': 134–135, 147; FTC, *Proposed Guides for the Use of U.S. Origin Claims*: 49.

[69] FTC, *Proposed Guides for the Use of U.S. Origin Claims*: 17; FTC, 'Made in the USA': 173. The FTC's reliance on 'deceptive' includes themes which are almost incomprehensible to non-lawyers. In a US context, see, for example, R. Craswell, 'Interpreting Deceptive Advertising', *Boston University Law Review*, 65 (1985): 657–732.

automatically undermined the reliability of its conclusions.[70] Noting these caveats, it is apparent that there was a divergence between consumers and the FTC on the meaning of 'Made in the USA'. For example, only 5 per cent of the sample understood it to mean 'all or virtually all'. A substantial percentage of respondents had only a general understanding of what 'Made in the USA' meant, and it was claimed that most consumers did not understand enough about manufacturing to provide intelligent answers about US-based processing. Further, it was suggested that consumer perceptions were inaccurate. Thus, Nike is a famous US brand; its headquarters are located in Oregon; leading professional athletes wear its footwear, which is imported. Similarly, although Ford is a renowned US car manufacturer, there was no incentive to co-brand its automobiles 'Made in the USA' because of its inability to satisfy the FTC's regulations. Put another way, it was necessary to distinguish 'US-made' products from those manufactured by US-based companies.[71]

Nonetheless, there was greater consensus amongst consumers when survey questions directed them to consider whether different ratios of foreign and domestic inputs affected their perception of 'Made in the USA'. There was general agreement that consumers understood US-made to mean that a product had been 'assembled' in the United States. Many respondents were willing to accept 'Made in the USA' was an accurate designation of US-assembled products even when they contained significant foreign components. Thus, in coat manufacture, the production of cloth was secondary to where the cloth was made into a coat.[72] Howard Beales, representing the Bicycle Manufacturers Association of America, stated, '[f]rom the survey results we can tell that consumers understand the "Made in USA" as a claim about where the product came into being, not some specific part of it, but where the product as a whole came into being'.[73] The importance of assembly is shown in Table 9.2, from which a number of observations can be made. First, *irrespective* of the US share of total cost, US assembly was the most important factor justifying use of 'Made in the USA'. This observation also applies when comparing 'Country of assembly unspecified' and

[70] FTC, 'Made in the USA': 121–122.
[71] FTC, 'Made in the USA': 45, 87–90, 125–126, 303–304. The Nike and Ford examples suggest that company brands with strong American lineage were more important than country of origin.
[72] FTC, 'Made in the USA': 41, 82.   [73] FTC, 'Made in the USA': 85–86.

TABLE 9.2 *Percentage of respondents who agreed and disagreed with a 'Made in USA' label*

	Assembled in the United States		Country of Assembly Unspecified		Assembled in Foreign Country	
	Agree	Disagree	Agree	Disagree	Agree	Disagree
Total Cost						
90% US / 10% Foreign	75.0	22.0	63.9	31.5	54.6	33.3
70% US / 30% Foreign	67.0	31.0	50.9	43.5	38.9	50.0
50% US / 50% Foreign	36.0	46.0	28.7	57.4	18.5	63.9
30% US / 70% Foreign	25.0	68.0	20.4	72.2	10.2	83.3
10% US / 90% Foreign	20.0	74.0	19.4	74.1	10.2	84.3

Note: Percentages do not sum to 100. The survey data treated each question as separate, so the responses are not cumulative.
Source: FTC, *Proposed Guides for the use of U.S. Origin Claims.* May 1997: 45.
Downloaded from www.scribd.com/document/1182035/US-Federal-Trade-Commission-madeinus. Accessed October 2016.

'Assembled in a foreign country'.[74] However, assembly alone was not always sufficient to justify use of 'Made in the USA'. For example, 75 per cent of the sample agreed with the validity of 'Made in the USA' if 90 per cent of the total costs of manufacture occurred in the United States. Finally, for each of the three headings, the proportion of respondents agreeing with 'Made in the USA' showed the biggest decline when the US share of total costs declined from 70 to 50 per cent. This suggested that consumers believed a minimum threshold – greater than 50 per cent of domestic contribution to total cost – was necessary to justify use of 'Made in the USA'.

The results presented in Table 9.2 were not universally accepted by US manufacturers. United Technologies Carrier claimed that consumers understood that global supply chains meant there were few

---

[74] This difference is discussed later. Different criteria were used by US customs and the FTC to determine country of origin. The FTC also relied on the 'rebuttable presumption' that products not indicating country of origin were assumed by US consumers to be domestic.

wholly domestic products. Packard Bell Electronics reported that some of the components they used were no longer manufactured in the United States, and representatives of the footwear industry argued that the price differential between the United States and the Far East was of such magnitude that they could not remain in business without imported components. Richard Abbey, representing Stanley Works, argued that the FTC's standard adversely affected the competitiveness of this company and deceived consumers. Thus, if Stanley was forbidden to use 'Made in the USA' it would perpetuate the false impression that their tools were inferior to those branded US-made. Moreover, if foreign-made tools were cheaper than domestic tools but equivalent or superior in quality, reliance on 'Made in the USA' was simply a device to extract more money from US consumers. James Palmquist, representing Minnesota Mining and Manufacturing, argued that efforts to comply with the FTC's standard threatened the very existence of US-based companies: 'to apply the "virtually all" would in fact encourage us to close U.S. companies because there is no reason that exists, minus that, to have that U.S. company'.[75]

The FTC recognised the need to reconcile divergence between consumer understanding of 'Made in the USA' and the inability of manufacturers to comply with the regulations governing this indication of origin. It admitted, '[i]ncreasing globalization of production suggests that a requirement that even minor parts be all made in the United States is outdated and inflexible'.[76] But to what extent should the FTC lower its threshold, and which mechanism was to be employed to determine the new level? One methodology was the minimum percentage requirement test. Precedents for this test included the Buy American Act of 1933 and the North American Free Trade Agreement (NAFTA), which became effective in 1994.

The Buy American Act sought to protect US business and labour by restricting the purchase and employment of materials and final products that were not domestic – defined as those containing a minimum US proportion of 50 per cent of the total cost of components.[77] NAFTA specified a minimum regional value content governing the manufacture of

---

[75] FTC, *Proposed Guides for the Use of U.S. Origin Claims*: 13–15; FTC, 'Made in the USA: 253–254, 259, 276–280.

[76] FTC, 'Request for Public Comment on Proposed Guides for the Use of U.S. Origin Claims; Notice'. *Federal Register*, 7 May 1997: 25040.

[77] 47 Stat. 1520, ch. 212. The background to this legislation is discussed in Frank, *Buy American*.

products which were dependent on materials originating from outside Canada, Mexico, and the United States. The Agreement stipulated that unassembled products could be classed as 'originating' in these countries even when they contained 'non-originating' materials, provided they satisfied a minimum regional value content of 50 and 60 per cent, respectively, using net cost and transaction value methods.[78]

Both initiatives contained weaknesses. For example, the threshold of the Buy American Act applied only to federal procurement. It was not based on consumer perception and was, therefore, not directly relevant to the FTC's investigation.[79] Moreover, the Act was subject to significant criticisms. For example, how pertinent was it when US manufacturing was becoming 'de-Americanised'? By the mid-1980s, foreign investment in US manufacturing was $51 billion, and the statute may have encouraged US companies to inflate their prices when bidding for federal contracts.[80] However, the biggest single weakness in both approaches was that the percentage requirement was considered too low. Thresholds of 50 and 60 per cent conflicted with the data presented in Table 9.2, which show a marked decline in respondents' willingness to agree with 'Made in the USA' when the US share of total cost declined from 70 to 50 per cent. Steve Beckman of the United Auto Workers claimed that NAFTA was inadequate for 'guaranteeing that American consumers were buying products that were making a very valuable significant contribution to domestic employment and production'.[81] Moreover, the regulations governing 'Made in the USA' in the Buy American Act and NAFTA, were thought likely to increase consumer confusion: 'to pretend that something [which] is 50 per cent American content is American made [or] equivalent with something that is 100 per cent is very confusing'.[82]

An alternative approach was the 'substantial transformation' test used by US customs to determine the foreign origin of products. The McKinley and Smoot-Hawley Tariffs of 1890 and 1930, respectively, specified that products imported to the United States bear an English description of their

---

[78] US International Trade Commission, *Rules of Origin: Basic Principles*. www.usitc.gov /elearning/hts/media/2017/RulesofOrigina.pdf
[79] FTC, *Proposed Guides for the Use of U.S. Origin Claims*: 53.
[80] D. G. Goehle, 'The Buy American Act: Is It Relevant in a World of Multinational Corporations?', *Columbia Journal of World Business*, 24 (1989): 10–15.
[81] FTC, 'Made in the USA': 438–439.
[82] FTC, 'Made in the USA': 266. Other problems with a percentage standard included variations in exchange rates and uncertainty about the suitability of existing accounting procedures. FTC, *Proposed Guides for the Use of U.S. Origin Claims*: 22–29.

country of origin.[83] But growing importation of items subject to further processing in the United States generated a fundamental conflict between:

the desire of the Customs Service to prevent ... domestic importer-manufacturers from avoiding the marking requirements by performing minor adjustments on virtually completed items and the legitimate complaints of U.S. importers that articles undergoing substantial domestic processing are no longer of foreign manufacture.[84]

Resolution of this contest was achieved by employing the substantial transformation test, which determines whether a product loses its 'identity' when imported from one country and processed in another. In a US context, the criteria for assessing whether this transformation occurred involves name, character, and use. For example, a change in character must materially affect the original article, and may involve a change in chemical or physical identity.[85] Cases involving substantial transformation date to the late nineteenth century when a substantial body of court judgements emerged to guide US customs.[86]

Many witnesses perceived a fundamental conflict between customs and the FTC which they attributed to the different regulations governing the marking of products on importation and use of 'Made in the USA'. Customs laws required that each imported article indicate its country of origin, but imports that were to be substantially transformed within the United States were not required to display this indication. But this did not mean that such products could be marked 'Made in the USA': the substantial transformation test differed from the 'all or virtually all' criterion used by the FTC. Consequently, the origin message conveyed by a product legitimately marked 'Made in the USA' differed from the same product which was imported to the United States but marked 'Made in Japan'. Other differences between customs and FTC regulations exacerbated this disjuncture. For example, what inferences would domestic consumers make about a product not indicating its country of origin (because it

---

[83] These regulations were retained by the Omnibus Trade and Competitiveness Act, 19 USC s.1304 (1988), and 19 USC, s.1304 (1994), and remain current.

[84] R. F. Ruyack, 'United States Country of Origin Requirements: The Application of a Non-Tariff Trade Barrier', *Law and Policy in International Business*, 6 (1974): 509.

[85] L. A. Glick, *United States Customs and Trade Law after the Customs Modernization Act* (The Hague: Kluwer Law International, 1997), 48, 51–53.

[86] The earliest cases involved the importation, cleaning, and polishing of shells, and the treatment of imported corks prior to their use in the brewing of beer. *Hartranft, Collector, etc.* v. *Wiegmann and another*, 121 U.S. 609 (1887); *Anheuser-Busch Brewing Association, Appt.* v. *United States*, 207 U.S. 556 (1908).

was imported and substantially transformed within the United States, but unable to satisfy the 'all or virtually all' criterion)? Traditionally, the 'rebuttable presumption' employed by the FTC was that US consumers perceived these products to be 'Made in the USA'.[87] Similarly, marking of imports was mandatory but domestic use of 'Made in the USA' was voluntary. Finally, although some manufacturers were unable to employ 'Made in the USA' on domestic sales, its utilisation was necessary to satisfy customs regulations in export markets.[88]

The FTC's adoption of the substantial transformation test would have brought it into greater alignment with customs and eradicated many of the problems discussed earlier. Representatives of Compaq, the Joint Industry Group, and the American Association of Exporters and Importers argued that the FTC should change its 'Made in the USA' regulations. It was claimed alteration would reduce the regulatory burden of dealing with two government agencies, and that many businesses were more familiar with customs regulations which were perceived to be more objective than the FTC's 'all or virtually all' standard.[89] It was also claimed that adoption of the substantial transformation test made US regulations consonant with those prevailing in other countries, thereby facilitating international trade.[90]

Nonetheless, the biggest weakness of the substantial transformation test was that it permitted products with significant foreign content to be labelled 'Made in the USA'. If assembly was the key criterion justifying use of this indication of origin, then 'virtually any product could have a new name, character, and use after its foreign components are finally assembled in the U.S.'. The data in Table 9.2 indicate that assembly *and* domestic share of total cost were important in consumer perception of 'Made in the USA'. In other words, reliance on assembly alone would have increased opportunities for consumer deception and possibly improved

---

[87] But this presumption might adversely affect firms proclaiming the US content of their products: a firm announcing it used a higher proportion of US-sourced components might lose sales to a rival using a smaller proportion, but choosing to remain silent. FTC, 'Made in the USA': 298–299.

[88] FTC, *Proposed Guides for the Use of U.S. Origin Claims*: 30–32; FTC, 'Made in the USA'; USITC, *Country of Origin Marking*: ix; FTC, 'Made in the USA': 160, 199–200.

[89] Legal studies suggest this claim is suspect. See, for example, C. E. Galfand, 'Heeding the Call for a Predictable Rule of Origin', *Journal of International Law*, 11 (1989): 469–493; C. N. Schnarr, 'Left Out in the Cold? The Customs' Country of Origin Marking Requirements, the Section 516 Procedure, and the Lessons of Norcal/Crosetti', *Washington University Law Review*, 73 (1995): 1679–1709.

[90] FTC, *Proposed Guides for the Use of U.S. Origin Claims*: 30–32.

the image of foreign products. Use of qualified statements, for example, 'Product of the US', or 'Country of Origin', were not attractive because they were considered inferior.[91]

After reviewing the evidence the FTC proposed a change to its 'all or virtually all' standard. The new policy was a compromise between consumer understanding that 'Made in the USA' represented a 'significant level of U.S.-derived content' and recognition that '[i]ncreasing globalization of production suggests that a requirement that even minor parts be all made in the United States is outdated and inflexible'.[92] The new regulations stipulated that unqualified use of US origin had to be based on a reasonable claim that the product was *substantially all* made in the United States'.[93] To comply with this regulation, firms had to satisfy one of two requirements, known as 'safe harbours'. The first 'safe harbour' stated that US costs be 75 per cent of the total manufacturing cost of making a product, and that product's last substantial transformation occur in the United States. This haven was suggested because it was aligned with consumer perception. The second 'safe harbour' emphasised processing and required that a product and each of its significant components be substantially transformed in the United States.[94]

But even this accommodation failed to assuage US manufacturers and consumers. It appears that the FTC's proposals galvanised substantial opposition which included 200 members of the House of Representatives, a Senate Resolution and eighteen attorneys general. This resistance was predicated on the belief that any change to the FTC's traditional policy facilitated the deception of US consumers who 'presently believe products bearing the "Made in USA" label were all or virtually all made in the United States'.[95] If accurate, this claim indicated that globalisation and its effects on US manufacturing had not altered consumer perception of 'Made in the

---

[91] FTC, *Proposed Guides for the Use of U.S. Origin Claims*: 34–36; 39; FTC, 'Made in the USA': 251–252, 378, 497.

[92] FTC, 'Request for Public Comment on Proposed Guides for the Use of U.S. Origin Claims; Notice', *Federal Register*, 7 May 1997: 25040.

[93] Emphasis added. 'Reasonable basis' required competent and reliable evidence. Claims relying on an assessment of US costs had to comply with accepted accounting principles. FTC, 'Request for Public Comment on Proposed Guides for the Use of U.S. Origin Claims; Notice', *Federal Register*, 7 May 1997, 25048.

[94] The proposed regulations also jettisoned the FTC's traditional reliance on the 'rebuttable presumption' doctrine. FTC, 'Request for Public Comment on Proposed Guides for the Use of U.S. Origin Claims; Notice', *Federal Register*, 7 May 1997: 25041, 25047.

[95] FTC, '"Made in USA" and Other U.S. Origin Claims; Notice', *Federal Register*, 2 December 1997: 63758.

USA'. Although some claimed that the proposals would harm the manufacturing base – because companies would have *less* incentive to use US labour and components – it is apparent that consumer perception of 'Made in the USA' was the principal reason for the FTC's decision to abandon its proposed changes:

An overwhelming number of consumers told the Commission ... that they prefer buying U.S. made goods; they want to be able to rely on a simple and clear standard; and, they feel very strongly that the current standard should be retained ... Thus the Commission concludes that the better course, and one equally consistent with the consumer perception evidence, is to retain and continue to enforce the Commission's traditional all or virtually all standard.[96]

Following publication of its Enforcement Policy Statement, the FTC instigated a 'vigorous enforcement and compliance program to ensure that domestic origin claims are truthful and substantiated'. From the mid-1990s, the FTC initiated more than forty investigations into companies making allegedly deceptive 'Made in the USA' claims or failing to make required disclosures about country of origin. Consent orders were issued against American Honda Motor Company, Johnson Worldwide Associates, Kubota Tractor Corporation, and USDrives Corporation for misleading 'Made in the USA' claims on publicity material or misuse of famous US images, for example, the American eagle, the American flag, or the Statue of Liberty, to convey a similar message.[97] More recently, the FTC took action against Chemence Inc. for misrepresenting that its glues were 'all or virtually all' made in the United States when imports accounted for 55 per cent of the cost of the chemicals, and claims made by Niall Luxury Goods that its watches comprising Swiss movements were 'Made in the USA'.[98]

---

[96] The FTC specified that products labelled 'Made in the USA' should only contain a *de minimis* amount of foreign content. Unqualified use of the term 'Assembled in USA' was reserved solely for products which were principally assembled in the United States and for which the last substantial transformation also occurred in the United States. FTC, '"Made in USA" and Other U.S. Origin Claims; Notice', *Federal Register*, 2 December 1997: 63764–63765, 63766–63770.

[97] FTC, U.S. Origin Claims: Enforcement and Compliance Activities since December, 1997. Downloaded from www.ftc.gov/sites/default/files/documents/reports/u.s.origin-claims-enforcement-and-compliance-activities-december-1997/musareport.pdf. Accessed January 2017.

[98] *FTC v. Chemence, Inc.*; www.ftc.gov/news-events/press-releases/2016/02/ftc-charges-manufacturer-kwik-frame-kwik-fix-krylex-glues-making; FTC to Braden Perry, downloaded from: www.ftc.gov/system/files/documents/closing_letters/nid/151120niall_letter.pdf. Similar actions were taken against E. K. Ekcessories, Inc., Shinola, Inc., and Wal-Mart stores.

'MADE IN EUROPE'?

The penultimate section of this chapter focuses on attempts by the EU to establish 'Made in the EU' for products manufactured within its borders. At first sight, this initiative does not appear aligned with 'Swiss made' or 'Made in the USA' because the EU is comprised of twenty-eight Member States. However, viewed from another perspective, it can be argued there was considerable congruence. In the Swiss and US cases discussed earlier, a fundamental issue was the extent to which company brands were subordinated to country of origin, whereas a major source of conflict within the EU was the extent to which individual countries were prepared to sacrifice their national identity to the 'EU' indication. Unlike Switzerland and the United States, the EU's task was complicated by the need to reconcile a range of conflicting national interests. Germany and Britain, for example, possess strong reputations for engineering and automobiles, and for luxury goods and textiles, respectively. Conversely, the 'new' manufacturing entrants to the EU – Bulgaria, Croatia, and Romania – have little (if any) renown. Unsurprisingly, therefore, attempts to introduce 'Made in the EU' have been vigorously and consistently rejected by Member States in northern Europe:

German cars, British tweed, Dutch electronics—all forcibly labelled 'Made in the European Union'? The very idea provoked tabloid outrage from London to Berlin amid fears that hard-won national marks of industrial quality would fall victim to Brussels bureaucrats bent on imposing the imprint of a European superstate.[99]

It should be emphasised that the plan to introduce 'Made in Europe' was fundamentally different to the efforts of Member States to promote domestic products using their own country of origin, for example, 'Made in Britain'. The former was to be mandatory and sought to enhance the reputation of EU products and combat misrepresentation which was adversely affecting EU consumers and industries. Initiatives such as 'Made in Britain' could only be voluntary: individual manufacturers and their trading associations were free to use 'British' or 'Made in Britain', but the British government was prohibited from making such use mandatory. The same restriction prevented other Member States compelling use of their own country of origin indicia.

---

[99] 'EU backs off idea of mandatory "Made in the EU" label', *Daily News*, 28 July 2004. Downloaded from www.hurriyetdailynews.com/eu-backs-off-idea-of-mandatory-made-in-the-eu-label.aspx?pageID=438&n=eu-backs-off-idea-of-mandatory-made-in-the-eu-label-2004-07-28. Accessed January 2017.

The EU is a customs union in which there is free trade between Member States, though a common tariff is imposed on products originating from outside. By the Treaty of Rome, '[q]uantitative restrictions on imports and all measures having equivalent effect shall, without prejudice to the following provisions, be prohibited between Member States'.[100] Trade restrictions could be justified on the grounds of public morality and public security and where health and life were endangered.[101]

Numerous non-fiscal restrictions can be applied to imports, including regulations limiting the channels of distribution, and price fixing. Such impediments are referred to as 'distinctly applicable measures' because they give more favourable treatment to domestic products compared to imports.[102] For my purposes 'origin marking rules' are pertinent because they encouraged the purchase of domestic products contrary to the Treaty of Rome. For example, faced with serious economic problems, the Irish government and the Irish Goods Council launched a 'Buy Irish' campaign in 1978 using a 'Guaranteed Irish' symbol. It was anticipated that this scheme would generate 10,000 jobs and transfer 3 per cent of total consumer spending from imports to Irish products. The ECJ ruled that the 'Buy Irish' initiative was contrary to the Treaty of Rome because it was 'a reflection of the Irish Government's considered intention to substitute domestic products for imported products on the Irish market and thereby to check the flow of imports from other Member States'.[103]

Use of compulsory indications of origin was forbidden even when deployed to combat fraud and consumer misrepresentation. The Trade Descriptions (Marking Order) (Miscellaneous Goods) Order enacted by the British government in 1981 prohibited the sale of clothing and textile goods, domestic electrical appliances, footwear, and cutlery, unless accompanied by an indication of origin.[104] Such products were bedevilled

---

[100] Treaty of Rome, Article 30. Articles 32–35 prevented the introduction of new quantitative restrictions or the tightening of existing measures; bilateral quotas between Member States were to apply to all such States and a phased reduction in quotas was provided for. www.cvce.eu/en/obj/treaty_establishing_the_european_economic_community_ro me_25_march_1957-en-cca6ba28-0bf3-4ce6-8a76-6b0b3252696e.html. The range of measures having 'equivalent effect' are discussed in C. Barnard, *The Substantive Law of the EU: The Four Freedoms* (Oxford: Oxford University Press, 2013), 71–117; Oliver and Jarvis, *Free Movement of Goods*, 157–214.

[101] *Treaty of Rome* (1957): Article 36.   [102] Barnard, *The Substantive Law of the EU*, 81.

[103] *Commission* v. *Ireland*, Case 249/81 (1982): 4022.

[104] Trade Descriptions (Origin Marking) (Miscellaneous Goods) Order 1981(Statutory Instrument 1981, No. 121).

by consumer complaints involving misrepresentation.[105] The British government defended this Order by arguing that it protected consumers, but this claim was flatly rejected by the European Court of Justice:

[I]f the national origin of goods brings certain qualities to the minds of consumers, it is in manufacturers' interests to indicate it themselves on the goods or on their packaging and it is not necessary to compel them to do so. In that case, the protection of consumers is sufficiently guaranteed by rules which enable the use of false indications of origin to be prohibited. Such rules are not called in question by the EEC Treaty.[106]

It appears that the first attempt to introduce obligatory indications of EU origin occurred in 1981. This initiative, motivated by a range of considerations, including the need to harmonise regulations, was directed to specific textile and clothing products made by Member States and imports from outside the EU. Textile manufactures had to be marked 'Made in the EEC', though firms were permitted to replace or complete this indication with the name of their Member State. Imports from outside the EU were required to bear the indication 'Made in . . . ' followed by the name of the country.[107] However, this scheme was opposed by the EC's Economic and Social Committee because price, composition, and quality were considered more important than country of origin as determinants of consumer expenditure. Additionally, this Committee noted that marking products according to customs requirements was itself a cause of consumer confusion: customs policies focused on the country where the last major processing operation occurred (substantial transformation), not the country where the raw material originated, or the location of spinning and weaving operations. This Committee was also concerned that marking EU textile products with an indication of origin might encourage other industries to apply for similar treatment – resulting in a clear breach of the Treaty of Rome.[108] Consequently, this country-of-origin scheme was

---

[105] For Sheffield cutlery, see D. M. Higgins, 'Made in Sheffield: Trade Marks, the Cutlers' Company and the Defence of 'Sheffield', in C. Binfield and D. Hey (eds.), *Mesters to Masters. A History of the Company of Cutlers in Hallamshire* (Oxford: Oxford University Press, 1997), 104–106. For French complaints involving textiles and clothing, see Written Question No 1116/79. *Official Journal*, 8 April 1980, No C 86/21–22.

[106] *Commission v. United Kingdom*, Case 207/83, 1985: 1212.

[107] 'Proposal for a Council Directive on the Approximation of Laws of the Member States Relating to the Indication of Origin of Certain Textile and Clothing Products', *Official Journal*, No. C 294/3, 13 November 1980.

[108] 'Opinion on the Proposal for a Council Directive on the Approximation of Laws of the Member States Relating to the Indication of Origin of Certain Textile and Clothing Products', *Official Journal*, No. C 185/32, 27 July 1981.

abandoned. Apart from proposals which focused on the textile sector, including suggestions that 'Made in France' and 'Made in Italy' could rejuvenate the clothing industries in these countries, indication of country of origin for non-foodstuffs remained dormant until the 2000s.[109]

In 2003, the EC revisited the question of 'Made in', noting that the existing framework governing this indication was in disarray. Thus, customs required a declaration of origin on goods being imported to the EU, after which there was no obligation for them to bear an indication of origin;[110] EU exports had to comply with the origin-marking requirements of third countries, but the EU did not impose similar obligations on imports from the latter; there was no legal basis for 'Made in the EU', and Member States differed in their use of this indication. Although compulsory origin marking was prohibited, there was nothing to prevent firms marking their products 'Made in Britain' or 'Made in Italy', if they thought this would act as a mark of distinction.

The EC justified its reappraisal of 'Made in the EU' by claiming this would introduce greater homogeneity between Member States, reinforce the concept of 'Made in Europe', enhance recognition of the EU's single customs union, and provide an additional means to combat consumer deception. It was also believed that the scheme would promote the image and attractiveness of EU products, thereby helping EU companies to compete with low-cost producers.[111] This latter claim was especially important to textile and clothing industries because of WTO plans to eliminate quotas by 2005:

An important part of EU production corresponds to the higher quality and fashion segments of textiles and clothing, where EU industry is the world leader and has therefore a comparative advantage. Due to its long tradition, diversity of products and constant innovation, European textiles and garments are often associated in the minds of the public with excellence and high-class design. A 'Made in Europe' label could help increase the confidence of consumers, that when they are purchasing a garment they are paying a price that corresponds to the highest standards of production and style expected from European manufacturing.[112]

[109] Opinion of the Economic and Social Committee, 'Plan of Action to Increase the Competitiveness of the European Textile and Clothing Industry', *Official Journal*, C 214/95, 10 July 1998. Of course, as noted in Chapters 7 and 8, the European Union introduced a substantial regime governing origin marking on food and wine.

[110] This is referred to as 'free circulation'. Zaimis, *EC Rules of Origin*, 117.

[111] European Commission, Directorate-General for Trade, '*Made in the EU Origin Marking – Working Document of the Commission Services*', 12 December 2003.

[112] Commission of the European Communities, 'The Future of the Textiles and Clothing Sector in the Enlarged European Union', COM (2003) 649 final, 29 October 2003: 33.

FIGURE 9.3 'Made in EU' was to be a signal of quality.
Permission/acknowledgement: © tpx/Fotolia.com

Apart from the status quo, three options were available to the EC. First, a voluntary scheme could be introduced applicable to products made by Member States and imports to the EU. The alternative was to make country-of-origin marking compulsory for both categories of products. An intermediate option specified compulsory country-of-origin marking on imported products, but voluntary adoption of 'Made in the EU' for products made by Member States. After reviewing the net gains of each scheme, the EC was unable to arrive at a firm conclusion, noting only that: 'The Commission believes that an EU origin marking scheme has in principle several merits and that the feasibility of such a scheme should be pursued further.'[113]

Subsequently, the EC launched a consultation exercise in 2004, involving European industry federations such as Association des Industries de Marque, the Federation of European Sporting Goods Industries, and Toy Industries of Europe, as well as trade unions, national consumer associations, and a few Member States, for example, Britain, Germany, and Italy, countries belonging to the European Free Trade Association, and Turkey. Arguments for and against 'Made in the EU' and whether its use should be compulsory or voluntary appear finely balanced. Those in favour claimed the scheme could facilitate a marketing campaign

---

[113] European Commission, Directorate-General for Trade, '*Made in the EU Origin Marking – Working Document of the Commission Services*', 12 December 2003.

enhancing the reputation of 'Europe' or 'European' as a brand,[114] increase recognition of EU origin in third countries, and equalise country-of-origin marking costs between industries located within and outside the EU. It was also suggested that adoption of 'Made in the EU' would encourage foreign direct investment. However, the scheme was criticised because 'Made in the EU' was not an acceptable replacement for esteemed indications of country of origin. Indeed, the proposal might adversely affect the latter, which were used on a voluntary basis and not governed by specific EU regulations. Additionally, the scheme increased costs because third countries might require Member States' indications of origin in addition to 'Made in the EU'. Finally, 'Made in the EU' was potentially misleading: if the final product was assembled in the EU using foreign components, non-preferential rules of origin permitted it to be marked 'Made in the EU'.[115]

Member States providing evidence were largely against the scheme. Britain, Germany, and the Netherlands argued Members' country-of-origin indications were more meaningful to consumers than 'Made in the EU'. Representatives of the German engineering and furniture industries argued, '[i]n the internal market and in third countries the mark "Made in Germany" represents quality and design'. Respondents from the European Free Trade Association argued that 'Made in the EU' was a non-tariff trade barrier. The Turkish thought the scheme would promote 'EU' as a mark of distinction while simultaneously prejudicing its exports to the EU. Only Italy favoured the indication because it would 'distinguish European products from imported ones'. The EC concluded that there was insufficient support for its scheme, and initiatives based on country of origin and 'Made in the EU' were to remain voluntary. It acknowledged concerns about growing misrepresentation in specific industries, and recommended further consultation on the desirability of imposing compulsory or voluntary indications of

[114] This claim had considerable support. An impact assessment on country of origin revealed that when price and quality were similar, 89.7 per cent of consumers preferred European Community products to those originating from third countries. Calculated from Commission Staff Working Document, *Annex to the Proposal for a Council Regulation on the Indication of the Country of Origin of Certain Products Imported from Third Countries*. SEC (2005) 1657. Brussels, 16 December 2005.
[115] 'Consideration of an EU Origin Marking Scheme: Consultation Process, Analysis and Next Steps': 6, 8. Downloaded from http://trade.ec.europa.eu/doclib/docs/2005/may/tradoc_118123.pdf. Accessed December 2016.

origin on imported and domestic textiles, clothing, leather goods, foot-wear, and ceramics.[116]

Currently, there is no compulsory scheme for 'Made in the EU'. In 2014, efforts were made to introduce mandatory 'Made in' labelling on non-food products. This initiative was designed to improve product safety and market surveillance, reduce counterfeiting, and improve consumer protection within the EU. Under this scheme, 'Made in' would be determined by the country of origin – the country in which a product underwent its last 'substantial, economically justified processing' resulting in a 'new product' or representing 'an important stage of manufacture'. Companies were permitted to use 'Made in the EU', instead of a specific country, if a product was produced in several Member States. The proposal received substantial support within the European Parliament: the Schaldemose and Pietikäinen Reports were approved by 485 to 130 and 573 to 18 votes, respectively.[117] However, the scheme remains blocked because Member States hold different views. Generally, southern European countries such as Italy, welcomed the proposals because they would reinvigorate its shoemaking and ceramics industries. However, sixteen Member States from northern and eastern Europe, including Britain and Germany, opposed the proposal. Ironically, it was argued that the proposals violated the founding principles of the EU. According to the conservative MEP Ashley Fox, '[c]alls for "made in" markings are only used to demonstrate a perceived higher quality associated with a given country. This is against the principles of the single market.'[118]

CONCLUSIONS

Academic studies demonstrate that country of origin influences consumers and it is for this reason that companies, including those owning prestigious brands, continue to use 'Made in' to promote their products. Nonetheless, accelerating globalisation has diluted the origin signals

---

[116] 'Consideration of an EU Origin Marking Scheme: Consultation Process, Analysis and Next Steps': 6, 8. Downloaded from http://trade.ec.europa.eu/doclib/docs/2005/may/tr adoc_118123.pdf. Accessed December 2016, 11–12, 26–29.

[117] Christel Schaldemose and Sirpa Pietikäinen are, respectively, Danish and Finnish Members of the European Parliament. www.europarl.europa.eu/news/en/news-room /20140411IPR43453/meps-push-for-mandatory-made-in-labelling-to-tighten-up-pro duct-safety-rules. Accessed December 2016.

[118] www.theguardian.com/world/2014/apr/15/european-plan-made-in-label-source-cou ntry. Accessed January 2017.

communicated by 'Made in'. This trend is of little consequence to MNCs who rely on brands, not country of origin, to promote their sales. But the same cannot be said of countries, such as the United States, which is forty times the size of Britain, or the EU, which is comprised of twenty-eight Member States.

In many respects it is unsurprising that Switzerland was better able to reconcile the competing interests of private brands and country of origin. A symbiotic relationship existed between leading watch manufacturers and the 'Swiss' watch industry; the brands of the former were indispensable to the renown of 'Swiss' watches. In contrast, the diverse manufacturing base of the United States prevented a similar consensus on 'Made in the USA'. Companies which were substantially integrated into global supply chains to remain competitive were unable to satisfy the FTC's 'all or virtually all' criterion. In a remarkable turn of events, Donald Trump's rallying cry to 'Make America Great Again' by repatriating offshore jobs appears hypocritical: his daughter's brand, Ivanka Trump, is applied to a diverse range of textiles and fashion accessories, all of which are made abroad![119] The EU faced greater difficulties in its attempt to launch a compulsory 'Made in the EU' scheme. In addition to its diverse manufacturing base, it had to reconcile the competing interests of Member States.

The three case studies examined in this chapter possess a common feature: to varying degrees all were motivated by concerns about consumer misrepresentation. The relationship between provenance and 'Made in' was either ambiguous, for example, when parts of Swiss watches were manufactured in the Far East, or deliberately subverted, as occurred when Chinese textile manufactures were sold as 'Italian'. One conclusion that emerged from my discussion of 'Buy British' in Chapter 5 was that requiring imports to be marked with their country of origin was a passive strategy to prevent consumer deception. A similar theme reappears in this chapter. Promotion of 'Made in the EU' can be viewed as a proactive strategy to increase consumer awareness of EU products and combat misrepresentation. However, the EU scheme was never implemented because it proved impossible to reconcile the differences between Member States.

---

[119] www.nytimes.com/2016/12/28/business/donald-trump-ivanka-clothes-global-trade-overseas-manufacturing.html?_r=1

Reflections on the History of IGOs

The notion that products have national origins is so deeply ingrained that governments, and the publics they represent, are unable to adjust to the emerging reality ... they continue to focus on the wrong question: Is it a 'foreign' or 'domestic' product? ... National champions everywhere are becoming global webs with no particular connection to any single nation.

R. B. Reich, *The Work of Nations: Preparing Ourselves for 21st Century Capitalism* (New York: Alfred A. Knopf, 1991), 118, 131

This study has analysed the evolution of IGOs from medieval times to the present. These indications communicate a relationship between product quality and place, which cannot lawfully be delocalised. Misrepresentation of products according to geographical origin was extensive from the nineteenth century. It involved produce such as Canadian bacon and ham, Jamaican rum, and US beef, as well as manufactures, including Sheffield edge tools and Swiss watches. Because quality was associated with origin, passing-off represented a double fraud on consumers and undermined the goodwill that communities had created in their IGOs. Protection of these indications required cooperation between rival producers. Private interests needed to be subsumed for the benefit of the industry. Competition between producers of the same product was replaced by conflict between products, for example, Danish versus New Zealand butter. Safeguarding also required more effective legislation at the national and then international level, but the provisions of the two systems were not always consonant. The major conclusions which emerge from my analysis are presented in what follows.

First, I have argued that state support can 'artificially' imbue produce with qualities which are as equally desirable to consumers as those provided by nature. Two categories of IGO were examined: GIs and country of origin. The former signify that the unique characteristics of a product are attributable to its geographical origin. Terroir is the exemplar of this relationship: 'Pauillac makes the most striking and brilliant wine of the Médoc [while] Margaux [makes] the most refined and exquisite.'[1] Country of origin simply indicates provenance; it does not indicate that products derive specific qualities from a particular location. However, especially for foodstuffs, official intervention meant that certain produce, for example, Danish butter and New Zealand lamb, were recognised as superlative.

A second conclusion is that fraudulent use of IGOs was a significant challenge to 'fair' market exchange. The possibility of market failure necessitated private and then public intervention to safeguard these indications and the quality messages they conveyed. A major theme which emerges from this study is the need to better understand how standards evolve to determine the qualities of particular products. IGOs epitomise the conflicts that can arise between private and public standards and are particularly important for foodstuffs. The PDO and PGI schemes, for example, are public standards: the EU enacted legislation which established the criteria governing the award of GI status. But, increasingly, global food supply chains are subject to private standards. For example, the Red Tractor symbol in Britain has 'been promoted as a general quality indicator for agricultural products', while the Label Rouge in France represents the 'promulgation of private product differentiation standards ... on the basis of regional identity or distinct production systems'.[2] Growing use of private standards by producers was complemented by the activities of supermarkets and food retailers, for example, Marks and Spencer's 'Field-to-Fork', Starbucks' 'Shared Planet', and Tesco's 'Nature's Choice/Nurture'.[3] Private standards alter power relationships within food supply chains and may conflict with those that are publicly set.

A further conclusion is that the evolution and protection of IGOs were integral to globalisation. From the nineteenth century, IGOs featured prominently in the marketing campaigns of the world's major food-

---

[1] Johnson and Robinson, *The World Atlas of Wine*, 92.
[2] S. Henson and J. Humphrey, 'Understanding the Complexities of Private Standards in Global Agri-Food Chains as they Impact Developing Countries', *Journal of Development Studies*, 26 (2010): 1639.
[3] Henson and Humphrey, 'Understanding the Complexities', 1632.

exporting nations – Australia, Canada, Denmark, and New Zealand. One component of IGOs – geographical indications – remains central to EU agricultural policy and has featured prominently in disputes settled before the WTO. Similarly, country of origin and the clamour for compulsory use of 'Made in' were conspicuous during the interwar period and they continue to generate economic tension and claims of unfair competition. In the United States, for example, some have claimed that the election of Donald Trump threatens the viability of domestic textile manufacturing: 'Is "Made in USA" in danger of becoming "Make Made in USA Great Again"? . . . U.S. apparel makers could benefit from an administration that favors local producers and makes domestic manufacturing more cost effective [but] these brands could lose their cool among their prime demographic if Trump turns "Made in America" into a political slogan.'[4]

One question which has underpinned this study is whether the type of protection afforded GIs matters. Differences between sui generis and trademark defence have not only strained relations between the EU and the United States but they also create dissonance between the interests of consumers and producers. The classic example of this conflict involves qualified use of a GI, for example, 'Australian Burgundy' or 'Sauterne, Product of the US'. In these cases, consumers are unlikely to be misled about the true origin of the wine. Nonetheless, producers in the EU claim that their goodwill is threatened because of the danger of genericide: absolute protection of GIs means that *any* type of misuse is intolerable. Moreover, under the EU scheme, once a GI is registered it cannot become generic. Upon registration, the product's exclusive connection with location becomes indisputable, even when natural and human factors are reproducible elsewhere as a result of technical progress.[5]

Undoubtedly, the higher protection afforded wines and spirits currently enshrined in TRIPS can be traced to the Madrid Agreement of 1891. This preferential treatment may seem odd: the definition of a GI is independent of the products to which it is applied. This book indicates that the stronger defence of 'products of the vine' is explained by regulatory capture – a polite term for 'hijack' – in which Europe's major wine producers, especially France, were prominent. It is incontrovertible that

---

[4] 'As Trump pushes for U.S. manufacturing, "Made in America" is losing its lustre in the fashion world'. *Los Angeles Times*, downloaded from: www.latimes.com/business/la-fi-trump-made-in-america-20170117-story.html.
[5] M. Gragnani, 'The EU Regulation 1151/2012 on Quality Schemes for Agricultural Products and Foodstuffs', *European Food and Feed Law Review*, 8 (2013): 380.

France pioneered the protection of GIs and that French legislation influenced other civil law countries. Nonetheless, it is hard to escape the conclusion that the 'French Connection' prejudiced the harmonious evolution of an international architecture for the protection of IGOs. France consistently rejected attempts to assimilate the provisions of the Madrid Agreement into the Paris Convention. One result of this resistance was that Czech beers were unable to benefit from higher protection until the Lisbon Agreement in 1958.

A further conclusion is that determining the validity of competing approaches to GI protection remains vexatious. Tomer Broude argued that the rapid growth of PDO and PGI registrations during the 1990s led to a general devaluation of GIs and a diminution in their ability to protect 'quality'. Broude further claimed that the low thresholds which appear to govern the award of GI status encouraged localities to 'invent tradition'.[6] If this argument is correct, the United States and other 'new' world countries may justifiably claim that the EU scheme is protectionist: by securing a monopoly on the use of GIs, Europe was undermining the competitiveness of imported foods. Ironically, if intensive registration did devalue EU food GIs, they became more able to compete on price terms with imports because they no longer command the price premia that GI status confers. Conversely, more stringent regulations governing the award of GI status increase cost of production, artificially restrict supply, and generate even higher premia for GI producers.[7]

Some scholars have argued that the alternative approaches to protecting GIs reflect fundamental differences in social norms and attitudes between the EU and the United States. Geert Hofstede demonstrated that US society was much more individualistic than the societies of France and Italy. This difference was especially pronounced in comparison to the societies of Spain and Portugal.[8] Such variation was used to advance the claim that in the United States use of certification marks to protect GIs was 'the least intrusive approach to accomplish a group action but imposes little restrictions on the individual'. Conversely, 'the societies of southern Europe and France are more collective ... These countries

---

[6] T. Broude, '"Taking Trade and Culture" Seriously: Geographical Indications and Cultural Protection in WTO Law', *University of Pennsylvania Journal of International Economic Law*, 26 (2005): 676–677.

[7] P. Mérel and R. J. Sexton, 'Will Geographic Indications Supply Excessive Quality?', *European Review of Agricultural Economics*, 39 (2012): 567–587.

[8] G. Hofstede, 'The Cultural Relativity of Organizational Practices and Theories', *Journal of International Business Studies*, 14 (1983): 80.

have developed institutions that emphasize the group over the individual. PDO/PGI imposes more restrictions on individual behaviour.'[9]

The EC system for protecting GIs affects the general operation of the global market in foodstuffs. Is it possible to reconcile the monopoly characteristics of GIs with WTO efforts to promote greater liberalisation in agriculture? It appears that the answer to this question is negative: GIs are inherently high-value products the ownership of which is dominated by the EU. Consequently, it has been claimed that EU policy on GIs is an attempt to monopolise high-value foodstuffs for European producers. The corollary of this is that freer entry to the EU market is possible, but only for countries exporting low-value, non-GI foodstuffs.[10] Viewed from this aspect, EU efforts to claw back generic food terms, for example, Feta, Mozzarella, Parmigiano Reggiano, and Prosciutto di Parma, are an attempt to extend and consolidate the EU's monopoly supply of GI products. Obviously, the principal beneficiaries of clawback are those Member States that have long-established GIs of considerable repute.[11] It is ironic that the EU is pursuing this approach: it resembles the US 'first in time, first in right' treatment of GIs – to which the EU is opposed.

Recent scholarship claims that clawback was motivated by a 'gastro-panic myth' which 'distorts and naturalizes certain world views, ideologies and interpretations to appear as indisputable facts'.[12] Emphasising the sociocultural foundations of GIs exacerbates the problem of separating 'fact from fiction'. For example, GI products 'are synonyms for cultural diversity, reflections of the evolution of a society, of its attachment to certain habits of consumption', while the collective nature of GIs 'makes these products a part of the local culture and helps to distinguish provenance (meaning to issue from a place) from origin (meaning to truly *be* from a place)'.[13] Nonetheless, whatever the *legal* merits of clawback, it appears indisputable that GIs are fundamentally

---

[9] P. Patel, L. House, and T. H. Spreen, 'How Do Different Countries Use Labelling Standards: A Case Study Comparing Wisconsin Real Cheese to Parmigiano-Reggiano', 291, 296. https://ageconsearch.umn.edu/bitstream/122015/2/20-Spreen%20et%20al.pdf.

[10] P. Evans, 'Geographic Indications, Trade and the Functioning of Markets', in M. P. Pugatch, *The Intellectual Property Debate* (Cheltenham: Edward Elgar, 2006), 359.

[11] M. Blakeney, 'Geographical Indications and TRIPS', in M. P. Pugatch, *The Intellectual Property Debate*, 301.

[12] S. G. Solecki, 'A Tale of Two Cheeses: Parmesan, Cheddar and the Politics of Generic Geographical Indications (GGIs)'. PhD thesis, University of Warwick, 2014, 17.

[13] Bérard and Marchenay, quoted in Barham, 'Translating Terroir', 132; Bowen and De Master, 'New Rural Livelihoods or Museums of Production?', 74.

inconsistent with globalisation. Sarah Bowen has argued that the struggle over GIs:

[symbolized] the conflict between the local and the global ... representing consumers' right to choose quality, healthy food over the homogenous, mass-produced commodities associated with industrial agricultural production ... Because GIs root production in particular places and protect the unique environmental and cultural resources that have developed over time in these places, scholars and development practitioners have framed them as a means of localizing production.[14]

Another finding which emerges from this study is that GIs do not simply communicate a product, but a series of social and cultural images, including artisanal production and heritage. Consider, for example, cherry production in Lari (Italy). Approximately 50 tons of this GI product are cultivated every year, and its economic value and impact is substantially less than its social importance: its primary value is that it acts as a cultural marker for the identity and social cohesion of the local population.[15] In this sense, GIs function as brands. However, whereas globalisation is associated with MNCs and global supply chains, GIs are produced by small-scale associations, often possessing a cooperative structure, in specific, rigorously demarcated geographical areas. No wonder, then, that the EU's policy on GIs is 'immediately troubling for many corporations in the US' who made substantial investment in promoting their brands that derive from geographical names.[16] A pertinent example of this unease is the conflict between the US corporation Anheuser Busch, and the original brewery bearing that name, Budweiser Budvar.

Despite the legal differences between the EU and the United States there are signs of gastronomic convergence. Between 2012 and 2014, retail spending in the US food and beverage industry grew at 2.6 per cent per annum. This trend conceals a shift in consumer expenditure: between 2009 and 2013, the twenty-five biggest US food and beverage manufacturers experienced a 1 per cent growth in consumer spending, compared to 4.9 and 4.0 per cent on smaller and private brands, respectively.[17] Part of the explanation for this redirection in consumer spending is the

[14] S. Bowen, 'Embedding Local Places in Global Spaces: Geographical Indications as a Territorial Development Strategy', *Rural Sociology*, 75 (2010): 210.

[15] A. Marescotti, 'Cherry of Lari (Italy)', in Barham and Sylvander, *Labels of Origin*, 161–166.

[16] Barham, 'Translating Terroir', 128.

[17] Deloitte, 'Capitalizing on the Shifting Consumer Food Value Equation', 1. www2.deloitte .com/content/dam/Deloitte/us/Documents/consumer-business/us-fmi-gma-report.pdf

different preferences of the millennials: 'They are bored by their parents' bland diets ... There is an increasing desire for variety, taste, and local products.'[18] Consumers in the United States are allocating up to 25 per cent of their food budget on 'high-value items', especially chocolate, olive oil, and cheese. The rapid growth in the craft beer market also exemplifies 'an increasing desire for variety, taste and local products'. The evidence suggests that there is greater interest in locally produced foods compared to their organic rivals, and there is a need to address fundamental questions, such as: what does local mean? And how relevant is this term to states which cover hundreds of square miles?[19] It is tempting to speculate that as US consumers seek greater differentiation in their foodstuffs, the federal government may view the EC's PDO/PGI scheme more favourably.

Unsurprisingly, EU policy and the TRIPS Agreement are in accord that the defining feature of a GI is that 'a given quality, reputation, or other characteristics of the good is essentially attributable to its geographical origin'.[20] All of these features are usually certified by the relevant trade body, but how meaningful are they to consumers? One problem is that GI schemes only denote that a product has a specific quality: they do not indicate that a GI product is superior. A second difficulty is how to disentangle the effects of a GI when it is used in conjunction with a company's brand. The public nature of GIs means that firms enjoy a collective reputation, whereas private brands confer benefits unique to specific producers. Research suggests that GIs are best used in conjunction with private brands, and that sui generis systems generate more information for consumers than certification schemes based on common law regimes.[21] In common with trademarks, even if GIs denote high quality, they do not guarantee consistency of quality.[22] The fine wine trade is exemplary in this respect: even a casual inspection of the wine press shows that the marks critics award to a particular chateau vary each year.

---

[18] J. J. McCluskey, 'Changing Food and Consumer Preferences', 2. www.kansascityfed.org/~/media/files/publicat/rscp/2015/mccluskey-paper.pdf?la=en

[19] McCluskey, 'Changing Food', 6–7, 11–12.

[20] TRIPS Agreement, Article 22; EU Regulation No. 1151/2012 on quality schemes for agricultural products and foodstuffs. *Official Journal*, L 343/1, 14 December 2012, Article 5 (b).

[21] L. Menapace and G. C. Moschini, 'Quality Certification by Geographical Indications, Trademarks and Firm Reputation', *European Review of Agricultural Economics*, 39 (2012): 539–566.

[22] J. Aldred, 'The Economic Rationale of Trade Marks: An Economist's Critique', in Bently, Davies, and Ginsberg, *Trade Marks and Brands*, 270.

The concerns raised in the preceding paragraph have a bearing on the growth prospects of less developed countries (LDCs). Since 2010, the United Nations Conference on Trade and Development (UNCTAD) has supported selected LDCs in their efforts to secure GI registration for their 'traditional' products, for example, Bhutanese red rice, Cambodian Kampot peppers, and Mozambique Tete goat meat. The characteristics of these products are closely related to their local ecosystems and some are of considerable lineage: Bhutanese red rice was produced 800 years BC.[23] However, the rigorous production standards, quality control, and certification procedures that need to be satisfied to enable these products to obtain registration as GIs within the EU, are almost insurmountable. UNCTAD stated, '[f]inancial resources and time efforts necessary for protecting GIs [under the EU scheme] are considerable ... and should be carefully gauged ... There is no value in having GIs ... without being able to effectively market them or without adequate enforcement mechanisms.'[24]

Country of origin was not recognised as a GI until the Lisbon Agreement of 1958. Consequently, for most of the period covered by this study, 'Made in' did not benefit from the higher legal protection afforded GIs. A further conclusion that emerges from this book is that, at least for foodstuffs, differences in the scope of legal protection appear inconsequential: Danish bacon and New Zealand lamb, for example, were safeguarded by the British Merchandise Marks Acts.[25] Moreover, the growth of brands which became synonymous with country of origin, for example, Anchor and the Lur Brand, indicate that the export success of some food products did not require GI status. Recently, however, the viability of this strategy has been undermined by the decision of Arla, owners of Anchor, to move butter production from New Zealand to Britain.

Delocalisation is debarred for GIs, and for country of origin, when applied to food products. But when we turn our attention to the manufacture of industrial products and consumer durables, the issues surrounding provenance become more complex. Another conclusion suggested by this study is that country of origin, or 'Made in', is closely associated with nationalism. It also raises important questions about the economic role of

---

[23] UNCTAD, *Why Geographical Indications for Least Developed Countries?* (New York: UNCTAD, 2016), 19.
[24] UNCTAD, *Why Geographical Indications for Least Developed Countries?*, 54.
[25] Anchor and Danish Bacon were registered as British trademarks in 1905 and 1922, respectively.

nation states in a globalised world. Kenichi Ohmae argued that nation states are almost irrelevant to economic transactions: 'On a political map, the boundaries between countries are as clear as ever. But on a competitive map, a map showing the real flows of financial and industrial activity, those boundaries have largely disappeared.'[26]

'Made in' continues to generate many ironies. The British Merchandise Marks Act of 1887 resulted in the 'Made in Germany' debacle: the Act was intended to prevent foreign competitors misusing British trademarks, but it inadvertently promoted German exports. Donald Trump vowed to 'Make America Great Again'. To encourage the repatriation of US manufacturing, he threatens to penalise companies that offshore production. But to remain competitive, many US companies rely on low-cost assembly in the Far East. Even luxury products are not immune to the need to offshore: Louis Vuitton claims that its 'Italian' shoes embody 'ancestral savoir faire', but they are mass-produced in a Romanian factory. The price of a pair of mid-range Louis Vuitton court shoes is equivalent to six months' pay for a Romanian textile worker.[27]

Campaigns to promote the purchase of domestic products occur at inopportune phases of the economic cycle. Consider, for example, the promotion of 'Buy British' in the 1930s, and again in the early 1980s. A compelling case can be made that these initiatives were fundamentally misguided: they were knee-jerk reactions, unable to overcome long-term weaknesses in the competitiveness of the British economy. Appeals to patriotism overlook a simple truth: if domestic products were competitive, imports of manufactures would not have grown so rapidly.

The growth of MNC's and the global trade in semi-manufactured products undermines consumer confidence regarding 'Made in'. Exacerbating matters, customs' determination of origin for tariff purposes can differ from those of other government departments. The United States is an exemplar in this regard: ordinarily, products imported to the United States must bear an indication of origin. But if the imported article undergoes 'substantial transformation', it need not be marked – and US consumers have traditionally assumed that such products are 'Made in the USA'. However, a product that is 'transformed' cannot be marked 'Made in the USA', unless it satisfies the FTC's requirement that it is 'all or virtually all' made in the United States.

---

[26] K. Ohmae, 'Managing in a Borderless World', *Harvard Business Review*, 67 (1989): 153.
[27] *The Guardian*, 17 June 2017, 31.

Another conclusion from this study is that the battle between private brands and country of origin is ongoing. I have argued that 'Swiss made' is unusual: Switzerland benefits from a well-established reputation in watch manufacture and its famous producers, for example, Omega, Rolex, and Tag Heuer, have an interest in upholding the integrity of 'Swiss-made' watches. In contrast, the United States has a much more diversified industrial base, and many of its leading companies, including Ford and Nike, eschew 'Made in the USA' because compliance with the FTC's regulations would undermine their competitiveness. The EU occupies the least enviable position as regards 'Made in': it has a diversified industrial base, it is home to many famous brands, but it faces the additional challenge of reconciling the interests of its Member States, each of which possesses different economic strengths.

The final conclusion which emerges from this study is that GIs and indications of origin can be vexatious for capitalist economies because they are more concerned with communities than corporations, and because historical traditions and reputations are their key assets. According to Elizabeth Barham:

Concepts of neo-liberal economic theory that lie behind the economic push towards globalization posit a frictionless economy where neither space nor time impedes the free flow of goods, labor and capital. However, as a form of collective property anchored to specific places, IGOs challenge this picture in significant ways.[28]

NOTES ON SOURCES

One of the chief sources used in this study is the press, especially the 'trade press'. In this regard, *The Grocer and Oil Trades Review*, and the *Meat Trades Journal and Cattle Salesman's Gazette*, have been invaluable. Both publications provide extensive commentary on Australasian, British, European, and US agricultural developments and legislation; they also contain detailed analysis of litigation launched in British courts. Such reporting is particularly valuable because actions involving misrepresentation of geographical origin were usually heard in magistrates' courts: they were not considered sufficiently serious to be heard – and therefore reported – in official law reports. Whereas infringement of 'technical' trademarks directly affects individual firms, misuse of IGOs undermines the goodwill that communities, industries, regions, and even nations have

[28] Barham, 'Translating Terroir', 129.

established for their products. Consequently, central government features prominently in national and international efforts to improve the legal regime protecting geographical indications. For this reason, extensive use is made of official publications, including the publications of the Australian Dairy Producers Control Board' New Zealand Dairy Produce Control Board; New Zealand Meat Producers Board; Reports of the Minister of Agriculture for the Dominion of Canada; US Department of Agriculture, as well as the publications of the UK's Ministry of Agriculture and Fisheries. Many of these reports contain the views of major agricultural bodies, and they inform the discussion in Chapters 3 and 4.

At the international level, from the nineteenth century to the Lisbon Conference of 1958, the major sources I consulted included the annual reports of: the Association Internationale pour la Protection de la Propriété Industrielle; the Annuaire de l'Association Internationale pour la Protection de la Propriété Industrielle, and the various Actes de la Conférence Internationale pour la Protection de la Propriété Industrielle. These publications are authoritative sources on contemporary legal discussion on all issues pertaining to IGOs. The Actes provide verbatim accounts of the negotiating positions of the officials representing Member States, and the final protocols adopted. Subsequently, the World Intellectual Property Organization was established in 1967; it is responsible for coordinating the international protection of intellectual property. The reports and discussions of this body, together with those of the World Trade Organization, formed·in 1995, were the main sources I consulted for the later twentieth century onwards. These latter documents were complemented by reports and commentary issued by the European Commission. These sources were used in Chapters 2, 6, 7, 8, and 9.

The views of major employers' federations in the UK, Switzerland, and the United States were obtained from the National Archives (London), the Modern Records Centre (Warwick, UK), and the Federation of the Swiss Watch Industry (www.fhs.swiss/eng/homepage.html), and via official reports and transcripts of evidence supplied by the US Federal Trades Commission. This evidence underpins the narrative in Chapters 5 and 10.

One of the benefits of the modern age is rapid Internet access to electronic databases. Many of the official reports of the European Commission, World Intellectual Property Organization, and World Trade Organization can now be accessed remotely.

Bibliography

ARCHIVAL SOURCES

Guildhall Library, London

Associated Chambers of Commerce. MS. 14476. *Meeting of the Executive Council.*
British Federation of Traders' Association. MS. 16781. *Minute Book.*
London Chamber of Commerce. MS. 16459/8. *Minutes of Meeting of Council.*
London Chamber of Commerce. MS. 16459/10. *Minutes of Meeting of Council.*
London Chamber of Commerce. MS. 1659. *Minutes of the Briar Pipe Trade Section.*
London Chamber of Commerce. MS. 16775. *Minutes of the British Toy Manufacturers Association.*

Modern Records Centre (University of Warwick)

Federation of British Industries
MRC/FBI. MSS.200/F/1/1/10. Minutes of the FBI Executive Committee, 1924–1927.
MRC/FBI. MSS.200/F/1/1/1/155. *Minutes of the Committee on Trade Marks and Merchandise Marks and Others, 1919–1926.*
MRC/FBI. MSS.200/F/1/1/175. *Minutes of Various Committees.*
MRC/FBI. MSS.200/F/3/D2/2/1. *Correspondence re: 'Buy British Campaign'.*
MRC/FBI. MSS.200/F/4/2/1. *Second Annual Report, 1918.*
MRC/FBI. MSS.200/F/4/2/8. *Ninth Annual Report, 1925.*
The United Manufacturers Journal.

The National Archives

BT 63/1/3. *Merchandise Marks. Electric Lamps. Marking of Origin.*
BT 63/2/1. *Merchandise Marks. Pumps. Report of the Standing Committee.*
BT 63/2/10. *Merchandise Marks. Wood Rulers as Used in Schools. Report of Standing Committee.*
BT 63/3/6. *Merchandise Marks. Firearms. Report of Standing Committee.*
BT 63/3/10. *Merchandise Marks. Certain Rubber or Part Rubber Articles. Application of Surgical Instruments Order.*
BT 63/3/11. *Merchandise Marks. Furniture Castors. Application of Marking Order.*
BT 63/6/1. *Merchandise Marks. Furniture Imported without an Indication of Origin. Prosecution.*
BT 63/6/2. *Merchandise Marks. Toys, Imported, Indication of Origin.*
BT 63/6/4. *Merchandise Marks. Imported Boxes, Cartons, Cases and Other Containers Made of Cardboard, etc.*
BT 63/8/6. *Merchandise Marks Act. Air and Gas Compressors, Pneumatic Tools. Report of Standing Committee.*
BT 63/9/4. *Merchandise Marks. Eggs. Inadequate Penalties for Fraudulent Removal of Marks.*
BT 63/9/14. *Merchandise Marks. Shaving Brushes Assembled from Imported Materials not 'British Made'.*
BT 63/11/8. *Merchandise Marks. 'British'. Use of Description on 'Empire' Goods. Summary of Board of Trade Replies.*
BT 64/39. *Merchandise Marks. Prosecutions by the Board of Trade, 1936–1938.*
BT 64/40. *Merchandise Marks Act. Motor-Cars, Motor-Cycles and Pedal Cycles Made from Foreign Components and Assembled in . . .:*
BT 209/785. *Revision at Lisbon: Preparatory Work on the Agenda: Lisbon Conference, Preliminary Documents.*
BT 209/788. *Preparatory Work on the Agenda: Preliminary Documents, Propositions and Observations of Other Governments: International Union for the Protection of Industrial Property: Lisbon Conference Preliminary Documents.*
BT 209/790. *Proposed Revision of the Arrangement of The Hague 1925 and Madrid Arrangement (Marks) of Origin. Revision of the Madrid Arrangement on False Indications of Origin.*
BT 209/793. *False Indications and Appellations of Origin.*
BT 209/832. *International Union for the Protection of Industrial Property, Lisbon Conference Preliminary Documents.*
BT 258/957. *Committee on Consumer Protection: Board of Trade Submission on Merchandise Marks Acts.*

OFFICIAL REPORTS

Australia

Commonwealth of Australia. *First Annual Report of the Dairy Produce Control Board, 1926.* Melbourne: Government Printer.

Commonwealth of Australia. *Third Annual Report of the Dairy Produce Control Board for the Year Ended 30 June 1928*. Melbourne: Government Printer.

Commonwealth of Australia. *Fourth Annual Report of the Dairy Produce Control Board for the Year Ended 30 June 1929*. Melbourne: Government Printer.

Commonwealth of Australia. *Fifth Annual Report of the Dairy Produce Control Board for the Year Ended 30 June 1930*. Melbourne: Government Printer.

Commonwealth of Australia. *Sixth Annual Report of the Dairy Produce Control Board for the Year Ended 30 June 1931*. Melbourne: Government Printer.

Commonwealth of Australia. *Eighth Annual Report of the Dairy Produce Control Board for the Year Ended 30 June 1933*. Melbourne: Government Printer.

Commonwealth of Australia. *Tenth Annual Report of the Dairy Produce Control Board for the Year Ended 30 June 1935*. Melbourne: Government Printer.

Royal Commission on the Butter Industry. *Minutes of Evidence and Appendix*. Victoria, 1905.

Canada

Report of the Minister of Agriculture for the Dominion of Canada for the Calendar Year 1876. 40 Victoria, Sessional Papers No. 8. Ottawa, 1877.

Report of the Minister of Agriculture for the Dominion of Canada for the Calendar Year 1877. 41 Victoria, Sessional Papers No. 9. Ottawa, 1878.

Report of the Minister of Agriculture for the Dominion of Canada for the Calendar Year 1878. 42 Victoria, Sessional Papers No. 9. Ottawa, 1879.

Report of the Minister of Agriculture for the Dominion of Canada for the Calendar Year 1879. 43 Victoria, Sessional Papers No. 10. Ottawa, 1880.

Report of the Minister of Agriculture for the Dominion of Canada for the Calendar Year 1885. 49 Victoria, Sessional Papers No. 10. Ottawa, 1886.

Report of the Minister of Agriculture for the Dominion of Canada for the Calendar Year 1897. 61 Victoria, Sessional Papers No. 8. Ottawa, 1898.

Report of the Minister of Agriculture for the Dominion of Canada for the Year Ended 31 October 1905. 5–6 Edward VII, Sessional Paper No. 15. Ottawa, 1906.

Report of the Minister of Agriculture for the Dominion of Canada for the Year Ended 31 March 1908. 8–9 Edward VII. Sessional Paper No. 15. Ottawa, 1908.

Report of the Minister of Agriculture for the Dominion of Canada for the Year Ending 31 March 1931. Ottawa, 1931.

Report of the Minister of Agriculture for the Dominion of Canada for the Year Ending 31 March 1934. Ottawa, 1934.

Report of the Minister of Agriculture for the Dominion of Canada for the Year Ending 31 March 1935. Ottawa, 1935.

European Union

European Commission. Press Release Database, 'Why Do Geographical Indications Matter to Us?', Memo /03/160, Brussels. 30 July 2003.

European Commission. Press Release Database, 'WTO Talks: EU Steps Up Bid for Better Protection of Regional Quality Products', IP 03/1178. 28 August 2003.

European Commission. *Fact Sheet: European Policy for Quality Agricultural Products* (European Commission, January 2007): 12.

European Commission. *Communication on Agricultural Product Quality Policy: Impact Assessment Report* (version 08–04-09).

European Commission. *Agricultural Product Quality Policy. Impact Assessment: Annex B: Geographical Indications*: 30.

European Commission. *Agricultural Product Quality Policy. Impact Assessment: Annex B: Geographical Indications*: 38.

European Commission. *Green Paper on Agricultural Product Quality: Product Standards, Farming Requirements and Quality Schemes*. Com. Brussels, 15 October 2008.

New Zealand

Agricultural and Pastoral Industries and Stock Committee. *Dairy Produce Export Control Bill (Together with Minutes of Evidence)*. New Zealand. 1923.

Extension of Commerce Committee. Appendix to the *Journals of the House of Representatives*, Session I-10a. Wellington, New Zealand, 1903.

Frozen Meat Committee. Appendix to the *Journals of the House of Representatives*, Session I, I-1. Wellington, New Zealand, 1902.

Industries and Commerce Report, New Zealand. Appendix to the *Journals of the House of Representatives*, Session II, H-17. Wellington, New Zealand, 1906.

New Zealand Dairy Produce Control Board. First Annual Report and Statement of Accounts for the Period of 18 Months from 31 January 1924 to 31 July 1925. Wellington, New Zealand.

New Zealand Dairy Produce Control Board. Third Annual Report and Statement of Accounts for the Period of 12 Months Ended 31 July 1927. Wellington, New Zealand.

New Zealand Dairy Produce Control Board. Fourth Annual Report and Statement of Accounts for the Period of 12 Months Ended 31 July 1928. Wellington, New Zealand.

New Zealand Dairy Produce Control Board. Fifth Annual Report and Statement of Accounts for the Period of 12 Months Ended 31 July 1929. Wellington, New Zealand.

New Zealand Dairy Produce Control Board. Seventh Annual Report and Statement of Accounts for the Period of 12 Months Ended 31 July 1931. Wellington, New Zealand.

New Zealand Dairy Produce Control Board. Eighth Annual Report and Statement of Accounts for the Period of 12 Months Ended 31 July 1932. Wellington, New Zealand.

New Zealand Dairy Produce Control Board. Ninth Annual Report and Statement of Accounts for the Period of 12 Months Ended 31 July 1933. Wellington, New Zealand.

New Zealand Dairy Produce Control Board. Tenth Annual Report and Statement of Accounts for the Period of 12 Months Ended 31 July 1934. Wellington, New Zealand.

New Zealand Dairy Produce Control Board. Eleventh Annual Report and Statement of Accounts for the Period of 12 Months Ended 31 July 1935. Wellington, New Zealand.

New Zealand Dairy Produce Control Board. Twelfth Annual Report and Statement of Accounts for the Period of 12 Months Ended 31 July 1936. Wellington, New Zealand.

New Zealand Dairy Produce Control Board. Fifteenth Annual Report and Statement of Accounts for the Period of 12 Months Ended 31 July 1939. Wellington, New Zealand.

New Zealand, Industries and Commerce Report, 28 August 1906.

The New Zealand Produce Trade in England. Appendix to the *Journals of the House of Representatives*, Session I, H-17. Wellington, New Zealand, 1898.

New Zealand Meat Producers Board. Second Annual Report and Statement of Accounts for the Year Ending 30 June 1924. Wellington, New Zealand.

New Zealand Meat Producers Board. Eighth Annual Report and Statement of Accounts for the Year Ending 30 June 1930. Wellington, New Zealand.

New Zealand Meat Producers Board. Ninth Annual Report and Statement of Accounts for the Year Ending 30 June 1931. Wellington, New Zealand.

New Zealand Meat Producers Board. Eleventh Annual Report and Statement of Accounts for the Year Ending 30 June 1933. Wellington, New Zealand.

New Zealand Meat Producers Board. Twelfth Annual Report and Statement of Accounts for the Year Ending 30 June 1934. Wellington, New Zealand.

New Zealand Meat Producers Board. Thirteenth Annual Report and Statement of Accounts for the Year Ending 30 June 1935. Wellington, New Zealand.

New Zealand Meat Producers Board. Fourteenth Annual Report and Statement of Accounts for the Year Ending 30 June 1936. Wellington, New Zealand.

New Zealand Meat Producers Board. Sixteenth Annual Report and Statement of Accounts for the Year Ending 30 June 1938. Wellington, New Zealand.

Second Annual Report, Department of Industries and Commerce. Appendix to the *Journals of the House of Representatives*, Session I, H-17. Wellington, New Zealand, 1902.

Sixth Annual Report of the Department of Industries and Commerce by James McGowan. Appendix to the *Journals of the House of Representatives*, Session I, H-17. Wellington, New Zealand, 1907.

Trade between New Zealand and the West-Coast Ports of the United Kingdom. Appendix to the *Journals of the House of Representatives*, New Zealand, (1908): 35–36.

United Kingdom

Agricultural Tribunal of Investigation. *Final Report*. P.P. VII.45. London: HMSO, 1924.

Board of Trade Merchandise Marks Act, 1926. *Report of the Standing Committee Respecting Gold and Silver Leaf.* P.P. XI.107. London: HMSO, 1927.

Board of Trade Merchandise Marks Act, 1926. *Report of the Standing Committee Respecting Iron and Steel.* P.P. XI. 113. London: HMSO, 1927.

Board of Trade Merchandise Marks Act, 1926. *Report of the Standing Committee Respecting Rubber Tyres and Tubes.* P.P. XI.167. London: HMSO, 1927.

Board of Trade Merchandise Marks Act, 1926. *Report of the Standing Committee Respecting Furniture and Cabinet Ware.* P.P. XI.199. London: HMSO, 1927.

Board of Trade Merchandise Marks Act, 1926. *Report of the Standing Committee Respecting Boots, Shoes and Slippers (Other than Rubber).* P.P. XI.543. London: HMSO, 1928.

Board of Trade Merchandise Marks Act, 1926. *Report of the Standing Committee Respecting Pottery.* P.P. XI.563. London: HMSO, 1928.

Board of Trade Merchandise Marks Act, 1926. *Report of the Standing Committee Respecting Insulated Electric Cables and Wires.* P.P. XI.575. London: HMSO, 1928.

Board of Trade Merchandise Marks Act, 1926. *Report of the Standing Committee Respecting Cast Iron Enamel Baths.* P.P. XI.611. London: HMSO, 1928.

Board of Trade Merchandise Marks Act, 1926. *Report of the Standing Committee Respecting Electric Incandescent Lamps.* P.P. XI.625. London: HMSO, 1928.

Board of Trade Merchandise Marks Act, 1926. *Report of the Standing Committee Respecting Surgical, Medical, Dental and Veterinary Instruments and Appliances* ... P.P. VIII.467. London: HMSO, 1928.

Board of Trade Merchandise Marks Act, 1926. *Report of the Standing Committee Respecting Cutlery.* P.P. VIII.475. London: HMSO, 1928.

Board of Trade Merchandise Marks Act, 1926. *Report of the Standing Committee Respecting Carpets, Rugs and Mats.* P.P. VIII. 537. London: HMSO, 1928.

Board of Trade Merchandise Marks Act, 1926. *Report of the Standing Committee Respecting Granite Monuments and Enclosures and Parts.* P.P. VIII.555. London: HMSO, 1928.

Board of Trade Merchandise Marks Act, 1926. *Report of the Standing Committee Respecting Spring Balances.* P.P. VIII.561. London: HMSO, 1929.

Board of Trade Merchandise Marks Act, 1926. *Report of the Standing Committee Respecting Rubber Manufactures.* P.P. VIII.575. London: HMSO, 1929.

Board of Trade Merchandise Marks Act, 1926. *Report of the Standing Committee Respecting Firearms and Parts Thereof.* P.P. VIII.601. London: HMSO, 1929.

Board of Trade Merchandise Marks Act, 1926. *Report of the Standing Committee Respecting Domestic, etc., Glassware and Glass Bottles.* P.P. XVI.13. London: HMSO, 1929.

Board of Trade Merchandise Marks Act, 1926. *Report of the Standing Committee Respecting Scientific Glassware.* P.P. XVI.27. London: HMSO, 1929.

Board of Trade Merchandise Marks Act, 1926. *Report of the Standing Committee Respecting Asbestos Cement Products.* P.P. XVI.35. London: HMSO, 1929.

Board of Trade Merchandise Marks Act, 1926. *Report of the Standing Committee Respecting Tools.* P.P. XVI.51. London: HMSO, 1929.

Board of Trade Merchandise Marks Act, 1926. *Report of the Standing Committee Respecting Portland Cement.* P.P. XVI.59. London: HMSO, 1929.

Board of Trade Merchandise Marks Act, 1926. *Report of the Standing Committee Respecting Machinery Belting.* P.P. XVI.83. London: HMSO, 1930.

Board of Trade Merchandise Marks Act, 1926. *Report of the Standing Committee Respecting Wall Papers, Ceiling Papers, etc.* P.P. XVI.109. London: HMSO, 1930.

Board of Trade Merchandise Marks Act, 1926. *Report of the Standing Committee Respecting Electricity Meters and Parts Thereof.* P.P. XV.807. London: HMSO, 1931.

Board of Trade Merchandise Marks Act, 1926. *Report of the Standing Committee Respecting Printing Blocks.* P.P. XIV.791. London: HMSO, 1933.

Board of Trade Merchandise Marks Act, 1926. *Report of the Standing Committee Respecting Measuring Tapes of Cotton or Linen.* P.P. X.805. London: HMSO, 1933.

Board of Trade Merchandise Marks Act, 1926. *Report of the Standing Committee Respecting Wooden Tobacco Pipes and Bowls Therefor.* P.P. XIV. 871. London: HMSO, 1933.

Board of Trade Merchandise Marks Act, 1926. *Report of the Standing Committee Respecting Clocks, Movements, Escapements and Synchronous Motors.* P.P. XIV.877. London: HMSO, 1933.

Board of Trade Merchandise Marks Act, 1926. *Report of the Standing Committee Respecting Hair Combs and Blanks Therefor.* P.P. XIV.227. London: HMSO, 1934.

Board of Trade Merchandise Marks Act, 1926. *Report of the Standing Committee Respecting Picture and Greeting Postcards.* P.P. XI.565. London: HMSO, 1937.

Board of Trade Merchandise Marks Act, 1926. *Report of the Standing Committee Respecting Sanitary Ware of Pottery.* XIII.721. London: HMSO, 1938.

Board of Trade Merchandise Marks Act, 1926. *Report of the Standing Committee Respecting Watch Straps etc.* P.P. XIII.707. London: HMSO, 1938.

Board of Trade Merchandise Marks Act, 1926. *Report of the Standing Committee Respecting Solid-Headed Pins of Brass, Iron or Steel.* P.P. XIII.699. London: HMSO, 1938.

Board of Trade Merchandise Marks Act, 1926. *Report of the Standing Committee Respecting Cased Tubes.* P.P. XIII.253. London: HMSO, 1939.

Board of Trade Merchandise Marks Act, 1926. *Report of the Standing Committee Respecting Spectacle Frames, Fronts, Slides, and Bridges; and Eyeglass Frames and Bridges.* P.P. V.1. London: HMSO, 1939.

Board of Trade. *International Convention for the Protection of Industrial Property and International Agreement Regarding False Indications of Origin.* London: HMSO, 1934.

Board of Trade. Safeguarding of Industries. *Report of the Committee on Cutlery.* P.P. XV.663. London: HMSO, 1925.

Board of Trade. Safeguarding of Industries. *Report of the Committee on Leather Gloves, Fabric Gloves, and Glove Fabric.* P.P. XV.601. London: HMSO, 1925.

British Trade after the War. *Report of a Sub-Committee of the Advisory Committee to the Board of Trade on Commercial Intelligence with Respect to Measures for Securing the Position, after the War, of Certain Branches of British Industry.* P.P. XV.591. London: HMSO, 1916.

British Trade after the War. *Summaries of the Evidence Taken by a Sub-Committee of the Advisory Committee to the Board of Trade on Commercial Intelligence in the Course of Their Enquiry with Respect to Measures for Securing the Position, after the War, of Certain Branches of British Industry.* P.P. XV.611. London: HMSO, 1916.

Committee on Industry and Trade. *Minutes of Evidence*, Vol. I. London: HMSO, 1931.

Committee on Industry and Trade. *Minutes of Evidence.* Vol. III. London: HMSO, XXX.

Committee on Commercial and Industrial Policy. *Interim Report on the Importation of Goods from the Present Enemy Countries after the War.* P.P. XIII.221. London: HMSO, 1918.

Conditions Under Which Trading Is Possible since the Raising of the Blockade. P.P. XLV.723. London: HMSO, 1919.

Correspondence Relative to the Protection of Industrial Property. P.P. XCVIII.385. London: HMSO, 1888.

Department of Agriculture and Technical Instruction for Ireland: *Report of the Departmental Committee on the Irish Butter Industry.* P.P. VIII.1. Dublin: HMSO, 1910.

Dominions Royal Commission. *Royal Commission on the Natural Resources, Trade and Legislation of Certain Portions of His Majesty's Dominions. Minutes of Evidence Taken in London during October and November, 1912. Part II. Natural Resources, Trade and Legislation.* P.P. XVI.393. London: HMSO, 1912.

Empire Marketing Board. *The Demand for Cheese in London.* London: HMSO, 1929.

Empire Marketing Board. *The Demand for Empire Butter.* London: HMSO, 1930.

Empire Marketing Board. *Note on the Work and Finance of the Board and Statement of Research and Other Grants Approved by the Secretary of State for Dominion Affairs from July 1926, to March 31, 1932.* P.P. XVIII.763. London: HMSO, 1932.

Final Report of the Committee on Industry and Trade. P.P. VII.413. London: HMSO, 1929.

First Report of the Royal Commission on Food Prices, Vol. I. P.P. XIII.1. London: HMSO, 1925.

Imperial Committee on Economic Consultation and Cooperation. *Report.* P.P. XI.415. London: HMSO, 1933.

Imperial Economic Committee. *Report of the Imperial Economic Committee on Marketing and Preparing for Market of Foodstuffs Produced in the Overseas Parts of the Empire. First Report.* P.P. XIII.799. London: HMSO, 1925.

Imperial Economic Committee. *Report of the Imperial Economic Committee on Marketing and Preparing for Market of Foodstuffs Produced within the Empire. Fourth Report – Dairy Produce.* P.P. XII.281. London: HMSO, 1926.

Imperial Economic Committee. *Mutton and Lamb Survey*. London: HMSO, 1935.

Industrial Property and Trade Marks. Papers Relative to the Recent Conference at Rome on the Subject of Industrial Property. P.P. LX.413. London: HMSO, 1886.

International Convention for the Protection of Industrial Property. P.P. LXXXVII.225. London: HMSO, 1884.

Merchandise Marks Act, 1926. *Report of the Standing Committee on Eggs*. P.P. XI.175. London: HMSO, 1927.

Merchandise Marks Act, 1926. *Report of the Standing Committee on Frozen or Chilled Salmon and Trout*. P.P. XV.785. London: HMSO, 1930.

Merchandise Marks Act, 1926. *Report of the Standing Committee on Butter*. P.P. XV.843. London: HMSO, 1931.

Merchandise Marks Act, 1926. *Report of the Standing Committee on Meat*. P.P. XIV.167. London: HMSO, 1933.

Merchandise Marks Act, 1926. *Report of the Standing Committee on Poultry*. P.P.XIV.887. London: HMSO, 1933.

Merchandise Marks Act, 1926. *Report of the Standing Committee on Grapes*. P.P. XIII.953. London: HMSO, 1936.

Merchandise Marks Committee. *Minutes of Evidence*. London: HMSO, 1920.

Merchandise Marks Committee. *Report to the Board of Trade of the Merchandise Marks Committee*. XVI. 615. London: HMSO, 1920.

Ministry of Agriculture and Fisheries. Departmental Committee on Distribution and Prices of Agricultural Produce. *Final Report*. P.P. VII.1. London: HMSO, 1924.

Ministry of Agriculture and Fisheries. *Report on the Marketing of Cattle and Beef in England and Wales*. London: HMSO, 1929.

Ministry of Agriculture and Fisheries. *Report on the Marketing of Dairy Produce in England and Wales: Part I, Cheese*. London: HMSO, 1930.

Ministry of Agriculture and Fisheries. *Report of an Interdepartmental Committee on the Grading and Marking of Beef*. P.P. VIII.167. London: HMSO, 1930.

Ministry of Agriculture and Fisheries. *Report on the Marketing of Dairy Produce in England and Wales: Part II, Butter and Cream*. London: HMSO, 1932.

Ministry of Agriculture and Fisheries. *Departmental Committee Distribution and Prices of Agricultural Produce. Interim Report on Meat, Poultry and Eggs*. P.P. IX.297. London: HMSO, 1923.

Ministry of Agriculture and Fisheries. *Report of the Committee Appointed to Review the Working of the Agricultural Marketing Acts*. London: HMSO, 1947.

Ministry of Agriculture and Fisheries and Scottish Office. *Report of the Second Interdepartmental Committee on the Grading and Marking of Beef*. P.P. VI.141. London: HMSO, 1932.

Papers and Correspondence Relative to the Recent Conference of the International Union for the Protection of Industrial Property Held at The Hague, October 8–November 6, 1925. London: HMSO, 1926.

Patent Office Inquiry. *Report of the Committee Appointed by the Board of Trade to Inquire into the Duties, Organisation, and Arrangements of the Patent Office under the Patents, Designs, and Trade Marks Act, so Far as Relates to Trade Marks, and Designs.* P.P. LXXXI.37. London: HMSO, 1888.

Report and Special Report from the Select Committee on the Agricultural Produce (Marks) Bill. P.P. VIII.227. London: HMSO, 1897.

Report from the Select Committee on Merchandise Marks Act, 1887. P.P. XV.19. London: HMSO, 1890.

Report from the Select Committee on Food Products Adulteration. P.P. X.73. London: HMSO, 1895.

Report from the Select Committee on Merchandise Marks. P.P. XI.29. London: HMSO, 1897.

Report of Proceedings of the 4th World's Poultry Congress. London: HMSO, 1930.

Report to the Board of Trade of the Merchandise Marks Committee. P.P. XXI.615. London: HMSO, 1920.

Safeguarding of Industries: Procedures and Enquiries. P.P. XV.573. London: HMSO, 1925.

Second Report of the Royal Commission Appointed to Inquire into the Depression of Trade and Industry. C. 4715. London: HMSO, 1886.

Select Committee of House of Lords on Marking of Foreign Meat. P.P. XII.341. London: HMSO, 1893.

Select Committee on Trade Marks Bill, and Merchandize Marks Bill. P.P. XII.431. London: HMSO, 1862.

Special Report from the Select Committee on Merchandize Marks Act (1862) Amendment Bill. P.P. X.357. London: HMSO, 1887.

United States

The Status of the World Trade Organization Negotiations on Agriculture. Hearings before the Committee on Agriculture House of Representatives, 108th Congress First Session, Serial No. 108–5, 21 May–22 July. Washington, DC: US Government Printer, 2003.

US Tariff Commission. *Watches, Watch Movements and Watch Parts. Report to the President on Investigation No. 337–19.* Washington, DC, 1966.

Yearbook of the United States Department of Agriculture, 1895. Washington, DC: Government Printing Office, 1896.

Yearbook of the United States Department of Agriculture, 1896. Washington, DC: Government Printing Office, 1897.

Yearbook of the United States Department of Agriculture, 1897. Washington, DC: Government Printing Office, 1898.

Yearbook of the United States Department of Agriculture, 1898. Washington, DC: Government Printing Office, 1899.

Yearbook of the United States Department of Agriculture, 1899. Washington, DC: Government Printing Office, 1900.

Yearbook of the United States Department of Agriculture, 1911. Washington, DC: Government Printing Office, 1912.
Yearbook of the United States Department of Agriculture, 1912. Washington, DC: Government Printing Office, 1913.
USDA, Yearbook for 1920. Washington, DC: Government Printing Office, 1921.
USDA, Yearbook for 1922. Washington, DC: Government Printing Office, 1923.
USDA, Agriculture Yearbook for 1923. Washington, DC: Government Printing Office, 1924.
USDA, Agriculture Yearbook for 1924. Washington, DC: Government Printing Office, 1925
USDA, Agriculture Yearbook for 1925. Washington, DC: Government Printing Office, 1926.
USDA, Yearbook of Agriculture for 1926. Washington, DC: Government Printing Office, 1927.

United International Bureau for the Protection of Intellectual Property (BIRPI) and World Intellectual Property Organization

Actes de la Conférence de Bruxelles 1897 et 1900. Bureau International de l'Union, Berne 1901.
Actes de la Conférence de la Haye. Bureau International de l'Union, Berne 1911.
Actes de la Conférence de Lisbonne. Bureau International de l'Union, Geneva, 1963.
Actes de la Conférence de Washington. Bureau International de l'Union, Berne 1926.
Actes de la Conférence Réunie à Londres. Bureau International de l'Union, Berne 1934.
Conférence Internationale de la Conférence de Madrid de 1890 de l'Union pour la Protection de la Propriété Industrille. Impr. Jent et Reinert, Berne, 1892.
Lisbon Council. 'Problems Arising from the Practical Application of the Lisbon Agreement'. July 1970 (document AO/V/5).
Lisbon Council. 'Report of the Fifth Session', 26 September 1970 (document AO/V/8).
Lisbon Council. 'Report of the Sixth Session', 2 October 1971 (document AO/VI/5).
Lisbon Council. 'Territorial Extension of the Lisbon Union', 25 June 1971 (document AO/VI/4).
Records of the Intellectual Property Conference of Stockholm. 11 June–14 July 1967. World Intellectual Property Organization: Geneva, 1971, 66–68.
World Intellectual Property Organization. 'Revision of the Lisbon Agreement for the Protection of Appellations of Origin and Their International Registration or the Drafting of a New Treaty', 30 June 1972 (document P/EC/VIII/6).
World Intellectual Property Organization. 'Present Situation and Possible New Solutions', 28 June 1974 (document TAO/1/2 [1974]).
World Intellectual Property Organization. 'Report adopted by the Committee of Experts', 15 November 1974 (document TAO/1/8).

World Intellectual Property Organization. 'Draft Treaty, on the Protection of Geographical Indications', 25 August 1975 (document TAO/II/2).

World Intellectual Property Organization. 'The Need for a New Treaty and Its Possible Contents', 9 April 1990 (document GEO/CE/I/2).

World Intellectual Property Organisation. *Study on the Protection of Country Names*, 8 July 2013 (document SCT/29/5 Rev).

World Intellectual Property Organisation. *The Protection of Country Names against Registration and Use as Trademarks*, 23 November 2015 (document Strad/INF/7).

World Trade Organization

World Trade Organization. Dispute Settlement Body, 'United States' Response to the European Communities' Request for a Preliminary Ruling', 15 March 2004 (document WT/DS174/R/Add.1).

World Trade Organization. Dispute Settlement Body, 'First Written Submission of the United States', 23 April 2004 (document WT/DS174/R/Add.1), Annex A-2.

World Trade Organization. Dispute Settlement Body, 'First Written Submission by the European Communities', 25 May 2004 (document WT/DS174/R/Add.2).

World Trade Organization. Dispute Settlement Body, 'Arguments of the Third Parties', 15 March 2005 (document WT/DS174/R/Add.3: Annex C).

World Trade Organization. 'European Communities – Protection of Trademarks and Geographical Indications for Agricultural Products and Foodstuffs. Complaint by the United States', 15 March 2005 (document WT/DS174/R).

World Trade Organization. 'Issues Related to the Extension of the Protection of Geographical Indications Provided for in Article 23 of the TRIPS Agreement to Products Other than Wines and Spirits', 18 May 2005 (document WT/GC/W/546TN/C/W/25).

World Trade Organisation. *Report of the Committee on Rules of Origin to the Council for Trade in Goods*, 10 October 2013 (document G/L/1047).

BOOKS

Anholt, S. *Competitive Identity: The New Brand Management for Nations, Cities and Regions*. London: Palgrave Macmillan, 2006.

Atkin, M. *Snouts in the Trough: European Farmers, the Common Agricultural Policy and the Public Purse*. Cambridge: Woodhead, 1993.

Barham E. and Sylvander, B. (eds.). *Labels of Origin for Food: Local Development, Global Recognition*. Wallingford: CABI Books, 2011.

Barnard, C. *The Substantive Law of the EU: The Four Freedoms*. Oxford: Oxford University Press, 2013.

Barnes, F. *New Zealand's London*. Auckland: Auckland University Press, 2012.

Belson, J. *Special Report: Certification Marks*. London: Sweet & Maxwell, 2002.

Bertoli, G. and Resciniti, R. *International Marketing and the Country of Origin Effect. The Global Impact of 'Made in Italy'*. Cheltenham: Edward Elgar. 2012.

Bielman, J. *Five Centuries of Farming: A Short History of Dutch Agriculture, 1500–2000*. Wageningen: Wageningen Academic Publishers, 2010.

Blakeney, M. *The Protection of Geographical Indications*. Cheltenham: Edward Elgar, 2014.

Blanco-White, T. A. *Kerly's Law of Trade Marks and Trade Names*. London: Sweet & Maxwell, 1966.

Bodenhausen, G., *Guide to the Application of the Paris Convention for the Protection of Industrial Property*. Geneva: United International Bureaux for the Protection of Intellectual Property, 1969; reprinted by the World Intellectual Property Organization, 1991.

Braithwaite, J. and Drahos, P. *Global Business Regulation*. Cambridge: Cambridge University Press, 2000.

Breidling, R. J. *Swiss Made*. London: Profile Books, 2013.

Britnell, R. H. *The Commercialisation of English Society*. Manchester: Manchester University Press, 1996.

Cain, P. J. and Hopkins, A. G. *British Imperialism: Innovation and Expansion, 1688–1914*. London: Longman, 1993.

Campo, I. S. and Aerni, P. *When Corporatism Leads to Corporate Governance Failure: The Case of the Swiss Watch Industry*. Cambridge: Banson, 2016.

Chandler, A. D. *Scale and Scope: The Dynamics of Industrial Capitalism*. Cambridge, MA: Harvard University Press, 1994.

Church, R. and Godley, A. *The Emergence of Modern Marketing*. Abingdon: Routledge, 2003.

Coddington, C. E. *A Digest of the Law of Trade Marks*. New York: Ward & Peloubet, 1878.

Comish, N. *Co-operative Marketing of Agricultural Products*. London: D. Appleton & Company, 1929.

Consitt, F. *The London Weavers' Company*. Oxford: Clarendon Press, 1933.

Cooper, A. *British Agricultural Policy, 1912–36*. Manchester: Manchester University Press, 1989.

Corley, T. A. B. *Quaker Enterprise in Biscuits*. London: Hutchinson & Company, 1972.

Cox, R. *A Manual of Trade-Mark Cases Comprising Sebastian's Digest of Trade-Mark Cases*. Boston, MA: Houghton, Mifflin & Company, 1881.

Critchell, J. T. and Raymond, J. *A History of the Frozen Meat Trade*. London: Constable and Company, 1912.

Cunningham, W. *The Growth of English Industry and Commerce during the Early and Middle Ages*. Cambridge: Cambridge University Press, 1905.

Dawson, N. *Certification Trade Marks*. London: Intellectual Property Publishing Ltd., 1988.

Digby, M. *Digest of Co-operative Law at Home and Abroad*. London: P. S. King & Son, 1933.

Documentation pour la reunion de la conference diplomatique internationale en vue de l'etablissement d'une convention pour le marquage des oefs dans le commerce international. Bruxelles: Au Palais Des Academies, 7 December 1931.

Donze, P. Y. *History of the Swiss Watch Industry: From Jacques David to Nicolas Hayek.* Bern: Peter Lang AG, 2012.

Drane, N. and Edwards, H. *The Australian Dairy Industry.* Melbourne: F. W. Cheshire, 1961.

Drummond, J. M. *British Economic Policy and the Empire, 1919–1939.* London: Allen & Unwin, 1972.

Echols, M. A., *Geographical Indications for Food Products.* Alphen aan den Rijn: Wolters Kluwer, 2008.

Eichengreen, B. *Golden Fetters: The Gold Standard and the Great Depression, 1919–1939.* Oxford: Oxford University Press, 1995.

Epstein, S. *Wage Labour and Guilds in Medieval Europe.* Chapel Hill: University of North Carolina Press, 1977.

Faber, H. *Cooperation in Danish Agriculture.* London: Longmans, Green & Company, 1918.

Fay, C. R. *Co-operation at Home and Abroad.* Vol. II, *1908–1938.* London: P. S. King & Son, 1939.

Ffoulkes, C. *The Armourer and His Craft.* New York: Benjamin Bloom, 1967.

Fitzsimmons, M. *From Artisan to Worker.* Cambridge: Cambridge University Press, 2010.

Forrester, R. B. *Report upon Large Scale Co-operative Marketing in the United States of America.* Ministry of Agriculture and Fisheries. Economic Series No. 4. London: HMSO, 1925.

Frank, D. *Buy American.* Boston, MA: Beacon Press, 1999.

French, M. and Phillips, J. *Cheated not Poisoned? Food Regulation in the United Kingdom, 1875–1938.* Manchester: Manchester University Press, 2000.

Gangjee, D. *Relocating the Law of Geographical Indications.* Cambridge: Cambridge University Press, 2012.

Gervais, D. *The TRIPS Agreement.* 3rd edn. London: Sweet & Maxwell, 1998.

Glasmeier, A. *Manufacturing Time.* New York: Guildford Press, 2000.

Glick, L. A. *United States Customs and Trade Law after the Customs Modernization Act.* The Hague: Kluwer Law International, 1997.

Guy, K. M. *When Champagne Became French.* Baltimore, MD: Johns Hopkins University Press, 2003.

Hannah, L. *The Rise of the Corporate Economy.* London: Methuen, 1983.

Hanson, J. R. *Trade in Transition: Exports from the Third World, 1840–1900.* New York: Academic Press, 1980.

Hayward, D. *Golden Jubilee: The Story of the Meat Producers Board, 1922–1972.* Wellington: Universal Printers Ltd., 1972.

Head, D. *Made in Germany: The Corporate Identity of a Nation.* London: Hodder and Stoughton, 1992.

Heick, W. *A Propensity to Protect: Butter, Margarine and the Rise of Urban Culture in Canada.* Ontario: Wilfrid Laurier University Press, 1991.

Henzell, T. *Australian Agriculture: Its History and Challenges.* Victoria: CSIRO Publishing, 2007.

Hesseltine, N. F. *A Digest of the Law of Trade-Marks and Unfair Trade.* Boston, MA: Little Brown and Company, 1906. Reprinted in the Making of the Modern Law Print Edition.

Hopkins, J. L. *The Law of Unfair Trade.* Chicago, IL: Callaghan & Company. 1900.

Hopkins, J. L. *The Law of Trademarks, Tradenames and Unfair Competition.* Cincinnati, OH: W. H. Anderson Company, 1924.

International Association for the Protection of Industrial Property. *AIPPI and the Development of Industrial Property Protection, 1897–1997.* Basle: AIPPI Foundation, 1997.

Jaffe, E. and Nebenzahl, I. *National Image and Competitive Advantage.* Copenhagen: Copenhagen Business School, 2001.

Jefferys, J. B. *Retail Trading in Britain, 1850–1950.* Cambridge: Cambridge University Press, 1954.

Jensen, E. *Danish Agriculture.* Copenhagen: J. H. Schultz Forlag, 1937.

Johnson, H. and Robinson, J. *The World Atlas of Wine.* 5th edn. London: Octopus Publishing Group, 2001.

Jones, G. *Entrepreneurship and Multinationals: Global Business and the Making of the Modern World.* Cheltenham: Edward Elgar, 2013.

Josling, T. E and Tangermann, S. *Transatlantic Food and Agricultural Trade Policy.* Cheltenham: Edward Elgar, 2015.

Kenwood, A. G. and Lougheed, A. L. *The Growth of the International Economy, 1820–1990.* London: Routledge, 1992.

Kerly, D. M. *The Law of Trade Marks and Trade Name.* London: Sweet & Maxwell, 1913.

Keynes, J. M. *The Economic Consequences of the Peace.* London: Macmillan, 1920.

Kindleberger, C. P. *The World in Depression, 1929–1939.* London: Allen Lane, 1973.

Kitchin, Blanco-White, D., Llewelyn, D., Mellor, J., Meade, R., Moody-Stuart, T., and Keeling, D. *Kerly's Law of Trade Marks and Trade Names.* London: Sweet & Maxwell, 2005.

Kitson, M. and Solomou, S. *Protectionism and Economic Revival: The Interwar British Economy.* Cambridge: Cambridge University Press, 1990.

Klein, N. *No Logo: No Space, No Choice, No Jobs.* London: Flamingo, 2001.

Knox, F. *The Common Market and World Agriculture.* London: Praeger, 1972.

Kornberger, M. *Brand Society: How Brands Transform Management and Lifestyle.* New York: Cambridge University Press, 2010.

Ladas, S. P. *Patents, Trademarks and Related Rights: National and International Protection.* Cambridge, MA: Harvard University Press, 1975.

Landes, W. M., and Posner, R. A. *The Economic Structure of Intellectual Property Law.* Cambridge, MA: Belknap Press, 2003.

Larson, J. *Geographical indications in situ Conservation and Traditional Knowledge.* Geneva: International Centre for Trade and Sustainable Development, 2010.

Lewis, D. and Bridger, D. *The Soul of the New Consumer.* London: Nicholas Brealey, 2001.

Lloyd, G. I. H. *The Cutlery Trades.* London: Longman, 1913.

da Silva Lopes, T. *Global Brands: The Evolution of Multinationals in Alcoholic Beverages.* New York: Cambridge University Press, 2007.

Lury, C. *Brands: The Logos of the Global Economy.* London: Routledge, 2004.

MacLachlan, I. *Kill and Chill: Restructuring Canada's Beef Commodity Chain.* London: University of Toronto Press, 2001.

Maizels, A. *Industrial Growth and World Trade.* Cambridge: Cambridge University Press, 1963.

Mantrov, V. *EU Law on Indications of Geographical Origin.* London: Springer, 2014.

Marrison, A. *British Business and Protection, 1903–1932.* Oxford: Clarendon Press, 1996.

Mason, L. M. and Brown, C. *Traditional Foods of Britain: A Regional Inventory.* Totnes: Prospect Books, 2004.

McCracken, G. *Culture and Consumption.* Bloomington: Indiana University Press, 1988.

Menzies, H. *By the Labour of Their Hands: The Story of Ontario Cheddar Cheese.* Ontario: Quarry Press, 1994.

New Zealand Meat Producers Board. *The Case for Closer Trade with Britain: Being Evidence Submitted to the Customs Tariff Commission by the New Zealand Meat Producers Board.* Wellington: New Zealand Meat Producers Board, 1933.

Nims, H. D. *The Law of Unfair Business Competition.* New York: Baker, Voorhis and Company, 1909.

O'Connor, B. *The Law of Geographical Indications.* London: Cameron May, 2004.

Organisation for Economic Co-operation and Development. *Agricultural Policies, Markets and Trade: Monitoring and Outlook 1988.* Organisation for Economic Co-operation and Development: Paris, 1988.

Organisation for Economic Co-operation and Development. *Implementing Change: Entrepreneurship and Local Initiative.* Organisation for Economic Co-operation and Development: Paris, 1990.

Organisation for Economic Co-operation and Development. *What Future for Our Countryside? A Rural Development Policy.* Organisation for Economic Co-operation and Development: Paris, 1993.

Pabst, W. R. *Butter and Oleomargarine: An Analysis of Competing Commodities.* New York: AMS Press, 1968.

Palen, M.-W. *The 'Conspiracy' of Free Trade: The Anglo–American Struggle over Empire and Economic Globalisation, 1846–1896.* Cambridge: Cambridge University Press, 2016.

Papadopoulos, N. and Heslop, L. A. *Product Country Images: Impact and Role in International Marketing.* New York: International Business Press, 1993.

Peaslee, A. *International Governmental Organisations: Constitutional Documents.* The Hague: Martinus Nijhoff, 1979.

Perren, R. *Taste, Trade, Technology: The Development of the International Meat Industry since 1840.* Aldershot: Ashgate, 2006.

Pike, A. *Origination: The Geographies of Brands and Branding*. Chichester: Wiley-Blackwell, 2015.

Pinner, H. L. *World Unfair Competition Law: An Encyclopedia*. Vol. 1. Leyden: A. W. Sijthoff, 1965.

Reich, R. R. *The Work of Nations: Preparing Ourselves for 21st Century Capitalism*. New York: Alfred A. Knopf, 1991.

Rooth, T. *British Protectionism and the International Economy: Overseas Commercial Policy in the 1930s*. Cambridge: Cambridge University Press, 1992.

Schechter, F. I. *The Historical Foundations of the Law Relating to Trade-Marks*. New York: Colombia University Press, 1925.

Schultz, M., Antorini, Y., and Csaba, F. *Corporate Branding*. Copenhagen: Copenhagen Business School, 2005.

Sebastian, L. B. *The Law of Trade Marks*. London. Stevens & Sons, 1899. Second edition published 1911.

Self, P. and Storing, H. J. *The State and the Farmer*. Berkeley: University of California Press, 1963.

Sell, S. *Private Power, Public Law*. Cambridge: Cambridge University Press, 2003.

Simpson, J. *Creating Wine: The Emergence of a World Industry, 1840–1914*. Princeton, NJ: Princeton University Press, 2011.

Smith, J. T. *English Guilds*. Oxford: Oxford University Press, 1870.

Stanziani, A. *Rules of Exchange: French Capitalism in Comparative Perspective, Eighteenth to Early Twentieth Centuries*. New York: Cambridge University Press, 2012.

Starch, D. *Principles of Advertising*. London: A. W. Shaw & Company, 1926.

Taillefer, A. and Claro, C. *Traité des Marques de Fabrique et de la Concurrence Déloyale en Tous genres, d'Eugène Pouillet*. Paris: Marchal et Godde, 1912.

Taubman, A., Wager, H., and Watal, J. *A Handbook on the WTO TRIPS Agreement*. Cambridge: Cambridge University Press, 2012.

Trentmann, F. *Free Trade Nation*. Oxford: Oxford University Press, 2008.

Trueb, L. *The World of Watches*. New York: Ebner Publishing International, 2005.

Unwin, G. *The Gilds and Companies of London*. London: George Allen & Unwin, 1938.

Unwin, T. *Wine and the Vine*. London: Routledge, 1991.

Vermulst, E., Waer, P., and Bourgeois, J. *Rules of Origin in International Trade: A Comparative Study*. Ann Arbor: University of Michigan Press, 1994.

Williams, E. E. *Made in Germany*. London: Heinemann, 1896.

Yates, P. L. *Forty Years of Foreign Trade*. London: George Allen & Unwin, 1959.

Zaimis, N. A. *EC Rules of Origin*. London: Chancery Law Publishing, 1992.

CHAPTERS IN BOOKS

Aldred, J. 'The Economic Rationale of Trade Marks: An Economist's Critique', in L. Bently, J. Davis, and J. C. Ginsbur (eds.), *Trade Marks and Brands:*

An Interdisciplinary Critique. Cambridge: Cambridge University Press, 2010, 267–281.

Arfini, F. 'The Value of Typical Products: The Case of Prosciutto di Parma and Parmigiano Reggiano Cheese', in B. Sylvander, D. Barjolle, and F. Arfini (eds.), *The Socio-Economics of Origin-Labelled Products in Agri-Food Supply Chains: Spatial, Institutional and Co-ordination Aspects*. Vol. 1. Versailles: European Association of Agricultural Economists, 2000, 77–97.

Baeumer, L. 'International Treaties Relating to Appellations of Origin and Indications of Source'. *WIPO Symposium on Appellations of Origin and Indications of Source, Bordeaux, France, 1988*. Geneva: World Intellectual Property Organization, 1989, 15–37.

Barjolle, D., Chappuis, J.-M., and Dufour, M. 'Competitive Position of Some PDO Cheeses on Their Reference Market: Identification of the Key Success Factors', in B. Sylvander, D. Barjolle, and F. Arfini (eds.), *The Socio-Economics of Origin-Labelled Products in Agri-Food Supply Chains: Spatial, Institutional and Co-ordination Aspects*. Vol. 2. Versailles: European Association of Agricultural Economists, 2000, 13–33.

Belletti, G. 'Origin Labeled Products, Reputation and Heterogeneity of Firms', in B. Sylvander, D. Barjolle, and F. Arfini (eds.), *The Socio-Economics of Origin-Labelled Products in Agri-Food Supply Chains: Spatial, Institutional and Co-ordination Aspects*. Vol. 1. European Association of Agricultural Economists. Versailles: European Association of Agricultural Economists, 2000, 77–97, 239–259.

Blakeney, M. 'Geographical Indications and TRIPS', in M. P. Pugatch (ed.), *The Intellectual Property Debate*. Cheltenham: Edward Elgar, 2006, 293–304.

Constantine, S. 'Bringing the Empire Alive: The Empire Marketing Board and Imperial Propaganda, 1926–33', in J. MacKenzie (ed.), *Imperialism and Popular Culture*. Manchester: Manchester University Press, 1986, 192–231.

Davis, J. and Maniatis, S. 'Trademarks, Brands and Competition', in T. da Silva Lopes and P. Duguid (eds.), *Trademarks, Brands, and Competitiveness*. Abingdon: Routledge, 2010, 119–137.

De Roest, K. 'The Dynamics of the Parmigiano-Reggiano Production System', in B. Sylvander, D. Barjolle, and F. Arfini (eds.), *The Socio-Economics of Origin-Labelled Products in Agri-Food Supply Chains: Spatial, Institutional and Co-ordination Aspects*. Vol. 1. Versailles: European Association of Agricultural Economists, 2000: 271–286.

Djelic, M. L. and Quack, S. 'Institutions and Transnationalization', in R. Greenwood, C. Oliver, R. Suddaby, and K. Sahlin (eds.), *The Sage Handbook of Organisational Institutionalism*. Los Angeles, CA: Sage, 2008, 299–323.

Drori, G. S. 'Institutionalism and Globalisation Studies', in R. Greenwood, C. Oliver, R. Suddaby, and K. Sahlin (eds.), *The Sage Handbook of Organisational Institutionalism*. Los Angeles, CA: Sage, 2008, 449–472.

Duguid, P., da Silva Lopes, T., and Mercer, J. 'Reading Registrations: An Overview of 100 Years of Trademark Registrations in France, the United Kingdom, and the United States', in T. da Silva Lopes and P. Duguid (eds.), *Trademarks, Brands and Competitiveness*. Abingdon: Routledge, 2010, 9–30.

Epstein, S. R. and Prak, M. 'Introduction: Guilds, Innovation, and the European Economy, 1400–1800', in S. R. Epstein and M. Prak (eds.), *Guilds, Innovation and the European Economy, 1400–1800.* Cambridge: Cambridge University Press, 2008, 1–24.

Evans, P. 'Geographic Indications, Trade and the Functioning of Markets', in M. P. Pugatch (ed.), *The Intellectual Property Debate: Perspectives from Law, Economics and Political Economy.* Cheltenham: Edward Elgar, 2006, 346–360.

Farmer, E. A. 'Local, Loyal, and Constant: The Legal Construction of Wine in Bordeaux', in R. E. Black and R. C. Ulin (eds.), *Wine and Culture: Vineyard to Glass.* London: Bloomsbury, 2013, 145–159.

Federico, G. 'Growth, Specialization, and Organization of World Agriculture', in L. Neal and J. G. Williamson (eds.), *The Cambridge History of Capitalism.* Vol. II. *The Spread of Capitalism from 1848 to the Present.* Cambridge: Cambridge University Press, 2014, 47–81.

Forden, S. 'Pride versus Profits: Italian Makers Confront Offshore Production', quoted in D. Besanko, D. Dranove, and M. Shanley (eds.), *Economics of Strategy.* London: Wiley, 2000, 133–134.

Gadd, I. A. and Wallis, P. 'Researching beyond the City Wall: London Guilds and National Regulation, 1500–1700', in S. R. Epstein and M. Prak (eds.), *Guilds, Innovation and the European Economy, 1400–1800.* Cambridge: Cambridge University Press, 2008, 288–315.

Gangjee, D. S. 'Genericide: The Death of a Geographical Indication?', in D. S. Gangjee (ed.), *Research Handbook on Intellectual Property and Geographical Indications.* Cheltenham: Edward Elgar, 2016, 508–548.

Giraud, G., Sirieix, L., and Lebecque, A. 'Consumers' Purchase Behaviour towards Typical Foods in Mass Marketing: The Case of PDO Camembert from Normandy', in B. Sylvander, D. Barjolle, and F. Arfini (eds.), *The Socio-Economics of Origin-Labelled Products in Agri-Food Supply Chains: Spatial, Institutional and Co-ordination Aspects.* Vol. 1. Versailles: European Association of Agricultural Economists, 2000, 117–125.

Griffiths, A. 'A Law-and-Economics Perspective on Trade Marks', in L. Bently, J. Davis, and J. C. Ginsbur (eds.), *Trade Marks and Brands: An Interdisciplinary Critique.* Cambridge: Cambridge University Press, 2010, 241–266.

Hansen, P. H. 'Cobranding Product and Nation: Danish Modern Furniture and Denmark in the United States, 1940–1970', in T. da Silva Lopes and P. Duguid, *Trademarks, Brands and Competitiveness.* Abingdon: Routledge, 2010, 77–101.

Heath, C. 'The Budweiser Cases: A Brewing Conflict', in C. Heath and A. Kamperman (eds.), *Landmark Intellectual Property Cases and Their Legacy.* Alphen aan den Rijn, The Netherlands: Kluwer Law International, 2011, 181–244.

Hey, D. 'The Establishment of the Cutlers' Company', in C. Binfield and D. Hey (eds.), *Mesters to Masters. A History of the Company of Cutlers in Hallamshire.* Oxford: Oxford University Press, 1997, 12–25.

Higgins, D. M. 'Made in Sheffield: Trade Marks, the Cutlers' Company and the Defence of "Sheffield"', in C. Binfield and D. Hey (eds.), *Mesters to Masters.*

A History of the Company of Cutlers in Hallamshire. Oxford: Oxford University Press, 1997, 85–114.

Hobsbawm, E. 'Introduction: Inventing Traditions', in E. Hobsbawm and T. Ragnger (eds.), *The Invention of Tradition.* Cambridge: Cambridge University Press, 1983, 1–14.

Ittersum, K. V., Candel, M. J. J. M., and Torelli, F. 'The Market for PDO/PGI Protected Regional Products: Consumers' Attitudes and Behaviour', in B. Sylvander, D. Barjolle, and F. Arfini (eds.), *The Socio-Economics of Origin-Labelled Products in Agri-Food Supply Chains: Spatial, Institutional and Co-ordination Aspects.* Vol. 1. Versailles: European Association of Agricultural Economists, 2000, 209–221.

Loureiro, M. and McCluskey, J. J. 'Effectiveness of PGI and PDO Labels as a Rural Development Policy', in B. Sylvander, D. Barjolle, and F. Arfini (eds.), *The Socio-Economics of Origin-Labelled Products in Agri-Food Supply Chains: Spatial, Institutional and Co-ordination Aspects.* Vol. 1. Versailles: European Association of Agricultural Economists, 2000, 159–162.

Marescotti, A. 'Cherry of Lari (Italy)', in E. Barham and B. Sylvander (eds.), *Labels of Origin for Food: Local Development, Global Recognition.* Wallingford: CABI Books, 2011, 161–166.

Nützenadel, A. 'A Green International? Food Markets and Transnational Politics, c.1850–1914', in A. Nützenadel and F. Trentmann (eds.), *Food and Globalization: Consumption, Markets and Politics in the Modern World.* Oxford: Berg, 2008, 153–171.

Nützenadel, A. and Trentmann, F. 'Introduction: Mapping Food and Globalization', in A. Nützenadel and F. Trentmann (eds.), *Food and Globalization: Consumption, Markets and Politics in the Modern World.* Oxford: Berg, 2008, 1–18.

O'Rourke, K. H. 'Late 19th Century Denmark in an Irish Mirror: Land Tenure, Homogeneity and the Roots of Danish Success', in J. L. Campbell, J. A. Hall, and O. K. Pedersen (eds.), *The State of Denmark: Small States, Corporatism and the Varieties of Capitalism.* McGill: Queen's University Press, 2006, 159–196.

O'Rourke, K. H. and Williamson, J. G. 'Introduction: The Spread of and Resistance to Global Capitalism', in L. Neal and J. G. Williamson (eds.), *The Cambridge History of Capitalism.* Vol, II: *The Spread of Capitalism from 1848 to the Present.* Cambridge: Cambridge University Press, 2014, 1–21.

Parry, B. 'Geographical Indications: Not All "Champagne and Roses"', in L. Bently, J. Davis, and J. C. Ginsburg (eds.), *Trade Marks and Brands: An Interdisciplinary Critique.* Cambridge: Cambridge University Press, 2008, 361–380.

Reith, R. 'Circulation of Skilled Labour in Late Medieval and Early Modern Central Europe', in S. R. Epstein and M. Prak (eds.), *Guilds, Innovation and the European Economy, 1400–1800.* Cambridge: Cambridge University Press, 2008, 114–142.

Rosa, F. 'Total Quality Management of the PDO Prosciutto San Daniele', in B. Sylvander, D. Barjolle, and F. Arfini (eds.), *The Socio-Economics of Origin-Labelled Products in Agri-Food Supply Chains: Spatial,*

Institutional and Co-ordination Aspects. Vol. 2. Versailles: European Association of Agricultural Economists, 2000, 35–49.

Schroeder, J., Borgerson, J., and Wu, Z. 'A Brand Culture Perspective on Global Brands', in F. D. Riley, J. Singh, and C. Blankson (eds.), *The Routledge Companion to Contemporary Brand Management.* Abingdon: Routledge, 2016, 153–163.

Thévenod, E. and Marie-Vivien, D. 'Legal Debates Surrounding Geographical Indications', in E. Barham and B. Sylvander (eds.), *Labels of Origin for Food: Local Development, Global Recognition.* Wallingford: CABI Books, 2011, 13–28.

Townshend, F. 'Food Standards: Their Importance, Limitations and Problems with Special Reference to International Work', in S. M. Herschdoerfer, *Quality Control in the Food Industry.* Vol. 1. London: Academic Press, 1967, 285–366.

Trentmann, F. 'Before "Fair Trade": Empire, Free Trade, and the Moral Economies of Food in the Modern World', in A. Nützenadel and F. Trentmann (eds.), *Food and Globalization: Consumption, Markets and Politics in the Modern World.* Oxford: Berg, 2008, 253–276.

Wilson, N., Van Ittersum, K., and Fearne, A. 'Cooperation and Coordination in the Supply Chain: A Comparison between the Jersey Royal and the Opperdoezer Ronde Potato', in B. Sylvander, D. Barjolle, and F. Arfini (eds.), *The Socio-Economics of Origin-Labelled Products in Agri-Food Supply Chains: Spatial, Institutional and Co-ordination Aspects.* Vol. 2. Versailles: European Association of Agricultural Economists, 2000, 95–102.

ARTICLES

Ahmed, S. A. and d'Astous, A. 'Antecedents, Moderators, and Dimensions of Country-of-Origin Evaluations'. *International Marketing Review,* 25 (2008): 75–106.

Aichner, T. 'Country-of-Origin Marketing: A List of Typical Strategies with Examples'. *Journal of Brand Management,* 21 (2014): 81–93.

Akerlof, G. A. 'The Market for "Lemons": Quality Uncertainty and the Market Mechanism'. *Quarterly Journal of Economics,* 84 (1970): 488–500.

Bade, D. L. 'Beyond Marking: Country of Origin Rules and the Decision in CPC International'. *The John Marshall Law Review,* 31 (1997): 179–205.

Baldwin, R. 'Trade and Industrialisation after Globalisation's 2nd Unbundling: How Building and Joining a Supply Chain Are Different and Why It Matters'. National Bureau of Economic Research, Working Paper 17716 (2011).

Bales, M. 'Implications and Effects of the FTC's Decision to Retain the "All or Virtually All" Standard'. *University of Miami Law School Institutional Repository,* 30 (1999): 727–747.

Barham, E. 'Translating Terroir: The Global Challenge of French AOC Labelling'. *Journal of Rural Studies,* 19 (2003): 127–138.

Barnes, F. and Higgins, D. M. 'Brand Image, Cultural Association and Marketing: 'New Zealand' Butter and Lamb Exports to Britain c 1920–1938'. *Business History*, (forthcoming).

Barney, J. 'Firm Resources and Sustained Competitive Advantage'. *Journal of Management*, 17 (1991): 99–120.

Barthélemy, J. 'The Impact of Technical Consultants on the Quality of Their Clients' Products: Evidence from the Bordeaux Wine Industry'. *Strategic Management Journal*, 38 (2017): 1174–1190.

Bendekgey, L. and Mead, C. 'International Protection of Appellations of Origin and Other Geographic Indications'. *Trade Mark Reporter*, 82 (1992): 765–792.

Benson, R. W. 'Toward a New Theory for the Protection of Geographical Indications'. *Industrial Property*, 4 (1978): 127–136.

Bérard, L. and Marcheny, P. 'Local Products and Geographical Indications: Taking Account of Local Knowledge and Biodiversity'. *International Social Science Journal*, 58 (2006): 109–116.

Beresford, L. 'Geographical Indications: The Current Landscape'. *Fordham Intellectual Property, Media and Entertainment Law Journal*, 27 (2007): 979–997.

Beverland, M. B. 'Crafting Brand Authenticity: The Case of Luxury Wines'. *Journal of Management Studies*, 42 (2005): 1003–1029.

Blakeney, M. 'Geographical Indications and Trade'. *International Trade Law and Regulation*, 6 (2000): 48–55.

Bostock, F. and Jones, G. 'Foreign Multinationals in British Manufacturing, 1850–1962'. *Business History*, 36 (1994): 89–126.

Bowen, S. 'Embedding Local Places in Global Spaces: Geographical Indications as a Territorial Development Strategy'. *Rural Sociology*, 75 (2010): 209–243.

Bowen, S. and De Master, K. 'New Rural Livelihoods or Museums of Production? Quality Food Initiatives in Practice'. *Journal of Rural Studies*, 27 (2011): 73–82.

Broude, T. 'Taking "Trade and Culture" Seriously: Geographical Indications and Cultural Protection in WTO Law'. *University of Pennsylvania Journal of International Economic Law*, 26 (2005): 623–692.

Brown, S., Kozinets, R. V., and Sherry, J. F., Jr. 'Teaching Old Brands New Tricks: Retro Branding and the Revival of Brand Meaning'. *Journal of Marketing*, 67 (2003): 19–33.

Buchheim, C. 'Aspects of XIXth Century Anglo–German Trade Rivalry Reconsidered'. *Journal of European Economic History*, X (1981): 273–89.

Buchnea, E. 'Transatlantic Transformations: Visualising Change over Time in the Liverpool–New York Trade Network, 1763–1833'. *Enterprise & Society*, 15 (2015): 687–721.

Callmann, R. 'Unfair Competition with Imported Trademarked Goods'. *Virginia Law Review*, 43 (1957): 323–351.

Caracausi, A. 'Information Asymmetries and Craft Guilds in Pre-Modern Markets: Evidence from Italian Proto-Industry'. *Economic History Review*, 70 (2017): 397–422.

Clemens, R. and Babcock, B. 'Country of Origin as a Brand: The Case of New Zealand Lamb'. MATRIC Briefing Paper 04-MBP 9, November 2004.

Coerper, M. G. 'The Protection of Geographical Indications in the United States of America, with Particular Reference to Certification Marks'. *Industrial Property*, 29 (1990): 232–242.

Constantine, S. 'The Buy British Campaign of 1931'. *Journal of Advertising History*, 10 (1987): 44–59.

Craswell, R. 'Interpreting Deceptive Advertising'. *Boston University Law Review*, 65 (1985): 657–732.

Daniels, L. E. 'The History of the Trademark'. *Bulletin of the US Trademark Association*, 7 (1911): 239–268.

Derenberg, W. J. 'The Influence of the French Code Civil on the Modern Law of Unfair Competition'. *American Journal of Comparative Law*, 4 (1955): 1–34.

Deselnicu, O. C., Costanigro, M., Souza-Monteiro, D. M., and McFadden, D. T. 'A Meta-Analysis of Geographical Indication Food Valuation Studies: What Drives the Premium for Origin-Based Labels'. *Journal of Agricultural and Resource Economics*, 38 (2013): 204–219.

Devlétian, M. A. 'The Protection of Appellations and Indications of Origin'. *Industrial Property Quarterly*, 1 (1957): 6–24.

Dichter, E. 'The World Customer'. *Harvard Business Review*, 40 (1962): 113–122.

Duguid, P. 'Developing the Brand: The Case of Alcohol'. *Enterprise and Society*, 4 (2003): 405–441.

Duguid, P. 'Networks and Knowledge: The Beginning and End of the Port Commodity Chain, 1703–1860'. *Business History Review*, 79 (2005): 493–526.

Duguid, P. 'Information in the Mark and Marketplace: A Multivocal Account'. *Enterprise and Society*, 15 (2014): 1–30.

Dupré, R. '"If It's Yellow, It Must Be Butter": Margarine Regulation in North America since 1886'. *Journal of Economic History*, 59 (1999): 353–371.

Espejel, J., Fandos, C., and C. Flavián. 'Spanish Air-Cured Ham with Protected Designation of Origin (PDO): A Study of Intrinsic and Extrinsic Attributes' Influence on Consumer Satisfaction and Loyalty'. *Journal of International Food & Agribusiness Marketing*, 19 (2007): 5–30.

Espejel, J., Fandos, C., and C. Flavián, 'Consumer Satisfaction: A Key Factor of Consumer Loyalty and Buying Intention of a PDO Food Product', *British Food Journal*, 110 (2008): 865–881.

Hamzaoui-Essoussi, L., Merunka, D., and Bartikowski, B. 'Brand Origin and Country of Manufacture Influences on Brand Equity and the Moderating Role of Brand Typicality'. *Journal of Business Research*, 64 (2011): 973–978.

Evans, G. E. and Blakeney, M. 'The Protection of Geographical Indications after Doha: Quo Vadis?', *Journal of International Economic Law*, 9 (2006): 575–614.

Federico, G. 'How Much Do We Know about Market Integration in Europe?'. *Economic History Review*, 65 (2012): 470–497.

Fernándes, E. and Simpson, J. 'Product Quality or Market Regulation? Explaining the Slow Growth of Europe's Wine Co-operatives, 1880–1980'. *Economic History Review*, 70 (2017): 122–142.

Fhima, I. S. 'The Actual Dilution Requirement of the United States, United Kingdom and European Union: A Comparative Analysis'. *Boston University Journal of Science & Technology Law*, 12 (2006): 271–309.

Fletcher, S. R. and Godley, A. 'Foreign Direct Investment in British Retailing, 1850–1962'. *Business History*, 42 (2000): 43–62.

Fonte, M. 'Knowledge, Food and Place: A Way of Producing, a Way of Knowing'. *Sociologia Ruralis*, 48 (2008): 200–222.

Galfand, C. E. 'Heeding the Call for a Predictable Rule of Origin'. *Journal of International Law*, 11 (1989): 469–493.

Gangjee, D. 'Melton Mowbray and the GI Pie in the Sky: Exploring Cartographies of Protection'. *Intellectual Property Quarterly*, 3 (2006): 291–309.

George, A. 'Editorial Brands: Interdisciplinary Perspectives on Trade Marks and Branding'. *Brand Management*, 13 (2006): 175–177.

Gervais, D. J. 'Reinventing Lisbon: The Case for a Protocol to the Lisbon Agreement (Geographical Indications)'. *Chicago Journal of International Law*, 11 (2010): 67–126.

Godey, B., Pederzoli, B., Aiello, G., Donvito, R., Chan, P., Oh, H., Singh, R., Skorobogatykh, I. I., Tsuchiya, J., and Weitz, B. 'Brand and Country of Origin Effect on Consumers' Decision to Purchase Luxury Products'. *Journal of Business Research*, 65 (2012): 1461–1470.

Godley, A. 'Foreign Multinationals and Innovation in British Retailing, 1850–1962'. *Business History*, 45 (2003): 80–100.

Goehle, D. G. 'The Buy American Act: Is It Relevant in a World of Multinational Corporations?'. *Columbia Journal of World Business*, 24 (1989): 10–15.

Goldberg, S. D. 'Who Will Raise the White Flag? The Battle between the United States and the European Union over the Protection of Geographical Indications'. *University of Pennsylvania Journal of International Economic Law*, 22 (2001): 107–151.

Goodman, A., Maro, F., Molander, R., Ojeda, J., and Tompkins, O. 'The Swiss Watch Cluster'. Harvard Business School: The Microeconomics of Competitiveness, 6 May 2010. Downloaded from www.isc.hbs.edu/resources/courses/moc-course-at-harvard/Documents/pdf/student-projects/Switzerland_Watchmaking_2010.pdf. Accessed September 2016.

Gracia, A. and Albisu, L. M. 'Food Consumption in the European Union: Main Determinants and Country Differences'. *Agribusiness*, 17 (2001): 469–488.

Gragnani, M. 'The EU Regulation 1151/2012 on Quality Schemes for Agricultural Products and Foodstuffs'. *European Food and Feed Law Review*, 8 (2013): 380.

Guerra, J. L. *Geographical indications in situ Conservation and Traditional Knowledge*. International Centre for Trade and Sustainable Development. Policy Brief No. 3 (2010).

Gustafsson, B. 'The Rise and Economic Behaviour of Medieval Craft Guilds: An Economic-Theoretical Interpretation'. *Scandinavian Economic History Review*, 35 (1987): 1–40.

Henriksen, I., Hviid, M., and Sharpe, P. 'Law and Peace: Contracts and the Success of the Danish Dairy Cooperatives'. *Journal of Economic History*, 72 (2012): 197–224.

Henriksen, I., McLaughlin, E., and Sharp, P. 'Contracts and Cooperation: The Relative Failure of the Irish Dairy Industry in the Late Nineteenth Century Reconsidered'. *European Review of Economic History*, 19 (2015): 412–431.

Henriksen, I. and O'Rourke, K. 'Incentives, Technology and the Shift to Year-Round Dairying in Late-Nineteenth Century Denmark'. *Economic History Review*, 58 (2005): 520–554.

Henson, S. and Humphrey, J. 'Understanding the Complexities of Private Standards in Global Agri-Food Chains as they Impact Developing Countries'. *Journal of Development Studies*, 26 (2010): 1628–1646.

Higgins, D. M. '"Made in Britain?" National Trade Marks and Merchandise Marks: The British Experience from the Late Nineteenth Century to the 1920s'. *Journal of Industrial History*, 5 (2002): 50–70.

Higgins, D. M. 'Mutton Dressed as Lamb? The Misrepresentation of Australian and New Zealand Meat in the British Market, c.1890–c.1914'. *Australian Economic History Review*, 44 (2004): 161–184.

Higgins, D. M. and Gangjee, D. '"Trick or Treat?" The Misrepresentation of American Beef Exports in Britain during the Nineteenth Century'. *Enterprise & Society*, 11 (2010): 203–241.

Higgins, D. M. and Mordhorst, M. 'Reputation and Export Performance: Danish Butter Exports and the British Market, c. 1880–c. 1914'. *Business History*, 50 (2008): 185–204.

Higgins, D. M. and Mordhorst, M. 'Bringing Home the "Danish" Bacon: Food Chains, National Branding and Danish Supremacy over the British Bacon Market, c.1900–c.1938'. *Enterprise & Society*, 16 (2015): 141–185.

Higgins, D. M. and Tweedale, G. 'Asset or Liability? Trade Marks in the Sheffield Cutlery and Tool Trades'. *Business History*, 37 (1995): 1–27.

Hofstede, G. 'The Cultural Relativity of Organizational Practices and Theories'. *Journal of International Business Studies*, 14 (1983): 75–89.

Holt, D. B. 'Why Do Brands Cause Trouble? A Dialectical Theory of Consumer Culture and Branding'. *Journal of Consumer Research*, 29 (2002): 70–90.

Holt, D. B. 'Toward a Sociology of Branding'. *Journal of Consumer Culture*, 6 (2006): 299–301.

Hudson, B. T. 'Brand Heritage and the Renaissance of Cunard'. *European Journal of Marketing*, 45 (2011): 1538–1556.

Hughes, J. 'Champagne, Feta, and Bourbon: The Spirited Debate about Geographical Indications'. *Hastings Law Journal*, 58 (2006): 299–386.

Ilbery, B. and Kneafsey, M. 'Niche Markets and Regional Speciality Food Products in Europe: Towards a Research Agenda'. *Environment and Planning A*, 31 (1999): 2207–2222.

Ilbery, B. and Kneafsey, M. 'Producer Constructions of Quality in Regional Speciality Food Production: A Case Study from South West England'. *Journal of Rural Studies*, 16 (2000): 217–230.

Ilbery, B. and Kneafsey, M. 'Registering Regional Speciality Food and Drink Products in the UK: The Case of PDOs and PGIs'. *Area*, 32 (2000): 317–325.

Irwin, D. A. 'Free Trade and Protection in Nineteenth Century Britain and France Revisited: A Comment on Nye'. *Journal of Economic History*, 53 (1993): 146–152.

Irwin, D. A. 'Higher Tariffs, Lower Revenues? Analyzing the Fiscal Aspects of "The Great Tariff Debate of 1888"'. *Journal of Economic History*, 58 (1998): 59–72.

Irwin, D. A. 'Did Late-Nineteenth Century U.S. Tariffs Promote Infant Industries? Evidence from the Tinplate Industry'. *Journal of Economic History*, 60 (2000): 335–360.

Jones, G. and Bostock, F. 'U.S. Multinationals in British Manufacturing before 1962'. *Business History Review*, 70 (1996): 207–256.

Kirk, M. K. 'Revision of the Paris Convention and Appellations of Origin'. *Patent, Trademark and Copyright Law Proceedings, American Bar Association* (1979): 185–203.

Klein, B. and Leffler, K. B. 'The Role of Market Forces in Assuring Contractual Performance'. *Journal of Political Economy*, 89 (1981): 615–641.

Koschate-Fischer, N., Diamantopoulos, A., and Oldenkotte, K. 'Are Consumers Really Willing to Pay More for a Favourable Country Image? A Study of Country-of-Origin Effects on Willingness to Pay'. *Journal of International Marketing*, 20 (2012): 19–41.

Kotler, P. and Gertner, D. 'Country as Brand, Product, and Beyond: A Place Marketing and Brand Management Perspective'. *Journal of Brand Management*, 9 (2002): 249–261.

Ladas, S. P. 'Pan American Conventions on Industrial Property'. *American Journal of International Law*, 22 (1928): 803–821.

Landes, W. M. and Posner, R. A. 'Trademark Law: An Economic Perspective'. *Journal of Law and Economics*, 30 (1987): 265–309.

Lenzen, L. 'Bachus in the Hinterlands: A Study of Denominations of Origin in French and American Wine-Labelling Laws'. *Trademark Reporter*, 58 (1968): 145–187.

Levitt, T. 'The Globalization of Markets'. *Harvard Business Review*, 61 (1983): 92–102.

Libecap, G. D. 'The Rise of the Chicago Packers and the Origins of Meat Inspection and AntiTrust'. *Economic Inquiry*, 30 (1992): 242–262.

Lindahl, M. L. 'The Federal Trade Commission Act as Amended in 1938'. *Journal of Political Economy*, 47 (1939): 497–525.

Lindquist, L. A. 'Champagne or Champagne? An Examination of U.S. Failure to Comply with the Geographical Provisions of the TRIPS Agreement'. *Georgia Journal of International and Comparative Law*, 27 (1999): 309–344.

Lloyd, A. G. 'The Marketing of Dairy Produce in Australia'. *Review of Marketing and Agricultural Economics*, 18 (1950): 6–92.

Loureiro, M. L. and McCluskey, J. J. 'Assessing Consumer Response to Protected Geographical Identification Labeling'. *Agribusiness*, 16 (2000): 309–320.

Magnusson, P., Westjohn, S. A., and Zdravkovic, S. '"What? I Thought Samsung Was Japanese": Accurate or Not, Perceived Country of Origin Matters'. *International Marketing Review*, 28 (2011): 454–472.

Maronick, T. J. 'An Empirical Investigation of Consumer Perceptions of "Made in USA" Claims'. *International Marketing Review*, 12 (1995): 15–30.

McCarthy, J. T. and Devitt, V. C. 'Protection of Geographic Denominations: Domestic and International'. *Trade Mark Reporter*, 69 (1979): 199–228.

Massey, D. 'A Global Sense of Place'. *Marxism Today* (June 1991): 24–29.

Medina-Albaladejo, F. J. and Menzani, T. 'Co-operative Wineries in Italy and Spain in the Second Half of the Twentieth Century: Success or Failure of the Cooperative Business Model'. *Enterprise and Society*, 18 (2017): 32–71.

Menapace, L. and Moschini, G. C. 'Quality Certification by Geographical Indications, Trademarks and Firm Reputation'. *European Review of Agricultural Economics*, 39 (2012): 539–566.

Mérel, P. and Sexton, R. J. 'Will Geographic Indications Supply Excessive Quality?' *European Review of Agricultural Economics*, 39 (2012): 567–587.

Mollanger, T. 'The Effects of Producers' Trademark Strategies on the Structure of the Cognac Brandy Supply Chain during the Second Half of the 19th Century: The Reconfiguration of Commercial Trust by the use of Brands'. *Business History* (forthcoming).

Moore, K. and Reid, S. 'The Birth of Brand: 4000 Years of Branding'. *Business History*, 50 (2008): 419–432.

Mordhorst, M. 'Arla and Danish National Identity: Business History as Cultural History'. *Business History*, 56 (2014): 116–133.

Notz, W. 'New Phases of Unfair Competition and Measures for Its Suppression – National and International'. *Yale Law Journal*, 30 (1920–1921): 384–394.

Ohmae, K. 'Managing in a Borderless World'. *Harvard Business Review*, 67 (1989): 153.

Olins, W. 'Branding the Nation: The Historical Context'. *Journal of Brand Management*, 9 (2002): 241–248.

Olsson, T. C. 'Peeling Back the Layers: Vidalia Onions and the Making of a Global Agribusiness'. *Enterprise & Society*, 13 (2012): 832–861.

O'Rourke, K. H. and Williamson, J. G. 'Once More: When Did Globalization Begin?'. *European Review of Economic History*, 8 (2004): 109.

Palen, M.-W. 'Protection, Federation and Union: The Global Impact of the McKinley Tariff upon the British Empire, 1890–94'. *Journal of Imperial and Commonwealth History*, 38 (2010): 395–418.

Papadopoulos, N. and Heslop, L. 'Country Equity and Country Branding: Problems and Perspectives'. *Journal of Brand Management*, 2 (2002): 294–314.

Parrott, N., Wilson, N., and J. Murdoch. 'Spatializing Quality: Regional Protection and the Alternative Geography of Food'. *European Urban and Regional Studies*, 9 (2002): 241–261.

Pattishall B. W. 'Geographical Indications of Origin'. *Proceedings of the American Bar Association, Patent, Trademark & Copyright Law Section* (1979): 197–203.

Peteraf, M. A. 'The Cornerstones of Competitive Advantage: A Resource Based View'. *Strategic Management Journal*, 14 (1993): 179–191.

Pharr, J. M. 'Synthesizing Country-of-Origin Research from the Last Decade: Is the Concept Still Salient in an Era of Global Brands?'. *Journal of Marketing, Theory and Practice*, 13 (2005): 34–45.

Pike, A. 'Placing Brands and Branding: A Socio-Spatial Biography of Newcastle Brown Ale'. *Transactions of the Institute of British Geographers*, 36 (2011): 206–222.

Prigent-Simonin, A. and Hérault-Fournier, C. 'The Role of Trust in the Perception of the Quality of Local Food Products: With Particular Reference to Direct Relationships between Producer and Consumer'. *Anthropology of Food*, May (2005): 1–16.

Ramello, G. B. 'What's in a Sign? Trademark Law and Economic Theory'. *Journal of Economic Surveys*, 20 (2006): 547–565.

Rangnekar, D. 'The Socio-Economics of Geographical Indications'. *International Centre for Trade and Sustainable Development*, 4 (2004).

Raustiala, K. and Munzer, S. R. 'The Global Struggle over Geographic Indications'. *The European Journal of International Law*, 18 (2007): 337–365.

Renaud, J. R. 'Can't Get There from Here: How NAFTA and GATT Have Reduced Protection for Geographical Trademarks'. *Brooklyn Journal of International Law*, 26 (2001): 1097–1123.

Rice, D. A. 'Consumer Unfairness at the FTC: Misadventures in Law and Economics'. *George Washington Law Review*, 52 (1983–1984): 1–66.

Richardson, G. 'Guilds, Laws and Markets for Manufactured Merchandise in Late Medieval England'. *Explorations in Economic History*, 41 (2004): 1–25.

Richardson, G. 'Brand Names before the Industrial Revolution'. *National Bureau of Economic Research*, Working Paper No. 13930 (2008).

Robins, J. E. 'A Common Brotherhood for Their Mutual Benefit: Sir Charles Macara and Internationalism in the Cotton Industry, 1904–1914'. *Enterprise & Society*, 16 (2015): 847–888.

Ruyack, R. F., 'United States Country of Origin Requirements: The Application of a Non-Tariff Trade Barrier'. *Law and Policy in International Business*, 6 (1974): 485–531.

Samiee, S. 'Resolving the Impasse Regarding Research on the Origins of Products and Brands'. *International Marketing Review*, 28 (2011): 473–485.

Schnarr, C. N. 'Left Out in the Cold? The Customs' Country of Origin Marking Requirements, the Section 516 Procedure, and the Lessons of Norcal/Crosetti'. *Washington University Law Review*, 73 (1995): 1679–1709.

Schooler, R. 'Product Bias in Central American Common Market'. *Journal of Marketing Research*, 2(4) (1965): 394–397.

Self, R. 'Treasury Control and the Empire Marketing Board'. *20th Century British History*, 5 (1994): 153–182.

Simon, L. E. 'Appellations of Origin: The Continuing Controversy'. *Northwestern Journal of International Law & Business*, 5 (1983): 132–156.

Simpson, J. 'Cooperation and Cooperatives in Southern European Wine Production'. *Advances in Agricultural History*, 1 (2000): 95–126.

Simpson, J. 'Selling to Reluctant Drinkers: The British Wine Market, 1860–1914'. *Economic History Review*, LVII (2004): 80–108.

Stanziani, A. 'Wine Reputation and Quality Controls: The Origin of the AOCs in 19th Century France'. *European Journal of Law and Economics*, 18 (2004): 149–167.

Stanziani, A. 'Information, Quality and Legal Rules: Wine Adulteration in Nineteenth Century France'. *Business History*, 51 (2009): 268–291.
Steel, F. '"New Zealand is Butterland": Interpreting the Historical Significance of a Daily Spread'. *New Zealand Journal of History*, 39 (2005): 1–12.
Thakor, M. V. and Kohli, C. S. 'Brand Origin: Conceptualisation and Review'. *Journal of Consumer Marketing*, 13 (1996): 27–42.
Tregear, A., Kuznesof, S., and Moxey, A. 'Policy Initiatives for Regional Foods: Some Insights from Consumer Research'. *Food Policy*, 23 (1998): 383–394.
Tyszynski, H. 'World Trade in Manufactured Commodities'. *Manchester School*, 19 (1951): 272–304.
Usunier, J.-C. 'Relevance in Business Research: The Case of Country-of-Origin Research in Marketing'. *European Management Review*, 3 (2006): 60–73.
Vincent, M. 'Extending Protection at the WTO to Products Other Than Wines and Spirits: Who Will Benefit?'. *The Estey Centre Journal of International Law and Trade Policy*, 8 (2007): 57–68.
Voronev, M., de Clercq, D., and Hinings, C. R. 'Conformity and Distinctiveness in a Global Institutional Framework: The Legitimation of Ontario Fine Wine'. *Journal of Management Studies*, 50 (2013): 607–645.
de Vries, J. 'The Limits to Globalization in the Early Modern World'. *Economic History Review*, 63 (2010): 710–733.
Wadleigh, H. 'The British Agricultural Marketing Act'. *Journal of Farm Economics*, 14 (1932): 558–573.
Wadlow, C. 'The International Law of Unfair Competition: The British Origins of Article 10bis of the Paris Convention for the Protection of Industrial Property'. Oxford Intellectual Property Research Centre, 19 November.
Wiedmann, K.-P., Hennigs, N., Schmidt, S., and Wuestefeld, T., 'Drivers and Outcomes of Brand Heritage: Consumers' Perception of Heritage Brands in the Automative Industry'. *Journal of Marketing, Theory and Practice*, 19 (2011): 205–220.
Wilkins, M. 'The Neglected Intangible Asset: The Influence of the Trade Mark on the Rise of the Modern Corporation'. *Business History*, 34 (1992): 66–95.

UNPUBLISHED THESES

Capie, F. H. 'The Development of the Meat Trade between New Zealand and the United Kingdom, 1860–1914' (unpublished MSc thesis, London School of Economics, 1969).
Solecki, S. G. 'A Tale of Two Cheeses: Parmesan, Cheddar and the Politics of Generic Geographical Indications (GGIs)' (PhD thesis, University of Warwick, 2014).

ONLINE SOURCES

Chever. 'Geographical Indications (GIs) in the European Union: Economic Aspects'. WIPO: Worldwide Symposium on Geographical Indications.

Downloaded from www.wipo.int/edocs/mdocs/geoind/en/wipo_geo_bud_15/wipo_geo_bud_15_8.pdf.

Consortium for Common Food Names. 'Senators Remind Negotiators of Need to Address GI Abuse in TTIP'. 1 June 2016. Downloaded from www.common foodnames.com/senators-remind-negotiators-of-need-to-address-gi-abuse-in-tt ip/.

Consortium for Common Food Names. 'TTIP Proposal Reinforces Desire to Block U.S. Food Exports'. 1 June 2016. Downloaded from www.commonfood names.com/eu-ttip-proposal-reinforces-desire-to-block-u-s-food-exports/.

European Union. 'Value of Production of Agricultural Products and Foodstuffs, Wines, Aromatised Wines and Spirits Protected by a Geographical Indication (GI)'. Downloaded from https://ec.europa.eu/agriculture/external-studies/valu e-gi_en.

von Graevenitz, F. G. 'State and Market in Agriculture – France and Germany in the Interwar Period'. Downloaded from www.ebha.org/ebha2007/pdf/vonGra evenitz.pdf.

Insight Consulting, *Study on the Protection of Geographical Indications for Products Other than Wines, Spirits, Agricultural Products or Foodstuffs.* November 2009. Downloaded from: www.trade.ec.europa.eu/doclib/docs/20 11/may/tradoc_147926.pdf.

Katia, M.-L. 'Are Geographical Indications on EU Food Labels Worth Obtaining?' Downloaded from www.linkedin.com/pulse/geographical-indica tions-eu-food-labels-worth-obtaining-katia.

P. Patel, House, L., and Spreen, T. H. 'How do Different Countries Use Labelling Standards: A Case Study Comparing Wisconsin Real Cheese to Parmigiano -Reggiano'. Downloaded from https://ageconsearch.umn.edu/bit stream/122015/2/20-Spreen%20et%20al.pdf.

Serra. 'The Protection'. European Association of Agricultural Economists, 145th seminar, 14–15 April 2015. Downloaded from: http://purl.umn.edu/206447.

Stringleman, H. and Scrimgeour, F. 'Dairying and Dairy Products: The Beginnings of New Zealand's Dairy Industry'. *Te Ara – the Encyclopedia of New Zealand.* Downloaded from www.teara.govt.nz/en/dairying-and-dairy-products/page-1.

US International Trade Commission. 'Rules of Origin: Basic Principles'. www.us itc.gov/elearning/hts/media/2017/RulesofOrigina.pdf

Watson, K. W. 'Geographical Indications in TTIP: An Impossible Task'. October 2015. Downloaded from www.cato.org/publications/cato-online-for um/geographical-indications-ttip-impossible-task.

Index

Printed in the United States
By Bookmasters